Essentials of the
U.S. Health Care System

FOURTH EDITION

Leiyu Shi, DrPH, MBA, MPA
Professor, Johns Hopkins Bloomberg School of Public Health
Director, Johns Hopkins Primary Care Policy Center for the Underserved
Johns Hopkins University
Baltimore, Maryland

Douglas A. Singh, PhD, MBA
Associate Professor Emeritus of Management
School of Business and Economics
Indiana University South Bend
South Bend, Indiana

JONES & BARTLETT
LEARNING

World Headquarters
Jones & Bartlett Learning
5 Wall Street
Burlington, MA 01803
978-443-5000
info@jblearning.com
www.jblearning.com

Jones & Bartlett Learning books and products are available through most bookstores and online booksellers. To contact Jones & Bartlett Learning directly, call 800-832-0034, fax 978-443-8000, or visit our website, www.jblearning.com.

Substantial discounts on bulk quantities of Jones & Bartlett Learning publications are available to corporations, professional associations, and other qualified organizations. For details and specific discount information, contact the special sales department at Jones & Bartlett Learning via the above contact information or send an email to specialsales@jblearning.com.

10066-2

Production Credits

VP, Executive Publisher: David D. Cella
Publisher: Michael Brown
Associate Editor: Lindsey Mawhiney
Associate Editor: Nicholas Alakel
Production Assistant: Rebecca Humphrey
Composition: Integra Software Services Pvt. Ltd.
Cover Design: Kristin E. Parker

Rights & Media Research Specialist: Merideth Tumasz
Media Development Editor: Shannon Sheehan
Cover Images: Flag: © Feng Yu/ShutterStock, Inc., DC Skyline: © holbox/Shutterstock Inc.
Printing and Binding: Edwards Brothers Malloy
Cover Printing: Edwards Brothers Malloy

Library of Congress Cataloging-in-Publication Data
Shi, Leiyu, author.
  Essentials of the U.S. health care system/Leiyu Shi and Douglas Singh. – Fourth edition.
      p.; cm.
  Essentials of the United States health care system
  Includes bibliographical references and index.
  ISBN 978-1-284-10055-6 (alk. paper)
  I. Singh, Douglas A., 1946-, author.   II. Title.   III. Title: Essentials of the United States health care system.
  [DNLM: 1. Delivery of Health Care–United States.   2. Health Policy–United States. W 84 AA1]
  RA395.A3

    362.10973–dc23

                                                                                201503207
6048

Printed in the United States of America

19 18 17   10 9 8 7 6 5 4

Contents

Preface

This text is a condensed and simplified version of our standard textbook on the U.S. health care system, *Delivering Health Care in America: A Systems Approach, Sixth Edition*, which has been widely used for teaching both undergraduate and graduate courses. While retaining the main themes of the larger book, this version covers the essential elements of U.S. health care in an easier to read format. This text leaves out much of the data and technical details found in the expanded version. Remaining comprehensive and focused, this condensed version is designed for maximum accessibility and flexibility.

This text retains the systems model to organize the major themes of U.S. health care delivery. The first three chapters lay the foundation that is necessary for understanding the U.S. health care delivery system, which is distinct from any other system in the world. "Major Characteristics of U.S. Health Care Delivery" (Chapter 1) gives an overview of U.S. health care and contrasts the American system with the three most commonly used models of health care delivery in other advanced nations, such as Canada, the United Kingdom, and Germany. "Foundations of U.S. Health Care Delivery" (Chapter 2) explains the different models for understanding health and its determinants. In the context of American beliefs and values, this chapter also discusses the issue of equity using the concepts of market justice and social justice and explains how health services are rationed in both market justice– and social justice–based systems. "Historical Overview of U.S. Health Care Delivery" (Chapter 3) traces the history of U.S. health care from colonial times to the present and includes an added section on health care reform. The key to understanding the nature of the current health care system and its likely future direction is to understand its evolutionary past. This chapter also includes current trends in corporatization, information revolution, and globalization as they pertain to health care delivery.

The next three chapters are about the resources—both human and non-human—employed in delivering health care. "Health Care Providers and Professionals" (Chapter 4) addresses the roles played by some of the major types of personnel in health care delivery. It also discusses some key issues pertaining to the number and distribution of physicians and the effect these factors have on the delivery of health care. "Technology and Its Effects" (Chapter 5) discusses medical technology and the various issues related to its development and dissemination. "Financing and Reimbursement Methods" (Chapter 6) explains the concept of health insurance, the major private and public health insurance programs in the United States, and methods of reimbursing providers.

The next five chapters describe the system processes, beginning with outpatient and primary care services (discussed in Chapter 7). Hospitals are the focus of Chapter 8. "Managed Care and Integrated Systems" (Chapter 9) examines managed care and integrated organizations, such as integrated delivery systems and the emerging accountable care organizations, as well as the different types of arrangements found in integrated organizations. "Long-Term Care Services" (Chapter 10) explores the meaning and scope of long-term care and provides an overview of community-based and institution-based long-term care services. "Populations with Special Health Needs" (Chapter 11) highlights vulnerable populations and their special health care needs. This chapter also includes a section on mental health.

The next two chapters deal with the main outcomes of the health care system and the ways in which those outcomes are addressed through health policy. The main outcomes associated with health care are presented in Chapter 12, "Cost, Access, and Quality." "Health Policy" (Chapter 13) gives an overview of health policy, including the major participants in its development and the process by which it is created, in the United States.

Finally, "The Future of Health Services Delivery" (Chapter 14) explores the future of health care in the United States in the context of forces of future change, health care reform, conflicting issues of cost and access, future models of care delivery, global challenges, and technological innovations.

For easy reference, an Appendix, "Essentials of the Affordable Care Act," is found at the end of the 14 chapters. It provides a topical summary of the ACA.

Leiyu Shi

Douglas A. Singh

New in the *Fourth Edition*

This edition has been updated with the latest health statistics and pertinent information available at the time the manuscript was prepared. Some key additions to the text include the following:

- Current status of managed care and integrated delivery system under the Affordable Care Act; current status of public health system; health care reform in selected countries (Chapter 1)

- Implementation of *Healthy People 2020*; assessment of the Healthy People initiative (Chapter 2)

- New sections: "Era of Health Care Reform" and "U.S. Health Care Today" discuss the current state of affairs in the context of historical developments (Chapter 3).

- Current U.S. physician workforce and challenges (Chapter 4)

- Addition of nanomedicine; clinical decision support systems; Health Information Technology for Economic and Clinical Health (HITECH) Act; update on remote monitoring; regulation of biologics; and the ACA and medical technology (Chapter 5)

- New sections: "The Affordable Care Act and Private Insurance"; "The Affordable Care Act and Public Insurance"; "The Affordable Care Act and Payment Reform" (Chapter 6)

- Community health centers' current scope, efficacy/values, and challenges (Chapter 7)

- Discussion on the performance of church-owned hospitals and physician-owned hospitals; new section: "The Affordable Care Act and Hospitals" (Chapter 8)

- Update on accountable care organizations; new section: "Managed Care and Organizational Integration Under the Affordable Care Act" (Chapter 9)

- New section: "The Affordable Care Act and Long-Term Care" (Chapter 10)
- Current disparities in literature (racial, socioeconomic status) in terms of access to care, quality of care, and health outcomes; programs (national, regional, local) that address disparities (racial, socioeconomic status) in terms of access to care, quality of care, and health outcomes (Chapter 11)
- Quality initiatives both from government (e.g., Agency for Healthcare Research and Quality) and private sectors and programs to contain health care costs (Chapter 12)
- Update health policy issues and challenges after ACA (Chapter 13)
- New section discusses the future of U.S. health care delivery in the context of forces of future change; challenges of coverage, access, and cost and future of health care reform—including prospects for a single-payer system—in the context of the Affordable Care Act; new section on care delivery of the future (Chapter 14)

Acknowledgments

We gratefully acknowledge Sylvia Shi for creating the cartoons for this book. We are also grateful for the valuable assistance of Gaida Mahgoub and Geraldine Pierre Haile. Of course, all errors and omissions remain the responsibility of the authors.

List of Exhibits

List of Tables

List of Figures

Chapter 1

Major Characteristics of U.S. Health Care Delivery

INTRODUCTION

The United States has a unique system of health care delivery compared with other developed countries around the world. Almost all other developed countries have universal health insurance programs in which the government plays a dominant role. Almost all of the citizens in these countries are entitled to receive health care services that include routine and basic health care. In the United States, the Affordable Care Act[1] (ACA) has expanded health insurance, but it still falls short of achieving universal coverage. Besides insurance, adequate access to health care services and health care costs at both the individual and national levels continue to confound academics, policy makers, and politicians alike.

---

[1]Patient Protection and Affordable Care Act of 2010 as amended by the Health Care and Education Reconciliation Act of 2010, often shortened as the Affordable Care Act and nicknamed Obamacare.

The main objective of this chapter is to provide a broad understanding of how health care is delivered in the United States. The U.S. health care delivery system is both complex and massive. Ironically, it is not a system in the true sense because the components illustrated in **Figure 1.1** are only loosely coordinated. Yet, for the sake of simplicity, it is called a system when its various features, components, and services are referenced.

Organizations and individuals involved in health care range from educational and research institutions, medical suppliers, insurers, payers, and claims processors to health care providers. There are nearly 18.4 million people employed in various health delivery settings, including professionally active doctors of medicine (MDs), doctors of osteopathy (DOs), nurses, dentists, pharmacists, and administrators. Approximately 451,500

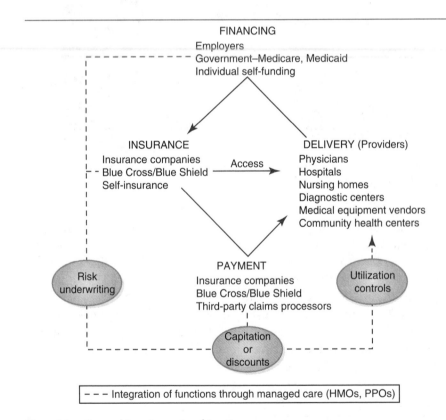

Figure 1.1   Managed Care: Integration of Functions

physical, occupational, and speech therapists provide rehabilitation services. The vast array of institutions includes 5,686 hospitals, 15,663 nursing homes, almost 2,900 inpatient mental health facilities, and 15,900 home health agencies and hospices. Nearly 1,200 programs support basic health services for migrant workers and the homeless, community health centers, black lung clinics, human immunodeficiency virus (HIV) early intervention services, and integrated primary care and substance abuse treatment programs. Various types of health care professionals are trained in 192 medical and osteopathic schools, 65 dental schools, 130 schools of pharmacy, and more than 1,937 nursing programs located throughout the country (Bureau of Labor Statistics, 2011; Bureau of Primary Health Care, 2011).

There are 201.1 million Americans with private health insurance coverage, most of whom are covered through their employers. An additional 103.1 million are covered under 2 major public health insurance programs—Medicare and Medicaid—managed by the U.S. government. Private health insurance can be purchased from approximately 1,000 health insurance companies. The private managed care sector includes approximately 452 licensed health maintenance organizations (HMOs) and 925 preferred provider organizations (PPOs). A multitude of government agencies are involved with the financing of health care, medical and health services research, and regulatory oversight of the various aspects of the health care delivery system (Aventis Pharmaceuticals, 2002; Bureau of Primary Health Care, 2011; Healthleaders, 2011; National Center for Health Statistics, 2007; Urban Institute, 2011; U.S. Bureau of the Census, 1998; U.S. Census Bureau, 2007).

SUBSYSTEMS OF U.S. HEALTH CARE DELIVERY

In the United States, multiple subsystems of health care delivery have developed, either through market forces or through government action to address the special needs of certain population segments.

Managed Care

Managed care seeks to achieve efficiency by integrating the basic functions of health care delivery, and it employs mechanisms to control (manage) utilization and cost of medical services. Managed care is the dominant health care delivery system in the United States today. It covers most Americans in both private and public health insurance programs through contracts with a managed care organization (MCO), such as an HMO or a PPO. The MCO, in turn, contracts with selected health care providers—physicians, hospitals, and others—to deliver health care services to its enrollees. The term *enrollee* (member) refers to the individual covered under a managed care plan. The contractual arrangement between the MCO and the enrollee—including descriptions of the various health services to which enrollees are entitled—is referred to as the *health plan* (or *plan* for short).

The MCO pays providers either through a capitation (per head) arrangement, in which providers receive a fixed payment for each enrollee under their care, or via a discounted fee arrangement. Providers are willing to discount their services for MCO patients in exchange for being included in the MCO network and being guaranteed a patient population. As part of their planning process, health plans rely on the expected cost of health care utilization, which always runs the risk of costing more than the insurance premiums collected. By underwriting this risk, the plan assumes the role of insurer.

Figure 1.1 illustrates the basic functions and mechanisms that are necessary for the delivery of health services within a managed care environment. The four key functions of financing, insurance, delivery, and payment make up the quad-function model. Managed care integrates the four functions to varying degrees.

Military

The military medical care system is available mostly free of charge to active-duty military personnel of the U.S. Army, Navy, Air Force, and Coast Guard, as well as to members of certain uniformed nonmilitary services such as the Public Health Service and the National Oceanographic and Atmospheric Association. It is a well-organized system that provides comprehensive services, both preventive and treatment oriented. Services are provided by salaried health care personnel. Various types of basic services are provided at dispensaries, sick bays aboard ships, first aid stations, medical stations, and base hospitals. Advanced medical care is provided in regional military hospitals.

Families and dependents of active-duty or retired career military personnel are either treated at the hospitals or dispensaries or are covered by

TriCare, a program that is financed by the U.S. Department of Defense. This insurance plan permits the beneficiaries to receive care from both private and military medical care facilities.

The Veterans Administration (VA) health care system is available to retired veterans who have previously served in the military, with priority given to those who are disabled. The VA system focuses on hospital care, mental health services, and long-term care. It is one of the largest and oldest (dating back to 1930s) formally organized health care systems in the world. Its mission is to provide medical care, education and training, research, contingency support, and emergency management for the U.S. Department of Defense medical care system. It provides health care to more than 9.6 million individuals at over 1,100 sites that include 153 hospitals, 807 ambulatory and community-based clinics, 135 nursing homes, 209 counseling centers, 47 domiciliaries (residential care facilities), 73 home health care programs, and various contract care programs. The VA budget exceeds $55 billion, and it employed a staff of about 280,000 in 2010 (Department of Veterans Affairs, 2011; National Center for Veterans Analysis and Statistics, 2007).

The entire VA system is organized into 21 geographically distributed *Veterans Integrated Service Networks (VISNs)*. Each VISN is responsible for coordinating the activities of the hospitals and other facilities located within its jurisdiction. Each VISN receives an allocation of federal funds and is responsible for equitable distribution of those funds among its hospitals and other providers. VISNs are also responsible for improved efficiency and cost containment.

Subsystem for Special Populations

Special populations, also called vulnerable populations, refer to those with health needs but inadequate resources to address those needs. For example, they include individuals who are poor and uninsured, those belonging to certain minority groups or of certain immigration status, or those living in geographically or economically disadvantaged communities. They typically receive care through the nation's safety net, which includes public health insurance programs such as Medicare and Medicaid, and providers such as community health centers, migrant health centers, free clinics, and hospital emergency departments. Many safety net providers offer comprehensive medical and enabling services—such as language assistance, transportation, nutrition and health education, social support services, and child care—according to individual needs.

As an example, federally qualified health centers have provided primary and preventive health services to rural and urban underserved populations for more than 50 years. The Bureau of Primary Health Care (BPHC), located within the Health Resources and Services Administration in the Department of Health and Human Services (DHHS), provides federal support for community-based health centers that include programs for migrant and seasonal farm workers and their families, homeless persons, public housing residents, and school-aged children. These services facilitate regular access to care for patients who are predominantly minority, low income, uninsured, or enrolled in Medicaid, the public insurance program for the poor. In 2012, the nationwide network of 1,198 community health organizations served 22 million people across 8,100 service sites and handled a total of 83.8 million patient visits. Approximately 93% of this population was living on incomes that were less than 200% of the federal poverty level, and 36% were uninsured (National Association of Community Health Centers, 2014). Health centers have contributed to significant improvements in health outcomes for the uninsured and Medicaid populations and have reduced disparities in health care and health status across socioeconomic and racial/ethnic groups (Politzer et al., 2003; Shi et al., 2001).

Medicare is one of the largest sources of public health insurance in the United States, serving the elderly, the disabled, and those with end-stage renal disease. Managed by the Centers for Medicare and Medicaid Services (CMS), another division within the DHHS, Medicare offers coverage for hospital care, post-discharge nursing care, hospice care, outpatient services, and prescription drugs.

Medicaid, the third largest source of health insurance in the country, covering approximately 17.3% of the U.S. population, provides coverage for low-income adults, children, the elderly, and individuals with disabilities (Smith and Medalia, 2014). This program is also the largest provider of long-term care to older Americans and individuals with disabilities. The program has seen significant expansion under the ACA.

In 1997, the U.S. government created the Children's Health Insurance Program (CHIP) to provide insurance to children in uninsured families. The program expanded coverage to children in families that have modest incomes but do not qualify for Medicaid. In 2014, the CHIP program spent $13 billion to cover approximately 8.1 million children (MACPAC, 2015).

Despite the availability of government-funded health insurance, the United States' safety net is by no means secure. The availability of safety net services varies from community to community. Vulnerable populations residing in communities without safety net providers must often forgo care or seek services from hospital emergency departments if available nearby. Safety net providers, in turn, face enormous pressure from the increasing number of poor and Medicaid-insured in their communities.

Integrated Systems

Organizational integration to form *integrated delivery systems (IDSs)*, or health networks, started in the early 2000s. An IDS has been defined as a network of health care providers and organizations that provides or arranges to provide a coordinated continuum of services to a defined population and is willing to be held clinically and fiscally accountable for the clinical outcomes and health status of the population served (Shortell et al., 1996). By gaining ownership of or forming strategic partnerships with hospitals, physicians, and insurers, IDSs aim to deliver a range of services. The ACA includes payment reform initiatives that encourage physician–hospital integration and coordination of services. It is hoped that integrated and coordinated care will increase cost-effectiveness and quality. A newer model of integrated organization—called an accountable care organization—is expected to respond to new payment incentives and be held accountable for better quality outcomes at reduced costs under a new Medicare Shared Savings Program. The ACA is also aimed to address issues related to fragmented care for individuals who suffer from co-occurring serious mental illness and substance use disorders. The most important principles in delivering integrated care that is specific to vulnerable populations include: (1) an emphasis on primary care; (2) coordination of all care, including behavioral, social, and public health services; and (3) accountability for population health outcomes (Witgert & Hess, 2012).

Long-Term Care Delivery

Long-term care (LTC) consists of medical and nonmedical care that are provided to individuals who have chronic health issues and disabilities that prevent them from doing regular daily tasks. Hence, LTC includes both health care and support services for daily living. It is delivered across a wide variety of venues, including patients' homes, assisted living facilities, and nursing homes. In addition, family members and friends provide the majority of LTC services without getting paid for them. Medicare does not cover LTC; thus, costs associated with this form of care can impose a major burden on families. Medicaid covers several different levels of LTC services, but a person must be an indigent to qualify for Medicaid. LTC insurance is offered separately by insurance companies, but most people do not purchase these plans because premiums can be unaffordable. By 2020, more than 12 million Americans are projected to require LTC, which will impose a severe strain on the nation's financial resources (CMS, 2011a).

Public Health System

The mission of the *public health system* is to improve and protect community health. The Institute of Medicine's *Future of Public Health in the 21st Century* has outlined the need for a more robust public health infrastructure and a population-based health approach for a healthier America (Centers for Disease Control and Prevention [CDC], 2013). The National Public Health Performance Standards Program identifies 10 essential public health services that a system needs to deliver:

1. Monitoring health status to identify and solve community health problems
2. Diagnosing and investigating health problems and hazards
3. Informing, educating, and empowering people about health problems and hazards
4. Mobilizing the community to identify and solve health problems
5. Developing policies and plans to support individual and community health efforts
6. Enforcing laws and regulations to protect health and safety
7. Providing people with access to necessary care
8. Assuring a competent and professional health workforce
9. Evaluating the effectiveness, accessibility, and quality of personal and population-based health services
10. Performing research to discover innovative solutions to health problems

In 2009, public health accounted for 3.1% of the nation's overall healthcare expenditures of $2.5 trillion (CMS, 2012). The amount of federal funding spent to prevent disease and improve health in communities varied significantly from state to state in 2013, with a per capita low of $13.67 in Indiana to a high of $46.48 in Alaska (TFAH & RWJF, 2014). To bolster the nation's public health efforts, the ACA established the Prevention and Public Health Fund to provide expanded and sustained national investments in prevention and public health, to improve health outcomes, and to enhance health care quality.

Expanded efforts are needed to combat antibiotic resistance, fight obesity and heart disease, curb prescription drug overdose, and deal with emerging issues such as chikungunya and e-cigarettes. Advanced information systems and data sharing have become increasingly more important in assuring a strong public health system.

CHARACTERISTICS OF THE U.S. HEALTH CARE SYSTEM

The health care system of a nation is influenced by external factors, including the political climate, level of economic development, technological progress, social and cultural values, the physical environment, and population characteristics such as demographic and health trends. It follows, then, that the combined interaction of these forces has influenced the course of health care delivery in the United States. This section summarizes the basic characteristics that differentiate the U.S. health care delivery system from that of other countries. There are 10 main areas of distinction (see **Exhibit 1.1**).

Exhibit 1.1   Main Characteristics of the U.S. Health Care System

- No central governing agency and little integration and coordination
- Technology-driven delivery system focusing on acute care
- High in cost, unequal in access, and average in outcome
- Delivery of health care under imperfect market conditions
- Government as subsidiary to the private sector
- Fusion of market justice and social justice
- Multiple players and balance of power
- Quest for integration and accountability
- Access to health care services selectively based on insurance coverage
- Legal risks influence practice behaviors

No Central Governing Agency; Little Integration and Coordination

The U.S. health care system stands in stark contrast to the health care systems of other developed countries. Most developed countries have centrally controlled universal health care systems that authorize the financing, payment, and delivery of health care to all residents. The U.S. system is not centrally controlled; it is financed both publicly and privately and, therefore, features a variety of payment, insurance, and delivery mechanisms. Private financing, predominantly through employers, accounts for approximately 57% of total health care expenditures; the government finances the remaining 43% (CMS, 2015).

Centrally controlled health care systems are less complex and less costly than the U.S. health care system. Centrally controlled systems manage their total expenditures through global budgets and can govern the availability and utilization of services. The United States has a large private infrastructure in which hospitals and physician clinics are private businesses that are independent of the government. Nevertheless, the federal and state governments in the United States play an important role in health care delivery. They determine public-sector expenditures and reimbursement rates for services provided to Medicaid and Medicare patients. The government also formulates standards of participation through health policy and regulation, which means that providers must comply with the standards established by the government to deliver care to Medicaid and Medicare patients. Certification standards are also regarded as minimum standards of quality in most sectors of the health care industry.

Technology Driven and Focusing on Acute Care

The United States is a hotbed of research and innovation in new medical technology. Growth in science and technology often creates a demand for new services despite shrinking resources to finance sophisticated care. Other factors contribute to increased demand for expensive technological care. For example, patients often assume that the latest innovations represent the best care, and many physicians want to try the latest gadgets. Even hospitals compete on the basis of having the most modern equipment and are often under pressure to recoup capital investments made in technology.

Legal risks for providers and health plans alike may also play a role in the reluctance to deny new technology.

Although technology has ushered in a new generation of successful interventions, the negative outcomes resulting from its overuse are many. For example, the use of high technology adds to the rising costs of health care. These costs are eventually borne by society. Technological innovation certainly has a place in medicine. However, given the fact that resources are limited, enough emphasis is not placed on primary care and public health, both of which produce better population-level outcomes and are more cost-effective than high-tech care.

High in Cost, Unequal in Access, and Average in Outcome

The United States spends more than any other developed country on medical services. Despite spending such a high percentage of the national economic output (almost 17% of the gross domestic product [GDP] in 2012—see **Figure 1.2**) on health care, many U.S. residents have limited access to even the most basic care.

Access refers to the ability of an individual to obtain health care services when needed. In the United States, access is restricted to those who (1) have health insurance through their employers, (2) are covered under a government-sponsored health care program (which includes health coverage under the ACA), (3) can afford to buy insurance out of their own private funds, (4) are able to pay for services privately, or (5) can obtain services through safety net providers. Health insurance is the primary—but not necessarily a sufficient—means for obtaining access. After the implementation of the ACA, the proportion of the U.S. population that was uninsured dropped from approximately 16% to roughly 12% in 2014 (Kutscher, Herman, & Meyer, 2015). However, despite expansion of health insurance, some people still face access barriers. For example, one-third of U.S. physicians do not accept new Medicaid-insured patients (Decker, 2012). For consistent basic and routine care, commonly referred to as primary care, the uninsured are unable to see a physician unless they can pay on an out-of-pocket basis. Those who cannot afford to pay generally wait until health problems develop, at which point they may be able to receive services in a hospital emergency department. Experts generally believe that inadequacy and disparity in access to basic and routine primary care services are the main reasons

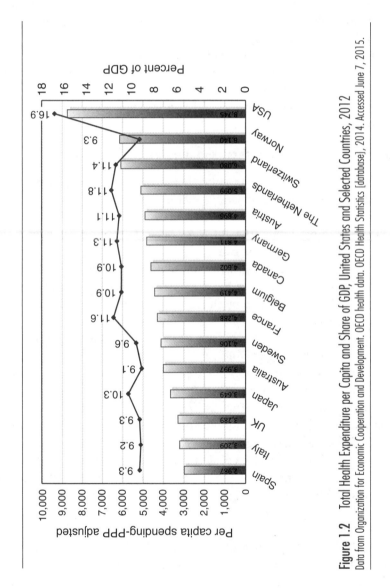

Figure 1.2   Total Health Expenditure per Capita and Share of GDP, United States and Selected Countries, 2012
Data from Organization for Economic Cooperation and Development. OECD health data. OECD Health Statistics [database], 2014. Accessed June 7, 2015.

that the United States lags behind other developed nations in measures of population health, (see **Figure 1.3** for U.S. racial disparity in life expectancy and **Figure 1.4** for death rates among children in ECD).

Imperfect Market Conditions

Under national health care programs, patients may have varying degrees of choice in selecting their providers; however, true economic market forces are virtually nonexistent. In the United States, even though the delivery of services is largely in private hands, health care is only partially governed by free market forces. Hence, the system is best described as a quasi-market or an imperfect market. The following key characteristics of free markets help explain why U.S. health care is not a true free market.

In a free market, multiple patients (buyers) and providers (sellers) act independently. In a free market, patients should be able to choose their providers based on price and quality of services. If matters were this simple, patient choice would determine prices by the unencumbered interaction of supply and demand. In reality, however, the payer is an MCO, Medicare, or Medicaid, rather than the patient. Prices are set by agencies external to the market; thus they are not freely governed by the forces of supply and demand.

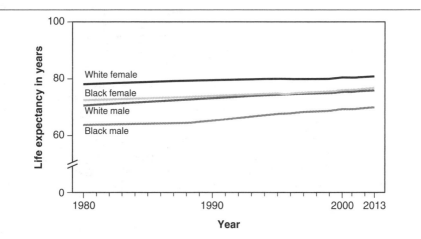

Figure 1.3   Life Expectancy at Birth

National Center for Health Statistics. Health, United States, 2014: In Brief. Hyattsville, MD. 2015, p 8. http://www.cdc.gov/nchs/data/hus/hus14_InBrief.pdf

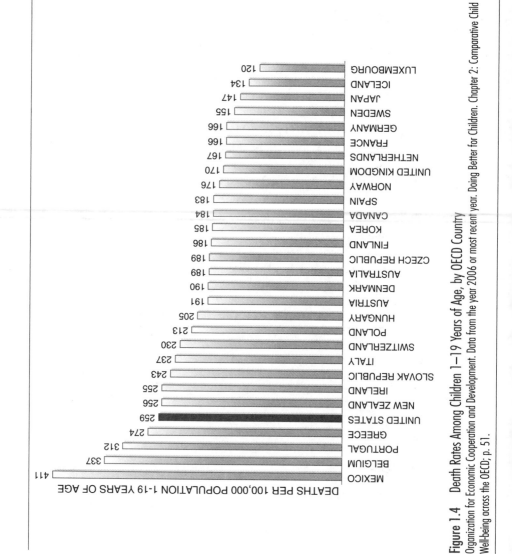

Figure 1.4 Death Rates Among Children 1–19 Years of Age, by OECD Country

Organization for Economic Cooperation and Development. Data from the year 2006 or most recent year. Doing Better for Children. Chapter 2: Comparative Child Well-being across the OECD; p. 51.

For the health care market to be free, unrestrained competition must occur among providers on the basis of price and quality. Generally speaking, free competition exists among health care providers in the United States. The consolidation of buying power into the hands of MCOs, however, is forcing providers to form alliances and IDSs on the supply side. In certain geographic locations of the country, a single giant medical system has taken over as the sole provider of major health care services, restricting competition. As the health care system continues to move in this direction, it appears that only in large metropolitan areas will there be more than one large integrated system competing for the business of the health plans.

Free markets operate best when consumers are educated about the products they are using, but patients are not always well informed about health care choices. The barrage of direct-to-consumer advertising about pharmaceuticals and other products is often confusing when it comes to making a decision as to what may be best. Choices involving sophisticated technology, diagnostic methods, interventions, and pharmaceuticals can be difficult and often require physician input. Acting as an advocate, physicians can reduce this information gap for patients. Increasingly, health care consumers have begun to take the initiative to educate themselves through the use of Internet resources for gathering medical information. However, one cannot always be sure about the reliability of such information.

In a free market, patients have information on price and quality for each provider. In the United States, however, the current pricing methods for health care services further confound free market mechanisms. Hidden costs make it difficult for patients to gauge the full expense of services ahead of time. *Item-based pricing*, for example, refers to the costs of ancillary services that often accompany major procedures such as surgery. Patients are usually informed of the surgery's cost ahead of time but cannot anticipate the cost of anesthesiologists and pathologists or hospital supplies and facilities, thus making it extremely difficult for them to ascertain the total price before services have actually been received. Package pricing and capitated fees can help overcome these drawbacks by providing a bundled fee for a package of related services. *Package pricing* covers services that are bundled together for one episode of care, which is less encompassing than capitation. *Capitation* covers all services an enrollee may need during an entire year.

In a free market, patients must directly bear the cost of services received. The fundamental purpose of insurance is to cover major expenses when unlikely events occur; but health insurance covers even basic and routine services, which undermines this fundamental principle. Health insurance coverage for minor services such as colds, coughs, and earaches amounts to prepayment for such services. A moral hazard exists, in that after enrollees have purchased health insurance, they typically use health care services to a greater extent than they would without health insurance.

In a free market, demand is determined by market forces—many individuals independently determine what to buy and when to buy a product or service. That is not the case in health care. First, decisions about the utilization of health care are often determined by need rather than by price-based demand. *Need* can be self-assessed or determined by a medical expert, such as a physician. But, many of the factors discussed previously affect whether or not the person actually obtains medical care. Second, the delivery of health care can actually result in creation of demand. For example, practitioners who have a financial interest in additional treatments may create artificial demand, commonly referred to as *provider-induced demand.*

Government as Subsidiary to the Private Sector

In most other developed countries, the government plays a central role in delivering health care. In the United States, the private sector plays the dominant role. This arrangement can partially be explained by the American tradition of reliance on individual responsibility and a commitment to limiting the power of government. As a result, government spending for health care has been largely confined to filling in the gaps left open by the private sector. These gaps include public health functions, such as clean water and sanitation; support for research and training; and care of vulnerable populations.

Fusion of Market Justice and Social Justice

Market justice and social justice are two contrasting theories that govern the production and distribution of health care services. The principle of *market justice* places the responsibility for fair distribution of health care on market forces in a free economy. In such a system, medical care and its benefits are distributed on the basis of people's willingness and ability to pay (Santerre & Neun, 1996, p. 7). In contrast, *social justice* emphasizes the well-being of the community over that of the individual; thus the inability to obtain medical services because of a lack of financial resources is considered unjust. In a system that blends public and private resources, the two theories often work well together, contributing ideals from both theories. As an example, employed individuals with middle-class incomes obtain employer-sponsored health insurance, whereas the most needy members of society depend on government-sponsored programs. On the other hand, the two principles of justice also create conflicts. For example, many of the small employers in the United States do not offer health insurance, or, if it is offered, many employees cannot afford the cost. Yet, these individuals do not qualify for government assistance in obtaining health care on account of their incomes exceeding certain threshold levels. The ACA is supposed to address this but it may take years to achieve the intended effect.

Multiple Players and Balance of Power

The U.S. health care system involves multiple players such as physicians, administrators of health service institutions, insurance companies, large employers, and the government. Big business, labor, insurance companies, physicians, and hospitals make up a set of powerful and politically active special-interest groups represented before lawmakers by high-priced lobbyists. Each player has a different economic interest to protect; however, problems frequently arise because the self-interests of the various players are often at odds. For example, providers seek to maximize government reimbursement for services delivered to Medicare and Medicaid patients, but the government wants to contain cost increases. The fragmented self-interests of the various players produce counteracting forces within the system. One positive effect of these opposing forces is that they prevent any single entity from dominating the system. In an environment that is rife with motivations to protect conflicting self-interests, achieving comprehensive, system-wide health care reforms is next to impossible, and cost containment remains a major challenge. Consequently, the approach to health care reform in the United States is best characterized as incremental or piecemeal and can sometimes be regressive when presidential administrations change. (Note: the ACA is really an example of incremental, not comprehensive, reform that primarily addresses insurance coverage.)

Quest for Integration and Accountability

Currently in the United States, there is a drive to use primary care as the organizing hub for continuous and coordinated health services. Although this model gained popularity with the expansion of managed care, its development stalled before reaching its full potential. The ideal role for primary care would include integrated health care in the form of comprehensive, coordinated, and continuous services offered with a seamless delivery (also termed medical home or health home for patients). Furthermore, this model emphasizes the importance of the patient–provider relationship and considers how it can best function to improve the health of each individual, thereby strengthening the population as a whole. Integral to this relationship is the concept of accountability. Accountability on the provider's part means providing quality health care in an efficient manner; on the patient's behalf, it means taking responsibility for one's own health and using available resources sensibly.

Access to Health Care Services Selectively Based on Insurance Coverage

Although the United States offers some of the best medical care in the world, this care is generally available only to individuals who have health insurance plans that provide adequate coverage or who have sufficient resources to pay for the procedures themselves. The uninsured have limited options when seeking medical care. They can either (1) pay physicians out of pocket at rates that are typically higher than those paid by insurance plans, (2) seek care from safety net providers, or (3) obtain treatment for acute illnesses at a hospital emergency department for which hospitals do not receive direct payments unless patients have the ability to pay. The Emergency Medical Treatment and Labor Act of 1986 requires screening and evaluation of every patient, provision of necessary stabilizing treatment, and hospital admission when necessary, regardless of ability to pay. Unfortunately, the inappropriate use of emergency departments results in cost shifting, whereby patients able to pay for services, privately insured individuals, employers, and the government ultimately cover the costs of medical care provided to the uninsured in emergency rooms.

Legal Risks Influence Practice Behaviors

Americans, as a society, are quick to engage in lawsuits. Motivated by the prospects of enormous jury awards, many people are easily persuaded to drag alleged offenders into the courtroom at the slightest perception of incurred harm. Private health care providers are increasingly becoming more susceptible to litigation, and the risk of malpractice lawsuits is a serious consideration in the practice of medicine. As a form of protection, most providers engage in what is known as *defensive medicine* by prescribing additional diagnostic tests, scheduling checkup appointments, and maintaining abundant documentation on cases. Many of these efforts are unnecessary and simply drive up costs and promote inefficiency.

HEALTH CARE SYSTEMS OF OTHER DEVELOPED COUNTRIES

Three basic models for structuring national health care systems prevail in Western European countries and Canada. In Canada, the government finances health care through general taxes, but the actual care is delivered by private providers. In the context of the quad-function model (see **Figure 1.1**), the Canadian system requires a tighter consolidation of financing, insurance, and payment functions, which are coordinated by the government; delivery is characterized by detached private arrangements.

In Germany, health care is financed through government-mandated contributions by employers and employees. Health care is delivered by private providers. Private not-for-profit insurance companies, called sickness funds, are responsible for collecting the contributions and paying physicians and hospitals (Santerre & Neun, 1996, p. 134). In this kind of socialized health insurance system, insurance and payment functions are closely integrated, and the financing function is better coordinated with the insurance and payment functions than it is in the United States. Delivery is characterized by independent private arrangements. The government exercises overall control.

In the United Kingdom, the government manages the infrastructure for the delivery of medical care, in addition to financing a tax-supported national health insurance program. Under such a system, most of the medical institutions are operated by the government. Most health care providers, such as physicians, are either government employees or are tightly organized in a publicly managed infrastructure. In the context of the quad-function model, the British system requires a tighter consolidation of all four functions, typically by the government.

Canada

In Canada, provinces and territories have introduced several initiatives to improve integration and coordination of care for chronically ill patients with complex needs. In 2004, as part of the 10-Year Plan to Strengthen Health

Care, all provincial and territorial governments agreed to provide at least half of their respective populations with access to multidisciplinary primary care teams. By 2007, about three-quarters of family physicians were working in physician-led, multiprofessional practices (Marchildon, 2013). Across the provinces, almost 60% of primary care physicians are using computerized medical records (Health Council of Canada, 2013; Mossialos et al., 2015).

As of April 2014, federal funding through the Canada Health Transfer has been distributed to provinces on a purely per-capita basis, ending previous compensations for variations in tax bases that benefited the less wealthy provinces (Mossialos et al., 2015). The objective of the new funding policy is to improve equity, but it has been criticized on the grounds that it reduces funding to less populated provinces with older populations and higher costs (Marchildon & Mou, 2013). There have been efforts across provinces to reduce the prices of generic drugs. Several provinces have significantly reduced prices in recent years; in Ontario, in 2010, the price ceiling was lowered to 25% of the price of the equivalent brand-name drug, and British Columbia lowered its price ceiling to 20% in 2014 (Mossialos et al., 2015).

Primary care reform has been under way across provinces since 2000, when the federal government invested CA$800 million (US$647 million) over 6 years through the Primary Care Transition Fund. Each province continues to reform its primary care systems, including provider payment methods, and to incentivize movement from solo to team-based practice, chronic disease management, and coordination of care with other health care providers (Hutchison et al., 2011; Sweetman & Buckley, 2014).

Germany

Germany implemented the General Law on Patients' Rights in 2013. It includes several measures designed to strengthen patients' rights. The most important one is the incorporation into the Civil Code of rights, duties, and forms of etiquette pertaining to relationships between providers and patients.

In July 2014, the federal cabinet passed the Bill of the First Act to Strengthen Long-Term Care. It aims to support families that provide care at home and to improve adult day care and short-term care by increasing the number of caregivers. Such benefits and services are to increase by 20%. The Second Act to Strengthen Long-Term Care is intended to redefine the need for care in view of the growing number of dementia patients.

The coalition agreement plan from 2013 includes proposals for various measures with a focus on the promotion of quality. In June 2014, the

Federal Joint Committee was commissioned to establish the Institute for Quality Assurance and Transparency in Health Care.

A new bill changes the way Social Health Insurance contribution rates are determined and shared between employer and employee to contain indirect labor costs. Beginning in 2015, the general contribution rate (14.6%) will be kept but both the special contribution rate for employees only (0.9%) and the supplementary premiums (and necessary specific social protection mechanisms) will be abolished (Mossialos et al., 2015). The latter two will be replaced by a supplementary income-dependent contribution rate, which will be determined by each sickness fund individually. For 2015, it is expected to be, on average, lower than 0.9%—that is, the insured will pay less than they did in 2014 (Mossialos et al., 2015).

United Kingdom

The purchasing and regulatory structures of the National Health Insurance in England have been significantly reformed under the Health and Social Care Act of 2012. The act abolished 150 primary care trusts and replaced them with clinical commissioning groups (of which there are currently 211 across England). These clinically oriented bodies are expected to make better use of resources in decisions about planning and purchasing a wide range of services for their local populations. Clinical commissioning groups differ from primary care trusts in their governance. All general practices are required to belong to a clinical commissioning group, and the groups' governing body must be chaired by a general practitioner and include other clinicians alongside managers. In 2013–2014, clinical commissioning groups controlled about half of the total NHS budget.

NHS-England was created to oversee the clinical commissioning groups. Reforms have also envisaged that all hospitals would become semi-autonomous foundation trusts, and that clinical commissioning groups would have more freedom to commission different kinds of providers and to enhance public scrutiny. However, evaluating the impact of the reform on cost, health outcomes, and quality of care will be complex, not least in the disentangling of the effects of the reform from the impact of financial pressures on health and social care services (National Audit Office, 2013).

Table 1.1 presents selected features of the national health care programs and health outcomes in Canada, Germany, and the United Kingdom and compares them with those in the United States.

Table 1.1   Health Care Systems of Selected Industrialized Countries

	United States	Canada	United Kingdom	Germany
Type	Pluralistic	National health insurance	National health system	Socialized health insurance
Ownership	Private	Public/private	Public	Private
Financing	Voluntary, multipayer system (premiums or general taxes)	Single-payer (general taxes)	Single-payer (general taxes)	Employer–employee (mandated payroll contributions and general taxes)
Reimbursement (hospital)	Varies (DRGs, negotiated fee-for-service, per diem, capitation)	Global budgets	Global budgets	Per diem payments
Reimbursement (physicians)	RBRVS, fee-for-service	Negotiated fee-for-service	Salaries and capitation payments	Negotiated fee-for-service
Consumer copayment	Small to significant	Negligible	Negligible	Negligible
Life expectancy for women	78.7	81.5	81.0	81.0
Infant mortality per 1,000 live births	6.1	4.8	4.1	3.3
Expenditures as a percentage of GDP	16.9	10.9	9.3	11.3

Note: DRGs, diagnosis-related groups; RBRVS, resource-based relative value scale.
Data from Organization for Economic Cooperation and Development. OECD health data. OECD Health Statistics [database], 2014, doi:10.1787/health_glance-2013-en. Accessed June 7, 2015.

SYSTEMS FRAMEWORK

A system consists of a set of interrelated and interdependent components designed to achieve some common goals. The components are logically coordinated. Even though the various functional components of the health services delivery structure in the United States are at best only loosely coordinated, the main components can be identified with a systems model. The systems framework used here helps understand that the structure of health care services in the United States is based on some basic principles, provides a logical arrangement of the various components, and demonstrates a progression from inputs to outputs. The main elements of this arrangement are system inputs (resources), system structure, system processes, and system outputs (outcomes). In addition, system outlook (future directions) is a necessary element of a dynamic system. This framework has been used as the conceptual base for organizing later chapters in this book (see **Figure 1.5**).

System Foundations

The structure of the current health care system is not an accident—historical, cultural, social, and economic factors explain its current structure. As discussed later in this text, these factors also affect forces that shape new trends and developments and those that impede change.

System Resources

Both human and nonhuman resources are essential for the delivery of health care services. Human resources consist of the various types and categories of workers directly engaged in the delivery of health care to patients. Such personnel—including physicians, nurses, dentists, pharmacists, other professionals trained at the doctoral level, and numerous categories of allied health professionals—usually have direct contact with patients. Numerous ancillary workers, such as those involved in billing and collection, marketing and public relations, and building maintenance, often play important but indirect supportive roles in the delivery of health care. Health care managers are needed to manage and coordinate various types of health care services.

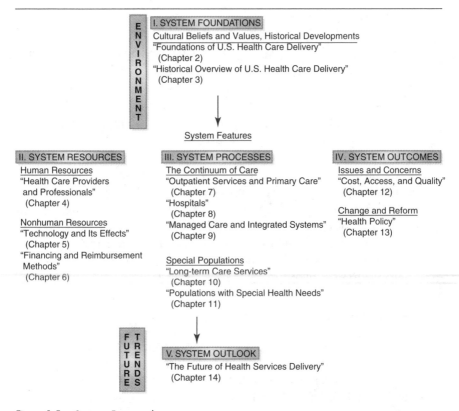

Figure 1.5   Systems Framework

System Processes

The system processes are carried out mainly through the health care delivery infrastructure consisting of hospitals, clinics, long-term care providers, etc. Most health care services are delivered in non-institutional settings, which are mainly associated with processes referred to as outpatient care. Institutional health services (inpatient care) are predominantly associated with acute care hospitals. Managed care organizations take responsibility for the actual delivery of health care, apart from their role in financing, insurance, and payment functions. Integrated systems are equipped to deliver a range of health care services. Special institutional and community-based settings have been developed for long-term care and mental health. The health care infrastructure must also support populations that have special needs.

System Outcomes

System outcomes refer to the critical issues and concerns surrounding what the health services system is able to accomplish—or not accomplish—in terms of its primary objective. The primary objective of any health care delivery system is to provide cost-effective health services that meet certain established standards of quality to an entire nation. The previous three elements of the systems model (foundations, resources, and processes) play a critical role in fulfilling this objective. Access, cost, and quality are the main outcome criteria for evaluating the success of a health care delivery system. Issues and concerns regarding these criteria trigger broad initiatives for reforming the system through health policy.

System Outlook

A dynamic health care system must look forward. In essence, it must project into the future the accomplishment of desired system outcomes in view of social, cultural, economic, and other main forces of change.

CONCLUSION

The United States has a unique system of health care delivery, but this system lacks universal access; therefore, continuous and comprehensive health care is not enjoyed by all Americans. Health care delivery in the United States is characterized by a patchwork of subsystems developed either through market forces or the need to take care of certain population segments. These components include managed care, the military and VA systems, the system for vulnerable populations, and the emerging IDSs. No country in the world has a perfect system. Most nations with a national health care program have a private sector that varies in size. The systems framework provides an organized approach to an understanding of the various components of the United States health care delivery system.

REFERENCES

Aventis Pharmaceuticals. *HMO-PPO Digest: Managed Care Digest Series.* Bridgewater, NJ: Aventis Pharmaceuticals; 2002; pp. 1–88.

Bureau of Labor Statistics. Occupational employment and wages: healthcare practitioners and technical occupations. http://www.bls.gov. Published 2011. Accessed December 1, 2011.

Bureau of Primary Health Care. *BPHC-UDS Annual Report.* Rockville, MD: Bureau of Primary Health Care, Health Resources and Services Administration; 2011.

Centers for Disease Control and Prevention (CDC). National Public Health Performance Standards Program. www.cdc.gov/nphpsp. Published 2013. Accessed June 7, 2015.

Centers for Medicare and Medicaid Services (CMS). Long term care. https://www.cms.gov/Regulations-and-Guidance/Legislation/CFCsAndCoPs/LTC.html. Published 2011a. Accessed August 2015.

Centers for Medicare and Medicaid Services (CMS). National Health Expenditure Data. https://www.cms.gov/Research-Statistics-Data-and-Systems/Statistics-Trends-and-Reports/NationalHealthExpendData/nationalHealthAccountsHistorical.html. Accessed August 2015.

Decker, SL. In 2011 nearly one-third of physicians said they would not accept new Medicaid patients, but rising fees may help. *Health Aff.* 2012;31(8):1673–1679.

Health Council of Canada. *How Do Canadian Primary Care Physicians Rate the Health System? Survey Results from the 2012 Commonwealth Fund International Survey of Primary Care Doctors.* Toronto, Canada: Health Council of Canada; 2013.

Healthleaders. Special data request via Kaiser. www.statehealthfacts.org. Published 2011. Accessed August 2011.

Hutchison B, Levesque J-F, Strumpf E, Coyle N. Primary health care in Canada: systems in motion. *Milbank Q.* 2011;89(2):256–288.

Kaiser Family Foundation (KFF). Medicaid managed care market tracker. http://kff.org/data-collection/medicaid-managed-care-market-tracker/. Published 2014. Accessed August 2014.

Kaiser Family Foundation and Health Research & Educational Trust. Employer health benefits 2009 annual survey. Exhibit 5.1. www.kff.org. Published 2009. Accessed August 2009.

Kutscher B, Herman B, Meyer H. Uninsured drop as ACA faces threats. *Mod Healthc.* 2015;45(22):1–11.

Marchildon G. Canada: health system review. *Health Syst Transit.* 2013;15(1): 1–179. http://www.euro.who.int/_data/assets/pdf_file/0011/181955/e96759. pdf. Accessed August 2013.

Marchildon GP, Mou H. The funding formula for health care is broken. Alberta's windfall proves it. *Globe and Mail.* http://www.theglobeandmail.com/globe -debate/the-funding-formula-for-health-care-is-broken-albertaswindfall-proves -it/article14764089/. Published October 9, 2013. Accessed October 10, 2014.

Medicaid and CHIP Payment and Access Commission (MACPAC). State Children's Health Insurance Program (CHIP) fact sheet. https://www.macpac .gov/wp-content/uploads/2015/03/CHIP-Fact-Sheet-April-2015.pdf. Published April 21, 2015. Accessed June 21, 2015.

Mossialos E, Wenzl M, Osborn R, Anderson C. 2014 international profiles of health care systems. The Commonwealth Fund. Pub. no. 1802. http:// www.commonwealthfund.org/~/media/files/publications/fund-report/2015/ jan/1802_mossialos_intl_profiles_2014_v7.pdf. Published January 2015. Accessed May 2015.

National Association of Community Health Centers. *A sketch of community health centers chart book 2014.* http://www.nachc.com/client/Chartbook_2014.pdf. Published 2014. Accessed June 7, 2015.

National Audit Office. Managing the transition to the reformed health system. Department of Health, United Kingdom, pp. 1–46, July 2013.

National Center for Health Statistics. *Health, United States,* 2007. Hyattsville, MD: Department of Health and Human Services; 2007.

National Center for Veterans Analysis and Statistics. *FY07 VA information pamphlet.* Washington, DC: Department of Veterans Affairs; 2007.

Politzer RM, et al. The future role of health centers in improving national health. *J Public Health Policy.* 2003;24(3):296–306.

Santerre RE, Neun SP. *Health Economics: Theories, Insights, and Industry Studies.* Chicago: Irwin; 1996. Published December 2013. Accessed.

Shi L, et al. The impact of managed care on vulnerable populations served by community health centers. *J Ambul Care Manage.* 2001;24(1):51–66.

Shortell SM, Gillies RR, Anderson D, Erickson K. *Remaking Health Care in America: Building Organized Delivery Systems.* Hoboken, NJ: Jossey-Bass; 1996.

Smith JC, Medalia C. Health insurance coverage in the United States. Current population reports. US Census Bureau. https://www.census.gov/content/dam/ Census/library/publications/2014/demo/p60-250.pdf. Issued September 2014. Accessed June 7, 2015.

Sweetman A, Buckley G. Ontario's experiment with primary care reform. *University of Calgary School Public Policy Research Papers.* 2014;7(11):1–37.

http://www.policyschool.ucalgary.ca/sites/default/files/research/ontario-health
-care-reform.pdf. Accessed August 2014.

Trust for America's Health (TFAH) and Robert Wood Johnson Foundation
(RWJF). Investing in America's health: a state-by-state look at public
health funding and key health facts. http://healthyamericans.org/assets/files
/TFAH2014-InvestInAmericaRpt08.pdf. Published May 2014. Accessed
August 2014.

Urban Institute. The Urban Institute and Kaiser Commission on Medicaid and
the Uninsured estimates based on data from Medicaid statistical information
system (MSIS) reports from the Centers for Medicare and Medicaid Services
(CMS). November 2011.

U.S. Bureau of the Census. *Statistical Abstract of the United States: 1998*. 118th ed.
Washington, DC: Bureau of the Census; 1998.

U.S. Census Bureau. Current populations report. In: *Income, Poverty, and Health
Insurance coverage in the United States: 2006*. Washington, DC: Government
Printing Office; 2007:60–233.

U.S. Centers for Medicare and Medicaid Services (CMS). National health
expenditure data. April 2012. Baltimore, MD; 2012. https://www.cms
.gov/Research-Statistics-Data-and-Systems/Statistics-Trends-and-Reports
/NationalHealthExpendData/downloads//tables.pdf. Accessed August 2012.

Welsh Government Programme for government. Cardiff, Welsh Government.
http://gov.wales/about/programmeforgov/?lang=en. Published 2011a.
Accessed August 2011.

Witgert K, Hess C. Including safety-net providers in integrated delivery systems:
issues and options for policymakers. The Commonwealth Fund. http://www
.nashp.org/sites/default/files/Including.SN_.Providers.in_.IDS_.pdf.
Published August 2012. Accessed December 2012.

Chapter 2

Foundations of U.S. Health Care Delivery

INTRODUCTION

From an economic perspective, curative medicine seems to yield decreasing returns on health improvement while health care expenditures increase (Saward & Sorensen, 1980). There is increasing recognition of the benefits to society that can result from the promotion of health and the prevention of disease, disability, and premature death. Although the financing of health care has primarily focused on curative medicine, slow progress continues toward an emphasis on health promotion and disease prevention. The progress has been slow due to the insurance system, cultural values, and medical practice that emphasize disease rather than health. The common definitions of health, as well as measures for evaluating health status, reflect similar inclinations.

This chapter explores the different aspects of what health is, main determinants of health, contrasting theories of market justice and social justice as they apply to health care delivery, and public health interventions to improve population health. Beliefs and values ingrained in the American culture have been influential in laying the foundations of a system that has remained predominantly private, as opposed to a tax-financed national health care program. In recent years, however, societal values have slowly shifted toward a social justice mind-set, and the expectations of many Americans suggest that a gradual departure from traditional American values of self-reliance may be giving way to greater dependence on the government. Passage of the Affordable Care Act (ACA) presages a gradual shift from market justice to social justice in the U.S. health care system.

WHAT IS HEALTH?

In the United States, the concepts of health and health care have largely been governed by the medical model or, more specifically, the bio-medical model. Under the *medical model*, health is defined as the absence of illness or disease. It emphasizes clinical diagnosis and medical intervention to treat disease or its symptoms. The implication is that optimal health exists when a person is free of symptoms and does not require medical treatment. Thus, when the term *health care delivery* is used, it actually refers to the delivery of medical care or illness care. Accordingly, prevention of disease and health promotion are relegated to a secondary status; a measure that is often used to indicate lack of health in a population is mortality or death (see **Figure 2.1** for death rates by age and cause in the United States).

Medical sociologists have gone a step further by defining health as the state of optimal capacity of an individual to perform his or her expected social roles and tasks, such as work, school, and household chores (Parsons, 1972). A person who is unable (as opposed to unwilling) to perform his or her social roles in society is considered sick even though many people continue to engage in their social obligations despite suffering from pain, cough, colds, and other types of temporary disabilities, including mental distress. Hence, a person's engagement in social roles does not necessarily signify that the individual is in a state of optimal health.

An emphasis on both the physical and mental dimensions of health is found in the definition of health proposed by the Society for Academic Emergency Medicine (SAEM). This organization defines health as "a state

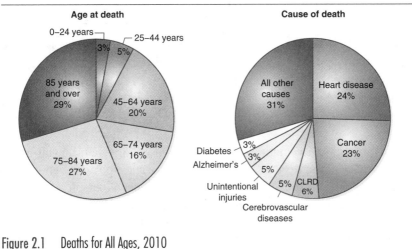

Figure 2.1 Deaths for All Ages, 2010

Note: CLRD: chronic lower respiratory diseases. Centers for Disease Control and Prevention, National Center for Health Statistics. Health, United States, 2013, Data from the National Vital Statistics Systems.

of physical and mental well-being that facilitates the achievement of individual and societal goals" (SAEM, 1992, p. 1386).

The World Health Organization's (WHO's) definition of health is most often cited as the ideal that health care delivery systems should try to achieve. WHO (1948) defines *health* as "a complete state of physical, mental, and social well-being, and not merely the absence of disease or infirmity" (p. 100). This definition includes physical, mental, and social dimensions, which constitute the biopsychosocial model of health. WHO has also defined a *health care system* as all of the activities aimed at promoting, restoring, or maintaining health (McKee, 2001). As this chapter points out, health care should include much more than medical care.

There has been a growing interest in holistic or comprehensive health, which emphasizes the well-being of every aspect of what makes a person whole and complete. *Holistic medicine* seeks to treat the individual as a whole person (Ward, 1995). Holistic health incorporates the spiritual dimension as a fourth element in addition to the physical, mental, and social aspects necessary for optimal health. Hence, the holistic model provides the most complete understanding of what health is (see **Exhibit 2.1** for some key examples of health indicators). A growing volume of medical literature now points to the healing effects of a person's religion and spirituality on morbidity and mortality (Levin, 1994). Numerous studies have

Exhibit 2.1   Indicators of Health

- Self-reported health status
- Life expectancy
- Morbidity (disease)
- Mental well-being
- Social functioning
- Functional limitations
- Disability
- Spiritual well-being

identified an inverse association between religious involvement and all-cause mortality (McCullough et al., 2000). Religious and spiritual beliefs and practices have been shown to positively influence a person's physical, mental, and social well-being—they may affect the incidences, experiences, and outcomes of several common medical problems (Maugans, 1996).

The spiritual dimension is often tied to one's religious beliefs, values, morals, and practices. More broadly, it is described as meaning, purpose, and fulfillment in life; hope and will to live; faith; and a person's relationship with God (Marwick, 1995; Ross, 1995; Swanson, 1995). The holistic approach to health also alludes to the need for incorporating alternative therapies into the predominant medical model.

Illness and Disease

The terms *illness* and *disease* are not synonymous, although they are often used interchangeably, as they are throughout this text. Illness is recognized by means of a person's own perceptions and evaluation of how he or she feels. For example, an individual may feel pain, discomfort, weakness, depression, or anxiety, but a disease may or may not be present; however, the ultimate determination that disease is present is based on a medical professional's evaluation rather than the patient's assessment. Certain diseases, such as hypertension (high blood pressure), are asymptomatic and are not always manifested through illness. A hypertensive person has a disease but may not know it. Thus it is possible to be diseased without feeling ill. Likewise, a person may feel ill, yet not have a disease.

Acute and Chronic Conditions

Disease can be classified as acute, subacute, or chronic. An *acute condition* is relatively severe, episodic (of short duration), and often treatable (Timmreck, 1994, p. 26). It is subject to recovery, and treatment is generally provided in a hospital. Examples of acute conditions include a sudden interruption of kidney function or a myocardial infarction (heart attack). A *subacute condition* lies between the acute and chronic extremes on the disease continuum, but has some acute features. Subacute conditions can be postacute, requiring further treatment after a brief stay in the hospital. Examples include ventilator and head trauma care. A *chronic condition* is less severe but of long and continuous duration (Timmreck, 1994, p. 26). The patient may not fully recover from such a condition. The disease may be kept under control through appropriate medical treatment, but if left untreated, it may lead to severe and life-threatening health problems. Examples include asthma, diabetes, and hypertension.

Quality of Life

The term *quality of life* is used in a denotative sense to capture the essence of overall satisfaction with life during and after a person's encounter with the health care delivery system. Thus the term is used in two different ways. First, it is an indicator of how satisfied a person was with his or her experiences while receiving health care services. Specific life domains such as comfort factors, dignity, privacy, security, degree of independence, decision-making autonomy, and attention to personal preferences are significant to most people. These factors are now regarded as rights that patients can demand during any type of health care encounter. Second, quality of life can refer to a person's overall satisfaction with life and with self-perceptions of health, particularly after some medical intervention. The implication is that desirable processes during medical treatment and successful outcomes would subsequently have a positive effect on an individual's ability to function and carry out social roles and obligations.

DETERMINANTS OF HEALTH

The *determinants of health* have made a major contribution to the understanding that a singular focus on medical care delivery is unlikely to improve the health status of any given population. Multiple factors determine health and well-being. Hence, a more balanced approach must emphasize health determinants at an individual level as well as broad policy interventions at the population level (**Figure 2.2**).

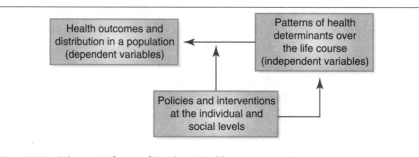

Figure 2.2   Schematic Definition of Population Health
Reproduced from Kindig D, Stoddart G. What is Population Health? Am J Public Health. 2003; 93 (3): 380-833

The leading determinants of health (see examples in **Exhibit 2.2**) can be classified into four main categories: environment, behavior and lifestyle, heredity, and medical care.

Environment

Environmental factors encompass the physical, socioeconomic, socio-political, and sociocultural dimensions of life. Physical environmental factors such as air pollution, food and water contaminants, radiation, and toxic chemicals are easily identified as factors that can significantly influence health; however, the relationship of other environmental factors to health may not always be so obvious. For example, socioeconomic status is related to health and well-being. People who have higher incomes often live in areas where they are less exposed to environmental risks and have better access to health care. The association of income inequality with a variety of health indicators such as life expectancy, age-adjusted mortality rates, and leading causes of death is well documented (Kaplan et al., 1996;

Exhibit 2.2   Examples of Health Determinants

• Physical activity	• Mental health
• Overweight/obesity	• Injury and violence
• Tobacco use	• Environmental quality
• Substance abuse	• Immunization
• Responsible sexual behavior	• Access to health care

Kawachi et al., 1997; Kennedy et al., 1996; Mackenbach et al., 1997). The greater the economic gap between the rich and poor in a given geographic area, the worse the overall health status of the population in that area will be.

The relationship between education and health status is also well established. Less educated Americans die younger than their better educated counterparts. One possible explanation for this relationship is that better educated people are more likely to avoid risky behaviors such as smoking and drug abuse.

The environment can also have a significant influence on developmental health. Neuroscientists have found that good nurturing and stimulation during the first 3 years of life—a key period for brain development— activate the brain's neural pathways and may even permanently increase the number of brain cells. Early childhood development has an enormous influence on a person's future health.

Behavior and Lifestyle

Individual lifestyles or *behavioral factors* include diet, exercise, a stress-free lifestyle, risky or unhealthy behaviors, and other individual choices that may contribute to significant health problems. Heart disease, diabetes, stroke, sexually transmitted diseases, and cancer are just some of the ailments with direct links to individual choices and lifestyles.

Heredity

Heredity is a key determinant of health because genetic factors predispose individuals to certain diseases. There is little anyone can do about the genetic makeup he or she has already inherited, but engaging in a healthy lifestyle and health-promoting behaviors can significantly influence the development and severity of inherited disease in those predisposed to it, as well as the risk for future generations.

Medical Care

Although environment, behavior and lifestyle, and heredity are more important in the determination of health, well-being, and susceptibility to premature death, access to medical care is nevertheless a key factor influencing health. Both individual health and population health are closely related to access to adequate preventive and curative health care services. Medical care alone, however, cannot ensure optimum health. Even preventive interventions are not adequate unless individuals take responsibility for their own health and well-being.

CULTURAL BELIEFS AND VALUES

A value system orients members of a society toward defining what is desirable for that society. The traditional cultural beliefs and values in America have been based on conservative principles that leaned toward market justice, with social justice principles (discussed in the next section) taking a secondary place. In recent years, the American society has been increasingly defined by several different subcultures that have grown in size because of a steady influx of new immigrants from different parts of the world. Such diversity promotes sociocultural variations in how people view their health and people's attitudes and behaviors concerning health, illness, and death (Wolinsky, 1988, p. 39). Driven by changing demographics, the foundational beliefs and values in the United States are in a state of flux. For example, the American Community Survey: 2009–2013 by the U.S. Census Bureau found that today's young adults—referred to as the millennial generation[1] by sociologists—differ considerably from previous generations, referred to as generation X and the baby boomers. Compared to previous generations, a much higher proportion of the millennials are foreign born, one in four speaks a language other than English at home, and one in five lives in poverty even though a higher proportion than previous generations have college degrees (U.S. Census Bureau, 2014). The millennials are more inclined toward social justice than the preceding generations. For example, the millennials, as well as minority groups in the United States, view the term *socialism* more positively than the general population; the same groups view the term *capitalism* negatively (Pew Research Center, 2011). A gradual shift in the traditional American beliefs and values is already at work in changing the way Americans will receive health care services in the future.

---

[1]The millennial generation, or millennials, commonly refers to those born between 1982 and 2000, and it numbers approximately 73 million.

DISTRIBUTION OF HEALTH CARE

In a perfect world, the production, distribution, and subsequent consumption of health care will have an equal impact on all members of a society. Unfortunately, no society has found a perfectly equitable method to distribute limited economic resources; in fact, any method of resource distribution leaves some inequalities. Societies, therefore, try to allocate resources according to some guiding principles acceptable to each society. Such principles are guided by a society's values and belief systems. It is generally recognized that not everyone can receive everything that medical science has to offer. The fundamental question that deals with distributive justice or equity is how a health care system can make essential services available to all members of society. The broad concern about equitable access to health care services is addressed by theories referred to as *market justice* and *social justice*.

Market Justice

The principle of market justice proposes that market forces in a free economy can best achieve a fair distribution of health care. Within such a system, medical care and its benefits are distributed on the basis of people's willingness and ability to pay (Santerre & Neun, 1996, p. 7). In other words, people are entitled to purchase a share of the available goods and services that they value. They must purchase these valued goods and services by using the financial resources acquired through their own legitimate efforts. This is how most goods and services are distributed in a free market. The free market implies that giving people something they have not earned would be morally and economically wrong. The principle of market justice is based on the following key assumptions:

- Health care is like any other economic good or service and, therefore, can be governed by the free market forces of supply and demand.
- Individuals are responsible for their own achievements. When individuals pursue their own best interests, the interests of society as a whole are best served (Ferguson & Maurice, 1970).
- People make rational choices in their decisions to purchase health care products and services to rectify their health problems and restore their health.

- People, in consultation with their physicians, know what is best for themselves. This assumption implies that people place a certain degree of trust in their physicians.
- A free market, rather than the government, can allocate health care resources in the most efficient and equitable manner.

Under market justice, the production of health care is determined by how much consumers are willing and able to purchase at prevailing market prices. It follows that in a free market system, individuals without sufficient income or who are uninsured face a financial barrier to obtaining health care (Santerre & Neun, 1996, p. 7). Thus prices and ability to pay combine to ration the quantity and type of health care services people consume. Such limitations to obtaining health care are referred to as *demand-side rationing* or price rationing. The key characteristics of market justice and their implications are summarized in **Table 2.1**.

Market justice emphasizes individual, rather than collective, responsibility for health. It proposes private, rather than government, solutions to the social problems of health.

The principles of market justice work well in the allocation of economic goods when their unequal distribution does not affect the larger society. For example, based on their individual success, people live in different sizes and styles of homes, drive different types of automobiles, and spend their money on different things; however, market justice principles generally fail to rectify critical human concerns such as crime, illiteracy, and homelessness, which can significantly weaken the fabric of a society. Many Americans believe that health care is also a social concern.

Social Justice

The idea of social justice is at odds with the principles of capitalism and market justice. According to the principle of social justice, the equitable distribution of health care is a societal responsibility. This goal can best be achieved by letting a central agency—generally the government—take over the production and distribution functions. Social justice regards health care as a social good—as opposed to an economic good—that should be collectively financed and available to all citizens regardless of the individual recipient's ability to pay for that care. Most industrialized countries long ago reached a broad social consensus that health care was a social good (Reinhardt, 1994). Public health also has a social justice orientation

Table 2.1   Comparison of Market Justice and Social Justice

Market Justice	Social Justice
Characteristics	
• Views health care as an economic good	• Views health care as a social resource
• Assumes free market conditions for health services delivery	• Requires active government involvement in health services delivery
• Assumes that markets are more efficient in allocating health resources equitably	• Assumes that the government is more efficient in allocating health resources equitably
• Production and distribution of health care are determined by market-based demand.	• Medical resource allocation is determined by central planning.
• Medical care distribution is based on people's ability to pay.	• Ability to pay is inconsequential for receiving medical care.
• Access to medical care is viewed as an economic reward of personal effort and achievement.	• Equal access to medical services is viewed as a basic right.
Implications	
• Individual responsibility for health	• Collective responsibility for health
• Benefits are based on individual purchasing power.	• Everyone is entitled to a basic package of benefits.
• Limited obligation to the collective good	• Strong obligation to the collective good
• Emphasis on individual well-being	• Community well-being supersedes that of the individual.
• Private solutions to social problems	• Public solutions to social problems
• Rationing based on ability to pay	• Planned rationing of health care

(Turnock, 1997). Under the social justice system, an inability to obtain medical services because of a lack of financial resources is considered unjust. The principle of social justice is based on the following assumptions:

- Health care is different from most other goods and services.
- Responsibility for health is shared. Individuals are not held totally responsible for their ill health because they do not control

factors such as economic inequalities, unemployment, unsanitary conditions, or air pollution.

- Society has an obligation to the collective good. An unhealthy individual is a burden on society; a person carrying a deadly infection, for example, poses a threat to society. Society is obligated to eliminate (cure) the problem by providing health care to the individual because doing so benefits the society as a whole.

- The government, rather than the market, can better decide through rational planning how much health care to produce and how to make it available to all citizens.

In a social justice–based system it is recognized that no country can afford to provide unlimited amounts of health care to all its citizens. Hence, the government must find ways to limit the availability of certain health care services by deciding, for instance, how technology will be dispersed and who will be allowed access to certain types of high-tech services, even though basic services may be available to all. This concept is referred to as *planned rationing* or *supply-side rationing*. The main characteristics and implications of social justice are summarized in **Table 2.1**.

Justice in the U.S. Health Care System

It is important to recognize that the current U.S. health care system is not a market justice–based system because American health care delivery does not follow free-market principles. A significant shift away from market justice began in 1965 with the creation of Medicare and Medicaid. Since then the move toward social justice has been gradual and ongoing, most recently espoused in the ACA. Currently, a little less than half of the financing for health care services in the United States comes from the government. The government also plays a major role in exercising a significant degree of control over the system through various policies governing insurance, payment to providers, availability of new drugs and procedures, mandating the use of information systems, funding for medical research, and quality initiatives, to name a few.

In the United States, the principles of market justice and social justice complement each other. Private, employer-based health insurance—mainly for middle-income Americans—is driven by market justice. Publicly financed Medicaid and Medicare coverage for certain disadvantaged groups and workers' compensation programs for those injured at work are based on social justice. The two principles collide, however, when a significant number of uninsured still cannot afford health insurance and do not meet the eligibility criteria for Medicaid, Medicare, or other public programs.

STRATEGIES TO IMPROVE HEALTH

Healthy People Initiatives

Since 1980, the United States has undertaken a series of 10-year plans outlining certain key national health objectives to be accomplished during each of the 10-year time frames. These initiatives have been founded on the integration of medical care with preventive services, health promotion, and education; integration of personal and community health care; and increased access to integrated services. Healthy People has established benchmarks and monitored progress over time in order to (1) encourage collaborations across communities and sectors; (2) empower individuals toward making informed health decisions; and (3) measure the impact of prevention activities (Office of Disease Prevention and Promotion, 2015a).

The *Healthy People 2010: Healthy People in Healthy Communities* initiative was launched in January 2000. Its objectives were defined in the context of changing demographics in the United States, reflecting an older and more racially diverse population. *Healthy People 2010* specifically emphasized the role of community partners such as businesses, local governments, and civic, professional, and religious organizations as effective agents for improving health in their local communities.

The current initiative, *Healthy People 2020*, was launched in December 2010 and builds on the strength of *Healthy People 2010*. *Healthy People 2020* takes into account some of the achievements made over the previous decade, such as increased life expectancy and a decreased death rate from coronary heart disease and stroke, and identifies other areas for improvement over the next decade. *Healthy People 2020*'s objectives include identifying nationwide health improvement priorities; increasing public awareness and understanding of the determinants of health, disability, and disease; providing measurable objectives and goals that are applicable at all levels; engaging multiple sectors to take action to strengthen policies and improve practices that are driven by the best scientific evidence and knowledge; and identifying critical research, evaluation, and data collection methods. *Healthy People 2020* will assess progress through measures of general health status, health-related quality of life and well-being, determinants of health, and disparities (U.S. Department of Health and Human Services [DHHS], 2011).

The overarching goals of *Healthy People 2020* include the following:

- Attaining high-quality, longer lives free of preventable disease, injury, and premature death
- Achieving health equity, eliminating disparities, and improving the health of all groups
- Creating social and physical environments that promote good health for all
- Promoting quality of life, healthy development, and health behaviors across all life stages (Office of Disease Prevention and Promotion, 2015a)

The graphic framework for *Healthy People 2020* is presented in **Figure 2.3**.

Four foundational health measures serve as an indicator of progress toward achieving the aforementioned goals. These are general health status, health-related quality of life and well-being, determinants of health, and disparities among the population (Office of Disease Prevention and Promotion, 2015a). Overall progress includes fewer adults smoking cigarettes, fewer children exposed to secondhand smoke, more adults meeting physical activity targets, and fewer adolescents using alcohol or illicit drugs (U.S. DHHS, 2014).

Healthy People Consortium is a diverse group of organizations committed to promoting and implementing *Healthy People 2020*. As of March 2015, there were 2,411 consortium organizations. Consortium members work to ensure that Healthy People meets the needs of their region, state, or community; share how their organization implements the program, champion the goals and objectives, and participate in the program (Office of Disease Prevention and Health Promotion, 2015b).

The National Association of County & City Health Officials (NACCHO) established a partnership with *Healthy People 2020* to support and increase the use of the program among local health departments, nonprofit hospitals, and other organizations related to community health assessment and improvement planning (NACCHO, 2015). NACCHO activities include identifying barriers and challenges, assessing uptake

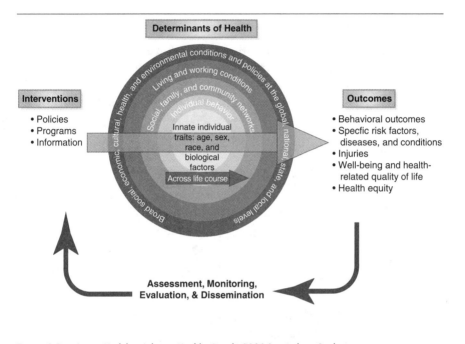

Figure 2.3   Action Model to Achieve *Healthy People 2020* Overarching Goals
Secretary's Advisory Committee on Health Promotion and Disease Prevention Objectives for 2020. Phase I report recommendations for the framework and format of Healthy People 2010, p. 8, Exhibit A. http://www.healthypeople.gov/2010/hp2020/Advisory/PhaseI/PhaseI.pdf.

at the local level, sharing examples of local use, promoting use through webinars and other means, offering training and technical assistance, and encouraging collaborative efforts (U.S. DHHS, 2012).

Public Health

In contrast to individual health, *public health* focuses on improving the health and well-being of the total population. As a prime example of social justice, government plays the central role in developing and enhancing the public health infrastructure—at the national, state, and local levels—through tax dollars. In evaluating the effectiveness of public health, indicators are developed along with a national surveillance system to consistently track the health indicators. Determinants of population health play a major role in evaluating a public health system.

Focus on Determinants

To improve the nation's health and minimize disparities among its vulnerable populations, development of a framework embodying social and medical determinants is warranted. This framework, presented in **Figure 2.4**, puts a balanced emphasis on both social and medical care

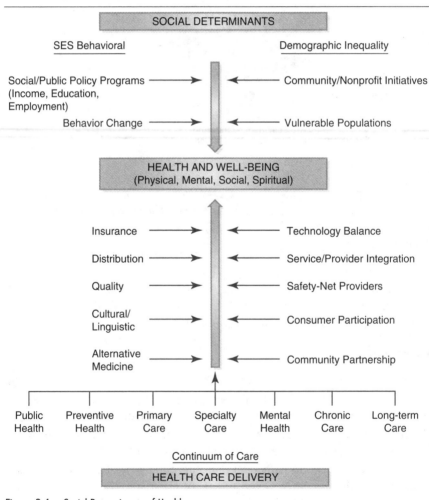

Figure 2.4   Social Determinants of Health

determinants because it is the combination of these factors that ultimately shapes health and well-being. This model synthesizes multiple health influences and highlights points for intervention. Health in this model is not just a state of being free of disease and disability, but also includes the positive concept of well-being and encompasses the physical, mental, social, and spiritual aspects of health.

Social Determinants of Health

The framework presented in **Figure 2.4** acknowledges the effects of (demographics) (socioeconomic status) /personal behavior,) and/community-level inequalities) and their defining influence on health. Personal demographics (e.g., race/ethnicity or age) directly contribute to vulnerability levels. Social and income inequalities have also been shown to contribute to disparities in health. Whether socioeconomic status is defined by education, employment, or income, both individual- and community-level socioeconomic status have independent effects on health. The health impact of personal behaviors—such as smoking or exercise—is rarely isolated from the social and environmental contexts in which choices are made. Accordingly, the WHO Commission on Social Determinants of Health (2007) concluded that the social conditions in which people are born, live, and work are the single most important determinant of one's health status.

Medical Care Determinants of Health

Although social determinants influence people's health status, the medical care system primarily focuses on treating illness or poor health. Preventive care is an exception to this rule, but understanding the influences of medical care on health should also take into consideration disparities that exist in basic health care access and quality. The framework includes a broad spectrum of medical care services and interventions to improve health. Whereas some services (preventive and primary care) contribute to general health status, others are more influential in end-of-life situations (hospice and long-term care). As patients move across the spectrum, they are likely to contend with issues of fragmentation, poor continuity of care, and insufficient coordination of care for multiple health needs. The Pan-American Health Organization (PAHO) and WHO have updated their primary health care strategy to focus on improving a country's capacity to implement coordinated, effective, and sustainable strategies. Based on the concept of universal coverage and access to services, these strategies aim to sustainably improve the health of populations and reduce health inequalities (PAHO, 2015). Services relating to mental health and chronic diseases are included in the primary health care framework (PAHO, 2015).

The relative value of each health service in the spectrum should be evaluated in determining health policy. For example, should equal investments be made in each service, or are some investments better than others (e.g., primary versus specialty care)? How can we optimize the medical system's potential for eliminating disparities with limited resources (e.g., focusing on primary care for all versus higher levels of technology care for certain populations)? Other health care factors, such as the quality of care, access to alternative therapies, and technology, will further affect a patient's health care experience and health outcomes.

Social and Medical Points of Intervention

Considering that social and medical determinants are responsive to numerous outside forces, the framework highlights important points for intervention. Dramatic reductions in health disparities are obtainable through interventions in both the social and medical domains and are grouped according to four main strategies: (1) social or public policy interventions, (2) community-based interventions, (3) health care interventions, and (4) individual interventions.

Policy Interventions   Product safety regulations, screening food and water sources, and enforcing safe work environments are just a few of the ways in which public policy directly guards the welfare of the nation. With fewer resources at their disposal, however, vulnerable populations are uniquely dependent on social and public policy to develop and implement programs that address basic nutritional, safety, social, and health care needs.

As an example of policy intervention, in 1970, the Occupation Safety and Health Act was passed, which created the Occupational Safety and Health Administration (OSHA). The goal of OSHA is to protect employees of companies from the potential dangers of an unsafe environment that may exist at the workplace. OSHA established the Injury and Illness Prevention Program that requires employers to implement a system that would ensure employees' compliance with a safe and healthy work environment. This is part of an overall effort to more effectively identify hazards in the workplace to protect employees who otherwise may be working in dangerous work environments (U.S. Department of Labor, 2011).

Community-Based Interventions   Many of the sources of health disparities may be addressed at the community or local level. Neighborhood poverty, lack of local health and social welfare resources, and societal incohesion are all likely to contribute to inequalities in a community. An understanding of the multidimensional risks and needs in a particular community can better equip local agencies responsible for designing interventions to successfully address health disparities in their communities (see the examples in **Exhibit 2.3**). Because community partnerships reflect the priorities of a local population and are often managed by members of the community, they minimize cultural barriers and improve community buy-in to the program.

Addressing disparities using community approaches has several other advantages. For example, local businesses and other partners often have a stake in contributing to local health causes that help needy members of the community. Community leaders can play a central role to help plan and manage strategies for health improvement. Community solutions also benefit from participatory decision making in which members of the community are involved. Moreover, many community programs are run by nonprofit organizations, and in exchange for providing services, these organizations are subsidized through federal, state, or local funds and receive tax exemptions. Thus they are able to offer services at lower cost than private health organizations that are obligated to their shareholders to price their services competitively.

As an example, in an effort to counteract the rise in childhood obesity rates, many schools are beginning classroom-conducted nutritional programs.

Exhibit 2.3   Strategies to Improve Health and Reduce Disparities

• Nutrition programs	• Patient safety/medical error reduction
• Work/environment safety efforts	• Prevention-oriented effort
• Community-based partnerships	• Coordinated care for chronically ill persons
• Culturally appropriate care	

These multicomponent nutritional interventions involve administrators, food services staff, teachers, parents, and students. Teaching students about proper nutrition in the classroom while concurrently educating parents increases the possibility of the program's success in fighting childhood obesity (DeMattia & Denney, 2008).

Health Care Interventions   As an example, interventions such as integrated electronic medical records systems can potentially improve patient care while also reducing waste in the health care system (Dorman & Miller, 2011; Hillestad et al., 2005; Sperl-Hillen et al., 2011). Electronic health records also hold the promise of improved quality through better coordination and integration of care among various providers. Coordinated and integrated care is particularly important in light of the increasing burden of chronic disease. For example, coordination of care and counseling for type 2 diabetes has been shown to improve blood glucose management in patients.

Individual-Level Interventions   Individual-level initiatives are critical in counteracting the effects of negative social determinants on health status. Altering individual behaviors that influence health (e.g., reducing smoking and increasing exercise) is often the focus of these individual-targeted interventions, and numerous theories have been promulgated to identify the complex pathways and barriers to eliciting changes or improvements in behavior. The integration of behavioral science into the public health field has been a valuable contribution, providing a toolbox of health-related, behavior-changing strategies.

CONCLUSION

Health and its determinants are multifactorial. Although important, medical care is only one factor that contributes to health and well-being. Factors such as physical, social, cultural, and economic environments; behaviors and lifestyles; and heredity play a large role in determining health and well-being for both individuals and populations. The delivery of health care is primarily driven by the medical model, which emphasizes illness rather than wellness. Even though major efforts and expenditures have been directed toward the delivery of medical care, they have failed to produce a proportionate impact on the improvement of health status. Holistic concepts of health care, along with integration of medical care with preventive and health promotional efforts, should be adopted to significantly improve the health of Americans; but such an approach would require a fundamental change in how Americans view health. It would also require taking individual responsibility for one's own health-oriented behaviors, as well as forging community partnerships to improve both personal and community health. An understanding of the determinants of health, health education, community health assessment, and national initiatives such as *Healthy People 2020* is essential for accomplishing such goals. Over the years, the U.S. health care system has been gradually transitioning toward social justice, yet not all Americans have equal access to health care services. To improve the nation's health and resolve disparities among its vulnerable populations, it is critical to address both the social and medical determinants of health.

REFERENCES

DeMattia L, Denney SL. Childhood obesity prevention: successful community-based efforts. *Ann Am Acad Politic Soc Sci.* 2008;615:83.

Dorman T, Miller BM. Continuing medical education: the link between physician learning and health care outcomes. *Acad Med.* 2011;86(11):1339.

Ferguson CE, Maurice SC. *Economic Analysis.* Homewood, IL: Richard D. Irwin; 1970.

Hillestad R, Bigelow J, Bower A, et al. Can electronic medical record systems transform health care? Potential health benefits, savings, and costs. *Health Aff.* 2005;24(5):1103–1117.

Kaplan GA, et al. Income inequality and mortality in the United States. *Br Med J.* 1996;312(7037):999–1003.

Kawachi I, et al. Social capital, income inequality, and mortality. *Am J Publ Health.* 1997;87:1491–1498.

Kennedy BP, et al. Income distribution and mortality: cross sectional ecological study of the Robin Hood Index in the United States. *Br Med J.* 1996;312(7037):1004–1007.

Levin JS. Religion and health: is there an association, is it valid, and is it causal? *Soc Sci Med.* 1994;38(11):1475–1482.

Mackenbach JP. Socioeconomic inequalities in morbidity and mortality in Western Europe. *Lancet.* 1997;349:1655–1660.

Marwick C. Should physicians prescribe prayer for health? Spiritual aspects of well-being considered. *JAMA.* 1995;273(20):1561–1562.

Maugans TA. The SPIRITual history. *Arch Fam Med.* 1996;5(1):11–16.

McCullough ME, et al. Religious involvement and mortality: a meta-analytic review. *Health Psychol.* 2000;19(3):211–222.

McKee M. Measuring the efficiency of health systems. *Br Med J.* 2001;323(7308):295–296.

National Association of County & City Health Officials (NACCHO). Healthy People 2020—NACCHO Partnership. http://www.naccho.org/topics /infrastructure/healthy-people/index.cfm. Published 2015. Accessed August 2, 2015.

Office of Disease Prevention and Promotion, Healthy People. About Healthy People. https://www.healthypeople.gov/2020/About-Healthy-People. Published March 2015a. Accessed August 2, 2015.

Office of Disease Prevention and Health Promotion, Healthy People. Healthy People 2020. Healthy People in action: consortium members. https://www .healthypeople.gov/2020/healthy-people-in-action/Consortium-Members. Published March 2015b. Accessed August 2, 2015.

PAHO. Primary health care strategy. WHO. Web. Published 2015. Accessed August 2015.

Parsons T. Definitions of health and illness in the light of American values and social structure. In: Jaco EG, ed. *Patients, Physicians and Illness: A Sourcebook in Behavioral Science and Health.* 2nd ed. New York: Free Press; 1972.

Pew Research Center. Little change in public's response to 'capitalism,' 'socialism.' http://www.people-press.org/2011/12/28/little-change-in -publics-response-to-capitalism-socialism/?src=prc-headline. Published 2011. Accessed July 2015.

Reinhardt UE. Providing access to health care and controlling costs: the universal dilemma. In: Lee PR, Estes CL, eds. *The Nation's Health.* 4th ed. Boston, MA: Jones and Bartlett; 1994:263–278.

Ross L. The spiritual dimension: its importance to patients' health, well-being and quality of life and its implications for nursing practice. *Intl J Nurs Stud.* 1995;32(5):457–468.

Santerre RE, Neun SP. *Health Economics: Theories, Insights, and Industry Studies.* Chicago: Irwin; 1996.

Saward E, Sorensen A. The current emphasis on preventive medicine. In: Williams SJ, ed. *Issues in Health Services*. New York: John Wiley & Sons; 1980:17–29.

Society for Academic Emergency Medicine (SAEM), Ethics Committee. An ethical foundation for health care: an emergency medicine perspective. *Ann Emerg Med*. 1992;21:1381–1387.

Sperl-Hillen J, Beaton S, Fernandes O, et al. Comparative effectiveness of patient education methods for type 2 diabetes: a randomized controlled trial. *Arch Intern Med*. 2011;171(22):2001–2010.

Swanson CS. A spirit-focused conceptual model of nursing for the advanced practice nurse. *Issues Comprehen Pediatr Nurs*. 1995;18(4):267–275.

Timmreck TC. *An Introduction to Epidemiology*. Boston, MA: Jones and Bartlett; 1994.

Turnock BJ. *Public Health: What It Is and How It Works*. Gaithersburg, MD: Aspen; 1997.

U.S. Census Bureau. New Census Bureau statistics show how young adults today compare with previous generations in neighborhoods nationwide. http://www.census.gov/newsroom/press-releases/2014/cb14-219.html. Published December 4, 2014. Accessed June 2015.

U.S. Department of Health and Human Services (DHHS). About *Healthy People*. http://www.healthypeople.gov/2020/about/default.aspx. Published 2011. Accessed December 10, 2011.

U.S. Department of Health and Human Services (DHHS). Office of Disease Prevention and Promotion, HealthyPeople. Using Healthy People 2020 to achieve your goals: implementation, action, and new tools. Presentation; November 2012. http://www.healthypeople.gov/sites/default/files/HP_Stakeholder%20Webinar_110712_508_PPT.pdf. Accessed December 2012.

U.S. Department of Health and Human Services (DHHS), Office of Disease Prevention and Health Promotion. Healthy People 2020 leading health indicators: progress update. http://www.healthypeople.gov/sites/default/files/LHI-ProgressReport-ExecSum_0.pdf. Published March 2014. Accessed Aug.2014.

U.S. Department of Labor. Injury and illness prevention programs. http://www.osha.gov/dsg/topics/safetyhealth/. Published 2011. Accessed December 10, 2011.

Ward B. Holistic medicine. *Austral Fam Phys*. 1995;24(5):761–762, 765.

WHO Commission on Social Determinants of Health. A conceptual framework for action on the social determinants of health. Geneva, Switzerland: World Health Organization; 2007. Available at http://www.who.int

/social_determinants/resources/csdh_framework_action_05_07.pdf. Accessed June 2015.

Wolinsky F. *The Sociology of Health: Principles, Practitioners, and Issues*. 2nd ed. Belmont, CA: Wadsworth; 1998.

World Health Organization (WHO). *Preamble to the Constitution*. Geneva, Switzerland: World Health Organization; 1948.

Chapter 3

Historical Overview of U.S. Health Care Delivery

INTRODUCTION

Knowledge of the history of health care is essential for understanding the main characteristics of the medical delivery system as it exists today. For example, the system's historical foundations explain why a government-run national health care system has not materialized in the United States. This is unlike what exists in Canada and Great Britain, for instance. Instead, the United States has predominantly a private health care industry that also receives a fairly substantial amount of financing from the government.

Traditionally held American cultural beliefs and values, social changes, technological advances, economic constraints, political opportunism, and ecological forces are the main historical factors that have continued to shape U.S. health care delivery (see examples in **Exhibit 3.1**). The ebb and flow of the same forces will shape health care's future direction.

Exhibit 3.1   Major Forces of Change in U.S. Health Care Delivery

• **Cultural beliefs and values**	• **Economic constraints**
• Self-reliance	• Health care costs
• Welfare assistance for the needy	• Health insurance
• **Social changes**	• Family incomes
• Demographic shifts	• **Political opportunism**
• Immigration	• President's agenda
• Health status	• Party ideology
• Urbanization	• Political maneuvers
• **Technological advances**	• Power of interest groups
• Scientific research	• Laws and regulations
• New treatments	• **Ecological forces**
• Training of health professionals	• New diseases
• Facilities and equipment	• Drug-resistant infections
• Information technology	• Global travel and transport

The agents of change just mentioned often interact in a complex manner. For example, President Barack Obama's political agenda trumped economic constraints and led to the enactment of the Affordable Care Act (ACA) in 2010 through political maneuvering. Historically, the beliefs and values espoused by the majority of Americans—such as capitalism, self-reliance, and limited government—have been primarily responsible for shielding the U.S. health care system from a major overhaul. Conversely, social, political, and economic forces led to certain compromises, as seen in the creation of Medicare and Medicaid and other public programs to extend health care to certain defined groups of people. The growing political clout of an increasing number of the elderly was instrumental in the addition of a prescription drug benefit to Medicare in 2003.

Advancements in science and technology have played a major role in shaping the U.S. health care delivery system. As a result, medical practice in the United States is highly specialized, while basic and routine primary care is given only secondary importance.

This chapter traces the evolution of health care delivery through four recognizable historical periods, each demarcating a major change in the structure of the medical delivery system. The first phase is the *preindustrial era*, which lasted from the middle of the 18th century until the latter part of the 19th century. The second phase is the *postindustrial era*, which began in the late 19th century. The third phase—called the *corporate era*—includes developments that started around 1970 and continue into the 21st century. The fourth phase, which is still in its infancy, is characterized by what is referred to as health care reform, currently enshrined in the ACA.

MEDICAL SERVICES IN PREINDUSTRIAL AMERICA

From colonial times to the late 1800s, medical education and practice were far more advanced in Great Britain, France, and Germany than they were in the United States. The practice of medicine in the United States had a strong domestic—rather than professional—character because medical procedures were rather primitive. As medical education was not grounded in science, medical practice was more a trade than a profession. The nation had only a handful of hospitals. There was no health insurance, private or public. Health care had to be purchased using personal funds, and health care was delivered in a free market. The main characteristics of health care delivery during this period are summarized in **Exhibit 3.2**.

Exhibit 3.2   Health Care Delivery in Preindustrial America

- Medical training and education were not grounded in science.
- Primitive medical procedures were practiced.
- Intense competition existed because any tradesman could practice medicine.
- People relied on family members, neighbors, and publications for domestic remedies.
- Physicians' fees were paid out of personal funds.
- Health care was delivered in a free market.
- Hospitals were few and located only in big cities.
- Hospitals had poor sanitation and unskilled staff.
- Almshouses served the destitute and disruptive elements of society and provided some basic nursing care.
- State governments operated asylums for patients with untreatable, chronic mental illness.
- Pesthouses quarantined people with contagious diseases.
- Dispensaries delivered outpatient charity care in urban areas.

MEDICAL TRAINING

Until around 1870, medical training was largely received through individual apprenticeship with a practicing physician rather than through university education. It is ironic that many of the preceptors under whom medical students apprenticed were themselves poorly trained (Rothstein, 1972, p. 86). Only a small number of medical schools existed at that time. To train a larger number of students than was possible through apprenticeship, American physicians began opening medical schools, albeit mainly to supplement their incomes by collecting student fees that were paid directly to the physicians.

These physicians did not have classroom facilities at their disposal, however, nor did they have the authority to confer the doctor of medicine (MD) degree. Hence, they had to affiliate with local colleges to use their facilities and confer degrees. As part of this approach, four or more physicians would get together to form a faculty. Medical schools were inexpensive to operate and often quite profitable. It is estimated that 42 such schools were in operation in the United States in 1850 (Rothstein, 1972, p. 91).

Medical education at this point was still seriously lacking in science. The 2-year MD degree required attending courses for 3 to 4 months during the first year and then essentially repeating the same coursework during the second year. Because fees were paid only as the student passed each course, low standards and a less-than-rigorous curriculum were necessary to attract and retain students. Even the best medical schools admitted students without a high school diploma. Training in the biological sciences was considered useful but not essential. Laboratories were nonexistent. Library facilities were inadequate, and clinical observation and practice were not part of the curriculum (Starr, 1982).

Medical Practice

As noted previously, the early practice of medicine was regarded more as a trade than a profession, and it most assuredly lacked the prestige it has today. First, it did not require the rigorous course of study, clinical practice, residency training, board exams, and licensing, without all of which it is impossible to practice medicine today. Second, medical procedures were primitive because medical science was still in its infancy. Bleeding, use of emetics, and purging with enemas and purgatives were popular forms of clinical therapy in early medicine. Surgery was limited because anesthesia had not yet been developed, and antiseptic techniques were not known. The stethoscope and x-rays had not been discovered. The clinical thermometer was not in use, and the microscope was not available for medical diagnosis. Physicians mainly relied on their five senses and experience to diagnose and treat medical problems. Hence, in most cases, physicians did not possess technical expertise any greater than that possessed by family members at home and experienced neighbors in the local community.

One of the main consequences of nonprofessional medicine was that anyone—trained or untrained—could practice as a physician. The clergy, for example, often combined medical services and religious duties. The generally well-educated clergymen and government officials were actually more learned in medicine than many physicians (Shryock, 1966, p. 252). Tradesmen such as tailors, barbers, commodity merchants, and those engaged in numerous other trades also practiced the healing arts by selling herbal prescriptions, nostrums, elixirs, and cathartics. The red-and-white striped poles (symbolizing blood and bandages) outside barber shops today are reminders that barbers also functioned as surgeons at one time, using the same blade to cut hair, shave beards, and perform bloodletting.

This system of free entry into medical practice created intense competition. Physicians did not enjoy the status, influence, and income that they do today. Indeed, many physicians found it necessary to engage in a second occupation because income from their medical practice alone was inadequate to support a family. It is estimated that most physicians' incomes in the mid-1800s put them in the lower echelon of the middle class (Starr, 1982, p. 84).

In the small communities of rural America, a spirit of strong self-reliance prevailed. Families and communities treated the sick using folk remedies that were passed on from one generation to the next. It was common for people to consult published books and pamphlets on home remedies (Rosen, 1983, p. 2). The market for physicians' services was also limited by affordability. Most families simply could not afford the cost because they had to pay for services out of pocket, without the help of health insurance. Also, most Americans resided in small rural communities, and summoning a physician could require traveling for several hours, and sometimes an entire day, which resulted in loss of work and income.

Medical Institutions

Before the 1880s, the United States had only a few isolated hospitals, which were found in large cities such as New York, Boston, New Orleans, St. Louis, and Philadelphia. In France and Great Britain, in contrast, general hospital expansion began long before the 1800s (Stevens, 1971, pp. 9–10). In Europe, medical professionals were closely associated with hospitals and readily adopted new advances in medical science. The situation was much different in the United States, where hospitals were characterized by deplorable sanitation conditions and poor ventilation. Unhygienic practices prevailed because nurses were generally unskilled and untrained. It was far more dangerous to receive care in a hospital than at home. Hospitals had a popular image as houses of death and institutions of welfare. People went to hospitals only because of dire circumstances, not by personal choice.

The forerunner of today's hospitals and nursing homes in the United States was the *almshouse* (also called a *poorhouse*). Almshouses existed in almost all cities of moderate size and were run by the local government. The almshouse was not a health care institution in the true sense, but rather a place where the destitute and disruptive elements of society were confined. The inmates, as they were called, included many of the elderly, the homeless, orphans, the ill, and the disabled. They were given food, shelter, and some basic nursing care if needed. In many cases, the almshouse was an infirmary, old-age facility, mental asylum, homeless shelter, and orphanage all rolled into one institution. Living conditions in these institutions were squalid, and they were a far cry from today's health care facilities. Thus the early health care institutions emerged mainly to take care of indigent people who could not be cared for by their own families.

An *asylum* was the forerunner of today's inpatient psychiatric facilities. Although almshouses were used to accommodate some mental patients, asylums were built by state governments for patients with untreatable, chronic mental illness. Attendants in these asylums employed physical and psychological techniques in an effort to return patients to some level of rational thinking. Techniques such as bleeding, forced vomiting, and hot and ice-cold baths were also used in these facilities (Sundararaman, 2009).

Another type of institution, the *pesthouse*, was operated by local governments to isolate people who had contracted a contagious disease such as cholera, smallpox, typhoid, or yellow fever. Their main function was to contain the spread of communicable disease and protect the inhabitants of a city.

Dispensaries were established as outpatient clinics to provide free care to those who could not afford to pay. They provided basic medical care and dispensed drugs to ambulatory patients (Raffel, 1980, p. 239). Around 1900 in the United States, approximately 100 dispensaries were located in large cities (Madison, 1990). Generally, young physicians and medical students desiring clinical experience staffed the dispensaries (as well as hospital wards) on a part-time basis for little or no income (Martensen, 1996). The dispensary can be regarded as the forerunner of today's more than 1,200 free and charitable clinics where services are delivered mainly by trained volunteer staff to the poor, the homeless, and the uninsured.

MEDICAL SERVICES IN POSTINDUSTRIAL AMERICA

The postindustrial era was marked by the growth and development of a medical profession that benefited from urbanization, new scientific discoveries, and reforms in medical education. American physicians formed professional organizations that acted as a powerful force in resisting proposals for a national health care program. The private practice of medicine, free from employment by hospitals and corporations, became firmly entrenched as physicians organized into a cohesive profession, opted for specialization, and gained power and prestige. The hospital emerged as a repository for high-tech facilities and equipment. Private and public health insurance took roots. Notable developments of this era are summarized in **Exhibit 3.3**.

Exhibit 3.3　Notable Developments During the Postindustrial Era

• Urbanization	• Powerful political interest group
• Scientific discoveries and their applications in medicine	• Support of licensing laws
• Advanced science-based treatments	• Opposition to national health insurance proposals
• Rising health care costs	• Support of private entrepreneurship in medical practice
• Imbalance between specialists and generalists	• Hospitals became true medical care institutions
• Medical education reform	• Growth of private health insurance
• Power and prestige of physicians	• Creation of Medicare and Medicaid
• Organized medicine	
• Control over medical training	

Medical Profession

Notably, much of the transformation in U.S. medicine occurred in the aftermath of the American Civil War (1861–1865), as the country transitioned from a rural agricultural economy to a system of industrial capitalism. Urban development attracted increasingly more Americans to the growing towns and cities. In 1840, only 11% of the U.S. population lived in urban areas; by 1900, that share had increased to 40% (Stevens, 1971, p. 34).

Urbanization created increased reliance on the specialized skills of paid professionals, as this trend distanced people from family-based care. At the same time, urbanization led to the concentration of medical practice in cities and towns where office-based practice began to replace house calls. Closer geographic proximity to their patients enabled physicians to see more patients in a given amount of time. Greater productivity, in turn, produced higher incomes for the physicians.

As medicine became increasingly driven by science and technology, lay people could no longer deliver legitimate medical care. Science-based medicine also created an increased demand for the advanced services that only trained professionals could provide. Developments in bacteriology, antiseptic surgery, anesthesia, immunology, and diagnostic techniques, along with a growing array of new drugs, helped bring medical practice into the category of a legitimate profession. **Exhibit 3.4** summarizes some of the groundbreaking early scientific discoveries in medicine made during this era.

A preoccupation with science and technology in the American culture brought numerous benefits but also produced some undesirable effects. For example, an overemphasis on the use of technology in medical care delivery created a bias toward specialization in medical training, which ultimately ended up creating far too many specialists in relation to generalists. Technology and specialization also increased the cost of medical care, but without significantly improving the health status of Americans. In contrast, other developed nations emphasized primary care in which, apart from delivering routine and basic care, a primary care physician and trained nurses ensured the continuity, coordination, and appropriateness of medical services received by a patient.

The American Medical Association

The American Medical Association (AMA) historically played a critical role in galvanizing the profession and in protecting the interests of physicians.

Exhibit 3.4   Groundbreaking Medical Discoveries

- The discovery of anesthesia was instrumental in advancing the practice of surgery. Nitrous oxide (laughing gas) was first employed as an anesthetic around 1846 for tooth extraction by Horace Wells, a dentist. Later, ether and chloroform were used as anesthetics. Before the anesthetic properties of certain gases were discovered, strong doses of alcohol were used to dull the sensations. The surgeon who could do procedures, such as limb amputations, in the shortest length of time was held in high regard.

- Around 1847, Ignaz Semmelweis, a Hungarian physician practicing in a hospital in Vienna, implemented the policy of hand washing. Thus an aseptic technique was born. Semmelweis was concerned about the high death rate from puerperal fever among women after childbirth. Even though the germ theory of disease was unknown at this time, Semmelweis surmised that there might be a connection between puerperal fever and the common practice by medical students of not washing their hands before delivering babies and right after doing dissections. Semmelweis's hunch was right.

- Louis Pasteur is generally credited with pioneering the germ theory of disease and microbiology around 1860. Pasteur demonstrated sterilization techniques, such as boiling to kill microorganisms and withholding exposure to air to prevent contamination.

- Joseph Lister is often referred to as the father of antiseptic surgery. Around 1865, he used carbolic acid to wash wounds and popularized the chemical inhibition of infection (antisepsis) during surgery.

- Advances in diagnostics and imaging can be traced to the discovery of x-rays in 1895 by Wilhelm Roentgen, a German professor of physics. Radiology became the first machine-based medical specialty. Some of the first training schools in x-ray therapy and radiography in the United States attracted photographers and electricians to become doctors in roentgenology (a term from the inventor's name).

- Alexander Fleming discovered the antibacterial properties of penicillin in 1929.

The concerted activities of physicians through the AMA have been collectively referred to as *organized medicine* to distinguish them from the uncoordinated actions of individual physicians competing in the marketplace (Goodman & Musgrave, 1992, pp. 137, 139). Although it was founded in 1847, the AMA did not attain real strength until it delegated regional control by organizing its members into county and state medical societies. It first consolidated its power by controlling medical education. The AMA also vigorously pursued its objectives by supporting states in the establishment of medical licensing laws that made it illegal to practice medicine without a state-issued license.

Employment of physicians by hospitals and insurance companies was frowned upon. Physicians who attempted to seek salaried employment in a corporate setting were chastised by the medical profession and pressured into abandoning such practices. Independence from corporate control promoted private entrepreneurship and put American physicians in an envious strategic position in relation to organizations such as hospitals and insurance companies.

Thanks to the AMA's concerted activities, physicians' incomes grew sharply, and their supremacy as a profession finally emerged. The sphere of their influence expanded into nearly all aspects of health care delivery. For example, laws were passed that prohibited individuals from obtaining certain classes of drugs without a physician's prescription. Health insurance paid for treatments only when they were rendered or prescribed by physicians.

Educational Reform

Advances in medical science necessitated the reform of medical education, which began around 1870 when medical schools began affiliating with universities. In 1871, Harvard Medical School completely revolutionized the system of medical education. The academic year was extended from 4 to 9 months, and the length of medical education was increased from 2 to 3 years. Following the European model, laboratory instruction and clinical courses such as chemistry, physiology, anatomy, and pathology were added to the curriculum. Johns Hopkins University took the lead in further reforming medical education when it opened its medical school in Baltimore, Maryland, in 1893. For the first time, medical education became a graduate training program requiring a college degree, not a high school diploma, as an entrance requirement. Johns Hopkins also pioneered the practice of complementing classroom education with residency training in its own teaching hospital. Standards at Johns Hopkins became the model of medical education in other leading institutions around the country. Even so, in the early 1900s, fewer than half of the medical schools provided acceptable levels of training.

In 1910, a widely acclaimed report was published by Abraham Flexner under the auspices of the Carnegie Foundation for the Advancement of Teaching. The *Flexner Report*, as it came to be known, was based on an inspection of medical schools. It found widespread inconsistencies in medical education. By this time, the AMA had gained a firm foothold in medical training by creating the Council on Medical Education. It pushed for state laws that required graduation from a medical school accredited by the AMA as the basis for a license to practice medicine (Haglund & Dowling, 1993). Educational standards were formalized, and schools that did not meet the proposed standards were forced to close. As a note of interest, Howard University School of Medicine (1869) and the Meharry Medical College (1876) were established at the end of the American Civil War specifically to prepare black physicians to practice medicine.

Development of Hospitals

As had already occurred in Europe, the growth of hospitals in the United States came to symbolize the institutionalization of health care (Torrens, 1993). The hospital became the center around which other medical services were organized.

Advancements in medical science created the need to centralize expensive facilities and equipment in a medical institution, reflecting the reality that physicians could no longer afford to have the needed equipment and facilities in their own offices. The hospital became the center for advanced technology used in medical diagnosis and treatment and for the training of various types of health care personnel. The expansion of surgery, in particular, had profound implications for hospitals, physicians, and the public. Alongside these developments came remarkable progress in sanitation practices. The professionalization of nursing promoted healing and improved patient recovery. As a result of these changes, the growing appeal of hospital services in communities, sick patients' increasing need for hospital care, and the increasing professionalization of medical practice became closely intertwined.

Hospitals, for their part, depended on physicians to refer patients to keep their beds filled. These conditions created the need for informal alliances between hospitals and physicians. Physicians began to play a dominant role in hospital affairs even though they were not employees of the hospitals. As hospitals grew in number, physicians' ability to decide where to hospitalize their patients gave them enormous influence over hospital policy.

HISTORY OF HEALTH INSURANCE

There are several reasons why private health insurance (also called *voluntary health insurance*) took root and expanded in the United States. Later, the struggle to meet the medical needs of the elderly and the poor in an environment of rising health care costs prompted the U.S. Congress to create the publicly financed Medicare and Medicaid programs.

Workers' Compensation

The first broad-coverage health insurance in the United States emerged in the form of workers' compensation. It was originally designed to make cash payments to workers for wages lost because of job-related injuries and disease. Later, compensation for medical expenses and death benefits for survivors were added.

Between 1910 and 1915, workers' compensation laws made rapid progress in the United States (Stevens, 1971, p. 136). Looking at the trend, some reformers believed that because Americans had been persuaded to adopt compulsory insurance against industrial accidents, they could also be persuaded to adopt compulsory insurance against sickness. Workers' compensation served as a trial balloon for the idea of government-sponsored health insurance. However, the growth of private health insurance, along with other key factors discussed here, prevented any proposals for a national health care program from taking hold in the United States.

Emergence and Rise of Private Health Insurance

Private health insurance began in the form of disability coverage that provided income during temporary disability due to bodily injury or sickness. Just as with life insurance, people could purchase disability coverage out of personal funds. During the early 1900s, medical treatments and hospital care became a more entrenched part of American life. At the same time, they also became increasingly more expensive, and people could not predict their future needs for medical care or its costs. These developments pointed to the need for some kind of insurance to spread an individual's financial risk over a large number of people. Between 1916 and 1918, 16 state legislatures, including those in New York and California, attempted to enact legislation compelling employers to provide health insurance, but the efforts were unsuccessful (Davis, 1996).

First Hospital Plan and the Birth of Blue Cross

The dire economic conditions of the Great Depression set the stage for innovation in health insurance to cover hospitalization costs. Hospitals faced economic instability when they relied too much on philanthropic donations. On the other hand, individual patients faced not only loss of income from illness but also burdensome debt from medical care costs. In 1929, the blueprint for modern health insurance was conceived when Justin F. Kimball began a hospital insurance plan for teachers at the Baylor University Hospital in Dallas, Texas. Within a few years, it became the model for Blue Cross plans around the country (Raffel, 1980, p. 394). At first, other independent hospitals copied Baylor and started to offer single-hospital plans. Within a few years, plans sponsored by groups of hospitals became more popular because they offered consumers a choice of hospitals. The American Hospital Association supported these hospital plans and became the coordinating agency that united the plans into the Blue Cross network. The Blue Cross plans were nonprofit; that is, they had no shareholders to receive profit distributions. Later, control of the plans was transferred to a completely independent body, the Blue Cross Commission, which subsequently became the Blue Cross Association (Raffel, 1980, p. 395).

Hospital insurance quickly grew in popularity. In 1946, Blue Cross plans in 43 states served 20 million members. Within a few years, lured by the success of the Blue Cross plans, commercial insurance companies also started offering hospital insurance. Between 1940 and 1950 alone, the proportion of the U.S. population covered by hospital insurance increased from 9% to 57% (Anderson, 1990, p. 128). Private health insurance had received the AMA's endorsement, but the AMA had also made it clear that health insurance plans should include only hospital care.

First Physician Plan and the Birth of Blue Shield

In 1939, the California Medical Association started the first Blue Shield plan, which was designed to pay physician fees. By endorsing hospital insurance and by actively developing the first plans that covered physicians' services, the medical profession protected its own financial interests. The AMA ensured that private health insurance would be preserved and remained opposed to government-run national health insurance.

Starting in 1974, Blue Cross and Blue Shield plans began to merge. Now, in nearly every state, Blue Cross and Blue Shield plans are joint corporations or have close working relationships (Davis, 1996).

Employment-Based Health Insurance

Three main factors explain how health insurance in the United States became employer based:

- During the World War II period, the U.S. Congress imposed wage freezes in an attempt to control wartime inflation. In response, many employers started offering health insurance to their workers to compensate for the loss of raises in their salaries.
- In 1948, the U.S. Supreme Court ruled that employee benefits were a legitimate part of union–management negotiations. Health insurance thus became an important component of collective bargaining between unions and employers.
- In 1954, Congress amended the Internal Revenue Code to make employer-paid health coverage nontaxable. In economic value, employer-paid health insurance was equivalent to getting additional salary without having to pay taxes on it, which provided an incentive to obtain health insurance as an employer-furnished benefit.

In subsequent years, employment-based health insurance expanded rapidly, and private health insurance became the primary vehicle for the delivery of health care services in the United States.

Failure of National Health Insurance in the United States

In some Western European countries, national health insurance initiatives were closely associated with labor movements and worker sentiments. Notably in Germany and England, labor unrest threatened political stability. Universal health insurance for all citizens was seen as a means to obtain workers' loyalty and thwart any labor uprisings. By around 1912, national health insurance had spread throughout Europe, but political conditions in the United States were quite different. Unlike the situation in European countries, the American government was highly decentralized and engaged in little direct regulation of social welfare. Despite this fact, Theodore Roosevelt ran for the U.S. presidency in 1912 on a platform of social reform. Not surprisingly, Roosevelt was defeated by Woodrow Wilson. Even so, the Progressive movement favoring national health insurance remained alive for several more years.

The entry of the United States into World War I in 1917 dealt a political blow to the national health care movement as anti-German feelings were aroused and the U.S. government denounced German social insurance. Opponents of national health care called it a Prussian menace inconsistent with American values (Starr, 1982, pp. 240, 253). Any subsequent attempts to introduce national health insurance were met with the stigmatizing label of *socialized medicine*, a term that has since become synonymous with any large-scale government-sponsored expansion of health insurance. The traditional American values based on capitalism, self-determination, distrust of big government, and reliance on the private sector to address social concerns stood as a bulwark against broad-based government interventions. Conversely, during times of national distress, such as the Great Depression, pure necessity may have legitimized the advancement of social programs, such as Social Security and unemployment compensation.

The AMA played a leading role in opposing national health care, seeing it as a potential threat to the private practice of medicine. For example, the AMA was instrumental in the demise of several bills related to national health insurance that were introduced in Congress in the early 1940s during Franklin Roosevelt's presidency. In 1946, Harry Truman became the first president to make a direct appeal for a national health care program (Anderson, 1990, p. 119). Initial public reaction to Truman's plan was positive. However, when a government-controlled medical plan was compared with privately obtained insurance, polls showed a drastic decline in public support. The AMA was once again vehement in denouncing the plan. Other powerful health care interest groups, such as the American Hospital Association, also opposed the proposal. In 1948, Truman was reelected while promising national health insurance, which actually came as a surprise to many political observers. This time the AMA launched what was to become one of the most expensive lobbying efforts in U.S. history. The campaign directly linked national health insurance with communism until the idea of socialized medicine was firmly implanted in the public's minds. By 1950, national health insurance was a dead issue, and it remained so for decades.

After taking office in 1993, President Bill Clinton made national health insurance one of his top priorities, but his proposal was largely rejected by the American people. Defeat of the Clinton plan furnished another lesson on the power of beliefs and values prevalent in the United States. As a matter of principle, Americans have endorsed tax-supported health insurance to help needy citizens, but they also have been unwilling to pay, in the form of higher taxes, for what a universal health insurance program could realistically cost. Moreover, Americans have been uneasy about more government regulation and interference with employment-based private health insurance. In a 1999 national poll, half of the respondents—regardless of gender, race, age, or working status—indicated that employers were their preferred source of health insurance. Only 18% said they would prefer to rely on the government (Commonwealth Fund, 2000). **Exhibit 3.5** provides a summary of the main historical reasons for the failure of national health insurance in the United States.

Creation of Medicare and Medicaid

Before 1965, private health insurance was the only widely available source of payment for health care, and it was available primarily to middle-class working people and their families. The elderly, the unemployed, and the poor had to rely on their own resources, on limited public programs, or on charity from hospitals and individual physicians.

The earlier debates over national health insurance had made one thing clear: Most Americans did not desire government intervention in how they received health care, with one exception—they would be less opposed to

Exhibit 3.5   Reasons Why National Health Insurance Has Historically Failed in the United States

- Unlike in Europe, national health care failed to get an early footing because of labor and political stability in the United States.
- A decentralized American system gave the U.S. federal government little direct control over social policy.
- The German social insurance system was denounced during World War I. Since then, the term *socialized medicine* has been used as a synonym for national health insurance.
- The AMA opposed national health care initiatives.
- Middle-class Americans have traditionally espoused beliefs and values that are consistent with capitalism, self-determination, and distrust of big government.
- Middle-class Americans have been averse to higher taxes to pay for the increased cost of a national health care program.

reform initiatives for the underprivileged classes. In principle, the poor were considered a special class who could be served through a government-sponsored program. The elderly—those 65 years of age and older—were another group that started to receive increased attention in the 1950s. On their own, most of the poor and the elderly could not afford the increasing cost of health care. Also, because the health status of these population groups was significantly worse than that of the general population, their medical needs were more critical. The elderly, in particular, had a higher incidence and prevalence of disease than did younger age groups. Despite their greater need for health care, fewer than half of all elderly persons were covered by private health insurance. Even if they could afford it, many of them were unable to obtain private health insurance because of poor health status. Also, the growing elderly middle class was becoming a politically active force.

A bill introduced in Congress by Aime Forand in 1957 started the momentum for including necessary hospital and nursing home care as an extension of Social Security benefits (Stevens, 1971, p. 434). The AMA, however, undertook a massive campaign to portray a government insurance plan as a threat to the physician–patient relationship. The bill stalled initially, but public hearings around the country, which were packed by the elderly, produced an intense grassroots support to push the issue onto the national agenda (Starr, 1982, p. 368). A compromised legislation, the Medical Assistance Act, also known as the Kerr-Mills Act, went into effect in 1960. Under the act, federal grants were given to the states so they could extend health services under their welfare programs to low-income elderly persons. However, enrolling the elderly in a welfare program became controversial, as liberal congressional representatives voiced their opposition claiming that it was a source of humiliation to the elderly (Starr, 1982, p. 369). Within 3 years, the program was declared ineffective because many states did not even implement it (Stevens, 1971, p. 438). In 1964, health insurance for the aged and the poor became a top priority of President Lyndon Johnson's Great Society programs.

Eventually, Congress approved a three-part program that provided publicly financed health insurance to all elderly individuals, regardless of their income. Part A and Part B of Medicare (also known as *Title 18* of the Social Security Act of 1965) became the first two layers. *Part A* of Medicare was designed to use Social Security funds to finance hospital insurance and short-term nursing home coverage after discharge from a hospital. *Part B* of Medicare was designed to cover physicians' bills through government-subsidized insurance, in which the elderly would pay a small portion of the premiums. The *Medicaid* program (*Title 19* of the Social Security Act of 1965) was the third layer. It covered the eligible poor and was based on the earlier Kerr-Mills program. It would be financed through federal matching funds to the states in accordance with each state's per capita income.

Although adopted together, Medicare and Medicaid reflected sharply different traditions. Medicare enjoyed broad grassroots support and, being attached to Social Security, had no class distinction. Medicaid, in contrast, carried the stigma of public welfare. As a federal program, Medicare had uniform national standards for eligibility and benefits. State-administered Medicaid programs varied across states in terms of eligibility and benefits. Medicare covered anyone age 65 or older, whereas Medicaid became a *means-tested program*, which confined eligibility to people below a predetermined income level. Consequently, many of the poor did not qualify because their incomes exceeded the means-test limits.

Initially created to cover only the elderly, Medicare was expanded in 1973 to cover two other categories of people: (1) nonelderly disabled people receiving Social Security for at least 24 months, and (2) people with end-stage renal disease who needed dialysis or a kidney transplant. In 1997, Medicare added coverage options under Part C, and in 2003 a prescription drug benefit (Part D) was passed into law. The main characteristics of Medicare and Medicaid are summarized in **Exhibit 3.6**.

Soon after their inception, Medicare and Medicaid became instrumental in covering millions of Americans. By 1970, 20.4 million individuals received health care through Medicare and another 17.6 million through Medicaid. The increased coverage, however, came at a high price in the form of unrelenting government regulations and uncontrolled public expenditures.

The Medicare and Medicaid programs are financed by the government, but most beneficiaries receive health care services from private hospitals, physicians, and other providers. As a major payer of health care services, the government has implemented numerous regulations that govern the delivery of services and reimbursement to providers. As a result, the regulatory powers of government have increasingly encroached on the private sector. In 1977, the Health Care Financing Administration

Exhibit 3.6   Comparisons Between Medicare and Medicaid

Medicare	Medicaid
• Covers all elderly persons, nonelderly disabled persons on Social Security, and nonelderly persons with end-stage renal disease	• Covers only the very poor
• No income/means test	• Income criteria established by states (means test)
• No class distinction	• Public welfare
• Part A for hospitalization and short-term nursing home stay	• All services are covered under one program
• Part B for physician and other outpatient services	
• Nationally uniform federal program	• Program varies from state to state
• Title 18 of the Social Security Act	• Title 19 of the Social Security Act
• Part A financed through a payroll tax paid by employees, employers, and the self-employed	• Financed by the states, with matching funds from the federal government according to each state's per capita income
• Part B subsidized through general taxes, but the participants pay part of the premium cost	

(now called the Centers for Medicare and Medicaid Services) was created to manage Medicare and Medicaid separately from the Social Security Administration.

The creation of Medicare and Medicaid had a drastic impact on both federal and state budgets, but the federal government bore the brunt of this burden. As shown in **Table 3.1**, the gross domestic product—representing total economic consumption—grew at an average annual rate of 7.6% between 1965 and 1970. By comparison, total state and local government expenditures grew at an average annual rate of 13.6%, but health care expenditures grew at a somewhat slower rate of 12.5%. In the case of the federal government, however, health care expenditures increased at an average annual rate of 30%, whereas total federal expenditures increased at a rate of only 11.3%.

Table 3.1   Average Annual Percent Increase in Gross Domestic Product and Federal and State Expenditures Between 1965 and 1970

	Total (%)	Health Care (%)
Gross domestic product	7.6	—
Federal government expenditures	11.3	30.0
State and local government expenditures	13.6	12.5

National Center for Health Statistics. Health, United States, 1995, p. 235.

MEDICAL SERVICES IN THE CORPORATE ERA

The latter part of the 20th century and the beginning of the 21st century have been marked by the growth and consolidation of large business corporations and tremendous advances in global communications, transportation, and trade. These developments have changed the way health care is delivered in the United States and, indeed, around the world. The rise of multinational corporations, the information revolution, and globalization have been interdependent phenomena.

Corporatization of Health Care Delivery

Corporatization here refers to the ways in which health care delivery in the United States has become the domain of large organizations. Since the 1990s, managed care has become the primary source for health insurance and the delivery of medical services to the majority of Americans. The rise of managed care organizations (MCOs) consolidated immense purchasing power to obtain health care services at discounted prices and to implement various types of controls to reduce the rising costs of health care. To counteract this imbalance, providers began to consolidate as well, and larger, integrated health care organizations began forming. Large *integrated delivery systems* (IDSs) can provide a full array of health care services that include hospital inpatient care, surgical services in both inpatient and outpatient settings, primary care and multispecialty outpatient services, home health care, long-term care, and specialized rehabilitation services. Together, MCOs and IDSs have corporatized the delivery of health care in the United States. At the same time, they have made the health care system extremely complex.

In a health care landscape increasingly dominated by corporations, individual physicians have struggled to preserve their autonomy. As a matter of survival, many physicians had to consolidate into larger group practices, form strategic partnerships with hospitals, or start their own specialty hospitals. A growing number of physicians have become employees of large medical corporations.

Information Revolution

The delivery of health care is being transformed in unprecedented and irreversible ways by telecommunications. For example, telemedicine and e-health have been on the rise. *Telemedicine* came to the forefront in the 1990s with technological advances in the distant transmission of image data. This technology has made it possible to provide health care at a distance, such as real-time transmission of video examinations as well as telesurgery. *E-health* refers to health care information and services offered over the Internet by professionals and nonprofessionals alike (Maheu et al., 2001). These services include medical information from reliable sources such as the prestigious National Institutes of Health and the world-renowned Mayo Clinic through their websites, online purchase of health care products, online consultations with physicians, and online interaction with other consumers about health-related matters. The Internet has created a new revolution that is increasingly characterized by patient empowerment. Access to expert information is no longer strictly confined to the physician's domain, which in some ways has led to a dilution of the dependent role of the patient.

Globalization

Globalization refers to various forms of cross-border economic activities. It is driven by the global exchange of information, the production of goods and services more economically in developing countries, and the increased interdependence of mature and emerging world economies. It confers many advantages, but also has some downsides.

From the standpoint of cross-border trade in health services, Mutchnick and colleagues (2005) identified four different modes of economic interrelationships:

- Cross-country telemedicine and outsourcing of certain medical services have been made possible by advanced telecommunications technology. For example, teleradiology (the electronic transmission of radiological images over a distance) enables physicians in the United States to transmit radiological images overseas, where they are interpreted and reported back the next day (McDonnell, 2006). The radiologists residing overseas are licensed and credentialed in the United States.

- Consumers travel abroad to receive medical care (sometimes referred to as medical tourism). For example, countries such as India and Thailand offer surgeries in state-of-the-art medical facilities to foreigners at a fraction of what it would cost to have the same procedures done in the United States or Europe.

- Foreign direct investment in health services enterprises has become common. For example, Chindex International, a U.S. corporation, provides medical equipment, supplies, and clinical care in China. American providers such as Johns Hopkins Medicine International, the Cleveland Clinic, and Duke University's Global Health Institute support innovation and delivery of quality medical services through collaborative arrangements with other countries.

- Health professionals are choosing to move to other countries that offer high demand for their services and better economic opportunities than their native countries. Migration of physicians from developing countries helps alleviate at least some of the shortage in underserved locations in the developed world. On the downside, the developing world pays a price when emigration leaves these countries with shortages of trained professionals.

ERA OF HEALTH CARE REFORM

Health care reform refers to major changes undertaken by the government to expand health insurance to the uninsured and regulate the financing and delivery of health care. It results in numerous new regulations, expansion of the regulatory bureaucracy, and control over various aspects of health care delivery. The ACA represents the most sweeping reform since the creation of Medicare and Medicaid in 1965. Given that the presidency and the majority membership in the House and Senate were in the hands of the Democratic Party, the highly controversial ACA was passed without a single vote from Republicans. Surprisingly, this time the AMA caved in and supported the legislation. Since its heyday in political activism, the AMA has become a much weaker organization, supported by only 17% of U.S. doctors (Scherz, 2010).

After the ACA's enactment, more than half of the states and some private parties filed lawsuits challenging the constitutionality of the legislation. On June 28, 2012, the U.S. Supreme Court rendered a 5–4 decision, ruling that the majority of ACA provisions were constitutional. The Court, however, struck down a major provision of the law. The Court held that the federal government could not coerce states to expand their state Medicaid programs by threatening to eliminate funding for the existing Medicaid programs in states that would choose not to expand Medicaid coverage under the ACA (Anderson & Health Policy Institute of Ohio, 2012).

On June 30, 2014, in *Burwell v. Hobby Lobby Stores, Inc.*, the U.S. Supreme Court ruled against a controversial ACA requirement that forced certain employers to provide contraceptives that may be deemed to induce abortions. A lawsuit was initially brought by Hobby Lobby against the federal government. The Obama administration later appealed a lower court's verdict rendered against the government. The Supreme Court eventually ruled in a 5–4 decision that in case of a closely held corporation, the owners of which may have deeply held religious convictions against providing drugs or devices that may destroy an embryo, the ACA violated the Religious Freedom Restoration Act of 1993. Hobby Lobby had claimed that it faced annual fines of $475 million for failure to comply with the ACA (Liptak, 2014). The Court argued that the ACA imposed a substantial burden on religious liberty.

A major threat that could have unraveled the ACA, however, was cleared in June 2015. The U.S. Supreme Court rendered a 6–3 decision in *King et al. v. Burwell* that federal subsidies for certain low-income individuals were available to all eligible buyers of health insurance through government exchanges,[1] regardless of whether the exchanges in question were

---

[1]Health insurance marketplaces established to sell health insurance to people who otherwise may not be covered under an employer's plan, Medicare, Medicaid, etc.

established by the states or the federal government. The lawsuit was based on a language in the ACA law itself. The question was whether federal subsidies were to be restricted only to those who purchased health insurance "through an exchange established by the state" (Section 1401 of the ACA).

U.S. HEALTH CARE TODAY

Driven by the forces of change discussed earlier in this chapter, U.S. health care today is at the crossroads of ongoing struggles to provide health care to all Americans while maintaining acceptable standards of quality at a cost that is affordable to both individuals and the nation as a whole.

The chief agent of change in U.S. health care delivery today is the ACA. Yet, the reform effort falls far short of what was promised. According to a Gallup poll, nearly 12% of Americans still did not have health insurance during the first 3 months of 2015, 1 year after the insurance features of the ACA went into effect. The number of uninsured, however, dropped significantly from the third quarter of 2013 when the uninsurance rate was 18% (Hughes, 2015). Still, despite Obama's public statements that all Americans would have health insurance coverage under the ACA, it appears that the law itself was not designed to achieve such a promise. Health policy researchers Nardin and colleagues (2013) stated:

> Our finding...runs counter to the common perception that the ACA will cover virtually all legal residents. The ACA will leave tens of millions uncovered. It will do little to alter racial disparities in coverage...The ACA, whatever its merits, will fall well short of its stated goal of providing affordable care for all Americans.

The ACA has promoted greater corporatization of American medicine by authorizing the formation of accountable care organizations (ACOs) and by proposing changes in the way hospitals, physicians, and other health care providers are paid. As a result, the pace of organizational consolidation has quickened (Ginsburg & Pawlson, 2014). This has occurred on the provider as well as the insurance side. ACOs integrate groups of providers. These organizations then contract with the government to deliver coordinated services to Medicare beneficiaries and share in any resultant cost savings. Although Medicare continues to expand ACO contracts, and this model of care holds the promise to improve quality and realize cost savings, thus far the results are mixed.

With greater corporatization of American medicine, the era of health care reform may well sound the death knell of independently owned small physician practices. According to some industry observers, it is getting harder by the day for small physician practices to manage information technology and other regulatory demands (Graham, 2015).

CONCLUSION

In a little more than 100 years, health care delivery has come a long way in the United States, evolving from a primitive and family-oriented craft to a technology-driven service and the largest industry in the country. In the process, many medical procedures and services have become increasingly unaffordable. Both private and public health insurance have become firmly entrenched mechanisms to pay for costly health care. Medicare, Medicaid, and other public programs, however, cover only those individuals who meet established criteria for eligibility. Efforts to create a national health insurance program have repeatedly failed.

The 21st century has been characterized as the corporate era in the delivery of medical care. Corporatization has put the delivery of health care into the hands of large managed care and integrated health care organizations, and it has turned the delivery of health care into a complex enterprise. The information revolution has created advanced telecommunication technologies, whose application in health care has made the distant delivery of certain health care services possible. E-health has given consumers access to health care information over the Internet. Globalization has added a worldwide dimension to the delivery of medical care through telemedicine, outsourcing, and foreign direct investment in health care delivery.

An era of health care reform was inaugurated in the United States with the passage of the Affordable Care Act in 2010. However, contrary to the promises made by its supporters, the law fails to provide affordable coverage to millions of Americans, albeit it has significantly reduced the number of uninsured. Some features of the ACA go hand in hand with greater corporatization, but it is unknown at present as to what extent rising costs would be contained while improving quality.

REFERENCES

Anderson D and the Health Policy Institute of Ohio. The Supreme Court's ruling on the Affordable Care Act: A review of the decision and its impact on Ohio. http://a5e8c023c8899218225edfa4b02e4d9734e01a28.gripelements.com/pdf /publications/scotus_brief.pdf. Published 2012. Accessed April 2015.

Anderson OW. *Health Services as a Growth Enterprise in the United States Since 1875.* Ann Arbor, MI: Health Administration Press; 1990.

Commonwealth Fund. *1999 National Survey of Workers' Health Insurance.* New York: Commonwealth Fund; 2000.

Davis P. The fate of Blue Shield and the new blues. *S Dakota J Med.* 1996;49(9):323–330.

Ginsburg PB, Pawlson LG. Seeking lower prices where providers are consolidated: an examination of market and policy strategies. *Health Aff.* 2014;33(6):1067–1075.

Goodman JC, Musgrave, GL. *Patient Power: Solving America's Health Care Crisis.* Washington, DC: CATO Institute; 1992.

Graham J. Medicare's (stay) home savings plan. Investor's Business Daily. April 20, 2015:A13.

Haglund CL, Dowling WL. The hospital. In: Williams SJ, Torrens PR, eds. *Introduction to Health Services.* 4th ed. New York: Delmar; 1993:133–176.

Hughes BM. Gallup: Despite Obamacare, 11.9% still uninsured. CNSNews.com. http://cnsnews.com/news/article/brittany-m-hughes/gallup-despite-obama care-119-still-uninsured. Published April 13, 2015. Accessed June 28, 2015.

Liptak A. Supreme Court rejects contraceptives mandate for some corporations. *The New York Times.* http://www.nytimes.com/2014/07/01/us/hobby-lobby -case-supreme-court-contraception.html. Published June 30, 2014. Accessed April 2015.

Madison DL. Notes on the history of group practice: the tradition of the dispensary. *Med Group Manage J.* 1990;37(5):52–54, 56–60, 86–93.

Maheu MM, et al. *E-Health, Telehealth, and Telemedicine: A Guide to Start-up and Success.* San Francisco: Jossey-Bass; 2001.

Martensen RL. Hospital hotels and the care of the "worthy rich." *JAMA.* 1996;275(4):325.

McDonnell J. Is the medical world flattening? *Ophthalmol Times.* 2006;31(19):4.

Mutchnick IS, et al. Trading health services across borders: GATS, markets, and caveats. *Health Aff: Web Exclusive.* 2005;24(suppl 1): W5-42–W5-51.

Nardin R, et al. The uninsured after implementation of the Affordable Care Act: a demographic and geographic analysis. *Health Aff Blog*. http://healthaffairs .org/blog/2013/06/06/the-uninsured-after-implementation-of-the-affordable -care-act-a-demographic-and-geographic-analysis/. Posted June 6, 2013. Accessed June 28, 2015.

Raffel MW. *The U.S. Health System: Origins and Functions*. New York: John Wiley & Sons; 1980.

Rosen G. *The Structure of American Medical Practice 1875–1941*. Philadelphia: University of Pennsylvania Press; 1983.

Rothstein WG. *American Physicians in the Nineteenth Century: From Sect to Science*. Baltimore, MD: Johns Hopkins University Press; 1972.

Scherz H. Why the AMA wants to muzzle your doctor. *Wall Street Journal*. http:// online.wsj.com/article/SB10001424052748703961104575226323909364054 .html. Updated May 7, 2010. Accessed October 2011.

Shryock RH. *Medicine in America: Historical Essays*. Baltimore, MD: Johns Hopkins University Press; 1966.

Starr P. *The Social Transformation of American Medicine*. Cambridge, MA: Basic Books; 1982.

Stevens R. *American Medicine and the Public Interest*. New Haven, CT: Yale University Press; 1971.

Sundararaman R. The U.S. mental health delivery system infrastructure: a primer. Congressional Research Service. https://www.fas.org/sgp/crs/misc/R40536 .pdf. Published April 21, 2009. Accessed July 31, 2015.

Torrens PR. Historical evolution and overview of health services in the United States. In: Williams SJ, Torrens PR, eds. *Introduction to Health Services*. 4th ed. New York: Delmar; 1993.

Chapter 4

Health Care Providers and Professionals

INTRODUCTION

The U.S. health care industry is the largest employer in the nation. It employs at least 13% of the total labor force in the United States (U.S. Bureau of Labor Statistics, 2014). The health care sector of the U.S. economy will continue to grow because of (1) growth in the overall population, mainly due to immigration, (2) aging of the population, as the baby boomers continue to turn age 65 years and older through 2029, and (3) increased life expectancies.

Health professionals are among the most well educated and diverse of all labor groups. Almost all of the practitioner groups are now represented by professional associations. Health services professionals work in a variety of health care settings. According to 2009 data (**Table 4.1**), the majority of health professionals are employed by hospitals (39.9%), followed by nursing care facilities (11.1%), and physicians' offices and clinics (9.9%) (U.S. Bureau of Labor Statistics, 2014).

Table 4.1   Persons Employed at Health Services Sites

Site	1994		2001		2014	
	Number of Persons (in thousands)	Percentage Distribution	Number of Persons (in thousands)	Percentage Distribution	Number of Persons (in thousands)	Percentage Distribution
All health services sites	10,587	100.0	12,211	100.0	16,516	100.0
Offices and clinics of physicians	1,404	13.3	1,387	11.4	1,640	9.9
Offices and clinics of dentists	596	5.6	672	5.5	884	5.4
Offices and clinics of chiropractors	105	1.0	120	1.0	136	0.8
Hospitals	5,009	47.3	5,202	42.6	6,586	39.9
Nursing care facilities	1,692	16.0	1,593	13.0	1,836	11.1
Other health services sites	1,781	16.8	3,273	26.5	5,434	32.9

Data are from U.S. Bureau of Labor Statistics. Labor force statistics from the current population survey. http://www.bls.gov/cps/cpsaat18.htm. Published 2014. Accessed Aug. 2015.

The demand for health services professionals closely follows demographic trends, advances in research and technology, disease and illness trends, and changes in health insurance and the delivery of services. Demographic trends were mentioned previously. Advances in scientific research contribute to new methods of preventing, diagnosing, and treating illness. New and complex medical techniques and machines are constantly introduced, creating the need to update skills. Specialization in medicine has contributed to the proliferation of different types of medical technicians. In addition, the changing pattern of disease, from acute to chronic, has created a greater need for health services professionals who are formally prepared to address health risks, their consequences, and their prevention. Recent expansion of health insurance under the Affordable Care Act (ACA) will lead to greater utilization of health care services, hence, a greater demand for health care professionals. Delivery of health care through managed care and a greater emphasis on prevention in the ACA require additional primary care providers than previously.

This chapter provides an overview of the large array of health services professionals. It summarizes the training and practice requirements for these professionals, their major roles, the practice settings in which they are generally employed, and some critical issues concerning their professions. Emphasis is placed on physicians because they play a leading role in the delivery of health care. Nonphysician practitioners, who have advanced training, are also filling a critical need in the delivery of primary care services. The chapter also describes the imbalance between primary and specialty care services, the maldistribution of practitioners, and the looming personnel shortages.

PHYSICIANS

Physicians play a central role by evaluating a patient's health condition, diagnosing abnormalities, and prescribing treatment. Some physicians are engaged in medical education and research to find new and better ways to control and cure health problems.

All states require physicians to be licensed before they can practice medicine. The licensure requirements include graduation from an accredited medical school that awards a doctor of medicine (MD) or doctor of osteopathic medicine (DO) degree, successful completion of a licensing examination administered by either the National Board of Medical Examiners or the National Board of Osteopathic Medical Examiners, and completion of a supervised internship/residency program (Stanfield, 1995, pp. 102–104). *Residency* is graduate medical education in a specialty that takes the form of paid on-the-job training, usually in a hospital. Most physicians serve a 1-year rotating internship after graduation before entering a residency, which may last 2 to 6 years.

The number of active physicians, both MDs and DOs, has steadily increased in the United States, rising from 14.1 physicians per 10,000 population in 1950 to 28.3 physicians per 10,000 population in 2012 (**Table 4.2**). Of the 192 medical schools in this country, 163 teach allopathic medicine (see the next section for its definition) and award the MD degree, and 29 teach osteopathic medicine and award the DO degree.

Similarities and Differences Between MDs and DOs

Both MDs and DOs use traditionally accepted methods of treatment, including drugs and surgery. The two differ mainly in their philosophies and approaches to medical treatment. *Osteopathic medicine*, practiced by DOs,

Table 4.2   Active Physicians: Type and Number per 10,000 Population

Year	All Active Physicians	Doctors of Medicine	Doctors of Osteopathy	Active Physicians per 10,000 Population
1950	219,900	209,000	10,900	14.1
1960	259,500	247,300	12,200	14.0
1970	326,500	314,200	12,300	15.6
1980	457,500	440,400	17,100	19.7
1990	589,500	561,400	28,100	23.4
1995	672,859	637,192	35,667	25.6
2000	772,296	727,573	44,723	27.8
2012	826,001	763,000	63,000	28.3

Data are from the National Center for Health Statistics. Health, United States, 2014 (p. 307); Hyattsville, MD: U.S. Department of Health and Human Services; 2015.

emphasizes the musculoskeletal system of the body (e.g., the correction of joints or tissues). In their treatment plans, DOs stress preventive medicine such as diet and the environment as factors that might influence natural resistance. They take a holistic approach to patient care. In contrast, MDs are trained in *allopathic medicine*, which views medical treatment as an active intervention to produce a counteracting reaction in an attempt to neutralize the effects of disease. MDs, particularly generalists, may also use preventive medicine along with allopathic treatments. Approximately one-third of MDs and more than one-half of DOs are generalists (U.S. Bureau of Labor Statistics, 2002).

Generalists and Specialists

Whereas most DOs are generalists, most MDs are specialists. In the United States, physicians trained in family medicine/general practice, general internal medicine, and general pediatrics are considered primary care physicians or *generalists* (Rich et al., 1994). For the most part, primary care physicians provide preventive services (e.g., health examinations, immunizations, mammograms, Pap smears) and treat frequently occurring and less severe problems. Referrals are often made to specialists for problems that occur less frequently or that require complex diagnostic or therapeutic approaches.

Physicians in non-primary care specialties dealing with particular diseases or organ systems are referred to as *specialists*. Specialists must seek certification in an area of medical specialization, which commonly requires additional years of advanced residency training followed by several years of practice in the specialty. A specialty board examination is often required as the final step for becoming a board-certified specialist. The common medical specialties include anesthesiology, cardiology, dermatology, specialized internal medicine, neurology, obstetrics and gynecology, ophthalmology, pathology, pediatrics, psychiatry, radiology, and surgery. These specialties can be divided into six major functional groups: (1) the subspecialties of internal medicine; (2) a broad group of medical specialties; (3) obstetrics and gynecology; (4) surgery of all types; (5) hospital-based radiology, anesthesiology, and pathology; and (6) psychiatry (Cooper, 1994).

Hospitalists

One type of specialty not categorized by a specific organ, disease, or age is that of a *hospitalist*, whose specialty is organized around the site of care, the hospital. Hospitalists are involved in inpatient medicine, and their roles parallel those of primary care physicians in an outpatient setting, in that they manage the care of hospitalized patients. This specialty has long served a significant role in urban hospitals in Canada and the United Kingdom. It surfaced in the U.S. health care system to a significant extent only in the last decade when managed care began to dominate the health care system, placing an emphasis on cost-efficiency. Hospitalists seek to decrease overall cost and length of stay for patients, yet still maintain referring-physician satisfaction and the readmission rates of subspecialist colleagues. Most practicing hospitalists train under various primary care concentrations such as general internal medicine, family practice, or general pediatrics.

Differences Between Primary and Specialty Care

Primary care can be distinguished from specialty care by the time, focus, and scope of services provided to patients. The five main areas of distinction are as follows:

1. In linear time sequence, primary care is first-contact care and is regarded as the portal of entry to the health care system (Kahn et al., 1994). Specialty care, when needed, generally follows primary care.

2. In managed care and integrated delivery environments, primary care physicians serve as gatekeepers—an important role in controlling costs, utilization rates, and the rational allocation of resources. In the gatekeeping model, specialty care requires referral from a primary care physician.

3. Primary care is longitudinal in the sense that primary care providers follow a patient through the course of treatment and coordinate various activities, including initial diagnosis, treatment, referral, consultation, monitoring, and follow-up. Specialty care is episodic and, therefore, more focused and intense.

4. Primary care focuses on the person as a whole. The patient may have multiple health issues, a condition referred to as comorbidity. Primary care seeks to balance the patient's multiple health issues, including referrals to appropriate specialists when needed. Specialty care deals with particular diseases or organ systems of the body. It is limited in its scope to episodes of illness, specific organ systems, or the disease process. Specialty care is also associated with secondary and tertiary levels of services.

5. The difference in scope is reflected in how primary and specialty care providers are trained. Primary care medical students spend a significant amount of time in ambulatory care settings, familiarizing themselves with a variety of patient conditions and problems. Students in medical subspecialties spend significant time in inpatient hospitals, where they are exposed to state-of-the-art medical technology to diagnose and treat diseases and perform surgeries.

Work Settings and Practice Patterns

The variety of settings in which physicians work include hospitals, where they are employed as medical residents, staff physicians, or hospitalists. Others work in the public sector, such as federal government agencies, public health clinics, community and migrant health centers, schools, and prisons. Most physicians, however, are office-based practitioners in private clinics. In private practice, physicians are partners or salaried employees under contractual arrangements.

Table 4.3 shows that in 2010, physicians in general/family practice accounted for the greatest proportion of ambulatory care visits in the United States (21.1%), followed by those in internal medicine (13.9%) and pediatrics (12.4%).

Table 4.3   Ambulatory Visits by Generalists and Specialists in the United States, 2010

Obstetrics/gynecology	7.8%
Pediatrics	12.4%
Internal medicine	13.9%
General/family practice	21.1%
Specialists	44.8%
Total	100%

National Center for Health Statistics. Health, United States, 2014: With Special Feature on Adults Aged 55–64. Hyattsville, MD; 2015:267–268.

Imbalance and Maldistribution of Physicians

In 2013 there were approximately 767,100 licensed physicians under the age of 75 in active practice. Women comprised a third (31%) of the workforce. Physicians between ages 65 and 75 comprised 10% of the active workforce. Physicians between ages 55 and 64 comprised 26% of the active workforce, and many in this age group will retire within the next decade (IHS, 2015). In 2012, there were 260.5 active physicians per 100,000 population in the United States, ranging from a high of 421.5 in Massachusetts to a low of 180.8 in Mississippi. States with the highest number of physicians per 100,000 population are concentrated in the Northeast (AAMC, 2013).

Looming Shortages and the Affordable Care Act

Demand for physicians continues to grow faster than supply, leading to a projected shortfall of between 46,100 and 90,400 physicians by 2025. Projected shortfalls in primary care will range between 12,500 and 31,100 by 2025, and between 28,200 and 63,700 in various specialties. Expanded medical coverage achieved under the ACA will likely increase demand by about 16,000 to 17,000 physicians (2.0%) over and above the increased demand resulting from changing demographics. Physician shortages are projected to persist even with the rapid growth in the supply of advanced-practice clinicians who can fill in for some of the roles of physicians (IHS, 2015).

To better plan for future workforce needs, it is critical to study some of the patterns of change: (1) how physician retirement patterns might change over time based on economic factors, work satisfaction, trends in health and mortality, and cultural norms regarding retirement; (2) whether younger physicians will continue to have similar work–life balance expectations as older cohorts; (3) how clinician staffing patterns, including those of advanced-practice clinicians, are likely to evolve over time; (4) the effects of different payment methods, which are changing under the ACA; and (5) the potential impact of emerging care delivery models, such as accountable care organizations (ACOs) emphasized under the ACA (IHS, 2015).

The ACA includes some provisions to address the looming shortages, although it is not clear how and to what extent they would be successful. The law seeks to modify federal Medicare payments for medical residency training and to authorize additional funding for medical residency training programs. The ACA also seeks to expand the nonphysician workforce of clinicians with advanced training. For example, the ACA includes provisions to expand the number of primary care providers under the National Health Service Corps to work in geographic areas where shortages exist (Heisler, 2013).

The ACA included the establishment of the National Health Care Workforce Commission, which is tasked with developing a national health care workforce strategy. The law also established the National Center for Health Workforce Analysis to develop information describing and analyzing the health care workforce and related issues, oversee the health care workforce development grant program, develop performance measures, and establish a national Internet registry of grants awarded. To date, almost $12 million have been spent (ACP, 2013).

Geographic Maldistribution

Physicians often choose to concentrate in metropolitan and suburban areas rather than in rural and inner-city areas because the former generally offer greater prospects for better living standards, professional interaction, access to modern facilities and technology, and professional growth.

The demand for physicians' services is primarily determined by the population's health care needs. The actual delivery of services, however, is based on people's ability to pay for them, mainly through health insurance. The need-based model assumes an even distribution of physicians in the projection of workforce requirements, whereas demand factors affect more favorably the distribution of physicians in metropolitan and suburban areas where most of the well-insured populations live. This leaves rural areas and inner cities with provider shortages.

Specialty Maldistribution

Besides geographic maldistribution of physicians, a considerable imbalance exists between primary and specialty care in the United States. From 1965 to 1992, the number of primary care physicians increased by only 13%, whereas the number of specialists increased by 121% (Rivo & Kindig, 1996). The supply of primary care physicians sharply dropped between 1949 and 1970 and has slowly declined since then. The number of positions filled in family practice residency programs showed an increase during the first few years of the 1990s but has experienced a slow decline since 1998 (Pugno et al., 2001). Other areas in primary care training show similar trends. The trends portray a declining interest in primary care among medical graduates.

In the United States, approximately 38% of physicians are generalists, and the remaining 62% are specialists (National Center for Health Statistics, 2015). Other industrialized countries typically have generalists accounting for over 50% of their physician workforce.

Specialty maldistribution has become ingrained in the U.S. health care delivery system for three main reasons: medical technology, reimbursement methods and remuneration, and specialty-oriented medical education. By comparison, the need for primary care physicians is determined mainly by the demographics of the general population. Because the population grows at a significantly slower rate than technological advancements, the gap between primary and specialty care physician workforces continues to expand.

The higher incomes earned by specialists relative to primary care physicians have led to the imbalance between primary care and specialty physicians. In addition, specialists have more predictable work hours and enjoy higher prestige, both among their colleagues and from the public at large (Rosenblatt & Lishner, 1991; Samuels & Shi, 1993). High status and prestige are accorded to tertiary care and specialties employing high technology. Perhaps not surprisingly, these considerations have influenced the career decisions of many medical students.

The imbalance between generalists and specialists has several undesirable consequences. Having too many specialists has contributed to the high volume of intensive, expensive, and invasive medical services as well as to the rise in health care costs (Greenfield & Nelson, 1992; Rosenblatt, 1992; Schroeder & Sandy, 1993; Wennberg et al., 1993). A greater supply of surgeons increases the demand for initial contacts and follow-up visits with surgeons. Seeking care directly from specialists is often less effective than using primary care physicians who often provide early intervention before complications develop (Starfield, 1992; Starfield & Simpson, 1993). Having higher numbers of primary care professionals is associated with lower overall mortality and lower death rates resulting from cardiovascular disease and cancer (Shi, 1992, 1994). Primary care physicians have also been the major providers of care to minorities, the poor, and people living in underserved areas (Ginzberg, 1994; Starr, 1982). Hence, the underserved populations suffer the most from shortages of primary care physicians.

DENTISTS

Dentists are the major providers of dental care. Their main role is to diagnose and treat problems related to the teeth, gums, and tissues of the mouth. All dentists must be licensed to practice. Licensure requirements include graduation from an accredited dental school that awards a doctor of dental surgery (DDS) or doctor of dental medicine (DMD) degree and successful completion of both written and practical examinations.

Eight specialty areas are recognized by the American Dental Association: orthodontics (straightening teeth), oral and maxillofacial surgery (operating on the mouth and jaws), pediatric dentistry (dental care for children), periodontics (treating gums), prosthodontics (making artificial teeth or dentures), endodontics (root canal therapy), public health dentistry (community dental health), and oral pathology (diseases of the mouth) (see **Table 4.4** for frequency distribution). The growth of dental specialties is influenced by technological advances, such as implant dentistry, laser-guided surgery, orthognathic surgery for the restoration of facial form and function, new metal combinations for use in prosthetic devices, new bone graft materials in tissue-guided regeneration techniques, and new materials and instruments.

Many dentists are involved in the prevention of dental decay and gum disease. Dental prevention includes regular cleaning of teeth and educating patients on proper dental hygiene. Hence, dental offices generally employ dental hygienists and assistants to perform many of the preventive and routine care services. Dentists also spot symptoms that require treatment by a physician.

Table 4.4   Specialties for Dentists, 2012

Dentists	125,800
Orthodontists	7,500
Oral surgeons	6,700
Dentists, all other	6,400
Total	146,400

Occupational employment and wages: national employment matrix. www.bls.gov. Accessed June 3, 2015.

Most dentists practice in private offices, either alone or in groups. As such, dental offices are operated as private businesses, and dentists often perform business tasks such as staffing, financing, purchasing, leasing, and work scheduling. Some dentists work within dental clinics in private companies, retail stores, franchised dental outlets, or managed care organizations (MCOs). Group dental practices—which typically offer lower overhead and increased productivity—have slowly grown. The federal government also employs dentists, mainly in the hospitals and clinics of the Department of Veterans Affairs and the U.S. Public Health Service.

The emergence of employer-sponsored dental insurance caused an increased demand for dental care because it enabled a greater segment of the population to afford it. The demand for dentists will continue to increase with the increase in populations having high dental needs, such as the elderly, the handicapped, the homebound, and patients with HIV. Other factors contributing to the increased demand for dentists include greater public awareness of the importance of dental care to general health status, the fairly widespread appeal of cosmetic and aesthetic dentistry, and the inclusion of dental care as part of many publicly funded programs (i.e., Head Start, Medicaid, community and migrant health centers, maternal and infant care).

PHARMACISTS

The traditional role of pharmacists has been to dispense medicines prescribed by physicians, dentists, and podiatrists and to provide consultation on the proper selection and use of medicines. All states require a license to practice pharmacy. Since 2005, the bachelor of pharmacy degree has been phased out, and a PharmD degree requiring 6 years of postsecondary education has become the standard. In addition to graduation from an accredited pharmacy program, licensure requirements include successful completion of a state board examination and practical experience or completion of a supervised internship. The 2011 annual salary range of pharmacists was between $51,000 and $130,000.

Although most pharmacists are generalists—dispensing drugs and advising providers and patients—some become specialists. Pharmacotherapists specialize in drug therapy and work closely with physicians. Nutrition-support pharmacists determine and prepare drugs needed for nutritional therapy.

Table 4.5   Sites of Employment for Pharmacists, 2012

Retail	192,200
Hospitals	69,800
Internet pharmacists, wholesalers, physician offices	17,100
Other	7,300
Total	286,400

Occupational employment and wages: national employment matrix. www.bls.gov. Accessed June 3, 2015.

Radiopharmacists or nuclear pharmacists produce radioactive drugs used for patient diagnosis and therapy.

Most pharmacists hold salaried positions and work in community pharmacies that are independently owned or are part of a national drugstore, supermarket, or department store chain. Pharmacists are also employed by hospitals, MCOs, home health agencies, clinics, government health services organizations, and pharmaceutical manufacturers (see **Table 4.5** for sites of employment for pharmacists).

The role of pharmacists has expanded over the last 2 decades from the preparation and dispensing of prescriptions to include drug product education and serving as experts on specific drugs, drug interactions, and generic drug substitution. In about half of all states, pharmacists have the authority to initiate or modify drug treatment, as long as they have collaborative agreements with physicians. Pharmacists play a critical role in informing consumers about prescription drugs and their potential misuse. This educating and counseling role of pharmacists is broadly referred to as *pharmaceutical care.*

OTHER DOCTORAL-LEVEL HEALTH PROFESSIONALS

In addition to physicians, dentists, and some pharmacists, some other health professionals have doctoral education, including optometrists, psychologists, podiatrists, and chiropractors (see **Table 4.6** for numbers of these professionals).

Table 4.6   Employment Levels of Doctoral-Level Health Professionals in the United States, 2012

Optometrists	33,100
Psychologists	146,700
Podiatrists	10,700
Chiropractors	44,400

Occupational employment and wages: national employment matrix. www.bls.gov. Accessed June 3, 2015.

Optometrists provide vision care such as examination, diagnosis, and correction of vision problems. They must be licensed to practice. The licensure requirements include the possession of a doctor of optometry (OD) degree and completion of a written and clinical state board examination. Most optometrists work in solo or group practices. Others work for the government, MCOs, optical stores, or vision care centers as salaried employees.

Psychologists provide patients with mental health care. They must be licensed or certified to practice. The ultimate recognition is the diplomate in psychology, which requires a doctor of philosophy (PhD) or doctor of psychology (PsyD) degree, a minimum of 5 years of postdoctoral experience, and the successful completion of an examination administered by the American Board of Examiners in professional psychology. Psychologists may specialize in several areas, such as clinical, counseling, developmental, educational, engineering, personnel, experimental, industrial, psychometric, rehabilitation, school, and social domains (Stanfield, 1995, pp. 280–282).

Podiatrists treat patients with diseases or deformities of the feet, by performing surgical operations, prescribing medications and corrective devices, and administering physiotherapy. They must be licensed. Requirements for licensure include completion of an accredited program that awards a doctor of podiatric medicine (DPM) degree and completion of a national examination administered by the National Board of Podiatry. Most podiatrists work in private practice, although some are salaried employees of health services organizations.

Chiropractors provide treatment to patients through chiropractic (Greek for "done by hand") manipulation, physiotherapy, and dietary counseling. They typically help patients with neurologic, muscular, and vascular disturbances. Chiropractic care is based on the belief that the body is a self-healing organism; thus chiropractors do not prescribe drugs or perform surgery. Chiropractors must be licensed to practice. Requirements for licensure include completion of a 4-year accredited program that awards a doctor of chiropractic (DC) degree and an examination by the state chiropractic board. Most chiropractors work in a private solo or group practice.

NURSES

Nurses constitute the largest group of health care professionals. The nursing profession developed around hospitals after World War I, and it primarily attracted women. Before World War I, more than 70 percent of nurses worked in private duty, either in patients' homes or for private-pay patients in hospitals. Hospital-based nursing flourished after the war as the effectiveness of nursing care became apparent. Federal support of nursing education increased after World War II, in the form of the Nursing Training Act of 1964, the Health Manpower Act of 1968, and the Nursing Training Act of 1971, but state funding remains the primary source of financial support for nursing schools.

Nurses are the major caregivers of sick and injured patients, addressing their physical, mental, and emotional needs. All states require that nurses be licensed to practice. The licensure requirements include graduation from an approved nursing program and successful completion of a national examination. Educational preparation distinguishes between two levels of nurses. Registered nurses (RNs) must complete an associate's degree (ADN), a diploma program, or a bachelor of science in nursing (BSN) degree. ADN programs take about 2 to 3 years and are offered by community and junior colleges. Diploma programs take 2 to 3 years and are offered by hospitals. BSN programs take 4 to 5 years and are offered by colleges and universities (Stanfield, 1995, pp. 126–199). Licensed practical nurses (LPNs)—called licensed vocational nurses (LVNs) in some states—must complete a state-approved program in practical nursing and take a national written examination. Most practical nursing programs last about 1 year and include both classroom study and supervised clinical practice.

Nurses work in a large variety of health care settings, and many still do private-duty nursing in patients' homes. They are often classified according to the settings in which they work—for example, hospital nurses, long-term care nurses, public health nurses, private-duty nurses, office nurses, and occupational health or industrial nurses. Head nurses act as supervisors of other nurses; for example, RNs supervise LPNs.

Because hospitals now treat much sicker patients than in the past, patient-to-nurse staffing ratios have increased, and caregiving has become more intensive. In addition, the remarkable growth in alternative settings has created new opportunities for nursing employment. The growing opportunities for RNs in supportive roles such as case management, utilization review, quality assurance, and prevention counseling have also expanded the demand for their services. Estimates show a current national shortfall of nurses, which is projected to increase (Sochalski, 2002). Sluggish wages, low levels of job satisfaction, and inadequate career mobility pose some major impediments to attracting and retaining nurses (Sochalski, 2002). Many U.S. hospitals turn to developing countries (such as the Philippines and China) for their nursing supply, and this trend is likely to continue.

Advanced-Practice Nurses

The term *advanced-practice nurse* (APN) is a general name for nurses who have education and clinical experience beyond that required of an RN. Four areas of specialization for APNs exist (Cooper et al., 1998): clinical nurse specialists (CNSs), certified registered nurse anesthetists (CRNAs), nurse practitioners (NPs), and certified nurse–midwives (CNMs). NPs and CNMs are also categorized as nonphysician practitioners; they are discussed in the next section. Besides being direct caregivers, APNs perform other professional activities such as collaborating and consulting with other health care professionals, educating patients and other nurses, collecting data for clinical research projects, and participating in the development and implementation of total quality management programs, critical pathways, case management, and standards of care (Grossman, 1995). According to the 2008 National Sample Survey of Registered Nurses, there are 251,000 APNs in the United States.

The main difference between CNSs and NPs is that CNSs work in hospitals, whereas NPs mainly work in primary care settings. CNSs can specialize in specific fields such as oncology, neonatal health, cardiac care, or psychiatric care.

NONPHYSICIAN PRACTITIONERS

The term *nonphysician practitioner* (NPP)—also called nonphysician clinician and midlevel provider—refers to clinical professionals who practice in many of the areas in which physicians practice but who do not have an MD or a DO degree. NPPs receive less advanced training than physicians but more training than RNs. They are also referred to as physician extenders because in the delivery of primary care they can, in many instances, substitute for physicians. They do not, however, engage in the entire range of primary care or deal with complex cases requiring the expertise of a physician (Cooper et al., 1998). Hence, NPPs often work in close consultation with physicians. NPPs typically include physician assistants (PAs), NPs, and CNMs.

NPs work predominantly in primary care, whereas PAs are evenly divided between primary care and specialty care. According to the 2008 National Sample Survey of Registered Nurses, there were 158,348 NPs, 70,383 PAs, and 8,000 CNMs in the United States (U.S. Bureau of Labor Statistics, 2011).

The American Academy of Physician Assistants (AAPA, 1986, p. 3) defines PAs as "part of the healthcare team ... [who] work in a dependent relationship with a supervising physician to provide comprehensive care." PAs are licensed to perform medical procedures only under the supervision of a physician. PAs assist physicians in the delivery of care to patients; the supervising physician may be either onsite or offsite. The major services provided by PAs include evaluation, monitoring, diagnostics, therapeutics, counseling, and referral (Fitzgerald et al., 1995).

In 2010, there were 142 accredited PA training programs in the United States, which were experiencing a steady growth in enrollment (U.S. Bureau of Labor Statistics, 2010). PA programs award bachelor's degrees, certificates, associate degrees, or master's degrees. In most states, PAs have the authority to prescribe medications.

The American Nurses Association defines NPs as individuals who have completed a program of study leading to competence as RNs in an expanded role. NPs constitute the largest group of NPPs and have also experienced the most growth (Cooper et al., 1998); since 1997, however, enrollments in NP preparatory programs have gradually dropped. The training of NPs may be a certificate program (at least 9 months in duration) or a master's degree program (2 years of full-time study). States vary with regard to the licensure and accreditation requirements for NPs. Most of these providers are now trained in master's- or post-master's-level nursing programs. In addition, NPs must complete clinical training in direct patient care. The primary function of NPs is to promote wellness and good health through patient education. NPs spend extra time with patients to help them understand the need to take responsibility for their own health. Hence, they are an important adjunct to the practice of primary care physicians. Another area where they provide service is nursing homes (Brody et al., 1976). NPs have statutory prescribing authority in almost all states.

CNMs are RNs with additional training from a nurse–midwifery program in areas such as maternal and fetal procedures, maternal and child nursing, and patient assessment (Endicott, 1976). CNMs deliver babies, provide family planning education, and manage gynecologic and obstetric care. They often substitute for obstetricians/gynecologists in prenatal and postnatal care, but refer abnormal or high-risk patients to obstetricians or jointly manage the care of such patients. Patients cared for by CNMs are less likely to have continuous electronic monitoring, induced labor, or anesthesia. These differences are associated with lower cesarean section rates and less resource use in areas such as length of hospital stay, operating room costs, and use of anesthesia staff (Rosenblatt et al., 1997).

Value of NPP Services

Efforts to formally establish the roles of NPs, PAs, and CNMs as nonphysician health care providers began in the late 1960s, when it was widely recognized that they could improve access to primary care, especially in rural and medically underserved areas. It helps alleviate some of the problems created by the geographic maldistribution of physicians. Studies have confirmed the efficacy of NPPs as many studies have demonstrated that they can provide both high-quality and cost-effective medical care. Compared to physicians, NPPs spend more time with patients and establish better rapport with them. NPs have been noted to have better communication and interviewing skills than physicians. These skills are considered particularly important in community and migrant health centers in assessing patients who are predominantly of minority origin and often have little education (Brody et al., 1976). Clients are more satisfied with NPs than with physicians because NPs are more likely to do comprehensive examinations. CNMs are considered effective in providing access to obstetric and prenatal services in rural and poor communities.

Among the issues that remain to be resolved before NPPs can be used to their full potential are legal restrictions on practice, reimbursement policies, and relationships with physicians. The lack of autonomy to practice is a noteworthy barrier facing midlevel providers as many states require physician supervision as a condition for practice. In some states, midlevel providers lack prescriptive authority. NPPs also face financial barriers related to reimbursement. Reimbursement for their services is generally indirect; that is, payments are made to the physicians with whom they practice.

ALLIED HEALTH PROFESSIONALS

In the early part of the 20th century, the health care provider workforce consisted of physicians, nurses, pharmacists, and optometrists. The growth in technology and specialized interventions subsequently placed greater demands on the time physicians and nurses could spend with their patients. Such time constraints created a need to train other professionals who could serve as adjuncts to or as substitutes for physicians and nurses. Allied health professionals received specialized training, and their clinical interventions were meant to complement the work of physicians and nurses. Thus physicians and nurses were relieved of time pressures so that they could attend to functions that they had the expertise to perform. The extra time also allowed them to keep abreast of the latest advances in their disciplines.

Allied health includes many health-related areas and constitutes approximately 60% of the U.S. health care work force. As noted in Section 701 of the Public Health Service Act, an *allied health professional* is someone who has received a certificate; associate's, bachelor's, or master's degree; doctoral-level preparation; or postbaccalaureate training in a science related to health care and has responsibility for the delivery of health or related services. These services may include those associated with the identification, evaluation, and prevention of diseases and disorders; dietary and nutritional services; rehabilitation; or health system management. Furthermore, these professionals differ from those who have received a degree in medicine (MD or DO), dentistry, optometry, podiatry, chiropractic, or pharmacy; a graduate degree in health administration; a degree in clinical psychology; or a degree equivalent to one of these. Allied health professionals can be divided into two broad categories: technicians and/or assistants and therapists and/or technologists.

Technicians and Assistants

Typically, technicians and assistants receive less than 2 years of postsecondary education and are trained to perform procedures. These individuals require supervision from therapists or technologists to ensure that care plan evaluation occurs as part of the treatment process. This group includes physical therapy assistants, certified occupational therapy assistants, medical laboratory technicians, radiological technicians, and respiratory therapy technicians.

Technologists and Therapists

Technologists and therapists receive more advanced training, including education in how to evaluate patients, diagnose problems, and develop treatment plans. They must also have training that enables them to evaluate the appropriateness and the potential side effects of therapy treatments and to teach procedural skills to technicians.

Some key allied health professionals are graduates of programs accredited by their respective professional bodies. For example, such programs train physical therapists (PTs), whose role is to provide care for patients with movement dysfunction. The earlier bachelor's degree has been phased out, and those pursuing this profession now enter master's degree (MPT or MSPT) or doctoral degree (DPT) programs in physical therapy. Passing a licensure examination administered by the American Physical Therapy Association is also required for licensure. Occupational therapists (OTs) help people of all ages improve their ability to perform tasks in their daily living and work environments. OTs help rehabilitate individuals who have conditions that are mentally, physically, developmentally, or emotionally disabling. OT interventions help people live independently or become more productive at their workplace. A bachelor's or master's degree in occupational therapy and passing a certification examination administered by the National Board for Certification in Occupational Therapy constitute the minimum requirements for entering the OT profession.

Dietitians, or nutritionists and dietetic technicians, ensure that institutional foods and diets are prepared in accordance with acceptable nutritional standards. Dietitians are registered by the Commission on Dietetic Registration of the American Dietetic Association.

Dispensing opticians fit eyeglasses and contact lenses. They are certified by the American Board of Opticianry and the National Contact Lens Examiners.

Speech–language pathologists treat patients with speech and language problems, whereas audiologists treat patients with hearing problems. The American Speech–Language–Hearing Association is the credentialing association for audiologists and speech–language pathologists.

Social workers help patients and families cope with problems resulting from long-term illness, injury, and rehabilitation, to name a few. The Council on Social Work Education accredits bachelor's and master's degree programs in social work in the United States.

PUBLIC HEALTH PROFESSIONALS

The field of public health employs a diversity of health professionals. Public health professionals focus on the community as a whole, rather than on treating the individual, and deal with issues such as access to health care, infectious diseases control, environmental health issues, and violence and injury issues. Public health professionals include physicians, researchers, administrators, lawyers, environmentalists, and social scientists. In addition to education in their primary profession, many people employed in public health have acquired a graduate degree from a school of public health. As of 2012, there were 49 accredited schools of public health in the United States. The five core disciplines in public health education are biostatistics, epidemiology, health services administration, health education/behavioral science, and environmental health (Association of School of Public Health [ASPH], 2011).

HEALTH SERVICES ADMINISTRATORS

Health services administrators are employed at the top, middle, and entry levels of various types of organizations that deliver health services. Top-level administrators provide leadership and strategic direction, work closely with governing boards, and are responsible for an organization's long-term success. They are responsible for the operational, clinical, and financial outcomes of the entire organization. Middle-level administrators may have leadership roles in major service centers such as outpatient, surgical services, or nursing services, or they may be departmental managers in charge of single departments such as diagnostics, dietary, rehabilitation, social services, environmental services, or medical records. Their jobs involve major planning and coordinating functions, organizing human and physical resources, direction and supervision of other employees, operational and financial controls, and decision making. They often have direct responsibility for implementing changes, enhancing efficiency, and developing new procedures with respect to changes in the health care delivery system. Entry-level administrators may function as assistants to midlevel managers and may supervise a small number of operatives. Their main function may be to oversee and assist with operations critical to the efficient operation of a departmental unit.

Health services administration is taught at the bachelor's and master's levels in a variety of settings, and the programs lead to several different degrees. The settings for such academic programs include schools of medicine, public health, public administration, business administration, and allied health sciences. Bachelor's degrees prepare students for entry-level positions. Mid- and senior-level positions require a graduate degree. The most common degrees held by health services administrators are the master of health administration (MHA) or master of health services administration (MHSA), master of business administration (MBA, with a health care management emphasis), master of public health (MPH), or master of public administration (or affairs; MPA) (Pew Health Professions Commission, 1998). The U.S. graduate schools of public health that are accredited by the Council on Education for Public Health play a key role in training health services administrators in their MHA/MHSA and MPH programs.

Growth of the elderly population, along with a current shortage of qualified administrators, is creating attractive opportunities in long-term care management. The training of nursing home administrators has been influenced to a great extent by government licensing regulations. Passing a national examination administered by the National Association of Boards of Examiners of Long-Term Care Administrators is a standard requirement; however, educational qualifications needed to obtain a license vary significantly from one state to another. Although the basic academic qualification required by most states is a bachelor's degree, acquiring adequate skills in nursing home administration requires a degree that specializes in long-term care administration or health care management (Singh, 2005).

CONCLUSION

Health services professionals in the United States constitute the largest proportion of the labor force. The growth and development of these professions are influenced by demographic trends, advances in research and technology, disease and illness trends, and the changing environment of health care financing and delivery. Physicians play a leading role in the delivery of health services. For a number of years now, maldistribution of physicians by both specialty and geography has persisted in the United States. A shortage of physicians and other health care professionals is foreseen as the number of insured has increased significantly since the implementation of the Affordable Care Act. In addition to physicians, many other health services professionals contribute significantly to the delivery of health care, including nurses, dentists, pharmacists, optometrists, psychologists, podiatrists, chiropractors, nonphysician providers, and various allied health professionals. These professionals require different levels of training and work in a variety of health care settings.

REFERENCES

American Academy of Physician Assistants (AAPA). *PA Fact Sheet*. Arlington, VA: AAPA; 1986.

American College of Physicians (ACP). National Health Care Workforce Commission. Accessed at http://www.acponline.org/advocacy/where_we_stand/assets/ii4-national-health-care-workforce.pdf. 2013. Accessed August 2013.

Association of American Medical Colleges (AAMC). *2013 State Physician Workforce Data Book*. https://members.aamc.org/eweb/upload/State%20Physician%20Workforce%20Data%20Book%202013%20(PDF).pdf. Published 2013. Accessed August 2013.

Association of Schools and Programs of Public Health (ASPH). About ASPH. www.asph.org. Published 2011. Accessed December 2011.

Brody SJ, et al. The geriatric nurse practitioner: a new medical resource in the skilled nursing home. *J Chronic Dis.* 1976;29(8):537–543.

Cooper RA. Seeking a balanced physician workforce for the 21st century. *JAMA.* 1994;272(9):680–687.

Cooper RA. Current and projected workforce of nonphysician clinicians. *JAMA.* 1998;280(9):788–794.

Endicott KM. In: Health Resources Administration, U.S. Public Health Service, *Health in America: 1776–1976.* DHEW Pub. No. 76616. Washington, DC: U.S. Department of Health, Education, and Welfare; 1976:138–165.

Fitzgerald MA. The midlevel provider: colleague or competitor? *Patient Care.* 1995;29(1):20.

Ginzberg E. Improving health care for the poor. *JAMA.* 1994;271(6):464–467.

Greenfield S, Nelson EC. Recent developments and future issues in the use of health status assessment measures in clinical settings. *Med Care.* 1992;30 (5 suppl):MS23–MS41.

Grossman D. APNs: pioneers in patient care. *Am J Nurs.* 1995;95(8):54–56.

Heisler E. Physician supply and the Affordable Care Act. Congressional Research Service. http://op.bna.com/hl.nsf/id/myon-93zpre/$File/crsdoctor.pdf. Published January 2013. Accessed August 2013.

IHS Inc. The complexities of physician supply and demand: projections from 2013 to 2025. Final report. https://www.aamc.org/download/426248/data/thecomplexitiesofphysiciansupplyanddemandprojectionsfrom2013to2.pdf. Published March 2015. Accessed August 2015.

Kahn NB, et al. AAFP constructs definitions related to primary care. *Am Fam Physician.* 1994;50(6):1211–1215.

National Center for Health Statistics. *Health, United States, 2014: With Special Feature on Adults Aged 55–64.* Hyattsville, MD; 2015.

Pew Health Professions Commission. Pew Commission urges increased action to cut U.S. physician supply. PT Bulletin, November 10, 1998:10.

Pugno PA, et al. Results of the 2001 national resident matching program: family practice. *Fam Med.* 2001;33:594–601.

Rich EC, et al. Preparing generalist physicians: the organizational and policy context. *J Gen Intern Med.* 1994;9(1 suppl):S115–S122.

Rivo ML, Kindig D. A report on the physician work force in the United States. *N Engl J Med.* 1996;334(13):892–896.

Rosenblatt RA. Specialists or generalists: on whom should we base the American health care system? *JAMA*. 1992;267(12):1665–1666.

Rosenblatt RA, Lishner DM. Surplus or shortage? Unraveling the physician supply conundrum. *Western J Med*. 1991;154(1):43–50.

Rosenblatt RA, et al. Interspecialty differences in the obstetric care of low-risk women. *Am J Public Health*. 1997;87(3):344–351.

Samuels ME, Shi L. *Physician Recruitment and Retention: A Guide for Rural Medical Group Practice*. Englewood, CO: Medical Group Management Press; 1993.

Schroeder S, Sandy LG. Specialty distribution of U.S. physicians: the invisible driver of health care costs. *N Engl J Med*. 1993;328(13):961–963.

Shi L. The relation between primary care and life chances. *J Health Care Poor Underserved*. 1992;3(2):321–335.

Shi L. Primary care, specialty care, and life chances. *Intl J Health Serv*. 1994;24(3):431–458.

Singh DA. *Effective Management of Long-Term Care Facilities*. Sudbury, MA: Jones and Bartlett; 2005.

Sochalski J. Nursing shortage redux: turning the corner on an enduring problem. *Health Aff*. 2002;21(5):157–164.

Stanfield PS. *Introduction to the Health Professions*. Sudbury, MA: Jones and Bartlett; 1995.

Starfield B. *Primary Care: Concepts, Evaluation, and Policy*. New York: Oxford University Press; 1992.

Starfield B, Simpson L. Primary care as part of US health services reform. *JAMA*. 1993;269:3136–3139.

Starr P. *The Social Transformation of American Medicine: The Rise of a Sovereign Profession and the Making of a Vast Industry*. New York: Basic Books; 1982.

U.S. Bureau of Labor Statistics, U.S. Department of Labor, *Occupational Outlook Handbook, 2014–15 Edition, Physicians and Surgeons*. http://www.bls .gov/ooh/healthcare/physicians-and-surgeons.htm. Published January 2015; accessed August 2015.

U.S. Bureau of Labor Statistics. Occupational employment statistics surveys. www.bls.gov. Published 2010. Accessed August 2010.

U.S. Bureau of Labor Statistics. 2008 national sample survey of registered nurses. www.bls.gov. Published 2011. Accessed December 1, 2011.

U.S. Bureau of Labor Statistics. Labor force statistics from the current population survey. http://www.bls.gov/cps/cpsaat18.htm. Published 2014. Accessed June 24, 2015.

U.S. Department of Labor, Bureau of Labor Statistics. Current population survey: employment and earnings, January 2010. http://www.bls.gov/cps/cpsa2009 .pdf. Published 2010. Accessed August 2010.

Wennberg JE, et al. Finding equilibrium in U.S. physician supply. *Health Aff.* 1993;(Summer):89–103.

Chapter 5

Technology and Its Effects

INTRODUCTION

Medical technology has brought numerous benefits to modern civilization. These benefits, however, have come at a price that society has to pay. Research and development (R&D) and the production of new technology are costly, although sophisticated advanced diagnostic procedures have reduced health complications and disability. New medical cures have increased longevity, and new drugs have helped stabilize chronic conditions and have given an improved quality of life to many. The fact that life expectancy almost doubled from 1900 to 1965 was as a result of advances in social conditions—improved sanitation, nutrition, and living conditions—rather than advances in medical treatment. The continuing increase in longevity since then, however, has been largely attributed to advances in medical technology as well as better nutrition and living conditions.

With the rising cost of medical care, at some point society will have to face the conflict between a commitment to medical innovation and the growth of new technology on the one hand and cost containment on the other hand. Bringing medical spending in the United States at par with other advanced nations has remained an elusive dream despite various efforts to contain rising costs.

Canadians and residents of other advanced nations in Europe, who have enjoyed universal health insurance for several decades, have been able to place limits on the availability and use of costly technology through supply-side rationing. In contrast, the notion of medical rationing has not been palatable to Americans. Hence, the idea of extending health care to all Americans presents a major predicament. Access to only basic health care for some and availability of technologically advanced services for others are impractical in the United States.

During the postindustrial era, developments in science and technology were instrumental in drastically changing the nature of health care delivery. Since then, the ever-increasing proliferation of new technology has continued to profoundly alter many facets of health care delivery. Following are some of the major changes triggered by technology:

- New technology has raised consumer expectations about what may be possible. Patients' expectations have considerable influence on their health care–seeking behavior, leading to greater demand for and utilization of the latest and best that technology can offer.

- Technology influences the organization and financing of medical services. Specialized services that previously could be offered only in hospitals are now available in outpatient and community settings.

- The introduction of advanced technology has influenced the scope and content of medical training and shaped the practice of medicine, fueling a trend toward specialization in medicine at the expense of public health, preventive medicine, and primary care.

- Although some medical technology may reduce costs, as a whole technology has contributed to health care cost escalation. For both the consumer and the provider, the cost of excessive treatment has generally been of little concern as long as a third party—either an insurance plan or the government—pays for it.

- Technology has raised complex moral and ethical dilemmas in medical research and decision making. For example, when critically ill patients are put on life support with little hope of full recovery, health care resources may be wasteful.

Economic globalization has also enveloped biomedical knowledge and technology. This is particularly true for the developed and developing nations where leading physicians have access to the same scientific knowledge through medical journals and the Internet. Most drugs and medical devices available in the United States are also available in many other parts of the world.

WHAT IS MEDICAL TECHNOLOGY?

Medical technology refers to the practical application of scientific knowledge to improve people's health and to create efficiencies in the delivery of medical care. Medical science has benefited from developments in other applied sciences, such as chemistry, physics, engineering, and pharmacology. For example, advances in organic chemistry made it possible to identify and extract the active ingredients found in natural plants to produce drugs and anesthetics. Developments in electrical and mechanical engineering led to such medical advances as radiology, cardiology, and encephalography (Bronzino et al., 1990, p. 11). Magnetic resonance imaging (MRI), a technology that had its origins in basic research on the structure of the atom, later was transformed into a major diagnostic tool (Gelijns & Rosenberg, 1994). Thedisciplines of computer science and communication systems have found their application in health information technology and telemedicine (Tan, 1995, p. 4).

Nanomedicine is an emerging area of medical technology that requires manipulation of materials at the atomic and molecular levels. Scientists are working on the use of nano[1] materials for accurate diagnosis and treatment of diseases, such as cancer.

In its narrow sense, medical technology includes sophisticated machines, pharmaceuticals, and biological therapies. In a broader sense, however, it also covers medical and surgical procedures used in rendering medical care, ultramodern facilities and settings of care delivery, health information systems, and management and operational systems that make health care delivery more efficient (**Exhibit 5.1**).

---

[1] A nanometer is one-billionth of a meter.

Exhibit 5.1   Examples of Medical Technology

- **Diagnostic equipment**
  - CT (computed tomography) scanner
  - MRI (magnetic resonance imaging)
- **Equipment and devices to render treatment**
  - Lithotripter
  - Heart and lung machine
  - Kidney dialysis machine
  - Pacemaker
- **Pharmaceuticals**
- **Medical procedures**
  - Open-heart surgery
  - Tissue transplants
  - Hip and knee replacements

- **Facilities and organizational systems**
  - Medical centers and systems
  - Laboratories
  - Managed care networks
  - Health information systems
  - Patient care management
  - E-health and e-therapy
  - Telemedicine
  - Distance education
  - Electronic medical records

HEALTH INFORMATION TECHNOLOGY

Information technology (IT) has become an integral part of health care delivery. IT involves computer applications that transform massive amounts of data into useful information. IT is indispensable for managing the vast array of information that is used in patient care delivery, quality improvement, cost containment, billing and collections, and other aspects of operating health care organizations. Most large health care organizations have information systems departments and managers who are charged with maintaining and improving the flow of information. In addition, IT applications are increasingly being used to link health care organizations to agencies outside those organizations. For example, it is a common practice to electronically transmit billing information to payers.

Major Categories

Specific IT system applications in health services delivery fall into four main areas:

1. *Clinical information systems* are IT applications that support patient care delivery. Electronic medical records, for example, can quickly

provide reliable information necessary to guide clinical decision making and to produce timely reports on the quality of care delivered. Computerized physician-order entry enables physicians to transmit orders electronically from the patient's bedside. Telemedicine is based on integrated applications of telecommunications and information technologies. *Health informatics* is the term now used for IT applications that are designed to improve clinical efficiency, accuracy, and reliability.

2. *Administrative information systems* are designed to assist in carrying out financial and administrative support activities such as payroll, patient accounting, staff scheduling, materials management, budgeting and cost control, and office automation.

3. *Decision support systems* provide information and analytical tools to support managerial decision making. Such tools are used to forecast patient volume, project staffing requirements, evaluate financial performance, analyze utilization, conduct clinical research, and improve quality and productivity.

4. *Clinical decision support systems* (CDSSs) are interactive software systems designed to help clinicians with decision-making tasks, such as determining a diagnosis or recommending a treatment for a patient (O'Sullivan et al., 2014). Their use, however, is not yet widespread. Internet and e-health applications enable patients and practitioners to access information, facilitate interaction between consumers or between patients and providers, add certain conveniences for both physicians and patients, and enable the possibility of *virtual visits* online between a patient and physician.

Electronic Health Records

Electronic health records (EHRs) replace the traditional paper medical records. In the United States, use of EHRs in health delivery organizations is well under way, but little progress has been made in the development of information-sharing networks. EHR networks make it possible to access individual records online from many separate, interoperable automated systems within an electronic network. The ability to share and access patient information by various users is referred to as *interoperability*. There is some evidence that EHR use produces improved patient care by enabling physicians to have timely access to patient records, alerting them to a potential for medical errors, and making critical lab values available when needed (King et al., 2014). On the downside, there is some indication that the use of EHRs may be time consuming, resulting in decreased productivity (Palmer, 2014). Also, the U.S. health care system has far to go in achieving interoperability because a significant number of physicians who use EHRs still do not get all the needed information electronically (Hsiao et al., 2015).

According to the Institute of Medicine (2003), a fully developed EHR system includes four key components:

- Collection and storage of health information on individual patients over time, where health information is defined as information pertaining to the health of an individual or health care provided to an individual
- Immediate electronic access to individual and population level information by authorized users
- Provision of knowledge and decision support that enhance the quality, safety, and efficiency of patient care (health informatics)
- Support of efficient processes for health care delivery

The Health Information Technology for Economic and Clinical Health Act

The Health Information Technology for Economic and Clinical Health (HITECH) Act of 2009 provides financial incentives to providers for adopting meaningful use of EHR technology. *Meaningful use* refers to specific criteria in quality, safety, efficiency, etc., that providers are required to meet.

The Health Insurance Portability and Accountability Act

To alleviate concerns about the confidentiality of patient information, the Health Insurance Portability and Accountability Act (HIPAA) of 1996 restricted the legal use of personal medical information for three main purposes: health care delivery to the patient, operation of the health care organization, and reimbursement. The HIPAA legislation mandated strict controls on the transfer of personally identifiable health data between two entities, provisions for disclosure of protected information, and criminal penalties for violation (Clayton, 2001). It also established certain patient rights, such as the right of patients to inspect and have copies of their protected health information, to request corrections to the records, and to restrict the use of the information. The HITECH law strengthened the civil and criminal enforcement of HIPAA by including increased penalties for violations.

The Internet, E-Health, and E-Therapy

The Internet has continued to revolutionize certain aspects of health care delivery. *E-health* refers to "all forms of electronic health care delivered over the Internet, ranging from informational, educational, and commercial 'products' to direct services offered by professionals, non-professionals, businesses, or consumers themselves" (Maheu et al., 2001). The use of e-health has grown as many providers have created secure Internet portals to enable patients to access their EHRs; allow patient–provider e-mail messaging; and use mobile apps for smartphones and tablets (Ricciardi et al., 2013).

E-therapy has emerged as an alternative to face-to-face therapy for behavioral health support and counseling (Skinner & Latchford, 2006). Also referred to as online therapy, e-counseling, teletherapy, or cyber-counseling, *e-therapy* refers to professional therapeutic interactions online between qualified mental health professionals and their clients. There is growing evidence that e-therapy is effective for a variety of psychosocial problems (Barak et al., 2008). The main difference between e-health and e-therapy is that the former is a self-help approach for obtaining Web-based information; the latter involves interaction with a health care professional.

By accessing self-help information from the Internet, patients have become more active participants in their own health care. Of course, while information empowers patients, it also has the potential to create conflict between patients and their physicians. Using the right source can provide valid and up-to-date information to both consumers and practitioners. For instance, departments of the U.S. government offer a wealth of research-based information.

The Internet is not merely a source of information; it also offers new ways to create efficiency. In practice settings, the Internet is being used to register patients, direct them to alternative care sites, transmit diagnostic results, and order pharmaceuticals and other products. In addition, by accessing patient information through the Internet from their homes or hospital lounges, physicians can get a head start on their hospital rounds (Morrissey, 2002).

Telemedicine and Remote Monitoring

Telemedicine, or distance medicine, employs telecommunications technology for medical diagnosis and patient care when the provider and client are separated by distance. It also enables a generalist to consult a specialist when a patient's illness and diagnosis are complex. Areas of specialized medical services in telemedicine include teleradiology, telepathology, and telesurgery. General adoption of telemedicine has been slow, however. Some of the main barriers have been licensure of physicians and other providers across state borders, concerns about legal liability, and lack of reimbursement for services provided via telemedicine. Also, the cost-effectiveness of most telemedicine applications remains unsubstantiated. Diagnostic and consultative teleradiology, in contrast, is almost universally reimbursed and has proven to be cost-effective (Field & Grigsby, 2002).

Remote in-home patient monitoring programs that monitor vital signs, blood pressure, and blood glucose levels, for example, are proving to be cost-effective (Haselkorn et al., 2007). Remote monitoring of cardiac implantable electronic devices, such as pacemakers and cardioverter defibrillators, has shown a high level of patient acceptance and satisfaction (Morichelli et al., 2014). Remote monitoring may also reduce hospital utilization (White-Williams, Unruh, & Ward, 2015). Tele-ICU is a relatively new development. It links intensivists[2] and other critical care professionals to a system network that enables remote monitoring of ICUs. The system provides real-time patient assessment capabilities and communication with bedside teams through ongoing virtual rounds (Goran, 2012). Tele-ICU programs have shown lower patient mortality, shorter lengths of stay, and increased patient safety (Lilly et al., 2014).

DIFFUSION AND UTILIZATION OF MEDICAL TECHNOLOGY

The development and dissemination of technology is called *technology diffusion*. This factor determines which new technology will be developed, when it will be made available for use, and where it can be accessed.

---

[2]Physicians who specialize in the care of critically ill patients.

High-tech procedures are more readily available in the United States than they are in most other countries, and little is done to limit the expansion of new medical technology. For example, compared with most hospitals in industrialized countries, American hospitals perform a far greater number of catheterizations, angioplasties, and heart bypass surgeries. The United States also has more high-tech equipment available for its population than most countries do. For example, in 2012, the United States had 1.4 times the number of MRI units per million population than Italy, which, after the United States, had the most MRI units among OECD[3] countries (OECD, 2015). To control medical costs, most nations have tried to limit—mainly through central planning (supply-side rationing)—the diffusion and utilization of high-tech procedures. For instance, the National Institute for Health and Clinical Excellence (NICE) of Great Britain decides whether the National Health Service should make certain medical technologies available (Milewa, 2006). Consequently, nations that employ central planning generally have "waiting lines" for specialized services. For example, in Canada, in 2014, the average wait to get an MRI scan was 8.7 weeks (20.0 weeks in the province of British Columbia) (Barua & Fathers, 2014). The rationing of medical technology through central planning curtails costs, but it also restricts access to care.

Spending on R&D drives innovation, which results in the development of new technology. Once technology has been developed, its use is almost ensured. In 2012, the United States spent $119.3 billion on biomedical R&D, of which 59% was spent by the private sector, such as the pharmaceutical and biotechnology industry; the remaining 41% came from the government (Chakma et al., 2014). Apart from private funding, the federal government, through the National Institutes of Health (NIH), is the largest source of funding biomedical research. The NIH has a budget of over $30 billion, 90% of which is used to support both intramural and extramural biomedical research (Owens, 2014).

R&D spending in the United States exceeds that in any other country. For example, U.S. R&D spending in 2014 exceeded by 46% the amount spent by all Europe. However, some concerns have been expressed that the share of U.S. spending has declined from 50% of global spending on medical R&D in 2007 to 44.4% in 2012 (Chakma et al., 2014). Yet, if the spending, even at reduced levels, is used more efficiently and productively than before, there should be little reason for concern.

---

[3]Organization for Economic Cooperation and Development is a forum of over 30 countries.

Exhibit 5.2   Mechanisms to Control the Growth of Technology

- Implement central planning to determine how much technology will be made available and where
- Withdraw federal funding for R&D
- Change the patterns of medical training, placing greater emphasis on primary care practice
- Reduce the number of specialty residency slots for medical graduates
- Curtail insurance payments for expensive medical treatments
- Impose controls on pharmaceutical prices, which in turn will make less money available for R&D and development of new drugs

The major reasons that the United States leads all other nations in the development and use of technology are (1) cultural beliefs and values, (2) medical training and practice, (3) insurance coverage, and (4) competition among providers. These factors are discussed in subsequent sections. **Exhibit 5.2** lists some interventions that the United States might potentially undertake to curtail the growth of technology. Implementing these measures, however, would go against the fundamental beliefs and values of Americans and would generate much controversy.

Cultural Beliefs and Values

American beliefs and values have been instrumental in determining the nature of health care delivery in the United States. Capitalism and limitations on government intervention promote innovation. An economic and political environment in which innovation thrives creates opportunities for scientists and manufacturers to develop new technology. Americans have high expectations of finding cures through science and technology, and they equate use of advanced medical technology with high-quality care. Consequently, Americans indicate overwhelmingly that advanced tests, drugs, medical equipment, and procedures are critical for improving the quality of health care (Schur & Berk, 2008). The desire to have state-of-the-art technology available, accompanied by the desire to use it despite its cost, is called the *technological imperative*.

Medical Training and Practice

The emphasis on specialty care over primary care and preventive services predominates in U.S. medical culture. This emphasis is reflected in the training of physicians. American medical graduates consistently choose to specialize rather than go into primary care practice. For example, it was estimated that only 20% of all 22,934 U.S. medical school graduates for 2012 would choose to practice primary care in 2015 (Schwartz, 2012). An oversupply of specialists has had important consequences for the development and use of new technology because primary care physicians use less technology than specialists, even for similar medical conditions.

Insurance Coverage

Both theory and empirical research have suggested that the generosity of insurance coverage stimulates technological change (Smith, Newhouse, & Freeland, 2009). In general, financing of health care through insurance, private or public, largely insulates both patients and providers from personal accountability for the utilization of medical services. Because out-of-pocket costs are of limited concern, patients expect their physicians to provide all that medical technology has to offer. Knowing that the services demanded by their patients are largely covered by insurance, providers generally show little hesitation in delivering the services. Other developed countries offer universal health insurance, but they use supply-side rationing to limit the overutilization of technology.

Competition Among Providers

Technology-based specialization has been used by the medical establishment as an enticement to attract insured patients by advertising the availability of the latest technology, which creates a perception of quality in the minds of consumers. State-of-the-art technology also plays a role in the ability of a hospital or clinic to recruit specialists. When hospitals develop new services and invest heavily in modernization programs, other hospitals in the area are generally forced to do the same, for competitive reasons. Such practices have resulted in a tremendous amount of duplication of services and equipment and have further contributed to medical specialization.

THE GOVERNMENT'S ROLE IN TECHNOLOGY DIFFUSION

Technology diffusion has been accompanied by issues of cost, safety, benefit, and risk. Federal legislation, in turn, has attempted to address these concerns. The government also plays a significant role in carrying out research and providing funding for research, as mentioned earlier.

Regulation of Drugs, Devices, and Biologics

The Food and Drug Administration (FDA) is an agency of the U.S. Department of Health and Human Services that is responsible for ensuring that drugs and medical devices are safe and effective for their intended use. The FDA also controls access to drugs by deciding whether a certain drug will be available by prescription only or as an over-the-counter purchase.

Legislation to Regulate Drugs

Exhibit 5.3 summarizes the main pieces of legislation that regulate drugs and medical devices. The regulatory functions of the FDA have evolved over time. Under the Food and Drugs Act of 1906, the Bureau of Chemistry (predecessor of the FDA) was authorized to take action only after drugs had been marketed to consumers. It was assumed that the

Exhibit 5.3   Summary of FDA Legislation

1906	*Food and Drugs Act*: FDA is authorized to take action only after drugs sold to consumers cause harm.
1938	*Federal Food, Drug, and Cosmetic Act*: Evidence of safety is required before new drugs or devices can be marketed.
1962	*Drug Amendments*: FDA takes charge of reviewing efficacy and safety of new drugs, which can be marketed only once approval is granted.
1976	*Medical Devices Amendments*: Premarket review of medical devices is authorized; devices are grouped into three classes.
1983	*Orphan Drug Act*: Drug manufacturers are given incentives to produce new drugs for rare diseases.
1990	*Safe Medical Devices Act*: Health care facilities must report device-related injuries or illness of patients or employees to the manufacturer of the device and, if death is involved, the incident must also be reported to the FDA.
1992	*Prescription Drug User Fee Act*: FDA receives the authority to collect application fees from drug companies to provide additional resources to shorten the drug approval process.
1997	*Food and Drug Administration Modernization Act*: Fast-track approvals for life-saving drugs are permitted when their expected benefits exceed those of existing therapies.

manufacturer would conduct safety tests before marketing the product. If innocent consumers were harmed, only then could the FDA take action (Bronzino et al., 1990, p. 198). The drug law was strengthened by the passage of the Federal Food, Drug, and Cosmetic Act of 1938 in response to the infamous Elixir Sulfanilamide disaster, which caused more than 100 deaths because of poisoning from a toxic solvent used in the liquid preparation (Flannery, 1986). Under the revised law, drug manufacturers were required to provide scientific evidence about the safety of new products before putting them on the market.

The drug approval system was further transformed by the 1962 drug amendments (Kefauver-Harris Amendments) to the Federal Food, Drug, and Cosmetic Act. The approval system authorized by these amendments essentially remains in place today for most new drugs. The law was tightened after the thalidomide tragedy. In the United States, thalidomide was a sleeping pill distributed as an experimental drug, but in Europe, it had been widely marketed to pregnant women as a means of preventing morning sickness. Thousands of deformed infants were born to mothers who had used this new drug. The 1962 drug amendments essentially stated that premarket notification was not sufficient. This legislation established a premarket approval system, giving the FDA authority to review the safety as well as the effectiveness of a new drug before it could be marketed. Its consumer protection role now enabled the FDA to prevent harm before it occurred. The new rule, however, was criticized for slowing down the introduction of new drugs and, consequently, denying patients the early benefit of the latest treatments.

In the late 1980s, pressure on the FDA from those wanting rapid access to new drugs for the treatment of HIV infection called for a reconsideration of the drug review process (Rakich et al., 1992, p. 186). The Orphan Drug Act of 1983 and subsequent amendments were passed to provide incentives, such as grant funding, for pharmaceutical firms to develop new drugs for rare diseases and conditions. As a result, certain new drug therapies, called *orphan drugs*, have become available for conditions that affect fewer than 200,000 people in the United States.

In 1992, Congress passed the Prescription Drug User Fee Act, which authorized the FDA to collect fees from pharmaceutical companies to review their drug applications. According to the U.S. General Accounting Office, these fees have allowed the FDA to make new drugs available more quickly by shortening the time it takes for approvals to be issued. On the flip side, there has been an increasing trend in the number of prescription and over-the-counter drug recalls (Nagaich & Sadhna, 2015). There is clearly a tradeoff between accelerating the review process and potential safety risks.

In 1997, Congress passed the Food and Drug Administration Modernization Act. This law provides for increased patient access to experimental drugs and medical devices. It also permits fast-track approvals when the potential benefits of new drugs for serious or life-threatening conditions are considered significantly greater than those for currently available therapies.

The FDA's drug approval process remains far from perfect, however. The agency does not carry out its own testing of new drugs, but instead evaluates the drug studies conducted by pharmaceutical companies. Many times drug recalls are issued by the manufacturer or the FDA years after a drug has been on the market and further research has shown the drug to be ineffective and/or unsafe.

Legislation to Regulate Devices

Medical devices include a wide range of products. They can be as simple as tongue depressors and bedpans and as complex as pacemakers and laser surgical equipment. Medical devices include general-purpose lab equipment, reagents, and test kits. Other examples include diagnostic ultrasound equipment, x-ray machines, and other imaging technology.

The FDA was first given jurisdiction over medical devices under the Federal Food, Drug, and Cosmetic Act of 1938. Initially, such jurisdiction was confined to the sale of products that were believed to be unsafe or that made misleading claims of effectiveness (Merrill, 1994). In the 1970s, however, several deaths and miscarriages were attributed to the Dalkon Shield, which had been marketed as a safe and effective contraceptive device (Flannery, 1986). The Medical Devices Amendments of 1976 extended the FDA's authority to include premarket review of medical devices divided into three classes:

- *Class I*: Devices that pose the lowest risk and are generally simple in design. These devices are subject to general controls regarding misbranding—that is, fraudulent claims regarding their therapeutic effects. Examples of Class I devices include enema kits and elastic bandages.

- *Class II*: Devices subject to requirements for labeling, performance standards, and postmarket surveillance. Examples include powered wheelchairs and some pregnancy test kits.
- *Class III*: Devices that come under the most stringent requirements of premarket approval regarding safety and effectiveness. Devices in this class support life, prevent health impairment, or present a potential risk of illness or injury (Rakich et al., 1992). Examples include implantable pacemakers and breast implants.

The Safe Medical Devices Act of 1990 has particular relevance for health care providers, who are required by law to report to the manufacturer, and in some cases to the FDA as well, all injuries and deaths caused by medical devices. Requirements under this act serve as an early warning system for any serious device-related problems that could potentially become widespread.

Legislation to Regulate Biologics

Biologics are derived from living organisms and include a wide range of products such as vaccines, blood and blood components, allergenics, somatic cells, gene therapy, tissues, and therapeutic proteins that are indicated for the prevention or treatment of a disease or health condition. Biologics are isolated from a variety of natural sources—human, animal, or microorganism. In contrast to most drugs that are chemically synthesized and have a known chemical structure, most biologics are complex mixtures that are not easily identified or characterized (FDA 2009). The FDA regulates the licensing of biologics under the Public Health Service Act of 1944. Similar to drugs, the safety and effectiveness of biologics are regulated according to the Food, Drug, and Cosmetic Act of 1938, discussed previously.

The Affordable Care Act and Medical Technology

In the area of medical technology, the ACA mainly affects devices and biologics. A 2.3% excise tax on the sale of certain medical devices by manufacturers and importers of these devices became effective on January 1, 2013. The higher costs associated with the tax will, of course, be passed on to the purchasers, mainly hospitals and physicians, and will eventually filter down to consumers through higher health insurance premiums.

The Biologics Price Competition and Innovation Act of 2009 (incorporated into the ACA) authorized the FDA to approve biosimilars under a process similar to the approval of generic drugs. Because of their complexity, the term *generic* cannot apply to biologics; hence, the term *biosimilar* was created to apply to products that are highly similar to, or are interchangeable with, an already approved biological product. The Biosimilar User Fee Act of 2012, passed subsequent to the ACA, authorized the FDA to charge biopharmaceutical firms a user fee to pay for the review of applications for biosimilar products. It is believed that the introduction of biosimilars will create competition and drive down the cost of biologics. The first biosimilar product to be approved in the United States in March 2015 was Zarxio—biosimilar to Neupogen—which can be prescribed for the treatment of certain cancers.

Research on Technology

The Agency for Healthcare Research and Quality (AHRQ), a division of the Department of Health and Human Services, is the lead federal agency charged with supporting research to improve the quality of health care, reduce health care costs, and improve access to essential services. The agency's reports on technology assessment are made available to medical practitioners, consumers, and other health care purchasers.

As previously discussed, the federal government is also a major provider of financial support to private and public institutions for biomedical research. The AHRQ and the NIH support both basic and applied biomedical research in the United States.

IMPACT OF MEDICAL TECHNOLOGY

The effects of advances in scientific knowledge and medical technology have been far-reaching and pervasive. The effects often overlap, making it difficult to pinpoint the precise impact of technology on the delivery of health care.

Impact on Quality of Care

Americans generally equate high-technology medicine to high-quality care, but such an association is not always accurate. Quality is enhanced only when new procedures can prevent or delay the onset of serious disease, provide better diagnosis, make quicker and more complete cures possible, increase safety of medical treatment, minimize undesirable side effects, promote faster recovery from surgery, increase life expectancy, and add to quality of life (**Exhibit 5.4**). Improvements in diagnostic capabilities increase the likelihood that timely and more appropriate treatments will be provided. Technology can provide new remedies where none existed before. It also offers improved remedies that are more effective, less invasive, or safer. The outcomes in such cases can include increased longevity and decreased morbidity, both of which are indicators of better quality of health care.

Exhibit 5.4   Criteria for Quality of Care

• Prevent or delay disease onset	• Increase safety of treatment
• Provide a more accurate diagnosis than is possible with currently available options	• Minimize side effects
	• Provide for faster recovery from surgery
• Provide a quicker cure	• Increase life expectancy
• Provide a more complete cure	• Add to quality of life

Numerous examples illustrate the role of technology in enhancing the quality of care. Tiny cardiac pacemakers and implantable cardioverter defibrillators can be placed in the human body to prevent sudden cardiac death. Angioplasty has reduced the need for open-heart bypass surgery. New imaging technologies such as positron emission tomography and single-photon emission computed tomography are available as advanced diagnostic tools to study brain function and identify the sources of both physical and mental disorders. Laser technology permits surgery to be performed with less trauma, better precision, and quicker postsurgical recovery. Advanced lasers are used for high-precision eye surgery. Molecular and cell biology are being employed to screen for genetic disorders and provide gene therapy. New specialty drugs offer therapeutic advances for a number of conditions such as cancer, hepatitis C, rheumatoid arthritis, and multiple sclerosis (Chambers et al., 2014).

Amid all the enthusiasm that emerging technologies might garner, some degree of caution must prevail. Past experience shows that greater proliferation of technology does not necessarily lead to higher quality of care. Unless the effect of each individual technology is appropriately assessed, some innovations may actually be wasteful, and others may possibly be harmful.

Impact on Quality of Life

Quality of life indicates a patient's overall satisfaction with life during and after medical treatment. For example, quality of life is enhanced when technology enables people to live normal lives despite disabling conditions affecting speech, hearing, vision, and movement. Major technological advances have furnished the clinical ability to help patients cope with diabetes, heart disease, end-stage renal disease, and HIV/AIDS. Thanks to modern treatments, HIV/AIDS has become a chronic disease, not a death sentence (Komaroff, 2005). New categories of drugs are also instrumental in relieving pain and suffering. For example, for cancer pain management, new opioids have been developed for transdermal, nasal, and nebulized administration that allow needleless means of controlling pain (Davis, 2006). Finally, minimally invasive surgical procedures, such as lithotripsy, which crushes kidney and bile stones by using shock waves, have improved quality of life by reducing pain and suffering and allowing a quicker return to normal life. Similarly, procedures such as coronary artery bypass graft surgery—an open-heart surgical procedure to correct blockage of coronary arteries—has made it possible for people with severe heart disease to return to normal activity within a few weeks after surgery. Previously, such patients would have required lifelong medication and suffered prolonged disability (Nitzkin, 1996).

Impact on Health Care Costs

Technological innovations have been the single most important factor in medical cost inflation (Institute of Medicine, 2002). In fact, they may have accounted for as much as half of the total rise in health care spending in recent years (Congressional Budget Office [CBO], 2008). Unlike other industries, in which new technology often reduces labor force and production costs, the addition of new technology in health care usually increases both labor and capital costs (Iglehart, 1982). **Exhibit 5.5** summarizes the main factors underlying technology-driven cost escalation. First, there is the cost of acquiring the new technology and equipment. Second, special training for physicians and technicians to operate the equipment and to analyze the results often leads to increases in labor costs. Third, new technology may require special space and facilities (McGregor, 1989). Finally, the utilization of new technology is assured when it is covered by insurance. From a systems perspective,

Exhibit 5.5   Cost Increases Associated with New Medical Technology

* Acquisition costs are often high because of R&D and precision manufacturing
* Training or hiring of technicians with special skills
* Facilities may require refurbishing or expansion to accommodate the new technology
* Utilization when covered by insurance (moral hazard and provider-induced demand)

costs associated with utilization of technology after it becomes available are more important than the purchase price.

Although it is true that many new technologies increase costs, others actually reduce costs when they replace treatments that are more expensive. For example, breakthroughs in antidepressant and antipsychotic drugs have saved money by reducing admissions for inpatient psychiatric care. **Exhibit 5.6** shows the main areas in which use of technology has saved health care costs. The cost-effectiveness of individual technologies is also being evaluated. For example, in comparing the costs of open partial nephrectomy and robotic partial nephrectomy, Mano and colleagues (2015) discovered that the robotic procedure resulted in shorter hospital stays. On other fronts, hospitals are gaining leverage on price negotiations and are clamping down on physician-preference items, such as expensive joint implants and cardiac devices (Lee, 2014; Sandier, 2015). Manufacturers from emerging economies are also putting competitive pressures in developed nations by producing and selling their products at lower cost. For example, General Electric has established a major research center in India to develop diagnostic and therapeutic radiology equipment that is less costly and does not require the services of highly skilled staff (Robinson, 2015).

Exhibit 5.6   Cost-Saving Medical Technology

* Replacement of earlier, more expensive procedures
* Minimally invasive procedures that eliminate the need for overnight hospital stays
* Technologies that shorten hospital stays
* Drugs that reduce inpatient psychiatric care
* Technologies that enable services to be rendered in outpatient and home care settings instead of hospitals

Impact on Access

Geographic access to health care can be improved for many people by providing mobile equipment or by using new communications technologies that allow remote access to centralized equipment and specialized personnel. Mobile equipment can be transported to rural and remote sites, making it accessible to those populations. Mobile cardiac catheterization laboratories, for example, can make the benefits of high technology available in rural settings.

Impact on the Structure and Processes of Health Care Delivery

Medical technology has transformed large urban hospitals into medical centers where the latest diagnostic and therapeutic remedies are offered, but technology also takes modern medicine to outpatient services and patients' own homes. This trend has led to reduced costs where similar technology was previously available only in hospitals. Without technological innovations, extensive adaptations of modern treatments in outpatient and home care would not have been possible. For example, monitoring devices can permit cardiac implants to transmit vital information over telephone lines, respirators can maintain breathing in the home, and kidney dialyzers are being used for some patients at home. Surgical procedures now commonly performed on an outpatient basis include hernia repair, surgery for kidney and gallbladder stones, cataract removal, tonsillectomy, carpal tunnel release, left heart catheterization, knee arthroscopy, and much gynecological surgery. Numerous diagnostic procedures, including some of the latest imaging procedures, are also performed in outpatient settings.

Impact on Global Medical Practice

As mentioned earlier, the United States leads the world in R&D spending and development of new medical technology. Many nations wait for the United States to develop new technologies that can then be introduced into their health care systems in a more controlled and manageable fashion. As a result of this practice, European and other economies get a free ride on U.S. biomedical R&D and obtain nearly all of the benefits of U.S. medical technology at much lower health care costs (Hay, 2006). On the other hand, research partnerships overseas are extending the boundaries of knowledge about disease and strategies for diagnosis, treatment, and prevention.

Such collaborations will take added significance as global health will increasingly have repercussions for the health of Americans (Glass, 2013). The home turf will no longer remain the domain of biomedical research and technological innovation.

Impact on Bioethics

Increasingly, technological change is raising serious ethical and moral issues. Gene mapping of humans, genetic cloning, stem cell research, genetic engineering, genetic testing, and so forth may hold potential benefits, but they also present serious ethical dilemmas. For example, research on embryonic stem cells may lead one day to the discovery of treatments and cures for diseases and other long-term degenerative illnesses such as cardiac failure, Parkinson's disease, spinal cord injury, and diabetes. However, the use of human embryos for research is highly controversial. Life support technology also raises serious ethical issues in medical decisions, including whether life support should continue when a patient may simply exist in a permanent vegetative state or whether life support should be discontinued, and if so, at what point.

ASSESSMENT OF MEDICAL TECHNOLOGY

Health technology assessment (HTA) refers to the evaluation of medical technology to determine its efficacy, safety, and cost-effectiveness. HTA also informs various stakeholders about the ethical, legal, and social implications of medical technologies (Lehoux et al. 2009). The objective of HTA is to establish the appropriateness of medical technology for widespread use. HTA becomes essential because many technologies have not produced health benefits; some may even be harmful. Hence, HTA should govern decisions to adopt and disseminate new technology.

Efficacy and safety are the basic starting points in evaluating the overall usefulness of medical technology. Cost-effectiveness goes a step further in evaluating the safety and efficacy of a technology in relation to its cost. Efficacy and safety are evaluated through clinical trials. A *clinical trial* is a carefully designed research study in which human subjects participate under controlled observations. Cost-effectiveness is determined by using economic models that compare the benefits of a treatment to its costs.

In the United States, it is primarily the private sector that conducts HTA; in contrast, European countries and Canada have centralized technology assessment agencies that perform this task. Since 2009, European nations have been attempting to coordinate their HTA efforts. The European Network for Health Technology Assessment was established as a facilitating organization for HTA collaboration and joint assessments in Europe.

Efficacy

Efficacy may be defined simply as the health benefit to be derived from the use of technology, or how effective a given technology is in diagnosing or treating a condition. If a product or service actually produces some health benefits, it can be considered efficacious or effective. Decisions about efficacy require that the right questions be asked. For example, is the current diagnosis satisfactory? What is the likelihood that a different procedure would result in a better diagnosis? If the problem is more accurately diagnosed, what is the likelihood of a better cure? Apart from evaluating the effects on mortality and morbidity, issues related to quality of life are important.

Safety

Safety refers to protection against unnecessary harm from the use of technology. As a primary benchmark, the benefits of any intervention must outweigh any negative consequences. After safety has been experimentally determined, the outcomes from the wider use of a certain technology are closely monitored over time to identify any problems.

Cost-Effectiveness

Cost-effectiveness, or cost-efficiency, goes a step beyond the determination of efficacy and safety by weighing benefits against costs. When a medical treatment is first introduced in caring for a patient, the benefits generally exceed the costs, and the use of technology is regarded as cost-effective. Over time, additional treatments then begin to lower the benefits in relation to rising costs. At some point along a time line, continued medical interventions yield benefits that are roughly equal to the additional costs. Optimal cost-effectiveness is achieved when additional benefits equal the additional cost of treatment. Beyond the optimal point, additional interventions either deliver no further benefits or the cost of providing additional care begins to exceed the benefits. In these cases, additional care becomes wasteful. In cost-effectiveness analysis, the potential risk from medical treatment can also be incorporated as a type of cost, recognizing that most medical procedures are associated with varying degrees of risk or potential harm.

Experts believe that much of the medical care delivered in the United States is wasteful because, after a certain point, additional care adds little or no health benefits while the costs continue to accumulate. One of the problems is that little is known about the cost-effectiveness of even well-established medical technologies. As the overall health care cost burden continues to mount, HTA will play a considerable role in future health care planning, policy, financing, and delivery. Establishing the cost-effectiveness of various treatments (called comparative effectiveness study) can potentially relieve physicians and insurers of the responsibility of making certain treatment decisions that might otherwise become controversial and lead to conflict and legal battles.

BENEFITS OF TECHNOLOGY ASSESSMENT

From the previous section, some of the main benefits of HTA become obvious. For example, establishing the safety and efficacy of new technology is essential to prevent potential harm to patients. Other beneficial effects discussed earlier, such as improved quality of care, better quality of life, better access, and control of costs, are all based on the use of technologies that pass rigorous examination of their safety, efficacy, and cost-effectiveness.

Delivering Value

Possibilities regarding what technology can achieve are limitless. However, health services decision making is increasingly being governed by the answer to the question, "What is appropriate?" rather than, "What is possible?" (Abele, 1995). The concept of *value*—improved benefits at lower costs and health risks—is becoming important to those who finance health care, including private employers, the government, and managed care organizations. Value can be increased by improving quality, reducing cost, or doing both. The problem is that insured patients often want to use all available medical resources, regardless of how little health benefit is received in relation to their cost. Physicians often find themselves in a precarious situation when they are required to withhold treatment because of its cost-inefficiency. Payers generally get blamed as uncaring profit mongers when they intervene in the delivery of medical care based on costs. Eventually the government may find itself in a central position of issuing practice guidelines based on cost-efficiency.

Cost Containment

Simply pointing to technology as the culprit for cost escalations and putting arbitrary restraints on technology development and dissemination would be a misdirected strategy. As stated earlier, technology has the potential to not only enhance health benefits but also reduce costs. Demands for reducing costs without sacrificing quality must influence technological change. Also, a greater emphasis should be placed on developing technology specifically for reducing costs.

Standardized Practice Protocols

Medical practice guidelines (or clinical practice guidelines) are systematically developed protocols to assist practitioners in delivering appropriate health care for specific clinical circumstances (Field & Lohr, 1990). HTA plays a significant role in the development of clinical protocols. Unlike in some other countries, however, cost-effectiveness has not taken central stage in health care delivery in the United States. Rising health care costs and excessive spending remain a top concern.

CONCLUSION

Medical technology includes drugs, devices, procedures, facilities, information systems, and organizational systems. Several factors have engendered the mind-set among Americans that all available medical technology must be used regardless of its cost. The United States has the world's foremost position in both the production and the utilization of medical technology. Other countries may then adopt the technology developed in the United States, thereby avoiding the high R&D costs necessary to create the technology in the first place. In addition, these nations use supply-side rationing to contain the diffusion and use of technology. Such an approach has been deemed unacceptable by most Americans. Consequently, medical technology has been one of the primary factors in the growth of health care expenditures in the United States. In the United States, the FDA regulates the introduction of new drugs, devices, and biologics based on their efficacy and safety, but without evaluating their cost-effectiveness. Under the Affordable Care Act, the FDA has also been given the authority to assess biosimilars and issue licenses for their adoption in medical practice. Experts believe that much of the medical care delivered in America is actually wasteful, but at this point, no one is quite sure how to contain Americans' insatiable demand for the almost indiscriminate use of technology.

REFERENCES

Abele J. Health reform and technology: what does it mean for us? *Biomed Instrument Tech*. 1995;29(6):476–478.

Barak A, et al. A comprehensive review and a meta-analysis of the effectiveness of Internet-based psychotherapeutic interventions. *J Technol Hum Serv*. 2008;26(2/4):109–160.

Barua B, Fathers F. *Waiting Your Turn: Wait Times for Health Care in Canada, 2014 Report*. Vancouver, British Columbia: The Fraser Institute; 2014.

Bronzino JD, et al. *Medical Technology and Society: An Interdisciplinary Perspective*. Cambridge, MA: MIT Press; 1990.

Chakma J, et al. Asia's ascent—global trends in biomedical R&D expenditures. *N Engl J Med*. 2014;370(1):3–6.

Chambers, JD, et al. Despite high costs, specialty drugs may offer value for money comparable to that of traditional drugs. *Health Aff*. 2014;33(10):1751–1760.

Clayton PD. Confidentiality and medical information. *Ann Emerg Med*. 2001;38(3):312–316.

Congressional Budget Office (CBO). *Technological Change and the Growth of Health Care Spending*. Washington, DC: Congressional Budget Office; 2008.

Davis MP. Management of cancer pain: focus on new opioid analgesic formulations. *Am J Cancer*. 2006;5(3):171–182.

Field MJ, Grigsby J. Telemedicine and remote patient monitoring. *JAMA*. 2002;288:423–425.

Field MJ, Lohr KN, eds. *Clinical Practice Guidelines: Directions for a New Agency*. Washington, DC: National Academy Press; 1990.

Flannery EJ. Should it be easier or harder to use unapproved drugs and devices? *Hastings Center Rep.* 1986;16(1):17–23.

Food and Drug Administration (FDA). What are "biologics" questions and answers. http://www.fda.gov/AboutFDA/CentersOffices/OfficeofMedicalProductsandTobacco/CBER/ucm133077.htm. Published 2009. Accessed April 2015.

Gelijns A, Rosenberg N. The dynamics of technological change in medicine. *Health Aff.* 1994;13(3):28–46.

Glass RI. What the United States has to gain from global health research. *JAMA.* 2013;310(9):903–904.

Goran, SF. Measuring tele-ICU impact: does it optimize quality outcomes for the critically ill patient? *J Nurs Manag.* 2012;20(3):414–428.

Haselkorn A, et al. The future of remote health services summary of an expert panel discussion. *Telemed J E-Health.* 2007;13(3):341–348.

Hay JW. Where's the value in health care? *Value Health.* 2006;9(3):141–143.

Hsiao CJ, et al. The role of health information technology in care coordination in the United States. *Medical Care.* 2015;53(2):184–190.

Iglehart JK. The cost and regulation of medical technology: future policy directions. In: McKinlay JB, ed. *Technology and the Future of Health Care.* Cambridge, MA: MIT Press; 1982:69–103.

Institute of Medicine. *Medical Innovation in the Changing Healthcare Marketplace.* Washington, DC: National Academy Press; 2002.

Institute of Medicine. *Key Capabilities of an Electronic Health Records System.* Washington, DC: National Academy Press; 2003.

King J, et al. Clinical benefits of electronic health record use: national findings. *Health Services Research.* 2014;49(1pt2):392–404.

Komaroff AL. Beyond the horizon. *Newsweek.* December 12, 2005;146:82–84.

Lee J. Supply chain: pressure to spend less…price transparency … economies of scale. *Mod Healthc.* 2014;44(1):20–21.

Lehoux P, et al. What medical specialists like or dislike about health technology assessment reports. *J Health Serv Res Policy.* 2009;14(4):197–203.

Lilly CM, et al. Critical care telemedicine: evolution and state of the art. *Crit Care Med.* 2014;42(11):2429–2436.

Maheu MM, et al. *E-Health, Telehealth, and Telemedicine: A Guide to Start-Up and Success.* San Francisco: Jossey-Bass; 2001.

Mano R, et al. Cost comparison of open and robotic partial nephrectomy using a short postoperative pathway. *Urology.* 2015;85(3):596–603.

McGregor M. Technology and the allocation of resources. *N Engl J Med.* 1989;320(2):118–120.

Merrill RA. Regulation of drugs and devices: an evolution. *Health Aff.* 1994;13(3):47–69.

Milewa T. Health technology adoption and the politics of governance in the UK. *Soc Sci Med.* 2006;63(12): 3102–3112.

Morichelli L, et al. Implantable cardioverter defibrillator remote monitoring is well accepted and easy to use during long-term follow-up. *J Interv Card Electrophysiol.* 2014:41(3):203–209.

Morrissey J. Hospitals offer remote control. *Mod Healthc.* 2002;32(51):32–35.

Nagaich U, Sadhna D. Drug recall: an incubus for pharmaceutical companies and most serious drug recall of history. *Int J Pharm Investig.* 2015;5(1):13–19.

Nitzkin JL. Technology and health care: driving costs up, not down. *IEEE Tech Soc Mag.* 1996;15(3):40–45.

Organization for Economic Cooperation and Development (OECD). 2015. Magnetic resonance imaging (MRI) units. https://data.oecd.org/healtheqt/magnetic-resonance-imaging-mri-units.htm. Accessed April 2015.

O'Sullivan D, et al. Professional issues: decision time for clinical decision support systems. *Clin Med.* 2014; 14(4):338–341.

Owens B. Mapping biomedical research in the USA. *Lancet.* 2014;384(9937):11–14.

Palmer PM. Electronic health records: the unintended consequences. *AAOS Now.* 2014; 8(12):34–35.

Rakich JS, et al. *Managing Health Services Organizations.* Baltimore, MD: Health Professions Press; 1992.

Ricciardi L, et al. A national action plan to support consumer engagement via e-health. *Health Aff.* 2013;32(2):376–384.

Robinson JC. Biomedical innovation in the era of health care spending constraints. *Health Aff.* 2015;34(2):203–209.

Sandier M. Device prices fall as hospitals' leverage grows. *Mod Healthc.* 2015;45(9):35.

Schur CL, Berk ML. Views on health care technology: Americans consider the risks and sources of information. *Health Aff.* 2008;27(6):1654–1664.

Schwartz MD. The US primary care workforce and graduate medical education policy. *JAMA.* 2012;308(21):2252–2253.

Skinner AEG, Latchford G. Attitudes to counselling via the Internet: a comparison between in-person counselling client and Internet support group users. *Counseling Psychother Res.* 2006;6(3): 92–97.

Smith S, Newhouse JP, Freeland MS. Income, insurance, and technology: why does health spending outpace economic growth? *Health Aff.* 2009;28(5):1276–1284.

Tan JKH. *Health Management Information Systems: Theories, Methods, and Applications.* Gaithersburg, MD: Aspen; 1995.

White-Williams C, Unruh L, Ward K. Hospital utilization after a telemonitoring program: a pilot study. *Home Health Care Serv Q.* 2015;34(1):1–13.

Chapter 6

Financing and Reimbursement Methods

INTRODUCTION

Financing refers to any mechanism that gives people the ability to pay for health care services. For most people, financing is necessary to access health care. Some uncompensated or charity care, mainly provided through free clinics, community health centers, and hospital emergency departments, is delivered to those who have little or no means to finance their health care. Such services, however, are not available in all geographic locations. In 2013—before the main insurance clauses of the Affordable Care Act (ACA) went into effect—the percentage of Americans without health insurance for the entire calendar year was 13.4%, or 42.0 million (Smith & Medalia, 2014). It is estimated that since the ACA's coverage provisions took effect, approximately 16.4 million people have gained health insurance (Department of Health and Human Services [DHHS], 2015).

The complexity of financing is one of the primary characteristics of medical care delivery in the United States. Most health insurance is privately financed. Certain categories of people, however, can become eligible for tax-supported public health insurance. Almost all Americans age 65 and older qualify for Medicare, which also covers some younger adults with disabilities. Medicaid is another major public insurance program that covers many of the poor, including children in low-income households. Other public programs, such as the Department of Veterans Affairs (VA) and the military health system, cover a relatively small number of people. Under the ACA, the public sector's role in providing health insurance has increased but by no means fills the gaps in enabling all Americans to have health insurance.

According to data compiled by the Office of the Actuary, Centers for Medicare and Medicaid Services (CMS)—an agency under the DHHS—in 2013, government financing accounted for 43% of total U.S. health care expenditures. The most notable shift from the private share of national health expenditures to the government's share occurred soon after the Medicare and Medicaid programs were created in 1965. Since then, the government has continued to liberalize benefits and has added new programs in a piecemeal fashion. Effects of the ACA on government financing for health care are yet unknown, but, based on history, the burden of health care expenditures will further shift to taxpayers.

Financing also includes the various methods of paying providers for the health care they deliver. Hence, the two functions encompassed in financing are purchase of health insurance and payment for the services delivered to insured patients.

The actual payments to providers of care are handled in numerous ways. In most cases, patients directly pay a relatively small portion of the total cost of the services they receive, although cost sharing by patients has increased significantly in recent years. Various private and public insurance plans pay the bulk of the cost of health care, and they use several different types of payment mechanisms. The financing of health care through the various private and public sources ultimately aggregates into national health expenditures, which comprise the total amount of money a nation spends on health care delivery and other health-related activities. **Figure 6.1** illustrates the relationships between financing, insurance, access, payment, and total expenditures.

Private employers and the government are the primary financiers of health care in the United States. From an economic perspective, one could

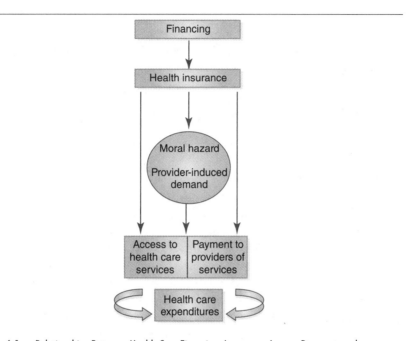

Figure 6.1   Relationships Between Health Care Financing, Insurance, Access, Payment, and Expenditures

argue that Americans, through employment and taxes, finance their own health care and subsidize health care for those who cannot afford it. For instance, employer-paid health insurance actually represents an exchange for salary. Working Americans also have a Medicare tax deducted from their paychecks, which amounts to prepayment of certain Medicare benefits they can expect to start receiving at age 65. General taxes collected from working Americans subsidize health care delivered to Medicaid recipients. Certain Medicare benefits are also subsidized by taxpayers.

EFFECTS OF HEALTH CARE FINANCING AND INSURANCE

Health care financing produces effects that go beyond merely providing access and paying the providers of care (**Exhibit 6.1**). It also produces some undesirable effects.

Exhibit 6.1   Health Care Financing and Its Effects

• Financing of private and public health insurance enables access to health care • Payment to providers • Moral hazard • Provider-induced demand	• Technology and services with liberal reimbursement proliferate • Total health care expenditures are greater than if the same services were to be paid by the patients

Taken together, financing and insurance are instrumental in creating the demand for health care services. Health insurance enables people to pay for health care, but it also desensitizes both consumers and providers to the price of those services. First, it creates excessive demand from consumers who want to use their health insurance benefits. Consumers are driven to utilize more health care services than they would if they had to pay the entire price out of their own pockets. Consumer behavior that leads to a higher utilization of health care services when the services are covered by insurance is referred to as *moral hazard* (Feldstein, 1993, p. 125).

Second, financing exerts powerful influences on supply-side factors, such as how much health care is delivered. Financing also indirectly affects the growth of medical technology, in that technology and services that are subject to more liberal reimbursement tend to proliferate rapidly. Conversely, when reimbursement is constrained, the supply of services is curtailed accordingly. Moreover, health insurance desensitizes the providers against the price of services, with the result that providers deliver additional and more expensive services. Again, if consumers had to pay for these services out of their own pockets, many of them would not be used. The providers' ability to create demand is referred to as *provider-induced demand*. These additional services often deliver little or no additional health benefits, however.

Financing eventually affects the total health care expenditures (also referred to as health care costs or national health care spending) incurred by a health care delivery system. Both moral hazard and provider-induced demand waste health care resources and add to the rising cost of health care. To counter these effects, countries with national health insurance implement *supply-side rationing*, which focuses on restricting the availability of expensive medical technology and specialty care. Otherwise, the health care expenditures in these countries would be astronomical. Without a centrally managed health care system, the United States cannot ration health care directly. However, utilization of services is curtailed to some extent because not all Americans have health insurance coverage, despite the ACA. This indirect type of rationing is called *demand-side rationing*. When they lack insurance, people face barriers to obtaining health care unless they can either pay for the services out of pocket or receive charity care. If health insurance is extended to everyone, without other restrictions, total health care expenditures will rise at a much faster rate than they now do.

INSURANCE: ITS NATURE AND PURPOSE

Basic Insurance Concepts

Insurance is a mechanism for protection against risk. In the context of insurance, *risk* refers to the possibility of a substantial financial loss from some event. In health care, illnesses requiring expensive treatments and hospitalization pose substantial financial risk to most people. Similarly, the cost of most surgeries and subsequent treatment would be beyond the means of many people to pay out of pocket. Insurance, in a general sense, is primarily designed to protect people against such eventualities. Health care providers are also subject to substantial risk when they are required to treat the sick and injured who cannot pay.

An individual who is protected by insurance against the possible risk of financial loss is called the *insured*. The insured may also be referred to as the *enrollee* or *member* (in a private health insurance plan) or the *beneficiary* (in a public health insurance plan). The insuring agency that assumes risk is called the insurer or underwriter. *Underwriting* is a systematic technique for evaluating, selecting (or rejecting), classifying, and rating risks. Four fundamental principles underlie the concept of insurance (Health Insurance Institute, 1969, p. 9; Vaughn & Elliott, 1987, p. 17):

- Risk is unpredictable for the individual insured.
- Risk can be predicted with a reasonable degree of accuracy for a group or a population.
- Insurance provides a mechanism for transferring or shifting risk from the individual to the group through the pooling of resources.
- Actual losses are shared on some equitable basis by all members of the insured group.

Based on underwriting, the insurer determines a fair price to insure against specified risks. The amount charged for insurance coverage is called a *premium*, which is usually paid every month. Including both the employer's and employee's share, the average monthly cost of health insurance premiums in 2014 was $502 for a single plan and $1,403 for a family plan (Claxton et al., 2014).

Cost Sharing

Insurance requires some type of *cost sharing* so that the insured assumes at least part of the risk. The purpose of cost sharing is to reduce the misuse of insurance benefits. Three main types of cost sharing are utilized in private health insurance: premium cost sharing, deductibles, and copayments.

In employer-sponsored health insurance, the employee is generally required to share in the total cost of the premium. Of the premium costs given previously, insured workers on an average paid 18% of the cost for single (individual) plans and 29% of the cost for family plans (Claxton et al., 2014). In addition to paying a share of the cost of premiums through payroll deductions, insured individuals also pay a portion of the actual cost of medical services out of their own pockets. These out-of-pocket expenses take the form of deductibles and copayments and are incurred only if and when medical care is used.

A *deductible* is the amount the insured must first pay before any benefits by the plan are payable. In most cases, the deductible must be paid on an annual basis. For example, in 2014, the average annual deductible for a single plan was $1,217. In this case, when the insured receives medical care, the plan starts paying for benefits only after the cost of medical services received by the insured has exceeded $1,217. The deductibles, however, vary considerably by the type of plan. A plan may also have separate deductibles for hospitalization and outpatient surgery. With few exceptions, all health insurance plans must provide certain recommended preventive services and immunizations without cost sharing, as mandated by the ACA.

Another type of shared cost is the *copayment*—the amount that the insured has to pay out of pocket each time health services are received after the deductible amount has been paid. For example, a plan may require a copayment of $25 for a primary care visit and $35 for a visit to a specialist. Copayment is cost sharing in the form of a dollar amount;

cost sharing in the form of a percent amount is called *coinsurance*. A plan with an 80:20 coinsurance, for example, pays 80% of all covered medical expenses after the deductible requirement has been met; the insured pays the remaining 20%. Most plans include a *stop-loss* provision, which is the maximum out-of-pocket liability an insured would incur in a given year. In case of a catastrophic illness or injury, the copayment amount can add up to a substantial sum. The purpose of the stop-loss provision is to limit the total out-of-pocket costs for the insured. Once the stop-loss limit has been reached, the plan pays 100% of any additional expenses. The ACA mandates health plans (with some exceptions) to limit the stop loss to no more than $6,350 for single plans and to no more than $12,700 for family plans.

Previously, $1 to $2 million lifetime limits on benefits were common. Under the ACA, lifetime limits are prohibited for all health plans sold or renewed on or after September 23, 2010.

The rationale for cost sharing is to control the utilization of health care services. Because insurance creates moral hazard by insulating the insured from the cost of health care, making the insured pay part of the cost promotes more responsible behavior in health care utilization. A comprehensive study employing a controlled experimental design conducted in the 1970s, known as the Rand Health Insurance Experiment, demonstrated that cost sharing had a material impact on lowering utilization without any significant negative health consequences.

PRIVATE INSURANCE

The modern health insurance industry is pluralistic; that is, private insurance includes many different types of health plan providers, such as commercial insurance companies (e.g., Aetna, Cigna, Metropolitan Life, Prudential), Blue Cross/Blue Shield, self-insured employers, and managed care organizations (MCOs). The nonprofit Blue Cross and Blue Shield Associations function much like private health insurance companies.

Private insurance is generally available in the form of single or family plans. A family plan covers the spouse and children of the subscriber in addition to the subscriber. In contrast, government programs such as Medicare and Medicaid do not offer family plans; each individual is an independent beneficiary. Five main types of private insurance are available: group insurance, self-insurance, individual private insurance, managed care plans, and high-deductible health plans (HDHPs). The distribution of health plan enrollments in 2006 (when HDHPs became available) and 2014 is illustrated in **Figure 6.2**.

Employment-based health insurance offer rates—percentages of employers who offer insurance—vary quite significantly according to employer characteristics (**Exhibit 6.2**). In 2014, 55% of all employers in the United States offered health insurance benefits, but this was before the ACA mandate for employers to provide health insurance, which was pushed back to 2015. In 2014, 98% of large employers (200 or more workers) offered health insurance to at least some of their workers; but only 54% of small employers (3 to 199 workers) did so. High cost of health insurance is the main reason small employers give for not offering it (Claxton et al., 2014). The offer rate is also lower among employers that employ a large percentage of low-wage earners. Also, only 24% of employers offered health insurance to part-time workers. Large employers are more likely than small employers to offer health insurance benefits to part-time workers. Health insurance offer rates are higher among workplaces that

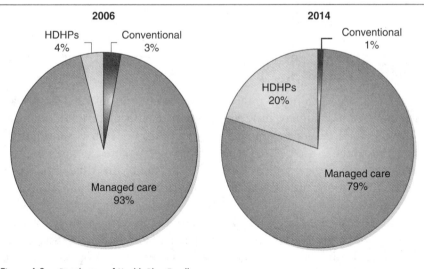

Figure 6.2   Distribution of Health Plan Enrollments

Exhibit 6.2   Employer Characteristics Associated with Health Insurance Offer Rates

• Large employers versus small employers   • Unionized versus nonunionized employers
• Greater number of high-wage earners versus   • Smaller percentage of young workers versus
low-wage earners   older workers
• Full-time workers versus part-time workers

are unionized. Offer rates are lower among employers that employ a large percentage of young workers aged 26 years and younger. Among employers that offer health insurance benefits, 53% also offer a separate dental plan (Claxton et al., 2014).

Group Insurance

Group insurance can be obtained through an organization such as an employer, a union, or a professional organization. A group insurance program anticipates that a substantial number of people in the group will participate in purchasing insurance through its sponsor. Risk and often the cost of insurance are shared by the members of the group.

Earlier health insurance plans were designed to protect the insured against financial hardships that could occur because of the high cost of hospitalization, extended illness, and expensive surgery. These plans were referred to as major medical plans. Since the 1970s, health insurance plans have commonly combined major medical coverage with all-inclusive comprehensive coverage that includes basic and routine physician office visits and diagnostic services.

Self-Insurance

A large employer often has a workforce that is big enough and sufficiently well diversified in terms of risk to warrant offering its own insurance. Rather than pay insurers a dividend to bear the risk, large employers can simply assume the risk by budgeting funds to pay medical claims incurred by their employees. This practice, which is referred to as *self-insurance*, gives employers better control over the health plan. Self-insured employers can protect themselves against any potential risk of high losses by purchasing *reinsurance* from a private insurance company. In 2014, 61% of workers were in self-insured employer plans (Claxton et al., 2014).

Individual Private Insurance

Although most Americans obtain health insurance coverage through employer-sponsored group plans or government programs, individually purchased (nongroup) private health insurance is an important source of coverage for many Americans. The family farmer, the early retiree, the employee of a business that does not offer health insurance, and the self-employed make up the bulk of the people who rely on private nonemployer-related health insurance. An estimated 17.6 million people had individual nongroup health insurance at the end of 2014. This represents an estimated growth of 5.3 million over the previous year (Mark Farrah Associates, 2014). This growth is attributed to the ACA. However, it is unclear how many of the new enrollees were previously uninsured or how many would have purchased individual coverage directly from an insurer in the absence of the ACA (Levitt, Cox, & Claxton, 2015).

Managed Care Plans

Managed care plans are offered mainly by health maintenance organizations (HMOs) and preferred provider organizations (PPOs). Such plans are a type of health insurance because they assume risk in exchange for an insurance premium. Unlike traditional insurance companies, however, MCOs assume the responsibility for obtaining health care services for their enrollees by contracting with a network of providers. MCOs also use a variety of mechanisms to monitor utilization and a variety of methods to reimburse providers for the services rendered.

High-Deductible Health Plans

HDHPs have grown in popularity because of their low premium costs. In 2014, 20% of employment-based health coverage was through an HDHP, up from 4% in 2006 (see **Figure 6.2**). Generally, health plans that carry at least $1,000 deductible for single coverage or $2,000 for family coverage are considered HDHPs. Two types of HDHP arrangements are available, both of which link a savings account to high-deductible insurance. The savings accounts give consumers greater control over how to use the funds. Savings are also used for relatively small and routine health care expenses. Hence, these plans are also referred to as *consumer-driven health plans*. HDHPs minimize moral hazard and make consumers responsible users of health care resources. Research findings by the RAND

Corporation showed strong evidence that consumer-directed health plans reduced health care spending and could lead to significant cost savings for the health care system (RAND Corporation, 2012).

The first type includes a health reimbursement arrangement (HRA—hence HDHP/HRA for the combination). The HRA is funded by the employer; employees are prohibited from contributing to it. The funds are used to reimburse the insured for qualified medical expenses, which include payment of HDHP premiums and premiums for long-term care insurance. Employees do not pay taxes on the payments made to them from HRAs. Although participants in an HRA are not required to have an HDHP, the arrangement commonly includes both. When coupled with an HDHP, the employee first pays for health care from the HRA and then pays for care on an out-of-pocket basis until the health plan deductible is met. Subsequently, HDHP kicks in. Unused HRA funds can generally be carried forward to the next year.

The second type of arrangement combines a health savings account (HSA) with an HDHP (HDHP/HSA) that meets federal standards. Federal regulations require caps on the yearly amounts contributed to an HSA ($3,350 for single coverage and $6,650 for family coverage in 2015; those 55 and older can contribute an additional $1,000). Employers may contribute to the account but are not required to do so. The funds belong to the account holder and can accumulate without limit. The minimum annual deductible in 2015 was $1,300 and $2,600 for single and family plans respectively. Out-of-pocket expenses are capped at a maximum. In 2015, annual out-of-pocket expenses for deductibles and copayments were capped at $6,450 and $12,900 for single and family plans, respectively. HSAs have significant tax advantages—namely, contributions are tax deductible, withdrawals used to pay for medical expenses are exempt from federal income taxes, and account earnings are tax exempt.

THE AFFORDABLE CARE ACT AND PRIVATE INSURANCE

Private health insurance remains the backbone for obtaining coverage under the ACA. That coverage is obtained either through one's employer, as in the past, or through government-run exchanges (called health insurance marketplaces[1]) in which private insurers participate.

---

[1]This is a misnomer because true markets must operate free of government control.

Insurance expansion is addressed through the following main mandates under the ACA:

1. Legal residents of the United States were mandated to have what is referred to as minimum essential coverage. Failing to comply results in an income tax penalty (called shared responsibility payment) when filing one's tax returns. For 2015 the penalty will amount to $325 per person (half of that amount for each child under 18) or 2% of yearly household income, whichever is higher. The minimum essential coverage requirement of the law refers to comprehensive coverage, which must include 10 categories of Essential Health Benefits that include preventive and wellness services. Ironically, plans must include maternity and newborn care and pediatric services, regardless of whether or not a person needs those services (e.g., single individuals or people who are past their childbearing age). The inability to choose makes health insurance more expensive for some than it otherwise would be. An exemption from the mandate can be granted based on established religious opposition to insurance, having to spend more than 8% of one's household income on insurance, and in some other situations.

2. To purchase health insurance through government-run exchanges, subsidies are made available to people with incomes between 100% and 400% of the federal poverty level (FPL).[2]

3. The exchanges offer four types of standardized plans—bronze, silver, gold, and platinum—tiered according to premium cost and cost sharing. The least expensive of the four, bronze plan, covers approximately 60% of a person's health care costs.

4. In an ACA provision that was delayed and changed by the Obama administration from implementation in 2014, employers with 100 or more full-time-equivalent workers must cover at least 70% of their full-time workers (full-time refers to 30 hours or more per week) starting in 2015 and 95% by 2016. Employers that have between 50 and 99 workers must comply by 2016. Failing these mandates, employers will have to pay heavy fines. Employers with less than 50 workers are exempt from this mandate. The insurance offered must comply with ACA requirements on coverage and cost.

---

[2] In 2015, the FPL was an annual income of $11,770 for a single person and $24,250 for a family of four ($27,890 in Hawaii and $30,320 in Alaska).

5. As early as 2010, the ACA had made it illegal to deny health insurance to people with preexisting medical conditions and had required children and young adults under the age of 26 to be covered under their parents' health insurance plans.

PUBLIC INSURANCE

This section discusses the financing, eligibility requirements, and covered services for the major public health insurance programs. In 2013, 64.2% of Americans were covered by private health insurance (53.9% were covered through their employers) and 34.3% were covered by public insurance (17.3% were covered by Medicaid and 15.6% by Medicare) (Smith & Medalia, 2014).

Public financing supports *categorical programs*, each of which is designed to provide benefits to a certain category of people who meet the eligibility criteria to become beneficiaries. The United States does not have publicly financed health insurance specifically for the unemployed. Even though public insurance is financed by the government, services are purchased from providers in the private sector, for the most part. One notable exception is the Department of Veterans Affairs (VA), which runs its own health care system to provide most of the services to its beneficiaries.

Medicare

The Medicare program, also referred to as Title 18 of the Social Security Act, finances medical care for three categories of people:

- Persons 65 years and older
- Disabled individuals of any age who are entitled to Social Security benefits
- People of any age who have permanent kidney failure (end-stage renal disease)

Medicare is a federal program administered by the CMS. In 1966, shortly after Medicare was created, it had 19.1 million beneficiaries. By 2013, the program had grown to 52.3 million beneficiaries (CMS, 2014). Although the program was initially created for the elderly population, 17% of the beneficiaries are now persons younger than 65 years of age who qualify on the basis of their disability. With the aging of the population, this program will continue to grow. Of all government programs, Medicare poses the single greatest future challenge to taxpayers as the growing number of beneficiaries is supported by fewer working adults. Approximately 4 workers per beneficiary are expected to decrease to 2.3 workers by 2030 (CMS, 2014).

Deductibles, copayments, premiums, and noncovered services can leave Medicare beneficiaries with substantial out-of-pocket costs. Noncovered services include vision care, eyeglasses, dental care, hearing aids, and many long-term care services. Even for covered services, Medicare has relatively high cost-sharing requirements. In 2010, the average out-of-pocket spending on services per beneficiary was $2,744 (Cubanski et al., 2014). To cover the high out-of-pocket costs, most beneficiaries have some source of supplemental coverage such as an employer-sponsored plan for retirees (35% of beneficiaries), Medicaid for low-income individuals (19% of beneficiaries), or a privately purchased supplemental insurance plan, known as *Medigap* (23% of beneficiaries) (Jacobson, Neuman, & Damico 2015).

For almost 30 years after its inception, Medicare had a dual structure comprising two separate insurance programs referred to as Part A and Part B. Now Medicare has a four-part structure.

Hospital Insurance (Part A)

Part A, the hospital insurance (HI) portion of Medicare, is financed by special payroll taxes paid equally by employers and employees. These taxes are paid by all working individuals, including those who are self-employed. All earnings are subject to the Medicare tax.

Part A is designed to cover hospitalization, short-term convalescence and rehabilitation in a skilled nursing facility (SNF), and home health care. For terminally ill patients, Medicare pays for care provided by a Medicare-certified hospice. **Figure 6.3** shows the distribution of Part A payments for various services (The managed care expenditures are for Medicare Advantage, which is discussed later).

The structure of Part A benefits is rather complex. For hospital and nursing home stays, the timing of benefits is determined by what is referred to as a *benefit period*. It begins on the day a beneficiary is hospitalized and ends when the beneficiary has not been in a hospital or an SNF for 60 consecutive days. If after 60 days the beneficiary is hospitalized again, a new

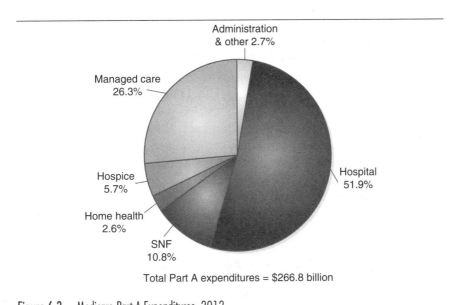

Total Part A expenditures = $266.8 billion

Figure 6.3 Medicare Part A Expenditures, 2012
Data from National Center for Health Statistics. Health, United States, 2014. Hyattsville, MD: U.S. Department of Health and Human Services; 2015:336.

benefit period begins. The number of benefit periods a beneficiary can have over his or her lifetime is unlimited. The following is a brief description of acute care, postacute skilled nursing care, home health, and hospice benefits under Part A.

Services received during a hospital stay are fully paid for the first 60 days in a benefit period after a deductible ($1,260 in 2015) has been met. Part A deductible applies to each benefit period. If ongoing hospitalization beyond 60 days is necessary, a copayment ($315 per day in 2015) must be paid from days 61 through 90. A benefit period has 90 days of maximum coverage. Beyond the 90 days, there is a lifetime reserve of 60 additional hospital inpatient days to which a higher copayment applies ($630 per day in 2015). Benefits for medical care in a psychiatric hospital are limited to 190 days in the beneficiary's lifetime.

For postacute care, Medicare pays for up to 100 days in a Medicare-certified SNF subsequent to inpatient hospitalization for at least 3 consecutive days, not including the day of discharge. Admission to the SNF must occur within 30 days of hospital discharge, and it must be related to the same condition for which the beneficiary was hospitalized. All covered services are fully paid for the first 20 days in the SNF. Beyond that, a copayment ($157.50 per day in 2015) must be paid from days 21 through 100.

Medicare pays for home health care when a person is homebound and requires intermittent or part-time skilled nursing care or rehabilitation therapy determined necessary by a physician. Services must be obtained from a Medicare-certified home health agency. Durable medical equipment (DME), such as wheelchairs, hospital beds, walkers, and medical supplies, is also covered. Home health visits do not have a deductible, but a 20% coinsurance applies to DME.

For terminally ill patients, Medicare pays for care provided by a Medicare-certified hospice. A small copayment applies for prescription drugs for these patients.

Supplementary Medical Insurance (Part B)

Part B, the supplementary medical insurance (SMI) portion of Medicare, is a voluntary program, financed partly by general tax revenues and partly by required premium contributions from the beneficiaries. Almost all persons entitled to hospital insurance also choose to enroll in SMI because they cannot get similar coverage at that price from private insurers. Coverage includes physician, ambulance, outpatient rehabilitation, an annual wellness exam, and medically needed preventive services; hospital outpatient services such as outpatient surgery, diagnostic tests, radiology, and pathology; emergency department visits; renal dialysis; prostheses; and medical equipment and supplies. Part B also covers limited home health services that are not associated with a hospital or SNF stay.

Part B premiums are income based. The standard premium for 2015 is $104.90 per month. For beneficiaries earning more than $85,000 and filing individual tax returns (or earning more than $170,000 and filing joint tax returns), 2015 premiums range between $146.90 and $335.70 depending on income. Part B also carries an annual deductible ($147 in 2015), and an 80:20 coinsurance applies to most services.

Medicare Advantage (Part C)

Part C is, in reality, not a program that offers specifically defined medical services. The program was formerly called Medicare+Choice, which took effect on January 1, 1998, and was mandated by the Balanced Budget Act of 1997. The law expanded the role of private managed care health plans such as HMO and PPO plans. To participate in Part C, a beneficiary must first be enrolled in both Part A and Part B. The beneficiary must pay Part B premiums to Medicare and an additional premium to the MCO (some plans have no premiums). Beneficiaries, however, do have the choice to remain in the original Medicare fee-for-service program.

By enrolling in Medicare Advantage, the beneficiary receives all Part A, Part B, and Part D services through an MCO. Medicare pays a set capitated amount of money each month to the participating managed care plans on behalf of each beneficiary. In turn, the plan manages Medicare benefits for its members. To attract Medicare enrollees, MCOs may offer extra benefits, such as basic dental and vision benefits, which may lower the beneficiaries' out-of-pocket costs. All Part C plans include a limit on out-of-pocket costs for covered services. Part C also eliminates the need for Medigap coverage. In 2014, 30% of the beneficiaries were enrolled in Medicare Advantage plans (Jacobson et al., 2014).

Prescription Drug Coverage (Part D)

Part D was added to the existing Medicare program under the Medicare Prescription Drug, Improvement, and Modernization Act of 2003 and was fully implemented in January 2006. The program is available to anyone, regardless of income, who has coverage under Part A or Part B. Coverage is offered through two types of private plans approved by Medicare. Standalone prescription drug plans that offer only drug coverage are available to those who want to stay in the original Medicare fee-for-service program. Alternatively, Medicare Advantage prescription drug plans are available to those who want to obtain all health care services through MCOs participating in Part C.

Like Part B, the Part D program is voluntary because it requires payment of a monthly premium. For 2015, the base premium was estimated to be $33 per month (Cubanski & Neuman, 2015), which is adjusted upward according to income and type of plan selected by the beneficiary. After an annual deductible ($320 in 2015), benefits are paid according to three layers of personal out-of-pocket spending on prescription drugs (see **Table 6.1**).

Table 6.1   Medicare Part D Benefits and Individual Out-of-Pocket Costs, 2015 (Illustrative Only)

	Drug Costs	Medicare Pays	Beneficiary Pays
Deductible	$320	None	$320
Initial coverage	Until the combined total paid by the plan and the beneficiary reaches $2,960	75%	25%
Coverage gap or "doughnut hole"	Until the beneficiary has spent $4,700 out of pocket for the year Drug discounts by the manufacturer count as out-of-pocket spending	None	45% for brand-name drugs; 65% for generic drugs
Catastrophic coverage—after the coverage gap ends		Approximately 95%	Approximately 5%

Notes: 1. The Extra Help feature of the program helps people with limited income and resources (e.g., someone who has full Medicaid coverage) to pay the Medicare prescription drug costs.
   2. Under the ACA, the coverage gap will gradually close. For example, in 2020, the beneficiary will pay 25% of the cost of all drugs. After 2020, the gap will be eliminated.

Medicaid

Also referred to as Title 19 of the Social Security Act, Medicaid is the United States' public health insurance program for the indigent. Each state has established its own criteria for determining eligibility according to income and other resources such as bank accounts, real property, and other assets. Federal law specifies coverage for low-income elderly, the blind, the disabled receiving Supplemental Security Income (SSI), and some pregnant women. Medicaid is also instrumental in providing health insurance to children in low-income families (**Figure 6.4**). In addition, most states, at their discretion, have

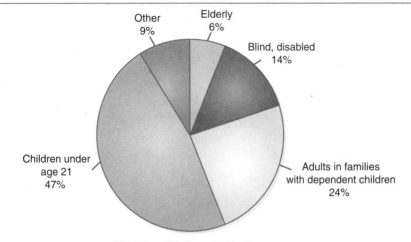

Total beneficiaries = 68.8 million

Figure 6.4   Medicaid Recipient Categories, 2011
Data from National Center for Health Statistics. Health, United States, 2014. Hyattsville, MD: U.S. Department of Health and Human Services; 2015:340.

defined other medically needy categories. Most important among these are individuals who are institutionalized in nursing or psychiatric facilities and individuals who are receiving community-based services but would otherwise be eligible for Medicaid if institutionalized. All of these people have to qualify based on assets and income, which must be below the threshold levels established by each state. Hence, Medicaid is a *means-tested program.*

The Medicaid program is jointly financed by the federal and state governments. The federal government provides matching funds to the states based on the per capita income in each state. Wealthier states have a smaller share of their costs reimbursed by the federal government.

Each state administers its own Medicaid program. Hence, eligibility criteria, covered services, and payments to providers vary considerably from state to state. However, for a state to receive federal matching funds, the state must provide some specific health services (see **Table 6.2**).

Children's Health Insurance Program

The Children's Health Insurance Program (CHIP), codified as Title 21 of the Social Security Act, was enacted under the Balanced Budget Act of 1997. When the program was created, nearly one-fourth of the children

Table 6.2   Federally Mandated Services for State Medicaid Programs

- Inpatient hospital services
- Hospital outpatient services
- Physician, nurse midwife, and nurse practitioner services
- Federally qualified health center and rural health clinic services
- Outpatient laboratory and x-ray services
- Freestanding birth center services
- Nursing facility services for beneficiaries age 21 and older
- Home health services for those eligible for nursing facility services, including medical supplies and equipment
- Medical and surgical services of a dentist
- Preventive, diagnosis, and treatment services (including vaccinations) for children up to age 21
- Family planning services and supplies
- Pregnancy-related services; tobacco cessation counseling and pharmacotherapy for pregnant women

Adapted from Paradise J. Medicaid moving forward. http://kff.org/health-reform/issue-brief/medicaid-moving-forward/. Published March 9, 2015. Accessed July 5, 2015.

in low-income families were uninsured. CHIP offers additional federal matching funds to states to expand Medicaid eligibility to enroll children up to 19 years of age who otherwise would not qualify for coverage because their families' incomes exceed the Medicaid threshold levels. Certain adults, such as pregnant women, parents, and caretaker relatives, may also be covered under CHIP.

In 2015, most states provided CHIP coverage to children with family incomes at or above 250% of the FPL, or about $60,625 (higher in Alaska and Hawaii) for a family of four, and if they are not covered under a private insurance plan. States have the option to either operate CHIP as a separate program or run it in conjunction with the state's Medicaid program. In December 2013, almost 5.8 million children were enrolled in CHIP (Smith, Snyder, & Rudowitz, 2014).

THE AFFORDABLE CARE ACT AND PUBLIC INSURANCE

The main changes to the public insurance programs under the ACA are as follows:

1. Payment cuts to managed care plans participating in Medicare Advantage between 2012 and 2017. As a result, enrollment in Medicare Advantage was expected to decrease. Analysts had projected that the cuts would drive MCOs to raise premiums, reduce additional benefits, and even pull out of the Medicare Advantage program. To the surprise of many, however, enrollments actually increased by 41% between 2010 and 2014. Neuman and Jacobson (2014) cite two main reasons: (1) The CMS provided quality-related bonus payments to nearly all Medicare Advantage plans, which helped offset payment reductions. (2) Plans have made adjustments such as cost cutting and increasing cost sharing. Any material changes in these two factors could have the opposite effect.

2. Expansion of Medicaid under the penalty of losing matching funds if a state would not expand its Medicaid program was a significant part of the ACA. The law had also envisioned a minimum income eligibility standard of 138% of the FPL to qualify for Medicaid in any state nationwide. In its 2012 ruling, however, the U.S. Supreme Court struck down the Medicaid provision of the law, which left each state free to decide whether or not it would expand its existing Medicaid program. As of April 2015, only 29 of the 50 states and the District of Columbia had adopted the ACA's Medicaid expansion initiative. Presently, it is unknown how many previously uninsured individuals have gained Medicaid coverage under the ACA.

3. For people whose incomes range between 139% and 200% of the FPL—who would not otherwise qualify for Medicaid—the ACA allows states to set up a separate Basic Health Program. In this program, enrollees obtain health insurance through the state government, not through the exchanges even though they may qualify for exchange-offered insurance. The cost of the program is subsidized through federal funding. States would purchase insurance through MCOs that cover the state's Medicaid population. As of 2015, only Minnesota and New York had established the Basic Health Program.

REIMBURSEMENT METHODS

Insurance companies, MCOs, Blue Cross/Blue Shield, and the government (for Medicare and Medicaid) are referred to as *third-party payers*, with the other two parties in the arrangement being the patient and the provider (Wilson & Neuhauser, 1985, p. 118). Payment made by third-party payers to the providers of services is called *reimbursement*.

Fee for Service

Fee-for-service reimbursement is based on the assumption that services are provided in a set of identifiable and individually distinct units of services. For example, physician services may include units such as an examination, x-ray, urinalysis, and a tetanus shot. For surgery, individual services may include an admission kit, numerous medical supplies (each accounted for separately), surgeon's fees, anesthesia, anesthesiologist's fees, recovery room charges, and so forth. Each of these services is separately billed.

Initially, fee-for-service charges were set by providers, and insurers passively paid the claims. Later, insurers started to limit reimbursement to a usual, customary, and reasonable amount that was determined by each payer. In this case, providers would *balance bill*—that is, ask the patients to pay the difference between the actual charges and the payments received from insurers.

Historically, providers preferred the fee-for-service method, which fell into disfavor with payers because of cost escalations. In response, private payers as well as the government have devised other methods aimed at limiting the amount of reimbursement. Some modified versions of fee-for-service reimbursement are still in use.

Bundled Payments

In *bundled payments* or package pricing, a number of related services are included in one price. For example, normal vaginal delivery may have one set fee that includes predelivery and postdelivery care (Williams, 1995, p. 114). Optometrists sometimes advertise package prices that include the charges for eye exams, frames for eyeglasses, and corrective lenses. Research has shown that bundled payments can align incentives for providers to work closely together across specialties and health care settings. Consequently, Medicare is undertaking bundled payment initiatives that link payments for multiple services beneficiaries receive during an entire episode of care.

Resource-Based Relative Value Scale

Implemented in 1992 by Medicare, the resource-based relative value scale (RBRVS) reimburses physicians according to a relative value assigned to each physician service. Relative values are based on the time, skill, and intensity it takes to provide a service, and the actual reimbursement is derived using a complex formula. Each year, Medicare publishes the Medicare Fee Schedule, which gives the reimbursement amount for each of the services and procedures identified by a current procedural terminology (CPT) code. The reimbursement amounts are adjusted for the geographic area in which the practice is located.

Reimbursement Under Managed Care

Three distinct approaches are used by MCOs. PPOs use a variation of the fee-for-service method, in which the PPO establishes fee schedules based on discounts negotiated with providers participating in its network. HMOs sometimes have physicians on their staff who are paid a salary. *Capitation* is another mechanism used by HMOs. Under this reimbursement scheme, a provider is paid a set monthly fee per enrollee (sometimes referred to as per member per month [PMPM] rate), regardless of whether an enrollee sees the provider or not and regardless of how often an enrollee sees the provider. Capitation removes the incentive for provider-induced demand. It makes providers prudent and encourages them to provide only necessary services.

From Retrospective to Prospective Reimbursement

Traditionally, Medicare and Medicaid established *per diem* (daily) rates for reimbursing hospitals, nursing homes, and other inpatient facilities. The per diem rates were based on the actual costs the providers had incurred during the previous year. Because rates were set after evaluating the costs retrospectively, the method was referred to as *retrospective reimbursement.* Home health was also reimbursed on the basis of cost.

Because the retrospective method was based on costs that were directly related to length of stay, services rendered, and the cost of providing the services, providers had no incentive to control costs. Services were rendered indiscriminately because health care institutions could increase their profits by increasing costs. Because of the perverse financial incentives inherent in retrospective cost-based reimbursement, it has been largely replaced by prospective methods of reimbursement.

In contrast to retrospective reimbursement, where historical costs are used to determine the amount paid to providers, *prospective reimbursement* uses certain preestablished criteria to determine in advance the amount of reimbursement. Medicare has been using the prospective payment system (PPS) to reimburse inpatient hospital acute care services under Medicare Part A since 1983. Four main prospective reimbursement methods currently in use are based on diagnosis-related groups (DRGs), ambulatory payment classifications (APCs), resource utilization groups (RUGs), and home health resource groups (HHRGs).

Diagnosis-Related Groups

The DRG method is used to pay for hospital inpatient services. The predetermined rate is set according to DRGs. Instead of a per diem rate, the reimbursement method based on DRGs prospectively sets a bundled price according to the principal diagnosis at the time of admission. The hospital receives the predetermined fixed rate for that particular DRG classification.

The primary factor governing the amount of reimbursement is the main clinical diagnosis, but additional factors can create differences in reimbursement for the same DRG. Such factors include differences in wage levels between geographic areas, an urban versus a rural hospital location, whether the institution is a teaching hospital (i.e., it has residency programs for medical graduates; adjustments in reimbursement are based on the intensity of teaching), and an adjustment related to treating a disproportionately large share of low-income patients. In 2007, Medicare Severity Diagnosis-Related Groups (MS-DRGs) were implemented. MS-DRGs include patient severity to better reflect use of hospital resources.

The DRG-based prospective reimbursement has forced hospitals to control their costs. To keep the cost of services below the fixed reimbursement amount, this reimbursement method has also forced hospitals to minimize the length of inpatient stay. If the total cost of services is less than the DRG-based reimbursement amount, a hospital gets to keep the difference as profit. Conversely, a hospital loses money when its costs exceed the prospective reimbursement rate. As an example, if the prospective reimbursement rate for a given DRG is $3,500 and the costs associated with each day of hospital stay are as shown in **Table 6.3**, a patient admitted under this DRG should be hospitalized for no more than 4 days when the cumulative costs will equal $3,400. If the hospital discharges this patient after 3 days, it will make a profit of $700 ($3,500 − $2,800). If the patient is discharged after 5 days, the hospital will suffer a loss of $500 ($3,500 − $4,000).

Table 6.3 Hospital Days of Stay and Costs for a Given DRG

Days of stay	1	2	3	4	5	6
Cost per day	$1,200	$900	$700	$600	$600	$600

Hospitals now have disincentives to discharge patients too quickly. The ACA requires reduction in payments to hospitals that incur excessive Medicare readmissions within 30 days of discharge. Readmission can be to the same or another hospital and is related to the medical condition for which the patient was previously hospitalized.

Ambulatory Payment Classifications

The prospective payment method based on APCs, implemented in 2000, is associated with Medicare's Outpatient Prospective Payment System (OPPS) for services provided by hospital outpatient departments. The APC divides all outpatient services into more than 300 procedural groups. Reimbursement rates are associated with each APC group. The rates are also adjusted for geographic variations in wages. APC reimbursement includes services such as anesthesia, certain drugs, supplies, and recovery room charges in a package price established by Medicare.

In January 2008, Medicare implemented the OPPS to pay for facility services—such as nursing, recovery care, anesthetics, drugs, and other supplies—in freestanding (i.e., nonhospital) ambulatory surgery centers. The most common procedures performed in these centers are cataract removal and lens replacement, upper gastrointestinal endoscopy, and colonoscopy. Physician services are reimbursed separately under the physician fee schedule based on RBRVS (MedPAC, 2014).

Resource Utilization Groups

Medicare pays SNFs on the basis of RUGs, but the method differs from the way in which DRG-based payments are used for hospitals. Whereas a fixed amount of reimbursement is associated with each DRG, RUG categories are used for determining an SNF's overall severity of health conditions requiring medical and nursing intervention. The aggregate of clinical severity in a facility is referred to as its *case mix*. It is determined by first evaluating each patient's medical and nursing care needs. Based on this evaluation, each patient is classified into one of 66 RUGs (according to RUG-IV classifications). The case-mix composite of an institution is then used to determine a fixed per diem amount—an all-inclusive bundled rate—associated with that case mix. The higher the case mix score, the higher the reimbursement. Adjustments to the PPS rate are made for differences in wages prevailing in various geographic areas and for facility location in urban as opposed to rural areas.

Home Health Resource Groups

Implemented in October 2000, the PPS for home health care pays a fixed, predetermined rate for each 60-day episode of care, regardless of the specific services delivered. Thus all services provided by a home health agency are bundled under one payment made on a per-patient basis. An assessment instrument called the Outcomes and Assessment Information Set (OASIS) is used to rate each patient's functional status and clinical severity level. The assessment measures translate into points; the points are totaled to determine the patient's HHRG. Payment is based on the patient's specific HHRG category. The HHRG classification uses 153 distinct groups in which patients can be classified according to clinical severity, functional status, and the need for rehabilitation therapies.

THE AFFORDABLE CARE ACT AND PAYMENT REFORM

Value-based payment to providers is the next wave of change in U.S. health care delivery, as required by the ACA. These payment arrangements will be designed to incentivize and hold providers accountable for the total cost and quality of care for a population of patients. Risk will increasingly shift to providers. One challenge, of course, is how value will be measured. It will also require changing the culture in which health care is practiced— how physicians practice medicine and what patients expect. In spite of the challenges that must be overcome, experts agree that the current reimbursement system is not sustainable (Smith & Walker, 2015). According to the DHHS, the goal is to have 30% of Medicare payments tied to quality or value by 2016, and 50% by 2018, using alternative payment models in which providers are held accountable for quality and cost (Burwell, 2015). The new models would include bundled payments as well as shared-savings and shared-risk arrangements.

NATIONAL HEALTH EXPENDITURES

National health expenditures (also called national health spending or national health care costs) are an estimate of the amount spent for all health services and supplies and health-related research and construction activities in the United States during a calendar year. According to data from the CMS, in 2013, national health expenditures in the United States amounted to $2.9 trillion. To put some meaning into such large expenditures, it is common to compare the total health care expenditures to the total economic consumption. The gross domestic product (GDP) measures the total value of goods and services produced and consumed in a country. In 2013, the U.S. GDP was $16.8 trillion. Hence, 17.4% of the total economic output in the United States in 2013 was consumed by health care. Another way to look at health care expenditures is in terms of the average per capita spending, which controls for changes in the size of the population. In 2013, the average per capita spending for health care amounted to $9,255 for each American. National health expenditures from 1960 to 2013 are presented in **Table 6.4.**

Table 6.4 National Health Expenditures, Selected Years

Year	Amount ($ Billions)	Percentage of GDP	Amount per Capita
1960	27.4	5.2	$147
1970	74.9	7.2	356
1980	255.8	9.2	1,110
1990	724.3	12.5	2,854
2000	1,378.0	13.4	4,881
2010	2,604.1	17.4	8,428
2013	2,919.1	17.4	9,255

Data from Health, United States, 2013, p. 327. Hyattsville, MD: National Center for Health Statistics. CMS, Office of the Actuary. NHE summary including share of GDP, CY 1960–2013. http://www.cms .gov/Research-Statistics-Data-and-Systems/Statistics-Trends-and-Reports/NationalHealthExpendData/ NationalHealthAccountsHistorical.html. Accessed May 2015.

Figure 6.5 shows the breakdown of how 2010 national health dollars were used. Almost 85% of total national health expenditures were devoted to personal health services and products, which include services provided by hospitals, physician and clinical services, dental care, other professional services, nursing home care, home health care, prescription drugs, medical supplies, durable medical equipment (DME), and other personal health care products and services. The remaining 15% of national expenditures were accounted for by public health services, research, investment in structures and equipment, costs related to administration of government programs, and administrative costs of private insurance.

The annual growth in health care spending, or health care cost inflation, is a matter of concern for almost all developed nations because health care spending has been rising faster than people's incomes. Cost inflation in health care is evaluated by comparing it to the growth of the

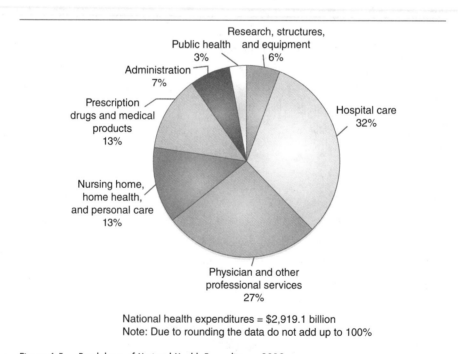

National health expenditures = $2,919.1 billion
Note: Due to rounding the data do not add up to 100%

Figure 6.5   Breakdown of National Health Expenditures, 2013
Data from Centers for Medicare and Medicaid Services, Office of the Actuary, National Health Statistics Group.

Table 6.5   Growth Comparisons of National Health Expenditures to the GDP and CPI, 2000–2013

	2000	2013
National health expenditures	$1,378.0 billion	$2,919.1 billion
Average annual increase		6.0%
GDP	$10,284.8 billion	$16,768.1 billion
Average annual increase		3.8%
Yearly average CPI	168.9	229.3
Average annual increase		2.4%

Data from Centers for Medicare and Medicaid Services, Office of the Actuary, National Health Statistics Group; Social Security Administration, Average CPI by quarter and year. http://www.ssa.gov/OACT/STATS/avgcpi.html. Accessed May 2015.

GDP as well as to the *consumer price index* (CPI), which measures inflation in the general economy. As **Table 6.5** shows, in the United States, health care cost inflation has exceeded the growth in the GDP and CPI.

CONCLUSION

Financing plays a critical role in health care delivery. For consumers, it pays for insurance coverage, which enables them to obtain health care services. For providers, it reimburses them for the services they deliver. The Affordable Care Act has been instrumental in expanding health insurance coverage; however, serious gaps still remain.

For most services, the methods of reimbursement were changed from retrospective to prospective mechanisms after it became widely known that cost-based methods and fee-for-service reimbursement contained perverse incentives for providers to increase the cost of health care delivery. Prospective payment methods, now widely in use, and capitation, used by health maintenance organizations, contain incentives for the delivery of cost-effective health care. Comprehensive health insurance also contains perverse incentives for consumers to use more health care than needed, a phenomenon known as moral hazard. Deductibles and copayments were instituted after payers realized that these methods of cost sharing reduce the excessive use of health care. In an effort to further improve efficiencies and quality, current emphasis is on creating value-based payment models.

The financing of health care is shared between private and public sources. Contrary to what many people might think, the government incurs a sizable proportion of total health care expenditures, estimated to be 43% of all health care spending in the United States. Hence, at least from a financing standpoint, the United States has a quasi-national health care system.

REFERENCES

Burwell SM. Setting value-based payment goals—HHS efforts to improve U.S. health care. *N Engl J Med.* 2015; 372(10):897–899.

Centers for Medicare and Medicaid Services (CMS). 2014 annual report of the boards of trustees of the Federal Hospital Insurance and Federal Supplementary Medical Insurance Trust Funds. http://www.cms.gov /Research-Statistics-Data-and-Systems/Statistics-Trends-and-Reports /ReportsTrustFunds/Downloads/TR2014.pdf. Published 2014. Accessed May 2015.

Claxton G, et al. *The Kaiser Family Foundation and Health Research and Educational Trust Employer Health Benefits 2014 Annual Survey.* Menlo Park, CA: Henry J. Kaiser Family Foundation/Chicago, IL: Health Research and Educational Trust; 2014.

Cubanski J, et al. How much is enough? Out-of-pocket spending among Medicare beneficiaries: a chartbook. http://kff.org/health-costs/report/how-much-is -enough-out-of-pocket-spending-among-medicare-beneficiaries-a-chartbook. Published July 21, 2014. Accessed May 2015.

Cubanski J, Neuman T. Medicare's income-related premiums: a data note. http://kff.org/medicare/issue-brief/medicares-income-related-premiums-a -data-note. Published June 3, 2015. Accessed May 2015.

Department of Health and Human Services (DHHS). Health insurance coverage and the Affordable Care Act. http://aspe.hhs.gov/health/reports/2015

/uninsured_change/ib_uninsured_change.pdf. Published May 5, 2015. Accessed July 7, 2015.

Feldstein PJ. *Health Care Economics*. 4th ed. New York: Delmar Publishers; 1993.

Health Insurance Institute. *Modern Health Insurance*. New York: Health Insurance Institute; 1969.

Jacobson G, et al. Medicare Advantage 2015 data spotlight: overview of plan changes. http://kff.org/medicare/issue-brief/medicare-advantage-2015-data -spotlight-overview-of-plan-changes. Published December 10, 2014. Accessed May 2015.

Jacobson G, Neuman T, Damico A. Medigap enrollment among new Medicare beneficiaries: How many 65-year olds enroll in plans with first-dollar coverage? http://kff.org/medicare/issue-brief/medigap-enrollment-among -new-medicare-beneficiaries. Published April 13, 2015. Accessed May 2015.

Levitt L, Cox C, Claxton G. Data note: how has the individual insurance market grown under the Affordable Care Act? http://kff.org/health-reform/issue-brief /data-note-how-has-the-individual-insurance-market-grown-under-the-afford able-care-act. Published May 12, 2015. Accessed July 7, 2015.

Mark Farrah Associates. Health insurance enrollment and marketplace estimates: December 2014 insights. http://www.markfarrah.com/healthcare-business -strategy/Health-Insurance-Enrollment-and-Marketplace-Estimates-December -2014-Insights.aspx. Published December 18, 2014. Accessed May 2015.

MedPAC. *Ambulatory surgical center services payment system*. Washington, DC: Medicare Payment Advisory Commission. http://www.medpac.gov /documents/payment-basics/ambulatory-surgical-center-services-payment -system-14.pdf?sfvrsn=0. Published October 2014. Accessed July 31, 2015.

Neuman T, Jacobson G. Medicare Advantage: take another look. http://kff.org /medicare/perspective/medicare-advantage-take-another-look. Published May 7, 2014. Accessed July 7, 2015.

RAND Corporation. Skin in the game: how consumer-directed plans affect the cost and use of health care. http://www.rand.org/content/dam/rand/pubs /research_briefs/2012/RAND_RB9672.pdf. Published 2012. Accessed May 2015.

Smith JC, Medalia C. *Health Insurance Coverage in the United States: 2013*. Washington, DC: U.S. Census Bureau; 2014.

Smith L, Walker T. Payment reform shifts to high gear. *Manag Healthc Executive*. 2015;25(4):6–15.

Smith V, Snyder, L, Rudowitz R. CHIP enrollment snapshot: December 2013. http://kff.org/medicaid/issue-brief/chip-enrollment-snapshot-december-2013. Published June 3, 2014. Accessed May 2015.

Vaughn EJ, Elliott CM. *Fundamentals of Risk and Insurance.* New York: John Wiley & Sons; 1987.

Williams SJ. *Essentials of Health Services.* Albany, NY: Delmar Publishers; 1995.

Wilson FA, Neuhauser D. *Health Services in the United States.* 2nd ed. Cambridge, MA: Ballinger Publishing; 1985.

Chapter 7

Outpatient Services and Primary Care

INTRODUCTION

Historically, outpatient care has been independent of most services provided in health care institutions. In earlier days, most physicians made home visits to treat patients, in addition to seeing patients in their clinics. Outpatient care now includes much more than primary care. With the advancement of medical science and for economic reasons, a variety of outpatient settings and services have become common. Because of technological innovation, health care delivery has increasingly shifted away from expensive stays in acute care hospitals. To capture lost revenues, hospitals gradually became dominant players in delivering not only inpatient care but outpatient services as well. For economic reasons, physician practices have become group practices, and very few solo practitioners are left. Group practices generally have several providers in primary care or a single specialty.

State and local government agencies have actively sponsored limited outpatient services to meet the needs of underserved populations, mainly indigent patients who lack the personal resources to obtain health care in the private sector. Community health centers, which primarily depend on federal and state funds including grants and Medicaid, serve a number of rural and inner-city areas and provide a wide array of outpatient services.

WHAT IS OUTPATIENT CARE?

The terms *outpatient* and *ambulatory* are used interchangeably, although the term *outpatient* is more comprehensive. Strictly speaking, *ambulatory care* consists of diagnostic and therapeutic services and treatments provided to the walking (ambulatory) patient. Yet, patients do not always ambulate to health service centers to receive ambulatory care. For example, in a hospital emergency department (ED), patients may arrive by land or air ambulance. In other instances, such as with mobile diagnostic units and home health care, services are taken to the patient, rather than the patient coming to receive the services. Hence, the term *outpatient service* refers to any health care services that do not require an overnight stay in an institution of health care delivery. The main settings and services for delivering outpatient care are listed in **Exhibit 7.1**.

SCOPE OF OUTPATIENT SERVICES

In 2008, according to the National Ambulatory Medical Care Survey, Americans made approximately 960 million visits, or more than 3 visits per person, to office-based physicians. Physicians in general and family

Exhibit 7.1   Outpatient Settings and Services

• Private practice	• Home care
• Hospitals	• Hospice care
• Outpatient clinics	• Outpatient long-term care services
• Freestanding facilities	• Public health services
• Mobile facilities for medical, diagnostic, and screening services	• Community health centers and free clinics
• Telephone triage	• Alternative medicine clinics

practice accounted for the largest share of these visits (23.5%), followed by physicians in internal medicine (16.0%), pediatrics (12.5%), and obstetrics and gynecology (8.6%). Doctors of osteopathy accounted for 7.3% of all visits. The South led the nation in share of physician visits (37.4%), followed by the West (22.0%), the Northeast (20.6%), and the Midwest (20.0%). Ambulatory visits per person were highest in the Northeast (3.6 visits) and lowest in the Midwest (2.9 visits). Most physician office visits (91.5%) took place in metropolitan areas. Visits per person were also higher in metropolitan areas (3.5) than in rural areas (1.6), reflecting poorer access to primary care in rural areas of the United States. Access to care remains problematic for some individuals, especially for the uninsured and racial/ethnic minorities (see **Exhibit 7.2**).

Most surgeries are now performed in outpatient settings, whereas many of these same procedures could previously be performed only in hospitals. This shift toward outpatient care is expected to continue. Hospital occupancy rates have declined for more than 2 decades, and hospital executives have increasingly viewed outpatient care as an essential portion of their health care business (Barr & Breindel, 1995). Previously, outpatient care was not considered a part of the hospital's core business.

The growth of nonhospital-based outpatient services has intensified competition for outpatient medical services between hospitals and community-based providers. Examples of such competition include home health care, ambulatory clinics for routine and urgent care, and outpatient surgery. On the other hand, several other services, such as dental care and optometric services, continue to be office based. Financing is the main reason that dental and optometric services have not been integrated with other outpatient medical services. Medical insurance plans have traditionally been separate from dental and vision care plans. Philosophical and technical differences account for other variations. For example, chiropractic care is generally covered by most health plans yet remains isolated from the mainstream practice of medicine. Other services, such as alternative therapies and self-care, are not covered by insurance, yet they continue to experience remarkable growth.

Several key changes have been instrumental in shifting the balance between inpatient and outpatient services. These factors can be broadly classified as reimbursement, technological factors, utilization control factors, and social factors.

Exhibit 7.2   Access to Primary Care

Did Not Get or Delayed Medical Care Due to Cost, 2012 (%)

Younger than 18 years	3.2
18–64 years	13.3
65 years and older	4.1
White	13.0
Black	14.8
Hispanic	14.8
Insured	8.1
Uninsured	33.4

Did Not Get Prescription Drugs Due to Cost, 2012 (%)

Younger than 18 years	2.2
18–64 years	9.4
65 years and older	3.4
White	8.4
Black	13.2
Hispanic	11.5
Insured	6.1
Uninsured	22.1

Did Not Get Dental Care Due to Cost, 2012 (%)

Younger than 18 years	5.5
18–64 years	14.8
65 years and older	6.1
White	13.7
Black	17.0
Hispanic	18.3
Insured	10.2
Uninsured	32.8

Data from Health, United States, 2013: With Special Feature on Prescription Drugs. National Center for Health Statistics (U.S.). Hyattsville, MD: National Center for Health Statistics (U.S.); May 2014:Table 74.

Reimbursement

Today, both private and public payers have a clear preference for outpatient treatment because it costs less than inpatient care. Quicker discharge of patients from hospital beds under prospective and capitated reimbursement methods created a substantial market for outpatient services. In response to changes in financial incentives for reimbursement of outpatient care, hospitals aggressively developed outpatient services to offset declining inpatient income.

Technological Factors

The development of new diagnostic and treatment procedures and less invasive surgical methods has made it possible to provide some services in outpatient settings that had previously required inpatient hospital stays. Shorter-acting anesthetics and the proliferation of minimally invasive technologies have made many surgical procedures less traumatic and require much shorter recovery times. Many office-based physicians have also acquired technology to deliver basic diagnostic, imaging, and surgical services.

Utilization Control Factors

Inpatient hospital stays are strongly discouraged by various payers. Prior authorization for inpatient admission and close monitoring during hospitalization have been actively pursued with the objective of minimizing a patient's length of stay.

Social Factors

Patients generally have a strong preference for receiving health care in home- and community-based settings. Indeed, most people do not want to be institutionalized unless absolutely necessary. Remaining in their own homes gives individuals a strong sense of independence and control over their lives—elements considered important for quality of life.

OUTPATIENT CARE SETTINGS AND METHODS OF DELIVERY

Certain outpatient services are now available in different settings. For example, agencies providing home health services may be freestanding, hospital based, or nursing home based. In many instances, physician group practices are merging with hospitals, and hospitals and freestanding surgical clinics often compete for various types of surgical procedures. Therefore, the classifications used in this section are merely illustrative—there are many exceptions to the arrangements presented here. Furthermore, in this constantly evolving system, new settings and methods are likely to emerge.

Private Practice

Physicians, as office-based practitioners, form the backbone of outpatient care. Most visits entail relatively limited examination and testing, and encounters with physicians are generally of a relatively short duration. The waiting time in the office is typically longer than the actual time spent with the physician.

In the past, the solo practice of medicine and small partnership arrangements attracted the most practitioners. Self-employment offered a degree of independence not generally available in large organizational settings. Now, group practices and institutional affiliations—such as employment by a hospital or managed care organization (MCO)—have become the norm. Several factors account for the shift away from solo practice: uncertainties created by rapid changes in the health care delivery system, contracting by MCOs with consolidated rather than solo entities, competition from large health care delivery organizations, the high cost of operating a solo practice, complexity of billings and collections in a multipayer system, and increased external controls over the private practice of medicine. Group practice and other organizational arrangements offer several benefits to providers, including patient-referral networks, negotiating leverage with MCOs, sharing of overhead expenses, ease of obtaining coverage from colleagues for personal time off, and attractive starting salaries along with benefits and profit-sharing plans.

Hospital Outpatient Clinics

Many hospital outpatient clinics, particularly those in inner-city areas, function as the community's safety net, providing primary care to the medically indigent and uninsured populations. On the other hand, outpatient services now constitute a key source of profits for many hospitals. Hospitals providing both inpatient and outpatient services have the advantage of enhancing their revenues by referring postsurgical cases to its affiliated units for rehabilitation and home care follow-up. Patients also prefer a seamless transition from the hospital to its affiliated outpatient services.

Hospital-based outpatient services can be broadly classified into five main types: clinical (typically for the uninsured or those participating in research studies), surgical (patients are discharged on the day of surgery), home health care (postacute care and rehabilitation), women's health, and traditional emergency care.

Freestanding Facilities

Various types of proprietary, community-based, freestanding medical facilities are found across the country. These settings can be differentiated as walk-in clinics, urgent care centers, and surgical centers. *Walk-in clinics* provide outpatient services ranging from basic primary care to urgent care and are generally used on a nonroutine, episodic basis. Primary care *retail clinics* are becoming available in stores such as Walmart, Walgreens, and CVS pharmacies. *Urgent care centers* generally offer a wide range of routine services for basic and acute conditions. The main advantages of walk-in clinics and urgent care centers are convenience of location, evening and weekend hours, and availability of services on a walk-in, no-appointment basis. *Surgicenters* are freestanding outpatient surgery centers that operate independently of hospitals. They usually provide a full range of services for the types of surgery that can be performed on an outpatient basis and do not require overnight hospitalization. Other types of outpatient facilities include outpatient rehabilitation centers, optometric centers, and dental clinics.

Mobile Facilities for Medical, Diagnostic, and Screening Services

Mobile health care services are transported to patients and constitute an efficient and convenient means for providing certain types of routine health services. These services include mammography, x-ray, dental care, and optometric care. They mainly benefit populations in small towns, rural communities, and nursing homes. Health screening vans, staffed by volunteers who are trained professionals, are generally operated by various non-profit organizations and are often seen at malls and fairgrounds where they do screening checks for blood pressure and cholesterol.

Telephone Triage

Telephone access, referred to as telephone triage, is a means of bringing expert opinion and advice on health care to the patient, especially during hours when physicians' offices are generally closed. Such a system is staffed by trained nurses who have access to patient medical records and provide guidance with the use of standardized protocols. They can consult with primary care physicians when necessary or refer patients to an urgent care facility or ED (Appleby, 1995).

Home Care

In home health care, services are brought to patients in their own homes. Without home services, the only alternative for such patients would be institutionalization in a hospital or nursing home. Home health care is consistent with the philosophy of maintaining people in the least restrictive environment possible. Home health services typically include nursing care, such as changing dressings, monitoring medications, and help with bathing; short-term rehabilitation, such as physical therapy, occupational therapy, and speech therapy; homemaker services, such as meal preparation, shopping, transportation, and some specific household chores; and certain medical supplies and equipment, such as ostomy supplies, hospital beds, oxygen tanks, and walkers and wheelchairs (the latter are referred to as durable medical equipment).

Hospice Care

The term *hospice* refers to a cluster of comprehensive services for terminally ill patients who have a life expectancy of 6 months or less. Hospice programs provide services that address the special needs of dying persons and their families. Hospice is a method of care, not a location, and services are taken to patients and their families wherever they are located. Hospice services include medical, psychological, and social services provided in a holistic context. The two primary areas of emphasis in hospice care are (1) pain and symptom management, which is referred to as *palliative care*, and (2) psychosocial and spiritual support.

Outpatient Long-Term Care Services

Long-term care (LTC) has typically been associated with care provided in nursing homes, but a number of alternative settings are also now available to address a variety of needs. Two types of ambulatory LTC services are *case management* and *adult day care*. Case management provides coordination and referral among a variety of health care services; the objective is to find the most appropriate setting in which to meet a patient's health care needs. Adult day care complements informal care provided at home by family members, with professional services available in adult day care centers during the day.

Public Health Services

Public health services in the United States are typically provided by local health departments, and the range of services offered varies greatly by locality. Generally, public health programs are limited in scope. They include well-baby care, venereal disease clinics, family planning services, screening and treatment for tuberculosis, and outpatient mental health care. States vary in the range and extent of public health services offered.

Community Health Centers

The federal government authorized the creation of community health centers (CHCs) during the 1960s, primarily to reach medically underserved regions of the United States. CHCs are supported by grant funding administered by the Bureau of Primary Health Care (BPHC), within the Department of Health and Human Services (DHHS). These centers are required by law to be located in medically underserved areas and to provide services to anyone seeking care, regardless of insurance status or ability to pay (McAlearney, 2001).

CHCs provide family-oriented preventive care, primary care, and dental care and serve as a primary care safety net. According to the BPHC, in 2014, 1,178 of these centers were funded through the program and provided care to approximately 22.9 million people through more than 90 million medical, dental, mental health, and substance abuse visits across the United States. Approximately 27.99% of these patients were uninsured, and an additional 47.3% were covered under Medicaid. The vast majority (92.4%) of patients who visited CHCs had incomes less than 200% of the federal poverty level, and more than 1 million were homeless.

Other health centers developed through federal funding include migrant health centers, serving transient farm workers in agricultural communities (approximately 891,796 patients were seen in 2014), and rural health centers located in isolated, underserved rural areas. One example is the Community Mental Health Center Program, which was established to provide outpatient mental health services in underserved areas.

Free Clinics

Approximately 1,200 free clinics provided services at little or no cost to needy people. These clinics are not operated or supported by the government. Services are delivered mainly by trained volunteer staff.

Alternative Medicine Clinics

Complementary and alternative medicine (CAM) refers to the broad domain of all health care resources, other than those intrinsic to biomedicine (CAM Research Methodology Conference, 1997). The treatment approaches purport to prevent or treat disease. Complementary interventions are used together with conventional medical treatments, whereas alternative interventions are used instead of conventional medicine. Alternative therapies include a wide range of treatments such as homeopathy, herbal remedies, natural products used as preventive and treatment agents, acupuncture, meditation, yoga exercises, biofeedback, and spiritual guidance or prayer (Barnes, Bloom, & Nahin, 2008). A significant number of adults in the United States use alternative medicine exclusively; one-fourth of all adults with no medical practitioner visits reported using CAM therapy in 2007. Alternative medicine is not yet a system of healing endorsed by most practitioners of conventional Western medicine, although interest in the efficacy of these treatments has been growing among the traditional medical establishment. Alternative treatments are generally not covered by health insurance.

PRIMARY CARE

Primary care is the conceptual foundation for outpatient services, but not all outpatient care is primary care. Services beyond primary health care have become an integral part of outpatient services. As the supply and use of specialist services increase, specialist physicians have become more integrated into the primary care system; however, much improvement is still needed for coordination of care between specialists and primary care providers (United States Pharmaceuticals & Healthcare Report, 2015). Primary care practice must evolve and adapt to recent changes in the health care system; this is particularly important in light of research predicting a shortage of more than 44,000 primary care physicians by 2035 (Petterson et al., 2015).

What Is Primary Care?

In a tri-level classification of care delivery, primary care is distinguished from secondary and tertiary care by its duration, frequency, and level of intensity. *Secondary care* is usually short term in nature, involving sporadic consultation from a specialist to provide expert opinions and/or surgical or other advanced interventions that primary care physicians are not equipped to perform. Secondary care includes hospitalization, routine surgery, specialty consultation, and rehabilitation. *Tertiary care* is the most complex level of care and is required for conditions that are relatively uncommon. Typically, tertiary care is institution based, highly specialized, and technology driven. Much of it is rendered in large teaching hospitals, especially university hospitals. Examples include trauma care, burn treatment, neonatal intensive care, tissue transplants, and open-heart surgery. In some instances, tertiary treatment may be long term in nature, and the tertiary care physician may assume long-term responsibility for the bulk of the patient's care.

Primary care is commonly viewed as a set of basic and routine services that include prevention, diagnostic and therapeutic services, health education and counseling, and minor surgery. However, primary care should be viewed as an approach to providing health care rather than as a set of specific services (Starfield, 1994). In this regard, definitions provided by the World Health Organization (WHO) and the Institute of Medicine (IOM) are useful.

WHO Definition

According to WHO, primary health care is essential health care that is based on practical, scientifically sound, and socially acceptable methods and technology. Such care should be universally accessible to individuals and families in the community by means acceptable to them and at a cost that the community and the nation can afford. Primary health care serves as the foundation of ambulatory services, characterized by the first level of contact between individuals, the family, and the community on the one hand and the health care delivery system on the other hand, bringing health care as close as possible to where people live and work. It constitutes the first element of a continuing health care process (WHO, 1978, p. 25).

IOM Definition

The IOM Committee on the Future of Primary Care defined primary care as the provision of integrated, accessible health care services by clinicians who are accountable for addressing the majority of personal health care needs, developing a sustained partnership with patients, and practicing in the context of family and community (Vanselow et al., 1995, p. 192).

Domains of Primary Care

For an understanding of primary care, the WHO and IOM definitions together highlight six key domains, as summarized in **Exhibit 7.3**.

Point of Entry

Primary care should be the point of entry into a health services system (Starfield, 1992, p. vii); that is, it is the first contact a patient makes with the health care delivery system. This first contact feature is closely associated with the gatekeeper role of the primary care practitioner. *Gatekeeping* implies that patients do not visit specialists and are not admitted to a hospital without being referred for such care by their primary care physicians. On the surface, gatekeeping may appear to be a controlling mechanism for denying needed care. In reality, in most cases, primary care protects patients from unnecessary procedures and overtreatment (Franks et al., 1992) because specialists use medical tests and procedures to a much greater extent than do primary care providers, and such interventions carry a definite risk of iatrogenic (i.e., caused by the process of health care) complications (Starfield, 1994). At the same time, appropriate technology must be incorporated into the delivery of primary care so that costly referrals to other components of the health delivery system are made only when necessary.

Exhibit 7.3   Domains of Primary Care

• Point of entry	• Essential care
• Community based	• Integrated care
• Coordination of care	• Accountability

Community Based

Primary care should be available in close proximity to where people live and work. Hence, primary care is characterized by convenience and easy accessibility. Also, to be widely available, to urban, suburban, and rural communities, primary care services must be basic, routine, and inexpensive.

Coordination of Care

One of the main functions of primary care is to coordinate the delivery of health services between the patient and the myriad components of the system. Hence, primary care professionals also serve as patient advisors and advocates. Besides making referrals, the primary care provider gives advice regarding various diagnoses and therapies, discusses treatment options, and provides continuing care for chronic conditions (Williams, 1993). Coordination of an individual's total health care needs is meant to ensure continuity and comprehensiveness. These desirable goals of primary care are best achieved when the patient and the provider have formed a close relationship over time. Primary care can be regarded as the hub of the health care delivery system wheel. The various components of the health care delivery system are located around the rim, with the spokes of the wheel signifying the coordination of continuous and comprehensive care (see **Figure 7.1**).

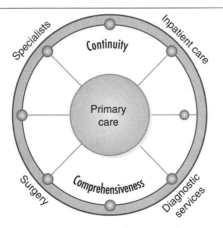

Figure 7.1   Coordination Role of Primary Care in Health Delivery

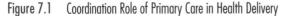

An ideal system of health care delivery is based on primary care but is closely linked with adequate and timely specialized services. Continuous and coordinated care requires that secondary and tertiary services be integrated with primary care through appropriate interaction and consultation among physicians. Coordination of health care has certain advantages. Studies have shown that both the appropriateness and the outcomes of health care interventions are better when primary care physicians refer patients to specialists, rather than when patients engage in self-referral (Bakwin, 1945; Roos, 1979).

Essential Care

Primary care is regarded as essential health care. When it is available to the vast majority of a nation's population, it optimizes population health. Countries whose health systems are more oriented toward primary care achieve better health outcomes, higher satisfaction with health services among their populations, and lower expenditures in the overall delivery of health care (Starfield, 1994). Even in the United States, those states with higher ratios of primary care physicians to patients show better health outcomes associated with the better availability of primary care (Shi, 1992, 1994). Higher ratios of family and general practice physicians in the population are also associated with lower hospitalization rates for conditions treatable with good primary care (Parchman & Culler, 1994). Adults who have primary care physicians as their regular source of care subsequently experience lower death rates and incur lower health care costs (Franks & Fiscella, 1998). In the United States, the mixture of public and private financing has created a fragmented system in which primary care does not form the organizing hub for continuous and coordinated health services.

Integrated Care

Integrated care embodies the concepts of comprehensive, coordinated, and continuous services that provide a seamless process of care. Primary care is comprehensive because it addresses any health problem at any given stage of a patient's life cycle. The coordinating function ensures the provision of a combination of health services to best meet the patient's needs. Continuity refers to care delivered over time by a single provider or a team of health care professionals.

Accountability

Both clinicians and patients have accountability. On the one hand, the clinical system is accountable for providing quality care, producing patient satisfaction, using resources efficiently, and behaving in an ethical manner. On the other hand, patients are responsible for their own health to the extent that they are capable of influencing it. Patients also have the responsibility to be judicious in their use of resources when they need health care. A desirable patient–provider relationship is based on mutual trust, respect, and responsibility. Apart from possessing the necessary knowledge and skills, primary care clinicians must use their best judgment to involve other practitioners in diagnosis, treatment, or both when it is appropriate to do so (Vanselow et al., 1995).

Community-Oriented Primary Care

Community-oriented primary care incorporates the elements of good primary care delivery and adds a population-based approach to identifying and addressing community health problems. Current thoughts about primary care delivery have extended beyond the traditional biomedical paradigm, which focuses on medical care for the individual in an encounter-based system. The broader biopsychosocial paradigm emphasizes the health of the population as well as that of the individual (Lee, 1994). The main challenge has been how to bring together individual health needs in the larger context of community health needs. Workforce shortages and financial incentives to go beyond individual health have been two major barriers.

EFFECTIVENESS OF PRIMARY CARE

Most preventive interventions are best carried out in primary care delivery even though some may suggest a specialty care focus. For example, cardiac care may be concerned with cholesterol levels; testing for cholesterol and interventions to bring the levels down to desired levels are routinely followed by primary care physicians. Primary care practitioners may also order further testing, such as electrocardiograms and cardiac stress tests, to assess the presence of heart disease. Referral to a cardiologist may be made when appropriate.

U.S. states with higher ratios of primary care physicians to the total population have lower smoking rates, less obesity, and higher seatbelt use than states with lower primary care physician-to-population ratios (Shi, 1994; Shi & Starfield, 2000). Continuity of care with a single provider was also positively associated with primary preventive care, including smoking cessation and influenza immunization, in a study of 60 U.S. communities (Saver, 2002). Studies have shown that an increase of one primary care physician per 10,000 population is linked to a reduction of 1.44 deaths per 10,000 population, a 2.5% reduction in infant mortality, and a 3.2% reduction in low birthweight infants on average. Similarly, population subgroups with a good primary care source have better birthweight distributions than comparable populations that have inadequate primary care. In 2000, it was shown that among white and black populations in both urban and rural areas of the United States, birthweights were higher when the source of care was a community health center designed to provide good primary care than they were in the comparable population as a whole (Politzer et al., 2001). The likelihood that disadvantaged children will have preventive care visits is much greater when their source of care is a good primary care practitioner (Gadomski, Jenkins, & Nichols, 1998). Early detection of breast cancer is also enhanced when the supply of primary care physicians (at least relative to specialists) is adequate, while a one-third increase in the supply of family physicians correlates to a 20% decrease in the mortality rates of cervical cancer in a population (Ferrante, Gonzalez, Pal, & Roetzheim, 2000; Macinko, Starfield, & Shi, 2007). Additionally, studies have suggested that as many as 127,617 deaths per year in the United States might be prevented with an increase of one primary care physician per 10,000 population (Macinko et al., 2007).

Hospitalizations and Use of Emergency Care

Strong evidence in the literature shows that lower rates of hospitalization for ambulatory care–sensitive conditions (i.e., hospitalizations that could be prevented with good primary care) are strongly associated with receiving primary care. Children receiving their care from a good primary care source have lower hospitalization rates for these conditions as well as lower hospitalization rates overall; these findings are associated with better receipt of preventive care from primary care providers (Gadomski et al., 1998). Rates of hospital admission are lower in U.S. communities in which primary care physicians are more widely involved in the care of children both before and during hospitalization (Perrin et al., 1996). Adolescents with the same regular source of care for preventive and illness care (i.e., a source of primary care) are much more likely to receive indicated preventive care and less likely to seek care in emergency rooms (Ryan et al., 2001). Thus strong and consistent evidence indicates that hospitalizations—and especially hospitalizations for ambulatory care–sensitive conditions—are less frequent when primary care is strong.

The geographic distribution of primary care physicians has also been found to be an important factor in determining the level of health for the local population. As an example, Parchman and Culler (1994, p. 45) demonstrated that geographic areas with more family and general care physicians per population had lower hospitalization rates for conditions that could be preventable with good primary care (including diabetes mellitus and pneumonia in children and congestive heart failure, hypertension, pneumonia, and diabetes mellitus in adults). Another study found that poor primary care resources were independently associated with higher rates of hospitalization for conditions that could be prevented by adequate primary care.

Cost of Care

Areas that have higher primary care physician-to-population ratios have lower total health care costs than other areas. This relationship has been demonstrated to hold among elderly in the United States who live in metropolitan areas, both for total costs (i.e., inpatient and outpatient) (Mark et al., 1996; Welch et al., 1993) and for the total population in the United States (Franks & Fiscella, 1998), as well as in international comparisons of industrialized countries (Starfield & Shi, 2002). Care for illnesses common in the population (e.g., community-acquired pneumonia) is more expensive if provided by specialists than if provided by generalists, with no difference in outcomes being noted based on the type of provider (Rosser, 1996; Whittle et al., 1998).

Morbidity

The supply of primary care physicians has been associated with lower rates of self-reported poor health in 60 representative U.S. communities, after controlling for a wide range of sociodemographic and socioeconomic characteristics (Shi & Starfield, 2000). Data from this same survey confirmed the positive impact of primary care by showing that those persons who actually experienced better primary care reported better health

(Shi et al., 2002). Birthweight and infant mortality were also associated with primary care physician supply in U.S. states. Higher primary care physician supply has been associated with lower low-birthweight percentages and lower infant mortality, even after controlling for educational levels, unemployment, racial/ethnic composition, income inequality, and urban–rural differences (Shi et al., 2004).

One population-based study (Roetzheim et al., 1999) in an entire U.S. state found that detection of colorectal cancer at earlier stages was better in areas that had a greater supply of primary care physicians. Conversely, diagnosis tended to be delayed in areas with more specialist physicians. The nature of their findings led the authors to conclude that a lower supply of specialists enhances the likelihood that primary care physicians will screen their patients for such cancers.

Several studies have shown the importance of primary care as an entry point to the health care system for a majority of conditions. For example, one study demonstrated that entry-level access is associated with better outcomes for 16 common conditions in children and youth (Starfield, 1985). Another study, conducted only among males, showed that men who lack a primary care provider were at greater risk for severe uncontrolled hypertension than those who lacked medical insurance or had alcohol-related problems (Shea, Misra, & Ehrlich, 1992).

Mortality

Perhaps the most frequent demonstration of the benefits of primary care has been with regard to mortality (i.e., death rates). One line of evidence comes from ecological studies of the relationship between primary care personnel-to-population ratios and various types of health outcomes in the United States. Two separate studies found better health outcomes in states with higher primary care physician-to-population ratios after controlling for sociodemographic measures (i.e., percentage of elderly, percentage of urban residents, percentage of minority individuals, education, income, unemployment, pollution) and lifestyle factors (i.e., seat belt use, obesity, and smoking) (Shi, 1992, 1994). The supply of primary care physicians has also been shown to exert a strong and significant direct influence on life expectancy, stroke, and postnatal and total mortality (Shi et al., 1999).

Studies using multiple years of data have also identified a relationship between primary care physician supply and mortality outcomes, where increases in the supply of primary care physicians are associated with decreases in overall and cause-specific population mortality rates (Shi et al., 2003; Villalbi et al., 1999). There is a significant positive association between life expectancy and higher numbers of primary care physicians. The greater the ratio of physicians per population, the greater the life expectancy of the population (Shi et al., 1999).

THE MEDICAL-HOME STRATEGY

As health care delivery becomes increasingly complex, a renewed proposal for coordinating care in a system termed *medical home* has gained support. In 2006, the American College of Physicians (ACP) recommended this care model as an improved fundamental change in the provision and financing of primary care. The ACP advocates the practice of patient-centered care based on a partnership between the patient and the provider and incorporating principles of the chronic care model. The chronic care model is based on the premise that chronic conditions are best managed with multidisciplinary practice-based teams, use of evidence-based guidelines, appropriate health information technology, and accountability for the quality and value of care provided (ACP, 2006). With one personal physician as their primary, continual medical contact, patients are wholly cared for by a directed team with coordination across all areas of the health system. In small-scale studies, the medical-home model has been found to improve patient health outcomes and satisfaction; reduce medical errors; and add value by producing cost savings without compromising health outcomes (Rosenthal, 2008). The medical-home model offers a long-term vision of reform that could help improve and revolutionize the primary care system.

ASSESSMENT OF COMMUNITY HEALTH CENTERS

Several recent studies have assessed the quality, accessibility, and cost-effectiveness of CHCs.

CHC Quality of Care

CHC patients report positive experiences overall, citing convenient locations and favorable interaction with providers. However, uninsured patients may be less likely to receive help from the staff in applying for government benefits and setting up appointments with other medical providers. Even though racial/ethnic and insurance coverage disparities are less prevalent at CHCs than at other primary care providers, better efforts need to be focused on assisting those without insurance in applying for benefits (Shi et al., 2013a). Results from another study showed that there was no significant difference in length of visit or number of services provided between patients seen at CHCs and those seen at office-based physician practices (Bruen et al., 2013). Across racial/ethnic groups, CHC patients were found to be more satisfied than the U.S. low-income patient population with the hours of operation and overall care received (Shi et al., 2013b).

Shin and colleagues (2013) compared CHCs' quality of care to national benchmarks of quality performance for Medicaid MCOs. Performance along three measures—diabetes control, hypertension control, and receipt of a Pap test—was evaluated. Nearly all health centers scored above the Medicaid MCO average benchmark. Only 4% of health centers ranked as low performers. In 2013, health centers had a lower percentage of low birthweight babies than the national estimates (HRSA, 2014). Additionally, 69% of diabetic patients had their diabetes under control, and 64% of hypertensive patients kept their blood pressure under control (HRSA, 2014).

CHC Access to Care

Access to preventative and primary services reduces the risk of increased disease severity, complications, and emergency medical utilization (Laiteerapong et al., 2014). Compared to the general U.S. low-income patient population, patients served by CHCs did not experience racial/ethnic or insurance-based disparities in access to primary care (Shi et al., 2013b). CHCs seem to be meeting the health care needs of vulnerable populations and reducing disparities in access to health care.

In comparing rates of inadequate hypertension control, poor diabetes control, and low birthweight across four racial/ethnic categories (non-Hispanic white, black/African American, Asian, and Hispanic/Latino), minimal differences and disparities for the clinical indicators were found among different races and ethnicities (Lebrun et al., 2013). Hence, CHCs seem to be successful in reducing racial/ethnic health disparities, especially when compared to disparities found nationwide. Moreover, increased federal funding for CHCs may have slowed the decline in access to care among low-income populations (McMorrow & Zuckerman, 2014).

CHC Cost-Effectiveness

CHC patients are found to have fewer office visits and hospitalizations and are three times as likely to receive breast cancer screening compared to non-CHC patients (Laiteerapong et al., 2014). Uninsured CHC patients have fewer outpatient visits and ED visits and are more likely to receive dietary advice and breast cancer screening than non-CHC patients (Laiteerapong et al., 2014). The findings suggest that CHCs focus on preventive care, which results in lower rates of medical care utilization by disadvantaged groups.

CHCs and the Affordable Care Act

The Affordable Care Act (ACA) created the Community Health Center Fund to provide $11 billion over a 5-year period for the operation, expansion, and construction of CHCs across the country, including the District of Columbia, Puerto Rico, the U.S. Virgin Islands, and the Pacific Basin. CHCs served 19.5 million people in 2010, which increased to 21.7 million in 2013 (HRSA, 2014). In 2014, the ACA provided $100 million for the establishment of 150 more health centers across the country (HRSA, 2014).

Despite the intents of the ACA, CHCs face significant financial challenges because Medicaid reimbursement has declined even as health center Medicaid patient load has increased (NACHC, 2012). Physicians at CHCs report overwhelming workloads and frustrations with administrative management (Cole et al., 2014). Unless these issues are resolved at a fundamental level, additional funding for the expansion of CHCs will likely accomplish little.

CONCLUSION

Outpatient services now transcend basic and routine primary care services. Many general medical and surgical interventions are provided in ambulatory care settings. In response to changing economic incentives in the health care delivery system, numerous types of ambulatory services have emerged, and a variety of settings for the delivery of services have developed. In most settings, patients visit delivery sites to receive services. In other cases, services are brought to the patients.

The effectiveness of primary care has been demonstrated in numerous ways. However, its predominant practice can no longer be confined to the way primary care has been traditionally practiced. The broader biopsychosocial paradigm emphasizes the health of the population as well as that of the individual. A medical-home model has been advocated to deliver primary care based on the principles of patient-centered care and team-based chronic disease management approaches. CHCs have been found to deliver high-quality care cost-effectively in underserved areas. The Affordable Care Act has authorized funds for the expansion of CHCs. Much remains to be done, however. The old as well as the newer approaches to primary care delivery face mounting challenges in the wake of workforce shortages and financial constraints.

REFERENCES

American College of Physicians (ACP). The advanced medical home: a patient-centered, physician-guided model of health care. http://www.acponline.org/. Published 2006. Accessed December 2006.

Appleby C. Boxed in? *Hosp Health Netw.* 1995;69(18):28–34.

Bakwin H. Pseudodoxia pediatrica. *N Engl J Med.* 1945;232:691–697.

Barnes PM, Bloom B, Nahin RL. Complementary and alternative medicine use among adults and children: United States, 2007. *Natl Health Stat Rep.* 2008;12:1–23.

Barr KW, Breindel CL. Ambulatory care. In: Wolper LF, ed. *Health Care Administration: Principles, Practices, Structure, and Delivery.* 2nd ed. Gaithersburg, MD: Aspen Publishers; 1995:547–573.

Bruen BK, Ku L, Lu X, Shin P. No evidence that primary care physicians offer less care to Medicaid, community health center, or uninsured patients. *Health Aff.* 2013;32(9):1624–1630.

Cole AM, Chen FM, Ford PA, Phillips WR, Stevens NG. Rewards and challenges of community health center practice. *J Prim Care Community Health.* 2014;5(2):148–151.

Complementary and Alternative Medicine (CAM) Research Methodology Conference. Defining and describing complementary and alternative medicine. *Altern Ther.* 1997;3(2):49–56.

Ferrante JM, Gonzalez EC, Pal N, Roetzheim RG. Effects of physician supply on early detection of breast cancer. *J Am Board Fam Pract.* 2000;13(6):408–414.

Franks P, et al. Gatekeeping revisited: protecting patients from overtreatment. *N Engl J Med.* 1992;327(4):424–429.

Franks P, Fiscella K. Primary care physicians and specialists as personal physicians: health care expenditures and mortality experience. *J Fam Pract.* 1998;47(2):105–109.

Gadomski A, Jenkins P, Nichols M. Impact of a Medicaid primary care provider and preventive care on pediatric hospitalization. *Pediatrics*. 1998;101(3):E1. http://www.pediatrics.org/cgi/content/full/101/3/e1. Accessed December 2000.

Health Resources and Services Administration (HRSA). The Affordable Care Act and Health Centers. http://bphc.hrsa.gov/about/healthcenterfactsheet.pdf. Published 2014. Accessed June 27, 2015.

Laiteerapong N, Kirby J, Gao Yue, et al. Health care utilization and receipt of preventive care for patients seen at federally funded health centers compared to other sites of primary care. *Heath Serv Res*. 2014;49(5):1498–1518.

Lebrun LA, Shi L, Zhu J, et al. Racial/ethnic differences in clinical quality performance among health centers. *J Ambul Care Manage*. 2013;36(1):24–34.

Lee PR. Models of excellence. *Lancet*. 1994;344(8935):1484–1486.

Macinko J, Starfield B, Shi L. Quantifying the health benefits of primary care physician supply in the United States. *Int J Health Serv*. 2007;37(1): 111–126.

Mark DH, Gottlieb MS, Zellner BB, et al. Medicare costs in urban areas and the supply of primary care physicians. *J Fam Pract*. 1996;43(1):33–39.

McAlearney JS. The financial performance of community health centers, 1996–1999. *Health Aff*. 2001;21(2):219–225.

McMorrow S, Zuckerman S. Expanding federal funding to community health centers slows decline in access for low-income adults. *Health Serv Res*. 2014;49(3):992–1010.

National Association of Community Health Centers (NACHC). Snapshot: health centers face declining Medicaid reimbursement. http://www.nachc.com/client//MedicaidReimbursement.pdf. Published October 2012. Accessed December 2013.

Parchman ML, Culler S. Primary care physicians and avoidable hospitalizations. *J Fam Pract*. 1994;39(2):123–128.

Perrin JM, et al. Primary care involvement among hospitalized children. *Arch Pediatr Adolesc Med*. 1996;150(5):479–486.

Petterson SM, et al. Estimating the residency expansion required to avoid projected primary care physician shortages by 2035. *Ann Fam Med*. 2015;13:107–114.

Politzer RM, Yoon J, Shi L, et al. Inequality in America: the contribution of health centers in reducing and eliminating disparities in access to care. *Med Care Res Rev*. 2001;58(2):234–248.

Roetzheim RG, et al. The effects of physician supply on the early detection of colorectal cancer. *J Fam Pract*. 1999;48(11):850–858.

Roos N. Who should do the surgery? Tonsillectomy and adenoidectomy in one Canadian province. *Inquiry.* 1979;16(1):73–83.

Rosenthal TC. The medical home: growing evidence to support a new approach to primary care. *J Am Board Fam Med.* 2008;21:427–440.

Rosser WW. Approach to diagnosis by primary care clinicians and specialists: is there a difference? *J Fam Pract.* 1996;42(2):139–144.

Ryan A, Riley A, Kang M, Starfield B. The effects of regular source of care and health need on medical care use among rural adolescents. *Arch Pediatr Adolesc Med.* 2001;155(2):184–190.

Saver B. Financing and organization findings brief. *Acad Res Health Care Policy.* 2002;5(1):1–2.

Shea S, Misra D, Ehrlich MH, et al. Predisposing factors for severe, uncontrolled hypertension in an inner-city minority population. *N Engl J Med.* 1992;327(11):776–781.

Shi L. The relation between primary care and life chances. *J Health Care Poor Underserved.* 1992;3:321–335.

Shi L. Primary care, specialty care, and life chances. *Int J Health Serv.* 1994;24(3):431–458.

Shi L, et al. Income inequality, primary care, and health indicators. *J Fam Pract.* 1999;48:275–284.

Shi L, et al. Primary care, self-rated health, and reductions in social disparities in health. *Health Serv Res.* 2002;37:529–550.

Shi L, Lebrun L, Rane S, Zhu J, Ngo-Metzger Q. The quality of primary care experienced by health center patients. *J Am Board Fam Med.* 2013a;26(6):768–777.

Shi L, Lebrun-Harris LA, Daly CA, et al. Reducing disparities in access to primary care and patient satisfaction with care: the role of health centers. *J Health Care Poor Underserved.* 2013b;24(1):56–66.

Shi L, Macinko J, Starfield B, et al. Primary care, infant mortality, and low birthweight in US states. *J Epidemiol Community Health.* 2004;58(5):374–380.

Shi L, Macinko, J, Starfield, B, Wulu, J, Regan, J, Politzer, R. The relationship between primary care, income inequality, and mortality in US states, 1980-1995. *Journal of the American Board of Family Practice,* 16(5):412–422, 2003.

Shi L, Starfield B. Primary care, income inequality, and self-rated health in the United States: A mixed-level analysis. *Int J Health Serv.* 2000;30:541–555.

Shin P, Sharac J, Rosenbaum S, Paradise J. Quality of care in community health centers and factors associated with performance. Kaiser Commission on Medicaid and the Uninsured Report #8447, available at http://kff.org/medicaid/issue-brief/quality-of-care-in-communityhealth-centers-and-factors-associated-with-performance/. Published June 2013. Accessed December 2013.

Starfield B. Motherhood and apple pie: the effectiveness of medical care for children. *Milbank Mem Fund Q: Health Soc.* 1985;63(3):523–546.

Starfield B. *Primary Care: Concept, Evaluation, and Policy.* New York: Oxford University Press; 1992.

Starfield B. Is primary care essential? *Lancet.* 1994;344(8930):1129–1133.

Starfield B, Shi L. Policy relevant determinants of health: an international perspective. *Health Policy.* 2002;60:201–218.

United States Pharmaceuticals & Healthcare Report. United States Pharmaceuticals & Healthcare Report [serial online]. January 2015;(1):1–119. Available from Business Source Complete, Ipswich, MA.

Vanselow NA, et al. From the Institute of Medicine. *JAMA.* 1995;273(3):192.

Villalbi JR, et al. An evaluation of the impact of primary care reform on health. *Aten Primaria.* 1999;24(8):468–474.

Welch WP, Miller ME, Welch HG, et al. Geographic variation in expenditures for physicians' services in the United States. *N Engl J Med.* 1993;328(9):621–627.

Whittle JC, et al. Relationship of provider characteristics to outcomes, process, and costs of care for community-acquired pneumonia. *Med Care.* 1998;36(7):977–987.

Williams SJ. Ambulatory health care services. In: Williams SJ, Torrens PR, eds. *Introduction to Health Services.* 4th ed. Albany, NY: Delmar Publishers; 1993.

World Health Organization (WHO). *Primary Health Care.* Geneva: WHO; 1978.

Chapter 8

Hospitals

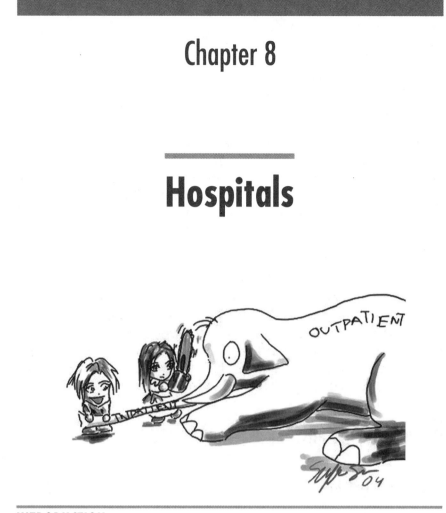

INTRODUCTION

The term *inpatient* refers to an overnight stay in a health care facility, such as a hospital or a nursing home, when the patient is formally admitted with a physician's order. *Outpatient*, in contrast, refers to services provided while the patient is not lodged in the hospital or some other health care institution. This chapter describes what a hospital is, its evolution, and its current role in health care delivery. Outpatient care is discussed in Chapter 7.

The American Hospital Association (AHA) defines a hospital as an institution with at least six beds whose primary function is "to deliver patient services, diagnostic and therapeutic, for particular or general medical conditions" (AHA, 1994). In addition, a hospital must be licensed, it must have an organized physician staff, and it must provide continuous nursing services under the supervision of registered nurses. A hospital must appoint a governing body or board that is legally responsible for the conduct of the hospital. It must also appoint a full-time chief executive officer (CEO) to be responsible for the hospital's operations. The hospital must maintain medical records on each patient, have pharmacy services available within the institution, and provide food services to meet the nutritional and therapeutic requirements of the patients (Health Forum, 2001). The construction and operation of the modern hospital is governed by federal laws, state health regulations, city ordinances, standards of the Joint Commission (formerly the Joint Commission on Accreditation of Healthcare Organizations [JCAHO]), and national codes for building, fire protection, and sanitation.

In the past 200 years or so, hospitals have gradually evolved from ordinary institutions of refuge for the homeless and poor to ultramodern facilities providing the latest medical services to the critically ill and injured. The term *medical center* is used by some hospitals, reflecting their high level of specialization and wide scope of services. Medical centers often engage in teaching and research. Since the 1980s, many hospitals have expanded their scope of services to include outpatient care.

EVOLUTION OF THE HOSPITAL IN THE UNITED STATES

The six major stages of hospital evolution in the United States are listed in **Exhibit 8.1**.

Stage 1

Before 1850 or so, only a few hospitals existed, all of which were found in major U.S. cities. The main health care institutions were the almshouses (also called poorhouses) run by local governments. Pesthouses were operated

Exhibit 8.1   *Major Stages of Hospital Evolution*

1. Almshouses as primarily institutions of social welfare
2. Community-owned private hospitals as charitable institutions supported by affluent donors
3. Institutions of medical practice and training serving the needs of all members of society and able to make a profit
4. Emergence of a relatively small number of physician-owned proprietary hospitals
5. University-based centers of medical research
6. Emergence of medical systems providing a large array of health services

to confine people with contagious diseases. Services in these institutions were more akin to social welfare than to medicine, consisting mainly of providing food and shelter to the destitute and some nursing care to the sick. Medicine and nursing as the professions we know today had not emerged. People generally stayed in these institutions for months rather than days.

Stage 2

During the latter half of the 1800s, hospitals evolved from the almshouses and pesthouses but continued to serve mainly the poor. At this time, hospitals began to transition from being primarily government-run institutions to community-owned institutions supported mainly through private charitable donations. Influential donors exercised control over the hospital as members of the board of trustees. Since this period, private (rather than government-owned) nonprofit hospitals have dominated the hospital landscape in America.

Stage 3

Medical discoveries during the latter half of the 1800s were instrumental in transforming hospitals into true institutions of medical practice. Discoveries that had a profound impact on hospital care included anesthesia, which aided significantly in advancing new surgical techniques, and the development of the germ theory of disease, which led to the subsequent discovery of antiseptic and sterilization techniques (Haglund & Dowling, 1993). From around 1850 onward, technological progress led to the development of advanced equipment, facilities, and personnel training, which became centered in the hospital. Hospitals established laboratories and x-ray units so that physicians could have convenient access to diagnostic technology. These advances made it necessary for community-based physicians to treat acute illnesses in hospitals, which also became centers where physicians received their practical training. From this point onward, hospitals came to be regarded as a necessity, because the superior medical services and surgical procedures offered there could not be obtained at home.

Stage 4

With advances in sanitation, nursing care, and medical services, hospitals began to attract well-to-do patients who could afford to pay for their care on an out-of-pocket basis. As these wealthier individuals began to use their services, hospitals found that they no longer had to depend totally on charitable contributions. They could now generate a profit. At this stage, some physicians started opening their own small hospitals, thereby laying the foundation for proprietary (for-profit) hospitals in the United States.

Stage 5

Many hospitals established formal affiliations with university-based medical schools and became centers of medical research where new discoveries were made. Even today, medical research plays a critical role in finding better cures and in disseminating research findings through publications in medical journals to advance new medical knowledge throughout the world.

During this stage, hospitals became complex organizations, and the field of hospital administration became a discipline in its own right. To manage hospitals, administrators needed expertise in financial management and good organizational and human relations skills. Also, departments such as food service, pharmacy, x-ray imaging, and the laboratory required well-trained professional staff to manage the delivery of services.

Stage 6

Since the 1990s, local market pressures have prompted many hospitals to merge or enter into formal affiliations with other hospitals. In urban areas, *medical systems* (or health systems) have formed. These systems are large organizations that may include more than one hospital to serve a large geographic area. They also provide a full array of health care services, including outpatient clinics, same-day surgery, outpatient imaging services, outpatient rehabilitation therapies, nursing home care, home health services, and hospice care. Many health systems have also opened special women's health centers and fitness centers. Increasingly, community services such as health education, promotion of healthy lifestyles, and prevention of disease have become an important part of a hospital's mission.

EXPANSION AND DOWNSIZING OF HOSPITALS IN THE UNITED STATES

The number of hospital beds in the United States grew from 35,604 in 1872 to 907,133 in 1929 (Haglund & Dowling, 1993). This phenomenal growth started once hospitals became institutions of medical practice, serving the needs of all members of society and making a profit (stage 4 in the six-stage model). Technological advances increased the volume of surgical work, which at that time could be done only in hospitals. As new facilities with additional beds were built, they were quickly filled by patients needing acute treatment or surgery. Advances in medical science, as well as professional training of nurses and other health care professionals, played an important role in creating a demand for more beds. Additional factors contributing to the growth of hospitals from the preindustrial era to around 1980 are listed in **Exhibit 8.2**.

After 1930, the wider availability of private health insurance enabled more and more people to pay for hospital services, which became increasingly more costly and unaffordable. Once people had health insurance, that fact in itself generated new demand. Early insurance plans provided generous coverage for inpatient care, and few restrictions were placed on the use of hospital–based services.

In the 1940s, the U.S. government recognized that a severe shortage of hospitals existed in the country. In response, Congress passed the Hospital Survey and Construction Act of 1946, commonly known as the Hill-Burton Act. It provided federal grants to the states for the construction of new hospital beds. The objective of the Hill-Burton Act was to increase the United States' hospital capacity to 4.5 beds per 1,000 population (Teisberg et al., 1991). Indeed, the Hill-Burton program has been regarded as the greatest single factor in increasing the nation's bed supply. This building program made it possible for even small and remote communities to establish their own hospitals (Wolfson & Hopes, 1994).

The creation of Medicare and Medicaid in 1965 made public health insurance available to a large segment of the U.S. population. Hospital demand, in turn, continued to grow. Between 1965 and 1980, the number of community hospitals in the United States increased from 5,736 (741,000 beds) to 5,830 (988,000 beds) (AHA, 1990). By 1980, the United States

Exhibit 8.2 Factors Contributing to the Growth of Hospitals

- Broad appeal once hospitals evolved into institutions of medical practice as a result of technological advances and professional training of health care professionals
- Private health insurance
- Hill-Burton Act
- Medicare and Medicaid

---

had also reached its goal of 4.5 community hospital beds per 1,000 civilian population (National Center for Health Statistics [NCHS], 2002).

In 1983, the U.S. government decided it needed to contain the exploding cost of hospital care, mostly because of its impact on the rising cost of Medicare (**Figure 8.1** shows the rise in costs that occurred between 1970 and 1980). This goal of cost containment was achieved through the enactment of the Social Security Amendments of 1983. The law required Medicare to stop paying hospitals per diem rates established on the basis of their costs of operation (retrospective reimbursement). Instead, a prospective payment system (PPS) was established to reimburse hospitals on the basis of diagnosis-related groups (DRGs). Under this method, hospitals received a preestablished fixed rate per admission. To ensure that they would not lose money, hospitals had to cut their costs of operation. They also had to discharge patients more quickly than before because keeping patients in the hospital longer than necessary cut into the hospital's profits. Many hospitals were forced to close when they had difficulty coping with the new method of reimbursement. Other hospitals continued

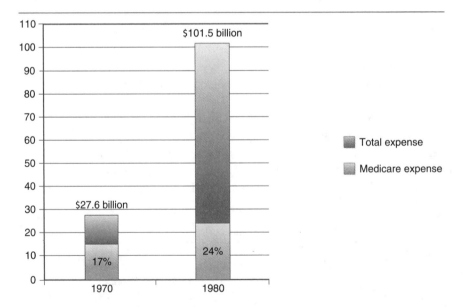

Figure 8.1   Medicare's Share of Hospital Expenses
Data from Department of Health and Human Services. Health, United States, 2003, p. 342; Table C-5: Selected data on community hospital expenses, 1965–95. http://aspe.hhs.gov.

to operate but had to take unused beds out of service. PPS triggered the downsizing phase in the U.S. hospital industry.

During the 1990s, the growth of managed care played a significant role in curtailing inpatient utilization even further. Managed care emphasized cost containment and efficient delivery of care through early discharge from hospitals, and, if necessary, continuity of care through home health agencies and skilled-care nursing homes. In other instances, the emphasis has been on using outpatient services whenever appropriate instead of admitting patients to hospitals.

The three main factors just discussed (and summarized in **Exhibit 8.3**) were largely successful in reducing the growth of national spending on hospital care. **Figure 8.2** illustrates the growth of spending on hospital inpatient

Exhibit 8.3   Factors Contributing to the Downsizing of Hospitals

- Change in Medicare reimbursement to hospitals from a retrospective to a prospective method, leading to shorter hospital stays
- Hospital closings
- Managed care's emphasis on cost containment and use of services such as outpatient, home health, and skilled nursing care

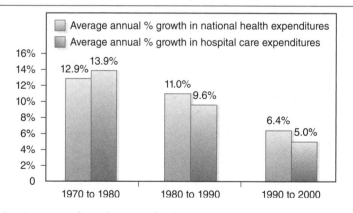

Figure 8.2   Comparison of Growth in Hospital and National Health Expenditures
Data from National Center for Health Statistics. Health, United States, 2002. Hyattsville, MD: Department of Health and Human Services, 2002:291.

care compared with the growth of national health expenditures. Notice the slower rates of growth after the implementation of the PPS between 1980 and 1990 and a further slowdown between 1990 and 2000 resulting from the advent of managed care.

ACCESS AND UTILIZATION MEASURES

Measures of Access

The total number of patient discharges per 1,000 population is an indicator of the level of access to hospital inpatient services. Because newborn infants are not included in admissions, discharges provide a more accurate measure of the number of people served by a hospital. *Discharges* refer to the total number of patients released from a hospital's acute care beds during a given period, including those patients who die while in the hospital. Discharges measure the number of patients who received hospital inpatient services.

Measures of Utilization

An *inpatient day* (also referred to as a patient day or a hospital day) is a night spent in the hospital by a patient. The average number of days a patient spends in the hospital is called the *average length of stay* (ALOS). The total number of inpatient days incurred by a population over a given period of time is referred to as *days of care*. Mathematically,

$$\text{Days of care} = \text{discharges} \times \text{ALOS}$$

National data on days of care per 1,000 population show that elderly individuals spend more time in hospitals than do younger people. Even after adjusting for childbearing among women 18 years of age and older, women are admitted to hospitals more often than men, but men incur longer stays. Hospital utilization is higher among blacks than whites and is also higher among the poor than the nonpoor. Various factors (e.g., education, socioeconomic status, behaviors, lifestyles, heredity, access to primary care) interact to produce differences in health status and onset of acute conditions for the various population groups; hence, some groups incur more frequent hospitalizations and require longer stays once admitted.

From this information, it can be concluded that overall hospital utilization is higher among Medicare and Medicaid recipients compared to the rest of the population. Demand for and utilization of hospital services are also influenced by overall population growth, advances in medical technology, and health insurance.

Since 2003, the ALOS for community hospitals in the United States has been 4.8 days, the lowest ever recorded. The PPS, as noted earlier, had a marked influence on the decline in the ALOS, as did the introduction of managed care during the 1990s. The sharp decline in ALOS during the 1990s became possible with the growth of alternative services, such as home health and subacute long-term care, which enabled people to be discharged earlier than was previously possible. Thanks to the development of these substitute sites of care and more advanced technology, there has been no evidence that quicker discharges of patients from hospitals under the PPS or managed care payment systems resulted in medical harm to patients.

Utilization of Hospital Capacity

Capacity refers to the number of beds set up, staffed, and made available by a hospital for inpatient use. Eighty-four percent of all community hospitals in the United States have fewer than 300 beds. The average size of a community hospital is approximately 160 beds (NCHS, 2015).

The term *census* refers to the number of patients in a hospital on a given day or the number of beds occupied on a given day. The cumulative census over a given period of time is called *patient days* or *days of care*. The average census over a period of time is called the *average daily census* (see **Table 8.1**). Mathematically,

Average daily census =
patient days over a given period ÷ number of days in the period

The *occupancy rate* is the percentage of capacity used during a given period of time. It is calculated by dividing the average daily census for that period by the capacity (see **Table 8.1**). The fraction is expressed as a percentage (percent beds occupied). An individual hospital's performance in capacity utilization can be meaningfully compared with local and national composite occupancy rates. In 2012, the occupancy rate for all U.S. community hospitals was 63.4% (NCHS, 2015).

. . . .

Table 8.1   Relationship Between the Selected Measures of Capacity Utilization

Day Number	Census	Patient Days
1	100	100
2	104	204
3	101	305
4	99	404
5	98	502
6	102	604
7	103	707

Patient days for this week: 707. Average daily census: $707 \div 7 = 101$. If hospital capacity is 153, the occupancy rate is 66% [$(101 \div 153) \times 100$].

. . . .

HOSPITAL EMPLOYMENT

Of the 143 million workers in the United States in 2010, almost 10% were employed in health occupation jobs. Among all health care workers, 40% were employed in various types of hospitals. Interestingly, between 2000 and 2010, while the overall employment in the United States declined by a little over 2%, hospital employment grew by almost 16% (overall health occupation jobs grew by 25%). Employment growth in the outpatient sector exceeds that in hospitals. Between 2010 and 2020, health occupation jobs in hospitals are expected to grow by over 16% (compared to 44% in the outpatient sector). The greatest need for new workers will be for registered nurses (Center for Health Workforce Studies, 2012).

TYPES OF HOSPITALS

The United States supports a variety of institutional forms, including both private and government-owned hospitals. A hospital can be classified under more than one category.

Exhibit 8.4   Characteristics of a Community Hospital

- Nonfederal: hospitals operated by local and state governments can be community hospitals
- Short stay: average length of stay must be ≤ 25 days
- Open to the general public
- Private for-profit or nonprofit; general or specialty

Community Hospitals

Over 87% of all U.S. hospitals are community hospitals. The identifying characteristics of these hospitals are listed in **Exhibit 8.4**. By definition, a *community hospital* is a nonfederal, short-stay hospital whose services are available to the general public. This definition excludes federal hospitals, such as those operated by the Department of Veterans Affairs (VA) and military systems, and hospital units of some institutions, such as prisons and infirmaries in colleges and universities, because their services are not available to the general public. In contrast, most hospitals operated by local and state governments are community hospitals. Also excluded from the definition of a community hospital are long-stay hospitals, such as psychiatric facilities, tuberculosis hospitals, and other chronic disease hospitals. In long-stay hospitals, the average length of stay is more than 25 days.

Public Hospitals

In health care, the word *public* connotes government ownership. *Public hospitals*, therefore, are hospitals owned by agencies of federal, state, or local governments. An estimated 22% of the U.S. hospitals are in the public sector (**Figure 8.3**).

A public hospital is not necessarily a hospital that is open to the general public. For example, because they are government owned, federal hospitals are classified as public hospitals, even though they do not serve the general public. Federal hospitals are maintained primarily for special groups of federal beneficiaries such as Native Americans, military personnel, and veterans. Of the 213 federal hospitals, 70% are VA hospitals.

State governments have generally limited themselves to the operation of mental and tuberculosis hospitals, reflecting the government's early role in protecting communities by isolating the mentally ill and persons with contagious diseases.

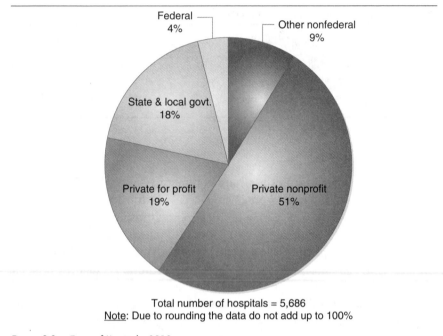

Total number of hospitals = 5,686
Note: Due to rounding the data do not add up to 100%

Figure 8.3   Types of Hospitals, 2013
Data from Health Forum LLC, an affiliate of the American Hospital Association. Fast facts on U.S. hospitals. 2015.

Local governments, such as counties and cities, operate hospitals that are open to the general public. Hence, these hospitals are also classified as community hospitals. Government-owned community hospitals are often located in large urban areas where they serve mainly the inner-city indigent and disadvantaged populations. Due to the generally poor health status of these populations and inner-city violence, these hospitals incur higher utilization than hospitals located in suburban areas. Most of these hospitals are of small to moderate size (the average size is approximately 115 beds). Some large public hospitals are affiliated with medical schools, and they play a significant role in training physicians and other health care professionals. Medicare, Medicaid, and state and local tax dollars finance most of the services these hospitals provide. These hospitals also provide a substantial amount of charity care and often suffer financial losses that are covered by funneling tax dollars into the operations. Because of increasing financial pressures, many public hospitals have undergone privatization or had to close in recent years. Consequently, the number of state and local government-owned community hospitals has steadily declined, from 1,444 in 1990 to 1,037 in 2012 (NCHS, 2015).

Private Nonprofit Hospitals

Private nonprofit hospitals are also called *voluntary hospitals*. A little over half of the hospitals in the United States are under private nonprofit ownership (see **Figure 8.3**). These hospitals are owned by nongovernment entities such as community associations, philanthropic foundations, or religious groups. The primary mission of these hospitals is to benefit the communities in which they are located. Their operating expenses are covered from patient fees, third-party reimbursement, donations, and endowments.

Church-owned hospitals play a significant role in delivering hospital services in the United States. For example, the Catholic Church operates over 600 hospitals (over 116,000 beds) in all 50 states and delivers care to one-sixth of all hospital patients each year (Catholic Health Association of the United States, 2015). Some Protestant denominations and Jewish philanthropic organizations also operate numerous community hospitals. These hospitals are not discriminatory in terms of access to care; however, they are generally sensitive to the special spiritual or dietary needs of the sponsoring denomination (Raffel & Raffel, 1994, pp. 131–132). Church-owned hospitals have been found to be superior than other ownership types in delivering high value to their communities with reliable high quality and efficiency and high patient perception of care at a reasonable cost (Foster, Zrull, & Chenoweth, 2013). According to the same report, government hospitals demonstrated the weakest balanced performance.

Lay people make a common assumption that nonprofit (sometimes referred to as not-for-profit) organizations do not make a profit. The fact is that every corporation, regardless of whether it is for profit or nonprofit, has to make a profit (a surplus of revenues over expenses) to remain operational over the long term. No business can survive for long if it continually spends more than it takes in. This statement is as true for nonprofit organizations as it is for the for-profit sector. The Internal Revenue Code, Section 501(c)(3), grants tax-exempt status to nonprofit organizations. As such, these institutions are exempt from federal, state, and local taxes such as income, sales, and property taxes. In exchange for the tax benefit these organizations receive, they must (1) provide some defined public good, such as service, education, or community welfare, and (2) not distribute the profits to any individual.

The rationale behind tax exemption is that these facilities provide an essential community benefit, principally for charitable, training, or research purposes. There are ongoing debates and court cases over what does or does not constitute a community benefit.

Research has shown considerable variation in the level of community benefits provided by nonprofit hospitals. A national study found that, on average, these hospitals spent 7.5% of their expenses on community benefits; more than 85% of these expenses were devoted to charity care and other patient care services (Young et al., 2013). Although for-profit and nonprofit hospitals engage in similar competitive behaviors, on average nonprofit hospitals do appear to spend more on charity care than their investor-owned counterparts, but the difference tends to be small (Rubin, Singh, & Young, 2015).

Private for-Profit Hospitals

Private for-profit hospitals, also referred to as *proprietary hospitals* or investor-owned hospitals, are owned by individuals, partnerships, or corporations. They are operated for the financial benefit of the entity that owns the institution—that is, the stockholders.

More than 260 hospitals in roughly 33 states are owned by physicians, representing about 5% of U.S. hospitals. These are relatively small hospitals that generally specialize in heart or orthopedic surgeries (Rau, 2013). According to the Physician Hospitals of America (PHA), a professional association representing this industry sector, 67% of the hospitals participating in the star-rating system developed by the Centers for Medicare and Medicaid Services (CMS) received 4 or 5 stars compared to 41% of all hospitals nationwide (PHA, 2015).

For-profit corporations operate some of the largest multihospital chains in the United States. The largest among them are Hospital Corporation of America (158 hospitals in 2013), Community Health Systems (198 hospitals), and Tenet Health System (76 hospitals). A significant trend over the past few years has been the building or acquisition of a substantial number of hospitals by large investor-owned corporations. Even so, most multihospital health care systems today are operated by nonprofit corporations. Although a major goal for a for-profit organization is to provide a return on investment to its shareholders, it achieves this goal primarily by excelling at accomplishing its basic mission. The basic mission of any health services provider is to deliver the highest quality of care possible at the most reasonable price possible.

General Hospitals

A *general hospital* provides diagnostic, treatment, and surgical services for patients with a variety of acute medical conditions. Its services may include general and specialized medicine, general and specialized surgery, and obstetrics. Most hospitals in the United States are general hospitals, but they are not all community hospitals because most federal hospitals are general hospitals, too.

The term *general hospital* does not imply that these hospitals are less specialized or that their care is inferior to that of specialty hospitals. The difference lies in the nature of services, not the quality. General hospitals provide a broader range of services for a larger variety of conditions, whereas specialty hospitals provide a narrow range of services for specific medical conditions or patient populations.

Specialty Hospitals

Specialty hospitals primarily engage in treating specific types of diseases or medical conditions—such as heart disease or cancer—or serving a specific patient population such as children. Specialty hospitals also provide services such as psychiatric care, rehabilitation, and orthopedic surgery. Specialty hospitals forge a distinct service niche in a given market. These hospitals are also considered community hospitals as long as they meet the criteria discussed previously. In some of the specialty areas, these hospitals compete with general hospitals that offer the same services.

Psychiatric Hospitals

The primary function of a psychiatric hospital is to provide diagnostic and treatment services for patients who have mental illnesses. Specifically, such an institution must have facilities to provide psychiatric, psychological, and social work services. A psychiatric hospital must also have a written agreement with a general hospital for the transfer of patients who may require medical, obstetric, or surgical care (Health Forum, 2001, p. A3). Historically, state governments took the primary responsibility for establishing facilities to care for the mentally ill, but as new therapies have become available to treat mental illness, private psychiatric facilities and outpatient treatment centers have assumed the task of delivering most mental health services.

Rehabilitation Hospitals

Rehabilitation hospitals specialize in intensive therapeutic services to restore the maximum level of functioning in patients who have suffered recent disability due to illness or accident. Such hospitals serve patients who generally cannot be cured but whose functioning can be improved. These patients include amputees, victims of accidents or sports injuries, stroke victims, and others. Patients often transfer to such facilities after undergoing orthopedic surgery or receiving trauma care in a general hospital. Facilities and staff are available to provide physical, occupational, and speech and language therapy.

Children's Hospitals

Children's hospitals are community hospitals that typically have special facilities and trained staff to deal with the unique medical problems of children, particularly those with complex and rare conditions. Most of the inpatients in children's hospitals are treated for chronic or congenital conditions. The remaining patients require intensive care for a variety of needs, such as cancer treatment, treatment of cystic fibrosis, and tissue transplants.

Children's hospitals have equipment and furnishings that are specially designed for children—from newborn babies requiring intensive care to teens with chronic illness. They also maintain a nurse staffing ratio that is higher than that in general hospitals because children require more nursing care than adults.

Rural Hospitals

A *rural hospital* is one that is located in a county that is not part of a metropolitan statistical area (MSA). The U.S. Bureau of the Census has defined an MSA as a geographic area that includes at least (1) one city with a population of 50,000 or more or (2) an urbanized area of at least 50,000 inhabitants and a total MSA population of at least 100,000. Compared with other hospitals, rural hospitals generally treat a larger percentage of poor and elderly patients. Remote geographic location, small size, and limited work-force, along with physician shortages and inadequate financial resources, pose a unique set of challenges for rural hospitals (AHA, 2011).

To save some of the very small rural hospitals from having to close, the Balanced Budget Act of 1997 allowed certain rural hospitals to operate as *critical access hospitals* (CAHs). According to Medicare rules, a CAH should have no more than 25 beds and must provide 24-hour emergency medical services. An additional 10 beds may be operated for psychiatric and/or rehabilitation services. CAHs are reimbursed according to the retrospective cost-plus method, instead of the PPS method.

Teaching Hospitals

To be designated as a *teaching hospital*, a hospital must offer one or more graduate residency programs approved by the American Medical Association. Hence, the primary role of a teaching hospital is to train physicians. Although these hospitals may also be actively involved in training nurses and other health professionals, such as therapists and dietitians, unless they train physicians, they cannot be called teaching hospitals.

Most major teaching hospitals are affiliated with medical schools of universities. The term *academic medical center* applies to an organization in which there is active collaboration among the university, medical school, hospital/health system, and health care professionals. An academic medical center is uniquely capable of conducting basic and applied clinical research, providing health care services, and offering medical education (Daniels & Carson, 2011). Among the largest and most prestigious teaching hospitals are the members of the Council of Teaching Hospitals and Health Systems, which has approximately 400 members in both the United States and Canada.

In addition to fulfilling a substantial teaching and research mission, teaching hospitals deliver specialized care for a variety of complex medical problems. These institutions often operate several intensive care units, possess the latest medical technologies, and attract a diverse group of physicians representing most specialties and many subspecialties. Major teaching hospitals also offer many unique tertiary care services not generally found in other institutions, such as burn care, trauma care, and organ transplantation.

Osteopathic Hospitals

Osteopathic medicine represents an approach to medical practice that employs all the methods traditionally associated with allopathic medicine, such as pharmaceuticals, laboratory tests, x-ray diagnostics, and surgery. Osteopathic medicine, however, takes a holistic approach and goes a step further in advocating treatment that involves correction of the position of the joints or tissues and in emphasizing diet and environment as factors that prevent disease and improve health. For many years after osteopathy was established as a separate branch of medicine in 1874, osteopaths had to develop their own hospitals because of antagonism toward their profession demonstrated by the established allopathic medical practitioners. In 1970, osteopathic hospitals became eligible to apply for registration with the AHA (AHA, 1994). Since then, allopathic and osteopathic physicians have been practicing side by side in the same clinics and hospitals.

For all practical purposes, osteopathic hospitals are community general hospitals. However, with the integration of medical practice, having separate hospitals has become economically unnecessary. Also, the operation of osteopathic hospitals has been found to be more costly and less productive in comparison to their counterparts (Sinay, 2005). Hence, a large number of osteopathic hospitals have closed.

THE AFFORDABLE CARE ACT AND HOSPITALS

The ACA has put new restrictions on physician-owned hospitals and imposed new requirements on nonprofit hospitals.

1. Effective January 1, 2011, no new physician-owned hospitals can be opened. To participate in Medicare, existing hospitals had to be certified by December 31, 2010. Restrictions have also been placed on expanding the capacity in existing physician-owned hospitals.

2. Nonprofit hospitals are required to assess community health needs and develop strategies to meet those needs, under a new section—501(r)—of the tax code. These hospitals must develop and publicize written financial assistance policies and limit billing and collection actions against patients who are eligible for assistance.

LICENSURE, CERTIFICATION, AND ACCREDITATION

A hospital is legally required to have a *license* from the state in which it operates. The licensure function is usually carried out by each state's department of health. State licensure standards strongly emphasize compliance with building codes, fire safety, climate control, space allocations, and sanitation. States have also established minimum standards for equipment and personnel that health care organizations must meet to be licensed.

Certification by the federal government gives a hospital the authority to participate in the Medicare and Medicaid programs. The DHHS has developed health, safety, and quality standards referred to as *conditions of participation* and has the authority to enforce those standards. Hospitals accredited by the Joint Commission or the American Osteopathic Association have been automatically deemed to meet all the health and safety requirements for participation in Medicare and Medicaid.

The Joint Commission, a private nonprofit body, was formed in 1951 with the approval of the various medical and hospital organizations. Upon compliance with its standards, the Joint Commission accredits most of the nation's general hospitals, as well as many of the long-term care facilities, psychiatric hospitals, substance abuse programs, outpatient surgery centers, urgent care clinics, group practices, community health centers, hospices, and home health agencies. Different sets of standards apply to each category of health care organization. Over the years, the Joint Commission has refined its accreditation standards and process of verifying compliance to put greater emphasis on quality of care. Seeking accreditation is voluntary, but Medicare regulations confer *deemed status* on accredited hospitals, allowing these hospitals to participate in Medicare and Medicaid without having to be certified.

HOSPITAL ORGANIZATION

Hospitals are complex organizations. A hospital is generally responsible to numerous external stakeholders, such as the community, the government, managed care organizations, and accreditation agencies. Internally, hospital governance involves three major sources of power, whose motivations are sometimes at odds. The organizational structure of a hospital also differs substantially from that of other large organizations. The CEO receives delegated authority from the governing body (board) and is responsible for managing the organization with the help of senior executives. In large hospitals, these senior executives often carry the title of senior vice president or vice president responsible for various key service areas, such as nursing services, rehabilitation services, human resources, finance, and so forth. Most physicians belong to a separate organizational structure that operates in parallel to the administrative structure (**Figure 8.4**). Such a dual structure is rarely seen in other types of businesses and presents numerous opportunities for conflict to arise between the CEO and the medical staff. Sometimes matters can be further complicated because most physicians are not employed by the hospital, yet they must be closely involved in its operations. Also, the nursing staff, pharmacists, diagnostic technicians, dietitians, and others are administratively accountable to the CEO but professionally accountable to the medical staff (Raffel & Raffel, 1994, p. 139).

One major exception to the medical staff organization described here occurs with employment of physicians on salary in organizations such as VA hospitals. Other hospitals employ a small number of salaried hospitalists, who manage the care of patients once they are hospitalized.

ETHICS AND PUBLIC TRUST

Ethical issues arise in all types of health services organizations, but the most significant ones occur in acute care hospitals. Advanced technologies create situations requiring decision making under complex circumstances. Constraints on reimbursement often make it essential to cut costs or eliminate unprofitable services, which also can raise ethical concerns. Many physicians must deal with issues such as legalized abortion, physician-assisted suicide, artificial prolongation of life, and experimentation.

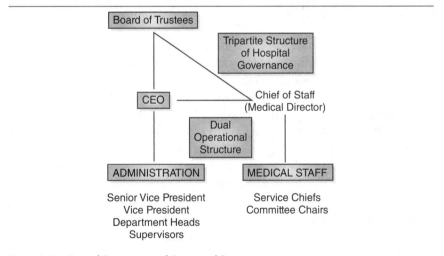

Figure 8.4   Hospital Governance and Operational Structure

Ethical Challenges

Physicians and other caregivers have moral responsibilities when delivering clinical care. These professionals are guided by the principles of beneficence and nonmaleficence. *Beneficence* means that a health services organization has an ethical obligation to do all it can to alleviate suffering caused by ill health and injury. This obligation includes providing essential services, such as emergency care, to needy individuals who do not have the ability to pay. Closely related to beneficence, *nonmaleficence* means that health services personnel have a moral obligation not to harm the patients. This principle requires physicians to use their best professional judgment in choosing interventions that maximize the potential health benefits at minimum risk.

No less challenging is the ethical issue surrounding the definition of extraordinary or heroic measures to sustain a person's life. Medical and legal experts differ on the controversial issue of withdrawing nutrition and other means of life support for dying patients (Bresnohan & Drane, 1986). The questions raised in such cases do not have easy answers, and most of the time physicians must follow their own consciences, apply their personal ethical values, or follow hospital policy. Other legal and ethical standards in medical treatment require the patient's consent before treatment is rendered, a discussion of the various treatment alternatives, and the patient's participation in decision making and the selection of treatment options. Health care providers are also duty bound to hold all patient information in strict confidence. Likewise, fairness, equality, and nondiscrimination are essential in the delivery of health care.

Addressing Ethical Issues

Many health care organizations, especially large acute care hospitals, have ethics committees. The *ethics committee* is charged with the responsibility of developing guidelines and standards for ethical decision making in the delivery of health care (Paris, 1995). Ethics committees are also responsible for resolving issues related to medical ethics. Such committees are interdisciplinary, involving physicians, nurses, clergy, social workers, legal experts, ethicists, and administrators.

Certain legal mechanisms are also available to help deal with difficult decisions about life and death. The Patient Self-Determination Act of 1990 applies to all health care facilities participating in Medicare or Medicaid.

This law requires hospitals and other facilities to provide all patients, on admission, with information on patients' rights.

Informed consent is a basic patient right. Every patient has the right to make an informed choice regarding his or her medical treatment, including the choice to refuse treatment. For a patient who is mentally capable, physicians must provide all the information the patient asks for or should have to make a properly informed decision.

Patients also have the right to formulate *advance directives*, allowing the patient to express in advance his or her wishes regarding continuation or withdrawal of treatment in the event that he or she becomes incompetent. When advance directives are not available, the burden of ethical decision making falls squarely on the shoulders of those responsible for providing health care services. In actual practice, however, discussions between physicians and patients about the prognosis at the end of life are infrequent and limited in scope (Bradley et al., 2001). Hence, relatively few people use advance directives. Physicians can play an important role by engaging their patients in discussions about the patients' preferences regarding end-of-life decisions.

Public Trust

Communities must place a high degree of trust in their hospitals, but occasionally the behavior of some hospitals has called this trust into question. Hospital administrators have a fiduciary responsibility. They are responsible for acting prudently in managing the affairs of the organization. Because a hospital's mission is to benefit the community, the hospital should be viewed as a community asset regardless of whether it is an investor-owned or nonprofit institution. When such a viewpoint is lost, and a hospital's board and its executives start placing other priorities ahead of their main responsibility to serve the community, a breach of public trust can occur. Although hospitals must maintain their financial and operational integrity, a real danger arises when financial concerns are put above a genuine concern for the welfare of the patients and the community. Because hospitals form the institutional hub of health care delivery, their integrity within the system is crucial. Scandals with regard to delays in care and alleged deaths resulting from such delays in VA hospitals received national media attention in 2014. When the critical services promised to the nation's veterans are not delivered, and there is little accountability for the billions of taxpayer dollars spent ineffectively, faith and confidence in the system are severely jeopardized.

CONCLUSION

Any facility that treats patients on the basis of an overnight stay is called an inpatient facility. The most common types of inpatient facilities are hospitals and nursing homes. Both of these institutions trace their beginnings to the almshouses of the 18th and 19th centuries, but as medical science advanced, hospitals emerged as institutions specializing in acute care and surgical services. In many parts of the United States, medical systems serve large geographic areas, delivering a full array of health care services.

Hospitals in the United States went through an expansion and then a contraction phase, both of which were triggered primarily by government policy. Hospital employment has steadily risen over time, and this trend is expected to continue.

Hospitals can be classified in a number of different ways. The majority of hospitals in the United States are private, nonprofit facilities. These hospitals have been required to provide community benefits; the Affordable Care Act has tightened this requirement. The ACA has also put severe restrictions on the expansion of physician-owned hospitals. Most hospitals are community hospitals, meaning that they are nonfederal, short stay, and open to the public. Licensure of hospitals is a legal requirement. Accreditation by the Joint Commission confers deemed status that enables a hospital to admit Medicare and Medicaid patients. Hospitals confront numerous ethical challenges and must operate in a way that strengthens public trust.

REFERENCES

American Hospital Association (AHA). *Hospital Statistics 1990–1991 Edition*. Chicago: AHA; 1990.

American Hospital Association (AHA). *AHA Guide to the Health Care Field 1994 Edition*. Chicago: AHA; 1994.

American Hospital Association (AHA). Section for small or rural hospitals: annual report for 2010. http://www.aha.org/content/11/2010-SRsectionAnnualReport .pdf. Published 2011. Accessed January 2012.

Bradley EH, et al. Documentation of discussions about prognosis with terminally ill patients. *Am J Med*. 2001;111(3): 218–223.

Bresnohan JF, Drane JF. A challenge to examine the meaning of living and dying. *Health Prog.* 1986;67:32–37, 98.

Catholic Health Association of the United States. Catholic health care in the United States. http://www.chausa.org/docs/default-source/general-files /cha-us-health-care-at-a-glance_january-2015.pdf?sfvrsn=0. Published January 2015. Accessed May 2015.

Center for Health Workforce Studies, University at Albany, State University of New York. Health care employment projections: an analysis of Bureau of Labor Statistics occupational projections 2010–2020. http://www.healthit .gov/sites/default/files/chws_bls_report_2012.pdf. Published March 2012. Accessed May 2015.

Daniels RJ, Carson LD. Academic medical centers: organizational integration and discipline through contractual and firm models. *JAMA.* 2011;306(17):1912–1913.

Foster D, Zrull L, Chenoweth J. Hospital performance differences by ownership. Truven Health Analytics. http://100tophospitals.com/portals/2/assets/HOSP _12678_0513_100TopHopPerfOwnershipPaper_RB_WEB.pdf. Published June 2013. Accessed May 2015.

Haglund CL, Dowling WL. The hospital. In: Williams SJ, Torrens PR, eds. *Introduction to Health Services.* 4th ed. Albany, NY: Delmar Publishers; 1993:135–176.

Health Forum. *AHA Guide to the Health Care Field.* 2001–2002 ed. Chicago: Health Forum; 2001.

National Center for Health Statistics (NCHS). *Health, United States, 2002.* Hyattsville, MD: Department of Health and Human Services; 2002.

National Center for Health Statistics (NCHS). *Health, United States, 2014.* Hyattsville, MD: Department of Health and Human Services; 2015.

Paris M. The medical staff. In: Wolper LF, ed. *Health Care Administration: Principles, Practices, Structure, and Delivery.* 2nd ed. Gaithersburg, MD: Aspen Publishers; 1995:32–46.

Physician Hospitals of America (PHA). Physician-owned hospitals excel in CMS star ratings. http://www.physicianhospitals.org/news/228189. Published 2015. Accessed May 2015.

Raffel MW, Raffel NK. *The U.S. Health System: Origins and Functions.* 4th ed. Albany, NY: Delmar Publishers; 1994.

Rau J. Doctor-owned hospitals prosper under health law. http://kaiserhealthnews .org/news/doctor-owned-hospitals-quality-bonuses. Published April 12, 2013. Accessed May 2015.

Rubin DB, Singh SR, Young GJ. Tax-exempt hospitals and community benefit: new directions in policy and practice. *Ann Rev Public Health.* 2015;36:545–557.

Sinay T. Cost structure of osteopathic hospitals and their local counterparts in the USA: are they any different? *Soc Sci Med.* 2005;60(8):1805–1814.

Teisberg ED, et al. *The Hospital Sector in 1992.* Boston: Harvard Business School; 1991.

Wolfson J, Hopes SL. What makes tax-exempt hospitals special? *Healthc Financ Manage.* July 1994:56–60.

Young GJ, et al. Provision of community benefits by tax-exempt U.S. hospitals. *N Engl J Med.* 2013;368(16):1519–1527.

Chapter 9

Managed Care and Integrated Systems

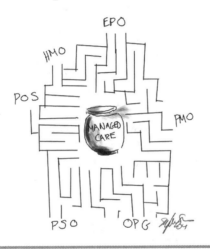

INTRODUCTION

Since around 1990, managed care has been the single most dominant force to fundamentally transform the delivery of health care in the United States. At first, some observers viewed the managed care phenomenon as an aberration. However, as private employers began to realize cost savings and public policy makers and administrators saw the opportunity to slow down the growth of Medicare and Medicaid expenditures, they increasingly turned to managed care. Managed care is now firmly entrenched in the U.S. health care system. Some features of managed care have also been adopted by other nations.

As employment-based private health insurance became dominant in the United States, neither the employers nor the insurance companies had any incentive to manage the delivery of services or payments made to providers. Providers showed a strong preference to be paid on a fee-for-service basis. Thus both the delivery of health care and payments for care got out of control. For example, between 1980 and 1990, the consumer price index—a measure of price increases (inflation) in the economy—rose by 59%, but inflation in medical care was 117% during the same time period (Department of Health and Human Services—DHHS, 1996, p. 241). Managed care was designed to slow down the rise in health care spending by limiting both the quantity of health care delivered and the amount of reimbursement to providers.

Managed care has experienced unprecedented success. For example, only 27% of all employees insured through employer-sponsored health insurance were enrolled in managed care plans in 1988. By 2002, however, 95% were enrolled in managed care. This growth occurred despite attacks on managed care from both physicians and consumers. Now, less than 1% of workers are enrolled in employer-sponsored conventional health insurance plans.

By enrolling a large segment of the insured U.S. population and taking responsibility to procure cost-effective health care for the enrollees, managed care organizations (MCOs) garnered enormous buying power. To a large extent, the organizational consolidation of providers represented a response to this growing power of MCOs. These changes have given rise to new organizational arrangements that are discussed in this chapter.

WHAT IS MANAGED CARE?

Managed care is a mechanism of providing health care services in which a single organization takes on the management of financing, insurance, delivery, and payment.

- *Financing.* Premiums are negotiated between employers and the MCO. Generally, a fixed premium per enrollee includes all health care services provided for in a contract.

- *Insurance.* The MCO collects premiums for insuring groups of enrollees. It then functions like an insurance company by assuming all risk. In other words, it takes financial responsibility if the total cost of services provided exceeds the revenue from fixed premiums. Under the Affordable Care Act (ACA), an MCO is allowed to retain no more than 20% of the premium dollar (15% for some MCOs) to manage risk and to cover its own administrative expenses. The remainder of the premium that is spent on health care services is called the *medical loss ratio.*

- *Delivery.* Unlike conventional insurance, the MCO arranges to provide health care to its enrollees. To do so, most MCOs establish contracts with physicians, clinics, hospitals, and medical systems. These providers operate independently but are linked to the MCO through legal contracts. Some very large MCOs have their own physicians on salary and operate their own clinics; in some instances, MCOs even operate their own hospitals. To keep costs under control, MCOs use various methods to manage the utilization of health care services.

- *Payment.* MCOs use three main types of payment arrangements with providers: capitation, discounted fees, and salaries. The three methods allow risk sharing in varying degrees between the MCO and the providers. Risk sharing puts the burden on the providers to be cost conscious and to curtail unnecessary utilization. Sometimes, a limited amount of fee-for-service is used for specialized services. Under *capitation,* the provider is paid a fixed monthly sum per enrollee, often called a per-member per-month (PMPM) payment. The provider receives the capitated fee per enrollee regardless of whether the enrollee uses health care services and regardless of the quantity of services used. The provider is responsible for providing all needed health care services determined to be medically necessary. A provider can lose money if services are delivered indiscriminately. The discounted fee arrangement uses a modified form of fee for service. After services have been delivered, the provider can bill the MCO for each service separately but is paid according to a schedule of fees. The fee schedule is prenegotiated and is based on discounts off the regular fees the provider would otherwise charge. Providers agree to discount their regular fees in exchange for the volume of patients the MCO brings them. In the third method of payment, salaries for physicians are often coupled with bonuses for efficient delivery of services.

The main characteristics of managed care are summarized in **Exhibit 9.1.**

Accreditation and Quality Indicators

Since 1991, MCOs have been accredited by the National Committee for Quality Assurance (NCQA). Accreditation is voluntary. The NCQA has also designed a set of standardized performance measures for MCOs. Commonly referred to as managed care report cards, the national standards and performance reports on individual MCOs are contained in the

Exhibit 9.1   Main Characteristics of Managed Care

MCOs manage financing, insurance, delivery, and payment for providing health care.

• Premiums are usually negotiated between MCOs and employers.

• MCOs function like an insurance company and assume risk.

• MCOs arrange to provide health care, mainly through contracts with providers.

• MCOs manage the utilization of health care services.

• Three main payment methods are capitation, discounted fees, and physicians on salary.

Healthcare Effectiveness Data and Information Set (HEDIS). The report cards are voluntary efforts that were begun out of concerns that controlling health care utilization could adversely affect the quality of care. HEDIS measures have been used quite extensively to evaluate and compare the quality of care in health plans.

The Centers for Medicare and Medicaid Services (CMS) rates the relative quality of Medicare Advantage plans (MA—Medicare Part C) on a one- to five-star scale, with five stars representing the highest quality. The star rating, which provides an overall measure of a plan's quality, is a cumulative indicator of the quality of care, access to care, responsiveness, and beneficiary satisfaction provided by the plan. The star rating incorporates HEDIS as one of the four measures. Ratings are available on Medicare's website to help beneficiaries choose from among the various MA plans if they want to enroll in Part C of Medicare. Under the ACA, the star ratings are used to reward higher-quality plans with incentive payments.

EVOLUTION OF MANAGED CARE

In the early 1900s, certain railroad, mining, and lumber companies located in isolated areas employed salaried physicians to provide medical care to their workers. In other instances, such companies contracted with physicians and hospitals at a flat fee per worker. Such arrangements can be viewed as prototypes of managed care.

The first known private health insurance plan started at the Baylor University Hospital in Dallas, Texas, in 1929 was also based on capitation. For a predetermined fixed fee per month, Baylor, and subsequently other hospitals, provided inpatient services.

Later, during the 1940s, some large health plans emerged in New York, California, Washington, and St. Louis. These plans also provided comprehensive health care to enrolled populations for a capitated fee. For example, the well-known Kaiser Permanente plan started in California in 1942 when the industrialist Henry J. Kaiser was faced with the problem of providing health care to his 30,000 workers. In 1945, the Permanente Health Plan was made available to the general public; today, the Kaiser Foundation Health Plan, operated by Kaiser Permanente, is the largest HMO in the United States. In the rest of the country, however, delivery of health care typically continued to follow the fee-for-service system. Commercial insurance companies were the dominant players in the private health insurance market.

The Health Maintenance Organization Act of 1973 was passed out of concern for escalating health care expenditures. Subsequent to the creation of Medicare and Medicaid, national health expenditures rose at more than double the rate of growth in the consumer price index during the 5-year period from 1966 to 1971 (**Figure 9.1**). The 1973 law was designed to provide an alternative to the traditional fee-for-service practice of medicine; it aimed to stimulate the growth of HMOs by providing federal funds to establish new HMOs (Wilson & Neuhauser, 1985, p. 206). The reasoning

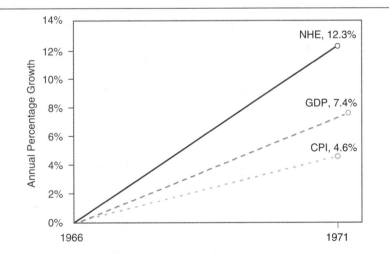

Figure 9.1   Average Annual Rates of Increase in National Health Expenditures (NHE), Gross Domestic Product (GDP), and Consumer Price Inex (CPI), 1966–1971
Data from Bureau of Labor Statistics, National Center for Health Statistics.

behind promoting HMO growth was that it would stimulate competition among health plans, increase efficiency, and slow the rate of growth in health care expenditures. The law's objective was to create 1,700 HMOs to serve 40 million members by 1976 (Iglehart, 1994). By the end of the 1970s, however, HMOs had enrolled fewer than 10 million members.

During the 1980s, managed care experienced relatively slow growth, but in states such as California and Minnesota, growth was faster than in most parts of the United States. As pointed out earlier, health care costs continued to rise uncontrollably, and private businesses were increasingly threatened by the erosion of profits resulting from double-digit increases in the cost of health insurance premiums. Consequently, employers started switching from traditional health insurance to managed care plans during the 1980s. It was not until the early 1990s, however, that a veritable managed care revolution got under way when private employers experienced a total increase of 217% (12.2% average annual increase) in the cost of health insurance between 1980 and 1990. **Figure 9.2** illustrates the growth of enrollment in managed care plans between 1988 and 2003.

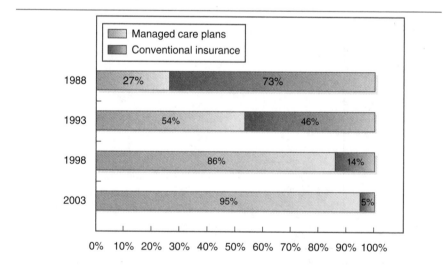

Figure 9.2   Enrollment of Worker in Employer-Sponsored Health Plans, Selected Years

Modified from Claxton G., et al. 2007. The Kasier Family Foundation and Health Research and Educational Trust Employer Health Benefits 2007 Annual Survey. Menlo Park, CA: Henry J. Kaiser Foundation and Chicago, IL; Health Research and Educational Trust, p. 65.

GROWTH AND TRANSFORMATION OF MANAGED CARE

As the market for managed care grew, competition among MCOs gave rise to new forms of managed care plans. To differentiate among themselves, some new organizations adopted variations in payment. Preferred provider organizations (PPOs), for example, differentiated themselves by using discounted fee payments instead of capitation. Other MCOs differentiated themselves according to how the medical care providers were organized. Still others offered their enrollees a choice between providers who were contractually affiliated with the organization and those who were not. MCOs also adopted various methods to control health care costs by actively monitoring utilization.

Private Insurance Enrollment

As pointed out previously, managed care has become the primary vehicle for delivering health care to the vast majority of Americans and is now a mature industry in the United States. In essence, private health insurance can now be equated with managed care, whether it is obtained through a small or large employer. High-deductible health plans are also commonly offered in the form of managed care plans.

Medicare Enrollment

Medicare beneficiaries have the choice of enrolling in a managed care plan under the MA program or remaining in the traditional fee-for-service program. Even though the latter option has been more popular with Medicare beneficiaries, enrollment in MA plans doubled between 2005 (14% of beneficiaries) and 2013 (28% of beneficiaries) (Sanofi-Aventis, 2014b).

Medicaid Enrollment

Waivers under the Social Security Act, particularly Sections 1115 and 1915(b), allowed states to enroll their Medicaid recipients in managed care plans. Later, the Balanced Budget Act of 1997 gave states the authority to implement mandatory managed care enrollments without federal waivers (Moscovice et al., 1998). Since then, enrollment in managed care has grown at a rapid pace. In 2013, 76% of Medicaid beneficiaries were enrolled in managed care plans (Sanofi-Aventis, 2014b).

Managed Care Backlash

Managed care made significant headway during the decade of the 1990s and achieved notable success in slowing down the growth of national health care expenditures. Toward the latter half of the 1990s, however, it drew a backlash from consumers, providers, and politicians. The American media also played a role in shaping public opinion against managed care by presenting, in many instances, one-sided and subjective "news" stories focusing on denial of services.

For consumers, dissatisfaction with managed care was associated mainly with the erosion of choice resulting from the limited number of providers associated with the plans and some restrictions in direct access to specialized services. Dissatisfaction on the part of physicians, hospitals, and other providers was related to the control that MCOs exerted over utilization and limits on reimbursement. Risk sharing under capitation became particularly controversial. Politicians responded by passing laws to contain some of the perceived excesses of managed care. In the process, however, all parties had to accept certain compromises.

Transformation of Managed Care

In response to the backlash, HMOs moved away from tight management of health care services but without totally abandoning utilization controls. They also incorporated fee-for-service reimbursement, along with capitation for certain services, within their payment schemes. PPOs emerged, offering greater choice of access to providers. Both consumers and providers welcomed these changes. In the end, enrollees had to give up unconditional freedom over choice, providers had to accept some controls over how they would practice medicine and settle for lower rates of reimbursement than what they were getting under fee-for-service arrangements, and MCOs had to relax tight management of health care utilization. Even though some differences between individual plans still exist, relaxed controls and flexibility have become common features of all plans. Managed care today is quite different from what it was initially intended to be: an organizational mechanism that would tightly control the financing and delivery of health care. It is because of these compromises that managed care became enormously successful—practically replacing traditional health insurance in the United States. The same compromises, however, eroded managed care's full potential to reverse the rising tide of health care spending.

UTILIZATION CONTROL METHODS IN MANAGED CARE

MCOs use three main approaches to monitor and control the utilization of services:

- Expert evaluation of which services are medically necessary in a given case. Such an evaluation ensures that only medically necessary services are actually provided.

- Determination of how services can be provided most inexpensively while maintaining acceptable standards of quality. For example, often similar services can be obtained as an outpatient or as an inpatient; outpatient services cost less. Similarly, generic drugs cost less than brand-name drugs.

- Review of the process of care and changes in the patient's condition to revise the course of medical treatment if necessary.

The methods most commonly used for utilization monitoring and control are gatekeeping and utilization review. Generally, HMOs employ tighter utilization controls than other types of managed care plans, which are discussed later in this chapter.

Gatekeeping

Commonly used by HMOs, *gatekeeping* is an arrangement that requires a primary care physician to coordinate all health care services needed by an enrollee. The physicians have contracts with the HMO as in-network providers. Gatekeeping also emphasizes preventive care, routine physical examinations, and other primary care services that are delivered by the primary care gatekeeper. Secondary care services, such as diagnostic testing, consultation from specialists, and admission to a hospital, are provided only on referral from the gatekeeper. In this way, the gatekeeper controls access to costly medical services.

Utilization Review

Utilization review is the process of evaluating the appropriateness of services provided. It is sometimes misunderstood to be a mechanism for denying services, but its main objective is actually to review each case and to determine the most appropriate level of services. Three main types of utilization review are employed: prospective, concurrent, and retrospective.

Prospective Utilization Review

Under this method, the medical necessity for certain treatments is determined before the care is actually delivered. An example of prospective utilization review is the decision by a primary care gatekeeper to refer or not refer a patient to a specialist. However, not all managed care plans use gatekeepers. Some plans require the enrollee or the provider to call the plan administrators for *precertification*—that is, approval before certain services are provided. Most plans use established clinical guidelines to determine the appropriateness of services. Preauthorization of hospital admissions and second opinions for surgical procedures are examples of precertification. In case of an emergency admission to an inpatient facility, plans generally require notification within 24 hours. One of the main objectives of prospective review is to prevent unnecessary or inappropriate institutionalization or other courses of treatment such as surgery.

Concurrent Utilization Review

Concurrent utilization review occurs when decisions regarding appropriateness are made during the course of health care utilization. The most common examples of this type of review involve monitoring the length of inpatient stays. When a patient is hospitalized, a certain number of inpatient days are generally preapproved. A trained nurse then monitors the patient's status and reviews the case with a physician if a longer stay is necessary. A decision is made to authorize or deny additional days.

Discharge planning is an important component of concurrent utilization review. A patient's prognosis for recovery, expected outcomes, and anticipated day of discharge are critical elements of concurrent review. Discharge planning deals with the patient's ongoing care and evaluates any special requirements that are necessary after discharge. For example, if a patient is admitted with a fractured hip, it is important to decide whether home health care or a skilled nursing facility would be more appropriate for convalescent care. If the patient requires care in a skilled nursing facility, then discharge planning must find out whether the appropriate level of rehabilitation services would be available and for how long insurance will pay for rehabilitation therapy in a long-term care setting.

Retrospective Utilization Review

Retrospective utilization review determines the appropriateness of utilization after services have already been delivered. Such review is based on an examination of medical records to assess the appropriateness of care. It may involve an assessment of individual cases. Large claims may be reviewed for billing accuracy. Retrospective review may also involve an analysis of data to examine patterns of excessive utilization or underutilization. *Underutilization* occurs when medically necessary care is not delivered. *Overutilization* occurs when medical services that are not necessary are delivered.

TYPES OF MANAGED CARE PLANS

Three main factors led to the development of different types of managed care plans. The first and most important involved the choice of providers. HMOs were the most common type of MCOs in the 1970s, but HMO plans had inherent weaknesses, especially with regard to choice of providers. Other types of MCO plans that offered greater choice were developed mainly to compete with the more restrictive HMO plans. Second, different ways of arranging the delivery of services led to different forms of MCOs because there is no single way to arrange providers into a delivery network. Payment and risk sharing make up the third major factor. The main differences between the three different types of managed care plans discussed in this section are presented in **Exhibit 9.2**.

HMO Plans

HMOs were the first type of managed care plans to appear on the market. An HMO is distinguished from other types of plans by its focus on wellness care. Such an organization not only provides medical care during illness but also offers a variety of services to help people maintain their health—hence the name "health maintenance organization." HMOs emphasize preventive and screening services through routine checkups and tests. Prevention of disease and early detection and treatment save health care costs in the long run when the course of a disease is checked before it turns into a more complex case. As an incentive to the enrollees to seek wellness care, HMO plans typically do not have annual deductibles, and they also have lower copayments than do other types of plans.

Exhibit 9.2   Differences Among the Three Main Types of Managed Care Plans

Main Distinguishing Factors
1. Choice of providers
2. Delivery of services
3. Payment and risk sharing

HMO Plans	PPO Plans	POS Plans
• Use of only in-network providers is permitted	• Use of both in-network and out-of-network providers is permitted	• Use of both in-network and out-of-network providers is permitted
• Providers on staff and/or contracted providers	• Contracted providers only	• Contracted providers only
• Use of gatekeeping	• No gatekeeping	
• Focus on prevention and primary care		
• Specialty services are obtained upon referral	• Unrestricted access to specialty services	• Unrestricted access to specialty services
• Providers are paid mostly under capitation: Some fee for service	• Providers are paid according to discounted fee schedules	• Combination of capitation and fee for service
• Risk sharing with providers under capitation	• No risk sharing	• Some risk sharing

Note: There may be some variations to the above for individual plans.

Initially, HMOs used only capitation to reimburse providers, but providers disliked the risk-sharing feature of capitation. HMOs, therefore, had to compromise by raising per-member per-month (PMPM) rates and, in many instances, switching to fee-for-service reimbursement. In 2013, 66% of HMOs used capitation; 58% used fee-for-service reimbursement to pay physicians (Sanofi-Aventis, 2014a).

HMO plans require that enrollees use in-network providers. The utilization of services is coordinated and managed by the HMO, mainly through primary care gatekeepers. Enrollees must obtain services from in-network hospitals, physicians, and other health care providers. Specialty services, such as mental health and substance abuse treatment, are frequently carved out. A *carve-out* is a special contract outside regular capitation, which is funded separately by the HMO. A state may also enroll its Medicaid beneficiaries into a specialized managed behavioral health organization (MBHO).

The four most widely used HMO models differ from each other according to the arrangements they make with participating physicians. These models are the staff, group, network, and independent practice association models.

Staff Model HMO

A staff model HMO employs its own salaried physicians. The physicians are typically paid fixed salaries. An HMO may also have a bonus program combined with the salary, in which case end-of-the-year bonuses are based on each physician's productivity and the HMO's profitability. Physicians work only for their employer HMO and provide services to that HMO's enrollees (Rakich et al., 1992, p. 281). Staff model HMOs must employ physicians in all of the common specialties to provide for the health care needs of their members. In addition, contracts with selected subspecialties are established for less frequently needed services. The HMO operates one or more outpatient clinics, which contain physicians' offices, support staff, and sometimes ancillary support facilities, such as laboratory and radiology departments. In most instances, the HMO contracts with area hospitals for inpatient services (Wagner, 1995).

Compared with other HMO models, staff model HMOs are able to exercise a greater degree of control over the practice patterns of their physicians. Hence, it is easier to monitor utilization. Even so, the fixed salary expense can be high, which requires that these HMOs have a large number of members to support the operating expenses. Enrollees generally have a limited choice of physicians. Because of its disadvantages, the staff model has been the least popular type of HMO.

Group Model HMO

A group model HMO contracts with a multispecialty group practice and separately with one or more hospitals to provide comprehensive services to its members. The group practice is an independent practice, employing its own physicians who can treat non-HMO patients as well. The

HMO generally pays an all-inclusive capitation fee to the group practice to provide physician services to its members. Under a different scenario, the HMO may own the group practice, which is organized as a separate corporation but one that is administratively tied to the HMO. In this case, the group practice may provide services exclusively to the HMO's members. Ownership or an exclusive contract enables the HMO to exercise better control over utilization. Even when it is not an exclusive contract, the HMO brings a block of business to the group practice, which gives the HMO a fair amount of leverage regarding financial terms and utilization controls.

Network Model HMO

Under the network model, the HMO contracts with more than one medical group practice. This model is particularly well suited for operations in large metropolitan areas and across widespread geographic regions where group practices are located. Each group practice is paid a capitation fee based on the number of enrollees. The group is responsible for providing all physician services. It can make referrals to specialists but is financially responsible for reimbursing them for any referrals it makes. The network model is generally able to offer enrollees a wider choice of physicians than the staff or group models. The main disadvantage is the dilution of utilization control.

Independent Practice Association Model HMO

Of the four HMO models, the independent practice association (IPA) model has been the most successful in terms of the largest share of enrollments. The IPA model became popular with both providers and enrollees. IPAs gave small groups and individual physicians the opportunity to participate in managed care and, therefore, were preferred by physicians. The enrollees generally have the greatest choice of providers under the IPA model.

An IPA is a legal entity separate from the HMO. The IPA, not the HMO, establishes contracts with both independent solo practitioners and group practices. The HMO, in turn, contracts with the IPA for physician services. Physicians do not have a contract with the HMO, but with the IPA. Hence, the IPA functions as an intermediary representing a large number of physicians. The IPA is generally paid a capitation amount by the HMO. The IPA retains administrative control over how it pays its physicians.

It may reimburse physicians through capitation or some other mechanism, such as modified fee for service. The IPA often shares risk with the physicians and assumes the responsibility for utilization management and quality assessment.

Under the IPA model, the HMO is still responsible for providing health care services to its enrollees, but the logistics of arranging physician services are shifted to the IPA. As a consequence, the HMO is relieved of the administrative burden of establishing contracts with numerous providers and controlling utilization. Financial risk is also shared with the IPA.

IPAs may be independently established by community physicians, or the HMO may create an IPA and invite community physicians to participate in it. An IPA may also be hospital based and structured so that only physicians from one or two hospitals are eligible to participate in it (Wagner, 1995). One major disadvantage of the IPA model is that if a contract is lost, the HMO loses a large number of participating physicians.

PPO Plans

PPO plans were created by insurance companies in response to the growth of HMOs. PPOs differentiated themselves by offering out-of-network options for enrollees. By the early 1990s, PPOs became more popular and their market share began to exceed that of HMOs.

PPO enrollees can either choose in-network preferred providers with whom the PPO has established contracts or use physicians and hospitals outside the network. Higher copayments apply for using nonpreferred providers. The additional out-of-pocket expenses largely act as a deterrent to going outside the network for care.

PPOs make discounted fee arrangements with providers. The discounts typically range between 25% and 35% off the providers' regular fees. Negotiated payment arrangements with hospitals can take a variety of forms, such as payments based on diagnosis-related groups, bundled charges for certain services, and discounts. Hence, no direct risk sharing with providers is involved. PPOs also apply fewer restrictions to the care-seeking behavior of enrollees. In most instances, they do not use gatekeeping, which allows enrollees to see specialists without being referred by a primary care physician. Precertification (prospective utilization review) is generally employed only for hospitalization and high-cost outpatient procedures (Robinson, 2002).

Point-of-Service Plans

Point-of-service (POS) plans combine features of classic HMOs with some of the characteristics of patient choice found in PPOs. Through this combination, POS plans overcome the drawback of restricted provider choice but retain the benefits of tight utilization management. Many POS plans are actually offered by HMOs to give members an optional plan that allows utilization of out-of-network providers. From the consumer's perspective, free choice of providers was a major selling point for POS plans, but after reaching a peak in popularity in 1998–1999, enrollment in POS plans gradually declined mainly because of the high out-of-pocket costs associated with them.

IMPACT ON COST, ACCESS, AND QUALITY

Influence on Cost Containment

Other countries assign the task of cost containment to the government, which controls health care expenditures by budgeting system-wide expenditures (global budgets) and imposing limits on services (supply-side rationing) and payments to providers. In the United States, the primary responsibility for cost containment falls on the private sector, but the government also has pioneered various approaches, mostly aimed at controlling Medicaid and Medicare costs. The private-sector approach to cost containment has involved the expansion of managed care, which has been widely credited for slowing down the rate of growth in health care expenditures during the 1990s. Because of the backlash against managed care, the full cost-containment potential of managed care was never realized.

From a cost-containment perspective, enrollment of Medicare and Medicaid beneficiaries in managed care has been controversial. However, some recent evidence suggests that MA plans offer care of equal or higher quality and for less cost than traditional fee-for-service Medicare, thus offering higher value (Newhouse & McGuire, 2014). On the other hand, the experience does not appear to be the same with Medicaid managed care. For example, a study encompassing all 50 states showed that shifting Medicaid recipients from fee for service into managed care did not reduce Medicaid spending (Duggan & Hayford, 2013).

Impact on Access

Baker and colleagues (2004) found that timely breast cancer and cervical cancer screenings were twice as likely for women receiving services in geographic areas with greater HMO market share, compared to women in areas with low managed care penetration. More recent studies report similar findings on health screenings, diabetes care, and favorable ratings of physicians by the patients (Ayanian et al., 2013). In MA plans, better access to primary care may have been responsible for lowering the risk of preventable hospitalizations, particularly for ethnic/minority groups (Basu, 2012). Behavioral health carve-outs have also been instrumental in addressing long-standing challenges in access and utilization of behavioral health care (Frank & Garfield, 2007). On the other hand, in Medicaid managed care, Caswell and Long (2015) found an increased probability of emergency department use (instead of primary care) and difficulty in seeing a specialist as an increasing number of beneficiaries were enrolled in managed care plans. Similarly, in one survey, only a quarter of the physicians participating in Medicaid managed care offered appointments within 2 weeks of the contact date (Taitsman, 2015).

Influence on Quality of Care

Despite anecdotes, individual perceptions, and isolated stories propagated by the news media, no comprehensive research to date has clearly demonstrated that the growth of managed care has come at the expense of _____ ericans. Actually, the available evidence _____: The quality of health care provided by _____ (Hofmann, 2002). Financial pressures _____ ges in physician behavior because under _____ responsibility for the patient's overall care

_____ of the literature by Miller and Luft (2002) _____ -HMO plans provide roughly equal quality of _____ nge of conditions, diseases, and interventions. At the same time, HMOs lower the use of hospital and other expensive resources. Hence, medical care delivered through managed care plans has been cost-effective. Evidence also suggests that the race, ethnicity, and socioeconomic status of managed care enrollees have little or no effect on the quality of care they receive (Balsa et al., 2007; Brown et al., 2005).

Conversely, evaluation of the existing literature does point to lower access and lower enrollee satisfaction ratings for HMO plans compared with non-HMO plans (Miller & Luft, 2002). Also, quality-based star ratings by the CMS are higher for nonprofit MA plans compared to for-profit plans (Peng et al., 2015). Earlier studies (e.g., Schneider et al., 2005) reached similar conclusions regarding quality of care in for-profit compared to nonprofit health plans. At present, the significant growth in Medicaid managed care enrollments by states across the country has become controversial as many observers have suggested that this is being done without consistent evidence that Medicaid managed care plans reduce expenditures and improve access and quality of care. The issue is particularly significant in the wake of Medicaid expansion under the ACA. Only future research will be able to clarify this issue.

INTEGRATED SYSTEMS

Organizational integration became necessary for economic reasons in a changing health care landscape. It began with hospital mergers and acquisitions during the 1990s. Subsequently, consolidation with physician group practices was viewed as beneficial for both hospitals and physicians as health care services increasingly moved from the inpatient to the outpatient sector. Diversification into services that an organization had not offered before was the next step in integration. Many of these transformations can be attributed to the growth of managed care, which came to dominate the U.S. health care system. For example, managed care gained enormous bargaining power over independent hospitals and physician clinics, and these organizations came under growing pressure to reduce costs and deliver services efficiently to populations spread over large geographic areas. More recently, the ACA has added another twist by requiring certain integrated organizations to be held accountable for people's health. Hence, today, we find two main types of highly integrated health care systems: integrated delivery systems (IDSs) and accountable care organizations (ACOs).

Since the passage of the ACA, consolidation through mergers and acquisitions has picked up in the health care industry. Hence, competition is being curtailed. It is not clear, however, whether the consolidation has occurred in response to the ACA.

Integrated Delivery Systems

An *integrated delivery system* (IDS) includes several organizations under ownership or contractual arrangements that provide an array of health care services to large communities. There can be degrees of integration, but a fully integrated health network operates in a one-stop shopping environment that is centered around one or more hospitals and includes outpatient clinics and surgical centers, one or more long-term care facilities, home health and hospice services, and ownership of or contract with one or more MCOs. Specialized cardiac care clinics and rehabilitation facilities may be included. Other services, such as imaging centers, dialysis centers, and mental health centers, may also be incorporated.

On the one hand, IDSs help achieve cost savings through resource sharing and elimination of duplication. On the other hand, these organizational networks tend to become complex and, therefore, difficult to manage. Yet, the number of various types of providers that are part of an IDS has continued to increase. For example, in 2014, almost 3,000 community hospitals and nearly 13,000 physician practices were affiliated with 342 IDSs nationwide (Sanofi-Aventis, 2015). Research shows that IDSs have positive effects on quality of care, as well as the potential to lower health service utilization and produce costs savings (Hwang et al., 2013).

Accountable Care Organizations

In a general sense, an *accountable c* integrated group of providers—includi postdischarge care delivery organizations coordinated care and take responsibility fo delivered. The ACA authorized formatio eficiaries enrolled in the traditional fee Medicare rules, an ACO must be a legal through contractual arrangements—suc tions, discussed later—do not qualify

The ACO must also have a governing body to provide oversight and be held legally accountable.

In conjunction with the formation of ACOs, the ACA authorized a Shared Savings Program that is designed to reward ACOs that lower the growth of health care expenditures while meeting performance standards on quality of care (CMS, 2015). This new model of care delivery is still in its infancy.

However, if successful, ACOs could potentially become the main providers of services to all Medicare beneficiaries. Using similar concepts, some states are experimenting with ACOs to serve their Medicaid populations.

More than 250 ACOs have formed across the nation. These organizations are more likely to form in geographic areas where IDSs that have experience working under capitation already exist (Auerbach et al., 2013). Growth of ACOs is also hinged on how they get to be regulated, which would include the shared savings formulas.

ACOs have already come under heavy criticism from providers. A survey by the National Association of ACOs indicated that two-thirds of the ACO participants were unlikely to remain in the ACO program. Yet, for the program to be successful, 800 to 900 Medicare ACOs would be needed by 2018 (Perez, 2015). Hence, much remains to be seen about what direction ACOs might go in the future.

TYPES OF INTEGRATION

Integration Based on Major Participants

Physicians and hospitals have been two key participants in the formation of integrated organizations because, in almost all instances, one entity cannot function without the other. Hence, a *physician–hospital organization* (PHO) has been a common type of integrated organization. A PHO is a legal entity that represents an alliance between a hospital and local physicians and combines their services under the aegis of a single organization. It allows both entities to have greater bargaining power in contract negotiations with MCOs. PHO formation is often initiated by the hospital, but it is unlikely to succeed without the participation of the medical staff leaders. PHOs provide the benefits of integration while preserving the independence and autonomy of physicians. The ACA specifies that PHOs can qualify as ACOs (Casalino et al., 2013).

Integration Based on Type of Ownership or Affiliation

The objectives of organizational integration can be accomplished in ways other than outright ownership. For example, relatively simple cooperative arrangements, sharing of resources, and joint responsibilities through contracts can be established.

Acquisitions and Mergers

Acquisition refers to the purchase of one organization by another. The acquired company ceases to exist as a separate entity and is absorbed under the name of the purchasing corporation. A *merger* involves a mutual agreement to unify two or more organizations into a single entity. The separate assets of two organizations are brought together, typically under a new name. Both former entities cease to exist, and a new corporation is formed.

Small hospitals may merge to gain efficiencies by eliminating the duplication of services. Acquisitions and mergers can also help an organization expand into new geographic markets. A large hospital may acquire smaller hospitals to serve as satellites in a large metropolitan area with sprawling suburbs. A regional health care system may be formed after a large hospital has acquired other hospitals and diversified into services such as outpatient care, long-term care, and rehabilitation.

Joint Ventures

A *joint venture* results when two or more institutions share resources to create a new organization to pursue a common purpose (Pelfrey & Theisen, 1989). Each of the participants in a joint venture continues to conduct business independently. The new company created by the participants also remains independent. Joint ventures are often used to diversify into new services when the participants can benefit by joining hands rather than competing against each other. For example, hospitals in a given region may engage in a joint venture to form a home health agency that benefits all partners. An acute care hospital, a multispecialty physician group practice, a skilled nursing facility, and an insurer may join to offer a managed care plan (Carson et al., 1995, p. 209). In this scenario, each of the participants would continue to operate its own business, and all would have a common stake in the new HMO or PPO.

Alliances

In one respect, the health care industry is unique because organizations often develop cooperative arrangements with rival providers. Cooperation instead of competition, in some situations, eliminates duplication of services while ensuring that all the health needs of the community are fulfilled (Carson et al., 1995, p. 217). An *alliance* is an agreement between two organizations to share their resources without joint ownership of assets. For example, a hospital may form an alliance with a physician group practice to conduct community health assessments, jointly create programs that minimize health risks, and work to improve the community's health.

Alliances are relatively simpler to form than mergers. An alliance may be a first step that gives both organizations the opportunity to evaluate the advantages of a potential merger. Alliances require little financial commitment and can be easily dissolved if the anticipated benefits do not materialize.

Virtual Organizations

When contractual arrangements between two or more organizations form a new organization, the resulting entity is referred to as a *virtual organization*, or an organization without walls. The formation of a health network based on contractual arrangements is called *virtual integration*. IPAs are a prime example of virtual organizations; a PHO may also be a virtual organization. The main advantage of virtual organizations is that they require less capital to enter new geographic or service markets (Gabel, 1997). They also help bring together scattered entities under one mutually cooperative arrangement.

Integration Based on Service Consolidation

Horizontal Integration

Horizontal integration is a growth strategy in which a health care organization extends its core product or service. For example, an acute care hospital that adds coronary bypass surgery to its existing surgical services or that builds a suburban acute care facility is integrating horizontally (Rakich et al., 1992, p. 326). Multihospital chains, nursing facility chains, and a chain of drugstores, all under the same management with member facilities offering the same core services or products, are other examples of horizontal integration. The main objective of horizontal integration is to achieve geographic expansion. Diversification into new products or services is not achieved through horizontal integration.

Vertical Integration

Vertical integration links services that are at different stages in the production process of health care—for example, organization of preventive services, primary care, acute care, and postacute service delivery around a hospital. The intended purpose of vertical integration is to increase the comprehensiveness and continuity of care. Vertical integration is a diversification strategy. It may be achieved through acquisitions, mergers, joint ventures, or alliances. To add just one or two new services, internal development strategies may be used. For example, CVS Health operates walk-in retail clinics inside its pharmacy stores in many locations. Health networks are also formed through vertical integration.

MANAGED CARE AND ORGANIZATIONAL INTEGRATION UNDER THE AFFORDABLE CARE ACT

The main implications of the ACA, as they pertain to organizational integration, apply to Medicaid and Mediare.

1. States are mandating Medicaid beneficiaries to enroll in managed care plans. As several states have chosen to expand their Medicaid programs under the ACA, the Medicaid population in the United States will also expand. Consequently, Medicaid HMO enrollments will grow.
2. ACOs are allowed to contract with the CMS to serve Medicare fee-for-service enrollees provided these organizations comply with CMS regulations.

CONCLUSION

Most insured Americans today—either through private or government sources—receive health care through a managed care organization. MCOs have been credited with cost containment in health care, and enrollment in managed care plans has continued to grow. Yet, the full potential of managed care was never realized because of widespread opposition.

Integrated delivery systems emerged as hospitals and physicians, in particular, faced growing pressures from managed care to deliver services at reduced costs. Integration has enabled large health care organizations to win sizable managed care contracts and, in some instances, to offer their own health insurance plans. However, the delivery of health care has become complex from the standpoint of providers and consumers. Through the Affordable Care Act, the U.S. government is now experimenting with accountable care organizations in the hope that it would reduce cost and improve quality. Some early challenges have emerged, but it is too early to tell whether care delivery through the ACOs will achieve the expected results.

REFERENCES

Auerbach DI, et al. Accountable care organization formation is associated with integrated systems but not high medical spending. *Health Aff.* 2013;32(10):1781–1788.

Ayanian JZ, et al. Medicare beneficiaries more likely to receive appropriate ambulatory services in HMOs than in traditional Medicare. *Health Aff.* 2013;32(7):1228–1235.

Baker L, et al. The effect of area HMO market share on cancer screening. *Health Serv Res.* 2004;39(6):1751–1772.

Balsa A, et al. Does managed health care reduce health care disparities between minorities and whites? *J Health Econ.* 2007;26(1):101–121.

Basu J. Medicare managed care and primary care quality: examining racial/ethnic effects across states. *Health Care Manag Sci.* 2012;15(1):15–28.

Brown AF, et al. Race, ethnicity, socioeconomic position, and quality of care for adults with diabetes enrolled in managed care. *Diab Care.* 2005;28(12):2864–2870.

Carson KD, et al. *Management of Healthcare Organizations.* Cincinnati, OH: South-Western College Publishing; 1995.

Casalino LP, et al. Independent practice associations and physician–hospital organizations can improve care management for smaller practices. *Health Aff.* 2013;32(8):1376–1382.

Caswell KJ, Long SK. The expanding role of managed care in the Medicaid program: implications for health care access, use, and expenditures for nonelderly adults. *Inquiry.* April 16, 2015; 52. Date of Electronic Publication: 20150416.:

Centers for Medicare and Medicaid Services (CMS). Shared savings program. http://www.cms.gov/Medicare/Medicare-Fee-for-Service-Payment/sharedsav ingsprogram/index.html. Published 2015. Accessed August 16, 2015.

Department of Health and Human Services (DHHS). *Health, United States, 1995.* Hyattsville, MD: DHHS; 1996.

Duggan M, Hayford T. Has the shift to managed care reduced Medicaid expenditures? Evidence from state and local level mandates. *J Policy Anal Manage*. 2013;32(3):505–535.

Eikel CV. Fewer patient visits under capitation offset by improved quality of care: Study brings evidence to debate over physician payment methods. *Findings Brief: Health Care Financing & Organization*. 2002;5(3):1–2.

Frank RG, Garfield RL. Managed behavioral health care carve-outs: Past performance and future prospects. *Ann Rev Public Health*. 2007;28(1): 303–320.

Gabel J. Ten ways HMOs have changed during the 1990s. *Health Aff*. 1997;16(3):134–145.

Hofmann MA. Quality of health care improving. *Bus Insurance*. 2002;36(38):1–2.

Hwang W, et al. Effects of integrated delivery system on cost and quality. *Am J Manag Care*. 2013;19(5):e175–e184.

Iglehart JK. The American health care system: managed care. In: Lee PR, Estes CL, eds. *The Nation's Health*. 4th ed. Boston, MA: Jones and Bartlett; 1994:231–237.

Miller RH, Luft HS. HMO plan performance update: an analysis of the literature, 1997–2001. *Health Aff*. 2002;21(4):63–86.

Moscovice I, et al. Expanding rural managed care: enrollment patterns and perspectives. *Health Aff*. 1998;17(1):172–179.

Newhouse JP, McGuire TG. How successful is Medicare Advantage? *Milbank Q*. 2014;92(2):351–394.

Pelfrey S, Theisen BA. Joint venture in health care. *J Nurs Admin*. 1989;19(4):39–42.

Peng X, et al. Relationship between Medicare Advantage contract characteristics and quality-of-care ratings: an observational analysis of Medicare Advantage star ratings. *Ann Int Med*. 2015;162(5):353–358.

Perez K. ACOs: from unicorns to pacesetters in four years. *Healthc Financial Manag*. 2015;69(5):108–109.

Rakich JS, et al. *Managing Health Services Organizations*. 3rd ed. Baltimore, MD: Health Professions Press; 1992.

Robinson JC. Renewed emphasis on consumer cost sharing in health insurance benefit design. *Health Aff Web Exclusives*. 2002;W139–W154.

Sanofi-Aventis. *Managed Care Digest Series: HMO-PPO Digest, 2014*. Bridgewater, NJ: Sanofi-Aventis US; 2014a.

Sanofi-Aventis. *Managed Care Digest Series: Public Payer Digest, 2014*. Bridgewater, NJ: Sanofi-Aventis US; 2014b.

Sanofi-Aventis. *Managed Care Digest Series: Hospitals/Systems Digest, 2015.* Bridgewater, NJ: Sanofi-Aventis US; 2015.

Schneider EC, et al. Quality of care in for-profit and not-for-profit health plans enrolling Medicare beneficiaries. *Am J Med.* 2005;118(12):1392–1400.

Taitsman J. Medicaid managed-care patients face hurdles in getting care. *Mod Healthc.* 2015;45(1):27.

Wagner ER. Types of managed care organizations. In: Kongstvedt PR, ed. *Essentials of Managed Health Care.* Gaithersburg, MD: Aspen Publishers; 1995:24–34.

Wilson FA, Neuhauser D. *Health Services in the United States.* 2nd ed. Cambridge, MA: Ballinger Publishing; 1985.

Chapter 10

Long-Term Care Services

INTRODUCTION

Long-term care (LTC) services are needed under three main circumstances: (1) Physical or mental deficits that limit a person's ability to do regular daily tasks; hence, creating the need for assistance. (2) Need for continuity of care after hospitalization because of severe illness, injury, or surgical episode. (3) Need for care in specialized environments. For example, elderly patients suffering from Alzheimer's disease or children and adolescents who suffer from birth-related disorders need specialized environments of care delivery. The elderly—people 65 years of age or older—are the primary clients of LTC. Most older adults, however, do not need LTC services. In fact, most elderly persons are physically and mentally healthy enough to live independently. On the other hand, many young adults are victims of debilitating diseases, such as multiple sclerosis, and serious injuries from vehicle crashes, sports mishaps, and industrial accidents. In many cases, these individuals require LTC services.

LTC is delivered in a variety of community-based settings as well as in nursing homes (skilled nursing facilities, subacute care facilities, and specialized care facilities). Hence, the LTC delivery system has two major components: community-based care and institutional care. In addition, most LTC in the United States is provided informally by family and friends, who receive no payment for their time and effort. It is estimated that 92% of community-dwelling elderly/disabled residents receive some sort of unpaid help from family members, relatives, friends, and volunteers (Kaye et al., 2010). Informal caregiver support forestalls institutionalization. Older people who have close access to informal support often continue to live in the community much longer than those who do not have such support.

In 2012, about 58,500 paid, regulated LTC providers served about 8 million people in the United States. The multifaceted LTC industry consisted of 15,700 nursing homes, 22,200 assisted living facilities, 12,200 home health agencies, 4,800 adult day care centers, and 3,700 hospices (Harris-Kojetin et al., 2013). Surveys over time have shown that the vast majority of older Americans wish to stay in their own home indefinitely. Hence, community-based services are preferred by most older people, and these services have grown more rapidly than LTC institutions. According to Kaye and colleagues (2010), compared to noninstitutional LTC populations, those receiving institutional care are older (median age 82 years), are single or widowed, and are more likely to have *cognitive impairment*, that is, a mental disorder indicated by memory and learning issues, ability to concentrate, and making decisions.

Even though most elderly are in good health, the aging process leads to chronic, degenerative conditions that resist cure. This means that as people grow older, the odds increase that they will require LTC. It also means that LTC cannot be an isolated component of the health care delivery system, but rather non-LTC services must be closely integrated with those of LTC. To address the total health care needs of LTC patients, the delivery system must allow ease of transition among various types of health care settings and services.

Chronic conditions are the leading cause of illness, disability, and death in the United States today. *Chronic conditions* are characterized by persistent and recurring health consequences lasting over a long period, which are generally irreversible. Arthritis, diabetes, asthma, heart disease, and dementia are some examples of chronic conditions, but a person's age or the mere presence of a chronic condition does not predict the need for LTC. However, as a person ages, chronic ailments, *comorbidity* (multiple health problems), disability, and

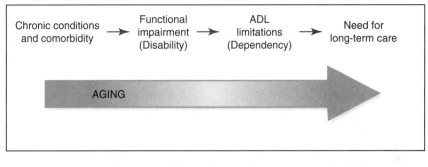

Figure 10.1 Progressive Steps Toward the Need for Long-Term Care Among the Elderly

dependency tend to follow each other, depending on the individual's lifestyle and compliance with medical directives. This progression increases the probability that a person will need LTC (**Figure 10.1**). Approximately one-third of the elderly have functional impairments of one kind or another; among those age 85 and older, two-thirds have functional impairments (Congressional Budget Office—CBO, 2013).

By 2050, 20% of the U.S. population will be elderly, up from 12% in 2000. The number of people age 85 and older will grow the fastest (CBO, 2013). Growth of the elderly population will bring a corresponding surge in the number of elderly people with functional and cognitive limitations. Thus, the need for LTC will increase sharply in coming decades. The rest of the developed world also faces aging-related problems and challenges in providing adequate LTC services very similar to those in the United States. Actually, the elderly population as a proportion of the total population in other developed countries, such as Japan, Germany, France, and Great Britain, is already higher than it is in the United States.

WHAT IS LTC?

LTC can be defined as a variety of individualized, well-coordinated services that promote the maximum possible independence for people with functional limitations and are provided over an extended period of time in accordance with a holistic approach, while maximizing their quality of life. The seven essential characteristics of LTC are summarized in **Exhibit 10.1** and are explained in this section.

Exhibit 10.1   Seven Essential Characteristics of Long-Term Care

- It includes a variety of health care services.
- Services are individualized.
- Services must be well coordinated.
- The goal is to promote maximum possible functional independence.
- Services are needed over an extended period of time.
- Patients' physical, mental, social, and spiritual needs must be met.
- Patients' quality of life must be maximized.

A Variety of Health Care Services

LTC clients need a variety of services for two main reasons:

- A variety of services is necessary because the need for services varies greatly from individual to individual. Even the elderly, who are the predominant users of LTC services, are not a homogeneous group. For example, some people just require supportive housing, whereas others require intensive treatments. Hence, LTC includes services such as housing programs, transportation, case management, recreation, nutrition, nursing, medical care, and social services.

- Even for the same individual, the need for the various types of services generally changes over time. Such change is not necessarily progressive, developing from lighter to more intensive levels of care. Depending on the change in condition and functioning, the individual may shift back and forth between the various levels and types of LTC services. For example, after hip surgery, a patient may require extensive rehabilitation therapy in a nursing facility for 2 or 3 weeks before returning home, where he or she receives continuing care from a home health agency. After that, the individual may continue to live independently but require a daily meal from Meals on Wheels. Later, this same person may suffer a stroke and after hospitalization have to stay indefinitely in an LTC facility.

LTC clients often require non-LTC services, such as primary care and acute care. Hence, LTC is not a self-contained system of comprehensive health care services, nor can it function independently of primary, acute, mental health, and ancillary services such as pharmaceuticals and diagnostics. LTC must also include both therapeutic and preventive services. The primary goal of preventive services is to prevent or delay the need for institutionalization in LTC facilities. Preventive measures call for ensuring that the elderly receive good nutrition and have access to preventive medical care. For example, older adults must have access to services such as vaccination against pneumonia, annual flu shots, glaucoma screening, diabetes screening, and cancer screening.

For those elderly persons who live independently, certain social support programs also serve a preventive function. Programs such as homemaker, chore, and handyman services can assist with a variety of tasks that older adults may no longer be able to perform. Examples include shopping, light cleaning, general errands, lawn maintenance, and minor home repairs.

Individualized Services

An assessment of the patient's physical, mental, and emotional condition and past medical and social history, former occupation, leisure activities, and cultural factors is used to determine which services would be most suitable for the individual. An individualized plan of care is developed, and services are rendered according to that plan.

Coordination of Services

The mere availability of a spectrum of services may not be sufficient to meet the varied and changing needs of LTC clients unless those services are well coordinated. As it is, many people find the health care delivery system difficult to navigate. Such difficulties are often compounded in the case of elderly and disabled individuals. For example, acute episodes, such as pneumonia, bone fracture, or stroke, require admission to a general hospital. Many acute care services are now delivered in a variety of outpatient settings instead of hospitals. After acute care delivery, a patient may be transferred to a hospital-based transitional care unit for intensive rehabilitation. The patient may subsequently have to be moved to an LTC facility for ongoing care. Depression may create a need to visit an outpatient mental health clinic. The same individual may also require dental or optometric care.

Maximum Possible Functional Independence

Two standard measures are used to determine a person's level of dependency. The first one is the activities of daily living (ADL) scale, which is used to assess a person's ability to perform certain common tasks referred to as *activities of daily living* (see **Exhibit 10.2**). Severe ADL limitations often indicate the need for institutional care. The second measure is the *instrumental activities of daily living* (IADL) scale. It incorporates activities that are necessary for living independently in the community, such as using the telephone, driving a car or traveling alone by bus or taxi, shopping, preparing meals, doing light housework, taking medicine, and handling money. IADLs are not generally used in institutional settings because institutionalized persons are not required to perform many IADLs (Ostir et al., 1999). The probability of having limitations in ADLs and IADLs increases significantly with age. The age-related progression of LTC intensity is illustrated in **Exhibit 10.3**.

The main goal of LTC is to enable the individual to maintain functional independence to the maximum level that is practicable. In many instances, a person's functional status can be improved by the use of adaptive devices, such as walkers, wheelchairs, special utensils, and many other types of equipment and modification of the living environment with safety features such as grab bars. However, as dependency increases, the need for LTC services also increases (see Figure 10.1).

Restoration of function may be possible to some extent through appropriate rehabilitation therapy, but in most cases a full restoration of normal functioning is an unrealistic expectation. Caregivers must render care and assistance wherever the patient is either unable to do things for himself or herself or absolutely

Exhibit 10.2   Activities of Daily Living

The classic ADL scale includes six basic activities:
• Eating
• Bathing
• Dressing
• Using a toilet
• Maintaining bowel and bladder control
• Transferring, such as getting out of bed and moving into a chair
Sometimes grooming and walking a distance of 8 feet are also included in the scale.

Exhibit 10.3   Age-Related Progression of Long-Term Care Intensity

- Independent living
- Decline in IADLs
  - Informal care for those who have adequate social support
  - Informal care supplemented by paid community-based services
- Decline in ADLs
  - For light ADLs (eating, dressing, using a toilet), informal care with supplemental services may continue
  - Institutionalization

refuses to do so. The focus should be on maintaining whatever functional ability the patient still has and on preventing further decline of that ability. Caregivers should motivate and help patients do as much as possible for themselves.

Extended Period of Time

Compared to acute care, LTC is sustained over a longer period of time. The period of care and institutional stays, when needed, generally extends to weeks, months, and years instead of days. Even when institutional LTC is indicated for a short period (90 or fewer days), LTC services may continue in the patient's own home after the patient has been discharged from a long-term care facility. At other times, long-range confinement to a nursing home may be necessary.

Holistic Approach

The holistic model of health focuses not merely on a person's physical and mental needs but also emphasizes well-being in every aspect of what makes a person whole and complete. A patient's physical, mental, social, and spiritual needs and preferences are incorporated into medical care delivery and the living environment. The following are brief descriptions of the four aspects of holistic caregiving:

1. *Physical.* The physical aspect refers to the technical aspects of care, such as medical examination, nursing care, medications, diet, and rehabilitation treatments. It also includes comfort factors such as appropriate temperature and cozy furnishings, cleanliness, and safety in home and institutional environments.

2. *Mental.* The emphasis with mental care is on the total mental and emotional well-being of each individual. Such care may include treatment of mental and behavioral problems, if necessary. Maintaining mental health goes beyond diagnosis and treatment of mental conditions, however. In an institutional setting, it includes appropriate layout, décor, and techniques that help overcome disorientation and confusion; mental stimulation to help overcome boredom and depression; and an environment that promotes positive feelings. For example, the living atmosphere can be enhanced through live plants, flowers, moving water, pleasant aromas, and soothing music. Pet animals, fish in aquariums, and birds create a vibrant living environment.

3. *Social.* Almost everyone enjoys warm friendships and social relationships. Visits from family, friends, or volunteers provide numerous opportunities for socializing. Many nursing homes have created indoor and outdoor spaces such as game rooms, alcoves, balconies, and patios where people can sit and enjoy one another's company.

4. *Spiritual.* The spiritual dimension operates at an individual level. It includes personal beliefs, values, and commitments in a religious and faith context. Spirituality and spiritual pursuits are very personal matters, but for most people, they also require continuing interaction with other members of their faith community.

Quality of Life

Quality of life refers to the total living experience that results in overall satisfaction with one's life. It is particularly relevant to LTC facilities because people typically reside there for an extended period. Quality of life factors include lifestyle pursuits, living environment, clinical palliation, human factors, and personal choices, as discussed here:

- Lifestyle factors are associated with personal enrichment and making one's life meaningful through enjoyable activities. For example, many older people still enjoy pursuing their former leisure activities, such as woodworking, crocheting, knitting, gardening, and fishing.

- The living environment must be comfortable, safe, and appealing to the senses. Cleanliness, décor, furnishings, and other aesthetic features are important.

- Clinical *palliation* should be available to provide relief from unpleasant symptoms such as pain or nausea, for instance, when a patient is undergoing chemotherapy.

- Human factors refer to caregiver attitudes and practices that emphasize caring, compassion, and the preservation of human dignity for the patient.

- Institutionalized patients generally find it disconcerting to have lost their autonomy and independence. Quality of life is enhanced when residents have some latitude to govern their own lives and make personal choices regarding food and daily routines. Residents in long-term care facilities also desire an environment that gives them adequate privacy.

COMMUNITY-BASED LONG-TERM CARE SERVICES

Community-based LTC services have four objectives: (1) to deliver LTC in the most economical and least restrictive setting whenever appropriate for the patient's health care needs, (2) to supplement informal caregiving when more advanced skills are needed to address the patient's needs, (3) to provide temporary respite to family members from caregiving stress, and (4) to delay or prevent institutionalization. These goals are accomplished through an administrative network that includes the Federal Administration on Aging, State Units on Aging, and Area Agencies on Aging. Nationally, more than 600 Area Agencies on Aging administer funds appropriated by the U.S. federal government under the Older Americans Act of 1965.

For the financially needy, Title III of the Older Americans Act may finance such community-based services as adult day care (ADC), home maintenance, health promotion and disease prevention (e.g., medication management, nutrition, and health screening), telephone reassurance, and transportation services. States may also have some federal funds available under Title XX Social Services Block Grants. In addition, community-based LTC services have grown under the Home and Community Based Services waiver program that was enacted under Section 1915(c) of the Social Security Act. Medicare and Medicaid may partially cover certain LTC services; the remainder must be covered by individual savings and private donations.

Home Health Care

Home health care refers to health care provided in the home of the patient by health care professionals. The organizational setup commonly requires a hospital-based or freestanding home health agency that sends health care professionals and paraprofessionals (such as home care aides) to patients' homes to deliver services approved by a physician.

Home health services typically include nursing care, such as changing dressings, monitoring medications, and providing help with bathing; short-term rehabilitation, such as physical, occupational, and speech therapy; homemaker services, such as meal preparation, shopping, transportation, and some specific household chores; and certain medical supplies and equipment, such as ostomy supplies, hospital beds, oxygen tanks, walkers, and wheelchairs. Not all home health agencies provide all of these services, however.

As the largest single payer for home health services, Medicare paid for 43% of home health expenditures in the United States in 2013 (National Center for Health Statistics—NCHS, 2015). To qualify for home care under the Medicare program, patients must (1) be homebound, (2) have a plan of treatment that is periodically reviewed by a physician, and (3) require intermittent or part-time skilled nursing and/or rehabilitation therapies.

Under Medicaid, states have several different options available to deliver home health services. In essence, states can develop programs to deliver services to Medicaid beneficiaries if these people would otherwise end up in an institution. In 2011, Medicaid paid for almost 37% of home health expenditures (NCHS, 2015).

Adult Day Care

Adult day care is a daytime, community-based, group program that is designed to meet the needs of functionally and/or cognitively impaired adults and to provide a partial respite to family caregivers. Such care is designed for people who live with their families but because of physical or mental conditions cannot remain alone during the day when the family members are working.

Most ADC services are highly focused on prevention and health maintenance, with the objective of preventing or delaying institutionalization, but they also incorporate nursing care, psychosocial therapies, and rehabilitation. As such, ADC services, in many instances, have become alternatives to home health care and assisted living and as a transitional step before placement in a long-term care institution. Nearly half of the participants have dementia, and 50% of ADC centers offer specialized programs for these patients (MetLife Mature Market Institute, 2010).

Adult Foster Care

Adult foster care is defined as a service characterized by small, family-run homes providing room, board, oversight, and personal care to nonrelated adults who are unable to care for themselves (AARP Studies Adult Foster Care, 1996). Foster care generally provides services in a community-based dwelling in an environment that promotes the feeling of being part of a family unit (Stahl, 1997). Participants in these programs are elderly or disabled individuals who require assistance with one or two ADLs, and many of the residents have a psychiatric diagnosis.

Typically, the caregiving family resides in part of the home. To maintain the family environment, most states license fewer than 10 beds per family unit. Each state has established its own standards for licensing foster care homes. As states have continued to shift Medicaid funds from institutional to community-based services, adult foster care use has grown. Medicare does not pay for services provided by the adult foster care home but may cover rehabilitation services.

Senior Centers

Senior centers are local community centers for older adults where seniors can congregate and socialize. Many centers serve a noon meal daily. Others sponsor wellness programs, health education, counseling services, recreational activities, information and referral, and some limited health care services. Health care services typically offered at senior centers include health screening, especially for glaucoma and hypertension.

Approximately 11,000 senior centers have been established across the United States, serving 1 million older adults every day. To maintain operations, senior centers rely on a variety of public and private sources of funding from various branches of government, businesses, donations, and volunteer hours (National Council on Aging, 2015).

Home-Delivered and Congregate Meals

The Elderly Nutrition Program operates under the U.S. Administration on Aging and serves congregate meals in senior centers and home-delivered meals, referred to as Meals on Wheels, to homebound elderly persons 60 years of age and older. The main goal of this program is to improve the dietary intake of older Americans. The program generally provides one hot noon meal for 5 days a week.

In the Meals on Wheels program, meals are prepared by local institutions and delivered by volunteers. The volunteers also offer an important opportunity to check on the welfare of homebound elderly and are encouraged to report any health or other problems that they may notice during their visits.

Homemaker and Handyman Services

Some older adults are relatively healthy but cannot carry out a few simple tasks necessary for independent living. These tasks may be as urgent as repairing a burst plumbing pipe or as mundane as cleaning the house. Some tasks, such as grocery shopping, must be performed often, whereas others, such as replacing storm windows, require attention just once or twice a year. Homemaker, household chore, and handyman services can assist older adults with a variety of such tasks, including shopping, light cleaning, general errands, and minor home repairs. Homemaker programs may be staffed largely or entirely by volunteers.

Emergency Response Systems

A personal emergency response system, also called a medical emergency response system, consists of an electronic device that enables people to summon help in an emergency. This kind of system is specifically designed for disabled or elderly people who live alone and may not otherwise need ongoing medical or supportive care. Other patients, after returning home from hospitals and nursing homes, are plagued by anxiety about relapses or accidents because they are often unprepared for self-management after returning home. Usually they either wear or carry a transmitter unit that enables them to send a medical alert to a 24-hour monitoring and response center. The system is available for a reasonable fee.

Case Management

In the LTC context, *case management* refers to a method of linking, managing, and coordinating services to meet the varied and changing health care needs of elderly clients (Zawadski & Eng, 1988). Case management services assess the special needs of older adults, formulate a care plan to address those needs, identify which services are most appropriate, determine eligibility for services, make referrals and coordinate delivery of care, arrange for financing, and ensure that clients are receiving services in accordance with the plan of care. Case managers often assist the adult children of disabled elderly persons who may be living far from each other.

INSTITUTIONAL LONG-TERM CARE

Generally, institutional LTC is more appropriate for patients whose needs cannot be adequately met in a less clinical, community-based setting. However, a variety of institutional options are available to meet the varying needs of the elderly who no longer can live alone safely. Available options today include retirement centers, residential or personal care facilities, assisted living facilities, and nursing homes. These facilities provide varying levels of assistance.

An evaluation of the extent of functional impairment often determines which services are best suited to the individual, but personal preferences, and often the availability of financing, also play a significant role. Because people generally prefer to receive care in their own home, when institutionalization becomes necessary, they prefer a homelike, nonclinical setting. Nevertheless, medical needs must often override personal preferences, especially when severe physical or mental problems develop. **Figure 10.2** illustrates, on a continuum, six types of elder care institutions that can be classified under three general categories: retirement homes, personal care homes, and nursing homes. Continuing-care retirement communities (CCRCs) offer all three options within one campus-like setting. Based on the concept of aging-in-place, CCRCs can address people's changing needs.

Retirement Facilities

Retirement facilities do not deliver nursing care services but emphasize privacy, security, independence, and active lifestyles. Some basic personal care such as assistance with bathing may be available in some retirement facilities, but in most instances, when additional nursing or rehabilitation services are needed, arrangements are made with a local home health agency.

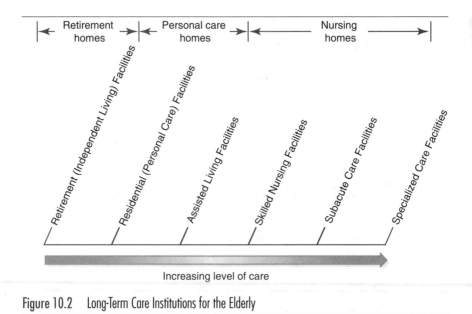

Figure 10.2   Long-Term Care Institutions for the Elderly

The special features and amenities in retirement facilities are designed to create a physically supportive environment that promotes independence. For example, the living quarters are equipped with emergency call systems. Many facilities provide monthly blood pressure and vision screenings. Most organize programs for socializing, physical fitness, recreation, and local outings for shopping and entertainment. Some basic hotel services, such as one meal a day and periodic housekeeping, are generally provided. Apartment units or detached cottages equipped with kitchenettes and private baths are the most common types of retirement facilities. Common laundry rooms are often shared with other residents. Many upscale retirement centers abound, in which one can expect to pay a fairly substantial entrance fee plus a monthly rental or maintenance fee. At the other end of the income scale, many communities have government-subsidized housing units for the low-income elderly and disabled individuals.

Personal Care Facilities

Personal care can be defined as nonmedical custodial care. *Custodial care* is confined to basic assistance provided in a protected environment and does not include active medical or rehabilitative treatments.

Facilities providing personal care may be called by different names, such as domiciliary care facilities, board-and-care homes, foster care homes, residential care facilities, or personal care facilities. These facilities provide physically supportive dwelling units, monitoring and/or assistance with medications, oversight, and light assistance with certain ADLs such as bathing and grooming. To maintain a residential rather than an institutional environment, many such facilities limit the admission of residents who use wheelchairs. Most of these facilities are relatively small and can be viewed as community-based alternatives rather than institutions. Staff members are mostly nursing paraprofessionals, such as personal care aides, who do not require a license or professional certification to deliver care. Similar workers employed in nursing homes must be certified by the state.

Assisted Living Facilities

An assisted living facility provides personal care, 24-hour supervision, social activities, recreational activities, and some nursing and rehabilitation services. The most common areas of assistance with ADLs are bathing, dressing, and toileting. These facilities maintain a skeleton staff of licensed nurses, generally licensed practical nurses (referred to as licensed vocational nurses in some states), to do admission assessments and deliver basic nursing care and medication management. Hence, these facilities can be classified on the LTC continuum somewhere between personal care homes and nursing homes. Advanced nursing care and rehabilitation therapies can be arranged through a home health agency. Approximately 59% of the residents eventually move into a skilled nursing facility and one-third pass away (National Center for Assisted Living, 2013).

Skilled Nursing Facilities

A skilled nursing facility is a typical nursing home that provides a full range of clinical LTC services, from skilled nursing care to rehabilitation to assistance with all ADLs. *Skilled nursing care* is medically oriented care provided by a licensed nurse. The plan of treatment is authorized by a physician. The majority of direct care with ADLs is delivered by paraprofessionals, such as certified nursing assistants and therapy assistants, but under the supervision of licensed nurses and therapists.

A variety of disabilities, including problems with ambulation, incontinence, and behavior, often coexist among a relatively large number of patients in need of skilled care. Compared to other types of facilities, these nursing homes have a significant number of patients who are cognitively impaired because of confusion, delirium, or dementia. The social functioning of many of the patients in such facilities is also in severe decline.

Licensed professionals who work in skilled care facilities include registered nurses (RNs), licensed practical/vocational nurses, and registered therapists (physical therapists, occupational therapists, respiratory therapists, and speech/language pathologists). Rehabilitation is often an important component of skilled care, as are therapeutic diets and nutritional supplements. The patient's assessment requires multidisciplinary input from various health care professionals, and the plan of care is highly individualized.

Subacute Care Facilities

Subacute care is a blend of intensive medical, nursing, and other services that are technically complex and provided in an LTC setting. Examples include complex wound care, intravenous therapy, blood transfusion, ventilator support, and AIDS care. Subacute care is a substitute for services that were previously provided in acute care hospitals; its popularity has grown because it is a cheaper alternative to a hospital stay.

Subacute care generally follows hospitalization and is required for a relatively short period of time, such as between 20 and 90 days. Services are available in three main settings:

1. Long-term care hospitals (LTCHs), according to federal regulations, must be certified as acute care hospitals and must have an average length of stay greater than 25 days.
2. Many skilled nursing facilities have opened subacute care units by raising the staff skill mix by hiring additional RNs and having therapists on staff.
3. Some subacute-type services are rendered by community-based home health agencies. Thanks to new technology, certain subacute services can be provided in a patient's own home.

Specialized Care Facilities

By their very nature, both subacute care and specialized care place high emphasis on medical and nursing services. Some skilled nursing facilities have opened specialized care units for patients requiring ventilator care, wound care, services for Alzheimer's disease, intensive rehabilitation, or closed head trauma care. Other freestanding facilities have chosen a niche, specializing only in Alzheimer's care, rehabilitation, or AIDS care.

LICENSING AND CERTIFICATION OF NURSING HOMES

Nursing homes are heavily regulated through licensure and certification requirements. In the United States, it is illegal to operate a nursing facility without a license. To serve Medicare and/or Medicaid beneficiaries, a facility must be certified by the federal government.

Licensing

Every state requires nursing homes to be licensed by the state. Annual renewal of a license is required for existing nursing homes. To keep their licenses in good standing, it is essential that facilities comply with the state's standards for nursing homes. These standards vary from state to state, except for national fire safety regulations. The Life Safety Code, published by the National Fire Protection Association, encompasses national building and fire safety rules that have become a part of licensure standards. In addition, each state has crafted basic standards for nursing care and other services. Compliance with standards is verified through periodic inspections, generally once a year. A state's department (board or division) of health or department of human services generally has nursing home licensing and oversight responsibilities.

Certification

The Centers for Medicare and Medicaid Services (CMS), an agency of the U.S. Department of Health and Human Services, is responsible for certifying a nursing home that wants to serve Medicaid and/or Medicare clients. To be certified, a nursing home must first be licensed by the state. Thus, licensure and certification serve different purposes. A license allows a facility to operate and do business, whereas certification allows a nursing home to admit patients who are on public assistance. It is possible for a facility to have only a license, but in that case, it cannot receive payments from Medicaid or Medicare.

Three distinct federal certification categories exist, and facilities in all three categories are generically referred to as nursing homes:

1. SNF certification allows a facility to admit patients whose care is financed by Medicare; Medicare pays for postacute skilled care only after a patient has stayed in a hospital for a minimum of 3 days, not counting the day of discharge. The maximum coverage in an SNF-certified facility is 100 days, but in actual practice the average length of stay is much shorter. This is due to complex Medicare rules that the facility must follow to determine the length of stay. Also, Medicare pays the full cost of skilled nursing care only for the first 20 days; the beneficiary must pay a substantial copayment ($157.50 per day in 2015) for days 21 through 100.

2. NF certification allows a facility to admit patients whose care is financed by Medicaid. Unlike Medicare, Medicaid allows patients to stay in an NF-certified nursing home indefinitely as long as the patient's physician authorizes the need for nursing care and the patient qualifies for Medicaid assistance. The beneficiary is required to turn over most of his or her monthly income to the facility; Medicaid pays the remaining costs. Many patients are initially admitted to a facility with a private-pay source of funding. When their private funds are exhausted, these patients generally become eligible for Medicaid assistance.

3. Intermediate Care Facility for Individuals with Intellectual Disabilities (ICF/IID)—previously called Intermediate Care Facility for the Mentally Retarded (ICF/MR)—certification allows a nursing facility to serve patients who are intellectually/developmentally disabled, also referred to as mentally retarded/developmentally disabled. *Developmental disability* is a physical incapacity that generally accompanies below-average intellectual functioning and often arises at birth or in early childhood. ICF/IIDs provide specialized programming and care modules for patients suffering from mental retardation and associated disabilities. The reimbursement is derived mostly from Medicaid.

Certification is granted on the basis of compliance with federal standards. The same standards apply to both SNF and NF certifications, but different standards apply to ICF/IID certification. A facility may be dually certified as both an SNF and an NF. Facilities having dual certification can admit Medicare and/or Medicaid patients to any part of the facility.

The small number of facilities that have elected not to be certified can admit only those patients who have a private source of funding for nursing home care. Such private-pay patients—those not covered by either Medicare or Medicaid for long-term nursing home care—are not restricted to noncertified facilities, however. In most certified nursing homes, private-pay patients are placed alongside those who depend on Medicare and Medicaid.

OTHER LONG-TERM CARE SERVICES

Respite Care

Family caregivers often experience physical and emotional problems. Caregiving responsibilities can ignite family conflicts and encroach on caregivers' employment and leisure activities. Under these circumstances, many caregivers experience stress and burnout. *Respite care* enables family caregivers to take some time off to deal with their feelings of stress and frustration. Virtually any kind of LTC service—adult day care, home health care, and temporary institutionalization—can be viewed as respite care as long as the focus is on giving informal caregivers some time off while meeting disabled persons' needs for assistance (Doty et al., 1996).

Restorative Care

Restorative care refers to therapeutic interventions designed to help patients regain or improve function. Restorative rehabilitation involves intensive short-term treatments rendered by physical therapists, occupational therapists, and speech/language pathologists. Examples of persons requiring rehabilitation therapy include individuals who have experienced orthopedic surgery, stroke, limb amputation, and prolonged illness. *Maintenance rehabilitation* has the goal of preserving the present level of function and prevent further decline. *Adaptive rehabilitation* improves function despite deficits that remain. Examples include adaptive equipment and training for their proper use, splints that can help a person use his or her arms to perform certain ADLs, and braces or orthotics to support the knee or foot so a person can ambulate safely.

Hospice Care

Approaches to terminal illness and death with the objective of maintaining the patient's dignity and comfort have received increased attention in the delivery of health care. Almost three-fourths of all deaths occur among those of age 65 and older. The common causes of death among the elderly are heart disease, cancer, chronic respiratory disease, stroke, and Alzheimer's disease (Murphy et al., 2013). Hence, dealing with death and dying is very much a part of LTC.

End-of-life care is commonly associated with *hospice*, a cluster of comprehensive services for terminally ill persons who have a life expectancy of 6 months or less. Hospice is a method of care, not a location, although some freestanding hospice facilities have been established. Hospice can be a part of home health care when the services are provided in the patient's home. In other instances, hospice services are taken to patients in nursing homes, retirement centers, or hospitals.

THE AFFORDABLE CARE ACT AND LONG-TERM CARE

The main implications of the ACA for long-term care services are as follows:

1. States have the option to provide home- and community-based attendant services under a program called Community First Choice through an increase in Medicaid federal matching payments.
2. The Elder Justice Act of 2010 was incorporated into the ACA to counter elder abuse, neglect, and exploitation. Nursing facilities that receive federal payments must comply with certain reporting and notification requirements.
3. All certified nursing facilities must comply with a Quality Assurance Performance Improvement (QAPI) requirement with the objective of preventing or decreasing the likelihood of quality problems.

NURSING HOME INDUSTRY AND EXPENDITURES

During the past several years, the number of nursing homes, bed capacity, number of residents in U.S. nursing homes, and occupancy rates have continued to decline (**Table 10.1**). This downward trend largely reflects the growth of community-based LTC alternatives and other institutional

Table 10.1 Nursing Home Trends (Selected Years)

	2000	2010	2013
Number of nursing homes	16,886	15,690	15,663
Number of beds	1,795,388	1,703,398	1,697,484
Average beds per nursing home	106.3	108.6	108.4
Number of residents	1,480,076	1,396,473	1,371,926
Occupancy rate*	82.4%	82.0%	80.8%

*Percentage of beds occupied (number of residents per 100 beds). These data do not include long-term care facilities that are not classified as nursing homes (**Figure 10.2**).
Data from National Center for Health Statistics. Health, United States, 2007 (pp. 370–371); Health, United States, 2012 (pp. 317–318); Health, United States, 2014 (pp. 300–301).

options and government policies that incentivize the use of community-based care. The need for various types of LTC services will continue to increase given a growing population with chronic conditions, comorbidities, and subsequent disability, but with increased life span.

The nursing home industry in the United States is dominated by private, for-profit nursing home chains. In 2012, 68% of the nursing homes had for-profit ownership; 25% were operated by private nonprofit entities. Only 7% were government owned, and most of these are owned and operated by local counties. Of all nursing homes, 97% were certified for Medicare, and among them 95% were also certified for Medicaid. Among nursing home residents, 85% were elderly, 68% were female, and almost half had a diagnosis of Alzheimer's disease or other dementias (Harris-Kojetin et al., 2013).

Nursing home expenditures are shown in **Table 10.2**. Over time, the share of U.S. nursing home expenditures has shifted from government to private sources and from Medicaid to Medicare. Although out-of-pocket payments constitute a substantial source of financing for nursing home care, Medicaid still remains the largest single source of financing. Medicare pays for eligible beneficiaries under Part A, but the coverage is for a short duration, representing mostly postacute care after discharge from a hospital. Only 8% of nursing home services are paid through

Table 10.2 Sources of National Nursing Home Expenditures for Nonhospital-Based Facilities, 2013

	Billions of Dollars	Percent
Total expenditures	155.8	
Medicare	34.6	22.2
Medicaid	46.9	30.1
Veterans Administration and Department of Defense	4.5	2.9
Total public sources		**55%**
Out of pocket	45.8	29.4
Private health insurance	12.6	8.1
Total private sources		**38%**
Other sources	**11.5**	**7.4%**

Data from National Center for Health Statistics. Health, United States, 2014: With Special Feature on Adults Aged 55–64. Hyattsville, MD. 2015. (p. 307).

private insurance. In 2009, only 7 million Americans (7% of those over age 50) had private LTC insurance coverage (National Health Policy Forum, 2011). Insurance premiums are generally expensive; hence, few people purchase LTC insurance.

CONCLUSION

LTC should be viewed not as an isolated component of the health care delivery system, but rather as a continuum of both community-based and institution-based services that are rationally linked to the rest of the health care delivery system. LTC includes medical care, social services, and housing alternatives. Hence, it involves a range of services that can vary according to individual needs. Chronic conditions and comorbidities can lead to physical and/or mental disability, which in turn may impair the performance of ADLs and IADLs. LTC services often complement what people with impaired functioning can do for themselves. Informal caregivers provide the bulk of these services. Respite care can provide family members temporary relief from the burden of caregiving. When the required intensity of care exceeds the capabilities of informal caregivers, available alternatives include professional community-based services to supplement informal care or admission to a long-term care facility. Services offered at these facilities range from basic personal assistance to more complex skilled nursing care and subacute care. Specialized facilities caring for patients with Alzheimer's disease, AIDS, intellectual/developmental disabilities, or head trauma have also proliferated. Some LTC patients require long-range custodial care without the prognosis of a cure; others may require short-term postacute convalescence and therapy. Still others may need end-of-life care through a hospice program. With the aging of the baby boom population, both demand and supply for LTC services are expected to grow at a rapid rate in the future. With rising costs, however, a greater emphasis is being placed on community-based services compared to nursing home care.

REFERENCES

AARP studies adult foster care for the elderly. *Public Health Rep.* 1996;111(4):295.

Congressional Budget Office (CBO). *Rising Demand for Long-Term Services and Supports for Elderly People.* Washington, DC: Congressional Budget Office; 2013.

Doty P, et al. Informal caregiving. In: Evashwick CJ, ed. *The Continuum of Long-Term Care: An Integrated Systems Approach.* Albany, NY: Delmar Publishers; 1996:125–141.

Harris-Kojetin L, et al. *Long-Term Care Services in the United States: 2013 Overview.* Hyattsville, MD: National Center for Health Statistics; 2013.

Kaye HS, et al. Long-term care: who gets it, who provides it, who pays, and how much? *Health Aff.* 2010;29(1):11–21.

MetLife Mature Market Institute. *The MetLife National Study of Adult Day Services.* Westport, CT: Metropolitan Life Insurance Company; 2010.

Murphy SL, et al. Deaths: final data for 2010. *Natl Vital Stat Rep.* 2013;61(4). Hyattsville, MD: National Center for Health Statistics.

National Center for Assisted Living. Resident profile. http://www.ahcancal.org/ncal/resources/Pages/ResidentProfile.aspx. Published 2013. Accessed August 16, 2015.

National Center for Health Statistics (NCHS). *Health, United States, 2014.* Hyattsville, MD: U.S. Department of Health and Human Services; 2015.

National Council on Aging. Fact sheet: senior centers. http://www.ncoa.org/assets/files/pdf/FactSheet_SeniorCenters.pdf. Published 2015. Accessed June 2015.

National Health Policy Forum. Private long-term care insurance: where is the market heading? *Forum Session,* April 15, 2011. Washington, DC: George Washington University; 2011.

Ostir GV, et al. Disability in older adults 1: prevalence, causes, and consequences. *Behav Med.* 1999;24(4):147–156.

Stahl C. Adult foster care: an alternative to SNFs? *ADV Occup Ther.* September 29, 1997.

Zawadski RT, Eng C. Case management in capitated long-term care. *Health Care Financing Rev Ann Suppl.* December 1988:75–81.

Chapter 11

Populations with Special Health Needs

INTRODUCTION

Certain population groups in the United States either face greater barriers than the general population in accessing timely and needed health care services or they have special health-related issues that may go unaddressed. These populations face greater risk of poor physical, psychological, and social health (Aday, 1994). These populations may be referred to as underserved populations, medically underserved, medically disadvantaged, underprivileged, and American underclasses. The causes of their vulnerability are largely attributable to unequal social, economic, health, and geographic conditions. These population groups encompass racial and ethnic minorities, uninsured women and children, persons living in rural areas, the homeless, the mentally ill, the chronically ill and disabled, and individuals with human immunodeficiency virus/acquired immunodeficiency syndrome (HIV/AIDS). This chapter defines these population groups, describes their health needs, and summarizes the major challenges that they typically face in the United States.

FRAMEWORK TO STUDY VULNERABLE POPULATIONS

The vulnerability model (see **Figure 11.1**) is an integrated approach to studying vulnerability. *Vulnerability* denotes susceptibility to negative events that result in poor health or illness. Poor health can be manifested physically, psychologically, and socially. Health needs are greater for those individuals who experience problems along multiple dimensions, because poor health along one dimension is often compounded by poor health along others. Vulnerability does not represent a personal deficiency inherent to certain populations, but rather the effects of interactions between multiple factors over which individuals may have little or no control (Aday, 1999).

Vulnerability is determined by a convergence of (1) predisposing, (2) enabling, and (3) need characteristics at both individual and ecological (contextual) levels (**Exhibit 11.1**). Not only do these predisposing, enabling, and need characteristics converge and determine individuals' access to health care, but they also ultimately influence individuals' risk of contracting illness or recovering from an existing illness. Individuals

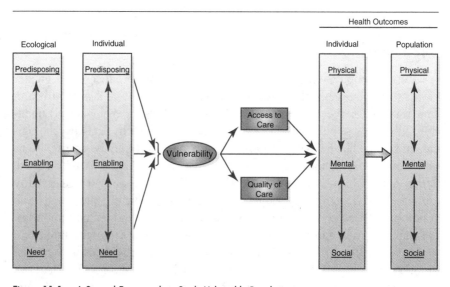

Figure 11.1   A General Framework to Study Vulnerable Populations

Exhibit 11.1 Predisposing, Enabling, and Need Characteristics of Vulnerability

• **Predisposing characteristics**   • **Need characteristics**

* **Predisposing characteristics**
  * Racial/ethnic characteristics
  * Gender and age (women and children)
  * Geographic location (rural health)
* **Enabling characteristics**
  * Insurance status (uninsured)
  * Homelessness
* **Need characteristics**
  * Mental health
  * Chronic illness/disability
  * HIV/AIDS

with multiple risks (i.e., a combination of two or more vulnerability traits) typically experience worse access to care, care of lesser quality, and inferior health status than those with fewer vulnerability traits.

Understanding vulnerability as a combination or convergence of disparate factors is preferred over studying individual factors separately, because vulnerability, when defined as a convergence of risks, best captures reality. Furthermore, this approach reflects the co-occurrence of risk factors and underscores the belief that it is difficult to address disparities in one risk factor without addressing others.

The vulnerability model presented here has a number of distinctive characteristics. First, it is a comprehensive model, including both individual and ecological attributes of risk. Second, it is a general model, focusing on the attributes of vulnerability for the total population rather than vulnerable traits of subpopulations. Although there are certainly individual differences in exposure to risks, a number of common, crosscutting traits affect all vulnerable populations. Third, the model emphasizes the effects of experiencing multiple vulnerability traits that have cumulative consequences.

PREDISPOSING CHARACTERISTICS

Attributes that predispose individuals to vulnerability include demographic characteristics, belief systems, and social structure variables. These attributes are associated with social position, access to resources, health behaviors, and variations in health status. Individuals have relatively little control over predisposing attributes. These attributes may lead to discrimination. Discrimination may be on account of race, gender, financial status, or sexual preference, for example. The following subsections discuss some of these predisposing characteristics, including race and ethnicity, gender, age, and geographic distribution.

Racial/Ethnic Minorities

The main categories for race recognized by the U.S. Census Bureau are white, black or African American, Hispanic or Latino, American Indian or Alaska Native, Asian, Native Hawaiian or other Pacific Islander, and a nondescript category called "some other race." *Asian* refers to persons originating from the Far East, Southeast Asia, or the Indian subcontinent, including those from Cambodia, China, India, Japan, Korea, Malaysia, Pakistan, the Philippine Islands, Thailand, and Vietnam. *Native Hawaiians or other Pacific Islanders* include persons originating from Hawaii, Guam, Samoa, or other Pacific Islands. *American Indian or Alaska Natives* include persons originating from North and South America (including Central America) who maintain tribal affiliation or community attachment. Nearly 30% of the U.S. population is made up of minorities: black or African American (12.3%), Hispanics or Latinos (16.3%), Asians (4.4%), Native Hawaiian and other Pacific Islanders (0.1%), American Indian and Alaska Natives (0.9%), or some other race (5.5%). In addition, 2.4% of the U.S. population identify themselves as being of two or more races (Mackun & Wilson, 2011).

Significant differences exist across the various racial/ethnic groups on health. Minority race and ethnicity often serve as a proxy for other factors such as socioeconomic status, language ability, or cultural behaviors that are correlated with health status and health care experiences. The available evidence suggests that racial/ethnic minorities generally have poorer access to health care, receive poorer quality care, and experience worse health outcomes (see **Exhibit 11.2**).

One of the most consistent findings across decades of research is that minorities have poor access to health services compared with their white counterparts, even after taking into account insurance, socioeconomic, and health status. A variety of studies have documented that minority Americans experience higher rates of illness and mortality than white Americans. Disparities in health exist between white and nonwhite

Exhibit 11.2 Racial and Ethnic Disparities

Black Americans
- More likely than whites to be economically disadvantaged.
- Shorter life expectancies than whites.
- Higher age-adjusted death rates for leading causes of death.
- Higher rates of premature death (death before age 75 years) from stroke and coronary heart disease than whites (CDC, 2013).
- More than double the infant mortality rate compared to non-Hispanic white women in both 2005 and 2008 (CDC, 2013).
- More likely than whites to report fair or poor health status.
- Males more likely than white males to smoke cigarettes (National Center for Health Statistics, 2015).
- 665% higher homicide rates among compared with non-Hispanic whites (CDC, 2013).

Hispanic Americans
- Nearly one-third have less than ninth-grade education.
- Approximately one-fourth of families live below the poverty line (National Center for Health Statistics, 2015).
- More likely to be uninsured and underinsured than non-Hispanic whites.
- AIDS is the leading cause of death.
- Homicide rate remains the second leading cause of death for young males (National Center for Health Statistics, 2015).
- Among individuals 18 years or older, a higher proportion of Hispanics are overweight or obese.
- Alcohol use is 43.0% in Hispanics (National Center for Health Statistics, 2015).
- Higher homicide rates compared to non-Hispanic whites (CDC, 2013).

Asian Americans
- Bipolar distribution of education, income, and health status.
- Asian/Pacific Islander category is extremely heterogeneous, encompassing 21 subgroups with different health profiles.
- In 2010, median family income was $64,308; a higher percentage (12.1%) live in poverty compared to non-Hispanic whites (9.9%) (DeNavas-Walt, 2011).
- Cambodian refugees have extremely high rates of posttraumatic stress disorder, dissociation, depression, and anxiety.
- As a whole, Asian/Pacific Islanders have the lowest smoking rates in the United States, but certain groups have higher smoking rates:
  - 92% of Laotians
  - 71% of Cambodians
  - 65% of Vietnamese (Yoon & Chien, 1996)
- Korean Americans have a fivefold incidence of stomach cancer and eightfold incidence of liver cancer compared with whites.

American Indians and Alaska Natives
- Poverty is associated with high injury-related mortality rate among these children.
- The rate of death due to alcohol is 7 times greater and the suicide rate is 3.5 times greater than the national averages (Pleasant, 2003).
- Higher rates for drug-induced deaths than among non-Hispanic whites (CDC, 2013).
- Higher homicide rates compared to non-Hispanic whites (CDC, 2013).
- Two to five times higher motor vehicle—related death rate as compared to other races/ethnicities (CDC, 2013).

Americans in terms of perceived health status as well as in traditional indicators of health such as the infant mortality rate, general population mortality rate, and birth weight.

One of the most commonly used measures of access to care is whether a person has a regular or usual source of care. In most research studies, a *usual source of care* is defined as a single provider or place where patients obtain, or can obtain, the majority of their health care. Having a usual source of care is associated with greater coordination of care.

Disparities persist not only in terms of mortality rates but also in terms of morbidity, exposure to environmental hazards, and social determinants of health. Additionally, disparities not only persist between racial/ethnic groups, as most commonly discussed, but also between genders, across socioeconomic statuses, and between rural and urban populations. Yet, the majority of federal initiatives have primarily served to draw national attention to racial disparities in health care (see **Exhibit 11.3**). Although federal programs are designed to address specific needs of the minorities, they nonetheless reflect a somewhat fragmented approach to addressing disparities in minority health and health care.

A report from the Agency for Healthcare Research and Quality (AHRQ, 2015) points out that the nation has made clear progress in improving the health care delivery system to achieve the three aims of better care, smarter spending, and healthier people. Still, more work needs to be done, particularly in addressing disparities in care.

Women and Children

Although women in the United States now enjoy a life expectancy almost 8 years longer than that of men, they suffer greater morbidity and poorer health outcomes than their male counterparts. Women also have a higher prevalence of certain health problems than men over the course of their lifetimes (Sechzer et al., 1996). Compared with men of comparable age, women develop more acute and chronic illnesses, resulting in a greater number of short- and long-term disabilities (National Institutes of Health [NIH], 1992). For example, in 2007, hospitalized women had higher mortality rates due to heart attacks than men (AHRQ, 2014). Women also have higher cholesterol levels than men at older ages (see **Figure 11.2**). Finally, women represent the fastest-growing population diagnosed with AIDS.

Exhibit 11.3 Selected Federal Programs to Eliminate Racial and Ethnic Disparities

U.S. Department of Health and Human Services Action Plan to Reduce Racial and Ethnic Health Disparities (HHS Disparities Action Plan) (2011)

- To reduce disparities in six key areas: infant mortality, cancer screening and management, cardiovascular disease, diabetes, HIV/AIDS, immunizations, through new opportunities such as the Affordable Care Act, *Healthy People 2020*, Let's Move!, the National HIV/AIDS Strategy, HHS Strategic Action Plan to End the Tobacco Epidemic, Efforts to Reduce Disparities in Influenza Vaccination, and Interagency Working Group on Environmental Justice (U.S. Department of Health and Human Services, 2011)

U.S. Office of Minority Health (1985)

- Mission is to improve the health of racial and ethnic minority populations through the development of effective health policies and programs that help eliminate disparities in health (U.S. Department of Health and Human Services, 2011)
- Program launched by the Centers for Disease Control and Prevention in 1999
- Aimed to support the goals of *Healthy People 2020* to eliminate racial disparities in health and health care

Minority Health Initiative (1992)

- Launched by the Office for Research on Minority Health at the National Institutes of Health to improve the national research agenda on minority health issues and strengthen the national commitment and responsiveness to the health and training needs of minority Americans

Indian Health Service

- An agency within the U.S. Department of Health and Human Services with the mission to be the principal advocate and provider of health services to American Indians and Alaska Natives

Migrant Health Center Program

- Was established by the Migrant Health Act (1962) to provide medical and support services to migrant farm workers and their families

Communities Putting Prevention to Work (CPPW)

- Funded by the CDC, American Recovery and Reinvestment Act, and the Affordable Care Act to support policy and environmental strategies in 50 communities to address obesity and tobacco use (U.S. Department of Health and Human Services, 2011)

Administration of Children and Families Head Start Program

- Serves to promote social and cognitive childhood development through education, health, nutritional, social, and other services for enrollees (U.S. Department of Health and Human Services, 2011)

Healthy Start

- Established by the National Institute of Health to address disparities in burden of asthma among minority children and children living in poverty (U.S. Department of Health and Human Services, 2011)

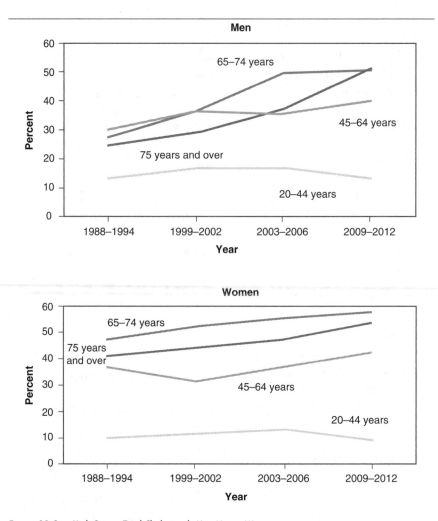

Figure 11.2   High Serum Total Cholesterol: Men Versus Women
Centers for Disease Control and Prevention, National Center for Health Statistics. Health, United States, 2014: With Special Feature on Adults Aged 55–64. Hyattsville, MD. 2015, Table 61.

Pronounced differences between men and women also exist in mental illness. For example, anxiety disorders and major depression affect twice as many women as men (Rodin & Ikovics, 1990). Adolescent females have a higher prevalence of depression, eating disorders, and suicidal ideation and attempts than adolescent males. Although females are more likely to have suicidal thoughts than males, males have suicide rates four times as high as women overall (AHRQ, 2014; Crosby et al., 2011).

The mission of the Office of Research on Women's Health, under the NIH within the U.S. Department of Health and Human Services (DHHS), is to stimulate, coordinate, and implement a comprehensive women's health agenda on research, service delivery, and education across agencies of the DHHS and other government agencies.

Children's health has certain unique aspects in terms of the delivery of health care, reflecting children's developmental vulnerability, dependency, and differential patterns of morbidity and mortality. *Developmental vulnerability* refers to the rapid and cumulative physical and emotional changes that characterize childhood, and the potential effects that illness, injury, or untoward family and social circumstances can have on a child's life-course trajectory. *Dependency* refers to the special circumstances that children face that require others to recognize and respond to their health needs. Children depend on their parents, school officials, caregivers, and sometimes neighbors to discover their need for health care, seek health care services on their behalf, authorize treatment, and comply with recommended treatment regimens. These relationships can affect the utilization of health services by children.

Children are increasingly affected by a broad and complex array of conditions that were not very prevalent among older generations, collectively referred to as *new morbidities*. *New morbidities* include drug and alcohol abuse, obesity, family and neighborhood violence, emotional disorders, and learning problems (see **Figure 11.3** for data on obesity among children). Addressing such conditions requires a continuum of comprehensive services that includes multidisciplinary assessment, treatment, rehabilitation, and community-based prevention strategies.

Geographic Distribution: Rural Health

Poverty is a common dimension of life in rural America. Rural residents earn, on average, $7,417 less than their urban counterparts, and 24% of rural children live in poverty (National Rural Health Association, 2011). Rural residents face a lack of public health infrastructure and poor access to health care (Davis et al., 2010). Rural communities face a higher burden of heart disease, stroke, diabetes, mental health disorders, tobacco usage, and substance abuse (Gamm et al., 2003).

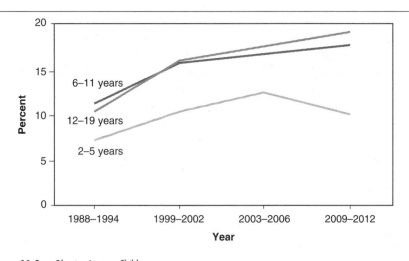

Figure 11.3   Obesity Among Children
Centers for Disease Control and Prevention, National Center for Health Statistics. Health, United States, 2014: With Special Feature on Adults Aged 55–64. Hyattsville, MD. 2015, Table 65.

One dimension of the barriers to health care access among rural residents is geographic maldistribution of health care professionals. An estimated 51 million Americans (approximately one-fifth of the total U.S. population) live in places classified as nonmetropolitan, and more than 20 million of these nonmetropolitan residents live in areas designated as having primary health care provider shortages. According to the National Rural Health Association, just 10% of all practicing physicians are based in rural areas. Low population density makes it difficult for such communities to attract physicians and for physicians to establish financially viable practices. Rural residents have particularly low access to specialist physicians.

As a result, rural populations face greater barriers in access to care. In fact, 73% of national- and state-level rural health experts recently named access to health care as a rural health priority.

Various measures have been undertaken to improve access to care in rural America, including the promotion of the National Health Service Corps, the designation of health professional shortage areas and medically underserved areas, the development of community and migrant health centers, and the enactment of the Rural Health Clinics Act.

ENABLING CHARACTERISTICS

Enabling characteristics include socioeconomic status, individual assets, and various mediating factors. *Socioeconomic status* is associated with social position, access to resources, and variations in health status (e.g., income, education, employment status, and occupation). Individual assets (i.e., human capital) contribute to an individual's ability to be economically self-sufficient (e.g., possessing inheritance, wealth, or certain skills). *Mediating factors* are associated with the use of health care services (e.g., health insurance, access to health care, quality of health care). The following section discusses enabling characteristics such as insurance status and homelessness.

The Uninsured

Even though a large segment of the previously uninsured has gained health insurance under the Affordable Care Act, a significant number of Americans remain uninsured. In general, the uninsured are likely to be poorer and less educated than insured populations and tend to work in part-time jobs and/or be employed by small firms. The uninsured also tend to be younger (25 to 40 years old) because most of the elderly (age 65 and older) are covered by Medicare. Ethnic minorities are also more likely to lack health insurance.

The uninsured face greater barriers to accessing needed health care and are more likely to report delays in seeking needed medical care or dental care (see **Figure 11.4** and **Figure 11.5**). The plight of the uninsured also affects those who have insurance. For example, community hospitals provide uncompensated care to the uninsured through emergency care; the cost of such care was estimated at $31 billion in 2009 (American Hospital Association, 2010). Much of this cost is currently shared by Medicaid, federal grants to nonprofit hospitals, and charitable organizations, although these costs are likely to be (at least partly) passed on to the U.S. public at large if the level of uncompensated care remains the same in the future.

Homelessness

Across the United States, approximately 578,424 people are homeless each night. Nearly 20% of this population consists of families with children or unaccompanied children and youth (National Alliance to End Homelessness, 2015). About 10.5% of this population are war veterans. Single women account for about 17% of the U.S. homeless adult population.

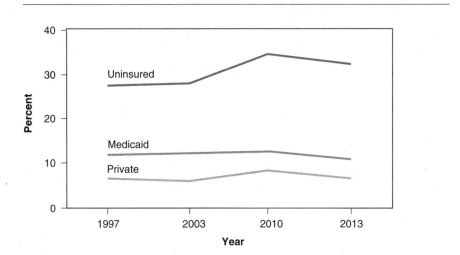

Figure 11.4   Delay in Seeking Needed Medical Care by Insurance Status
Data from Centers for Disease Control and Prevention, National Center for Health Statistics. Health, United States, 2014: With Special Feature on Adults Aged 55–64. Hyattsville, MD. 2015, Table 69.

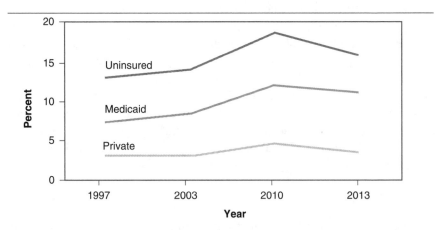

Figure 11.5   Delay in Seeking Needed Dental Care by Insurance Status
Data from Centers for Disease Control and Prevention, National Center for Health Statistics. Health, United States, 2014: With Special Feature on Adults Aged 55–64. Hyattsville, MD. 2015, Table 69.

Approximately 26% of all homeless persons have a severe mental illness, yet just 5% to 7% require institutionalization; the rest can live in the community with appropriate help (National Coalition for the Homeless, 2009a, 2009b).

The homeless face several barriers to adequate and appropriate health care. They have financial barriers and problems in satisfying eligibility requirements for health insurance. Accessible transportation to medical facilities is often unavailable to this population. The homeless usually suffer from a lack of proper sanitation, do not have a stable place to store medications safely, and are unable to obtain the proper food for a medically indicated diet necessary for conditions such as diabetes or hypertension. The homeless population suffers from a high prevalence of untreated acute and chronic medical, mental health, and substance abuse problems. Such persons are also at a greater risk of assault and victimization, as well as exposure to harsh environmental elements.

ELIMINATING SOCIOECONOMIC DISPARITIES

The U.S. Department of Health and Human Services (HHS) *Action Plan to Reduce Racial and Ethnic Health Disparities* (*Action Plan*) outlines goals and actions to reduce health disparities among racial and ethnic minorities. The *Action Plan* includes a continuous assessment of the impact of all policies and programs on racial and ethnic health disparities. It will promote integrated approaches, evidence-based programs, and best practices to reduce these disparities. The *Action Plan* builds on the strong foundation of the ACA and is aligned with other programs and initiatives such as *Healthy People 2020* and the president's national HIV/AIDS strategy. The five main goals of the *Action Plan* are: (1) transform health care; (2) strengthen the nation's HHS infrastructure and workforce; (3) advance the health, safety, and well-being of the American people; (4) advance scientific knowledge and innovation; and (5) increase the efficiency, transparency, and accountability of HHS programs.

Health Disparities and the Affordable Care Act

The ACA includes provisions related to disparities reduction, data collection and reporting, quality improvement, and prevention. The law is also expected to reduce health disparities by investing in prevention and wellness and giving individuals and families more control over their own care.

Other Federal Initiatives

- One of the four overarching goals of the *Healthy People 2020* initiative is "to achieve health equity, eliminate disparities and improve the health of all groups" (U.S. Department of Health and Human Services, 2010). The *Healthy People 2020* initiative will assess health disparities in the U.S. population by tracking rates of death, chronic and acute diseases, injuries, and other health-related behaviors for subpopulations defined by race, ethnicity, gender identity, sexual orientation, disability status or special health care needs, and geographic location.

- The Let's Move! initiative proposes to create a healthy start in life for children, from pregnancy through early childhood, serve healthier food in schools, and increase physical activity.

- President Obama's national HIV/AIDS strategy offers a vision that

> The United States will become a place where new HIV infections are rare and when they do occur, every person, regardless of age, gender, race and ethnicity, sexual orientation, gender identity, or socioeconomic circumstance, will have unfettered access to high-quality, life-extending care, free from stigma and discrimination (National HIV/AIDS Strategy for the United States, 2010).

- The DHHS has announced a strategic action plan to end the tobacco epidemic.

- The DHHS has launched efforts to maximize vaccinations in targeted racial and ethnic minority groups through coordinated efforts as well as private–public partnerships.

- The Interagency Working Group on Environmental Justice under Executive Order 12898 charges each federal agency to identify and address disproportionately high adverse human health or environmental effects on minority and low-income populations.

- The Office of Minority Health has launched the National Partnership for Action to End Health Disparities.

- An earlier program, Vaccines for Children, implemented in 1994, has been effective in reducing disparities in vaccination coverage among U.S. children.

Private Initiatives

- Heterosexual non-Hispanic black women in the United States are far more affected than women of other races or ethnicities by HIV. SisterLove, Inc., a community-based organization in Atlanta, Georgia, responded to this disparity early in the epidemic by creating the Healthy Love HIV and sexually transmitted disease prevention intervention in 1989. Since then, SisterLove has been delivering the intervention to black women in metropolitan Atlanta.

- A community-based organization in New York City evaluated and demonstrated the efficacy of its Many Men, Many Voices HIV/sexually transmitted disease prevention intervention in reducing sexual risk behaviors and increasing protective behaviors among black men who have sex with men.

NEED CHARACTERISTICS

Need attributes of individuals include their self-perceived or professionally evaluated health status and quality-of-life indicators. "Self-perceived or professionally evaluated health status" refers to self-perceived physical and mental health status and diagnoses of disease and illness from health professionals. *Quality-of-life indicators* include such factors as the ability to perform activities of daily living and instrumental activities of daily living; social limitations; cognitive limitations; and limitations in work, housework, or school.

Certain subpopulation groups are known to be at higher health risks. These potential threats include risks to physical health (e.g., high-risk mothers and infants, chronically ill and disabled individuals, and persons with HIV/AIDS), mental health (e.g., the mentally ill and disabled, alcohol or substance abusers, those who are suicide- or homicide-prone), and social well-being (e.g., abusive families, the homeless, and immigrants and refugees).

Mental Health

Mental disorders are common psychiatric illnesses affecting both adults and children, and they represent a serious public health problem in the United States. National studies have concluded that the most common mental disorders include phobias, substance abuse (including alcohol and drug dependence), and affective disorders (including depression). Schizophrenia is considerably less common, affecting approximately 1.1% of the population.

Mental illness ranks second, after ischemic heart disease, as a nationwide burden on health and productivity. An estimated 26.2% of the U.S. adult population has at least one diagnosable mental disorder in any given year, with 22.3% of those individuals (5.8% of the total population) facing a severe mental illness. Only 41% of those persons with a disorder receive any treatment (National Institute of Mental Health [NIMH], 2005). In 2006, 36.2 million people received $57.5 billion of mental health services, at an average cost of $1,591 per person (NIMH, 2006). Mental illness is a risk factor for death from suicide, cardiovascular disease, and cancer.

Most mental health services are provided in the general medicine sector—a concept first described by Regier and colleagues (1988) as the de facto mental health service system—rather than through formal mental health specialist services. The de facto system combines specialty mental health services with general counseling services, such as those provided in primary care settings, nursing homes, and community health centers by ministers, counselors, self-help groups, families, and friends. The nation's mental health system is composed of two subsystems—one primarily for individuals with insurance coverage or private funds and the other for those without private means of coverage.

Chronic Illness/Disability

Most people are vulnerable to *chronic illness* and disability during their lifetime. Overall, chronic diseases are responsible for 7 of 10 deaths in the United States every year. Almost half of all Americans have at least one chronic condition. Chronic disease deaths are largely attributable to preventable illnesses. Tobacco use, lack of physical activity, poor nutrition, and excessive alcohol consumption contribute to the major chronic disease killers: cardiovascular disease, cancer, diabetes, and chronic obstructive pulmonary disease (Centers for Disease Control and Prevention [CDC], 2010a) (see **Figure 11.6** for diabetes prevalence in the United States). An illness is considered chronic if a disease or injury with long-term (i.e., noticed for 3 months or more) conditions or symptoms is present. Other illnesses—namely, congenital anomalies, asthma, diabetes, and heart disease—have been specifically classified as chronic by the National Center

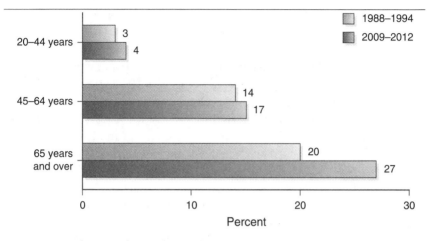

Figure 11-6   Diabetes Prevalence in the United States
Data from Centers for Disease Control and Prevention, National Center for Health Statistics. Health, United States, 2014: With Special Feature on Adults Aged 55–64. Hyattsville, MD. 2015, Table 44.

for Health Statistics, regardless of their duration (National Center for Health Statistics, 1999b, p. 5). Chronic illness and disability also pose unique challenges to a health care system that is primarily oriented toward treating acute illness.

HIV/AIDS

AIDS is caused by infection with HIV. HIV is an unusual type of virus, called a retrovirus, which causes immune system suppression leading to AIDS. Certain widely recognized risk factors promote the transmission of HIV, including male-to-male sexual contact, male-to-female sexual contact, drug use by injection, exposure to contaminated blood products, and perinatal transmission from mother to infant (during pregnancy, delivery, or breastfeeding).

The CDC estimates that more than 1 million adults and adolescents are currently living with HIV in the United States. Efforts at reporting and surveillance have been more successful in recent years, with data showing that more people infected with HIV know their positive status and that higher numbers of cases are being reported to the CDC—this trend is particularly due to increased and more widespread HIV testing (CDC, 2010b).

In addition, with the advent of combination antiretroviral therapy, AIDS surveillance data no longer reflect trends in HIV transmission because such therapy has been effective in delaying the progression of HIV to AIDS (CDC, 1999). Advancements in diagnosis and treatment have led to an increase in the number of people living with HIV/AIDS, although the incidence of new cases has remained relatively stable (CDC, 2010b).

The average cost of antiretroviral therapy is at least $15,000 per year, making such treatment difficult for many patients in the United States to obtain and keeping it out of reach in developing countries where more than 90% of the new HIV infections occur (Long, Brandeau, & Owens, 2010). Some patients temporarily stop treatment because the complicated drug regimen requires coordination of many pills and doses, making it easier to skip medications or doses. Other problems associated with HIV in the United States include issues of urban home health care; HIV infection in rural communities, children, and women; lack of HIV prevention programs; late diagnosis; discrimination; and the need for more HIV/AIDS-related research and health care provider training.

CONCLUSION

This chapter has examined the major characteristics of certain vulnerable U.S. population groups that face challenges and barriers in accessing health care services. These population groups may be organized along predisposing, enabling, and need characteristics and include racial/ethnic minorities, children and women, persons living in rural areas, the homeless, the mentally ill, and individuals with HIV/AIDS. The gaps that currently exist between these population groups and the rest of the population indicate the need for significant efforts to address the unique health concerns of vulnerable U.S. subpopulation groups.

REFERENCES

Aday LA. Health status of vulnerable populations. *Ann Rev Public Health.* 1994;15:487–509.

Aday LA. Vulnerable populations: a community-oriented perspective. In: Sebastian JG, Bushy A, eds. *Special Populations in the Community.* Gaithersburg, MD: Aspen; 1999;313–330.

Agency for Healthcare Research and Quality (AHRQ). Healthcare quality and disparities in women: selected findings from the 2010 national healthcare quality and disparities reports. Rockville, MD. Pub. No. 11-0005-1-EF. http:// www.ahrq.gov/research/findings/nhqrdr/nhqrdr10/women.pdf. Updated October 2014. Accessed June 20, 2015.

Agency for Healthcare Research and Quality (AHRQ). 2014 national healthcare quality & disparities report: executive summary. http://www.ahrq.gov /research/findings/nhqrdr/nhqdr14/exsumm.html. Reviewed April 2015. Accessed August 10, 2015.

American Hospital Association. Uncompensated hospital care cost fact sheet: health forum, AHA annual survey data, 1980–2009. www.aha.org/content /00-10/10uncompensatedcare.pdf. Published December 2010. Accessed August 10, 2015.

CDC health disparities & inequalities report—United States, 2013, *MMWR Morb Mortal Wkly Rep*. November 22, 2013;62(Suppl 3):1–187.

Centers for Disease Control and Prevention (CDC). Guidelines for national human immunodeficiency virus case surveillance, including monitoring for human immunodeficiency virus infection and acquired immunodeficiency syndrome. *MMWR Morb Mortal Wkly Rep*. 1999;48(RR-13):2–7.

Centers for Disease Control and Prevention (CDC). Chronic diseases and health promotion. http://www.cdc.gov/chronicdisease/overview/index.htm. Published 2010a. Accessed August 10, 2015.

Centers for Disease Control and Prevention. 2010b. HIV in the United States: an overview. http://www.cdc.gov/hiv/resources/factsheets/us.htm. Published 2010b. Accessed August 10, 2015.

Crosby AE, et al. Suicidal thoughts and behaviors among adults aged ≥ 18 years—United States, 2008–2009. *MMWR Surveill Summ*. 2011;60(no. SS-13). http://www.cdc.gov/mmwr/preview/mmwrhtml/ss6013a1.htm.

Davis JR, et al. The impact of disasters on populations with health and health care disparities. *Disaster Med Public Health Prep*. 2010;4(1):30–38.

DeNavas-Walt C, et al. *Income, Poverty, and Health Insurance Coverage in the United States: 2010*. Washington, DC: U.S. Census Bureau, Current Population Reports, P60-239, U.S. Government Printing Office; 2011.

Galloway-Gilliam L. Racial and Ethnic Approaches to Community Health. National Civic Review [serial online]. Winter2013 2013;102(4):46. Available from: MasterFILE Premier, Ipswich, MA. Accessed August 11, 2015.

Gamm LD, et al. *Rural Healthy People 2010: A companion document to Healthy People 2010*. Vol. 1. College Station, Texas: Texas A&M University System Health Science Center, School of Rural Public Health; 2003.

Long EF, Brandeau ML, Owens DK. The cost-effectiveness and population out-comes of expanded HIV screening and antiretroviral treatment in the United States. *Ann Intern Med.* 2010;153:778–789.

Mackun P, Wilson S. Population distribution and change: 2000 to 2010. In: *2010 census briefs.* Washington DC: U.S. Department of Commerce, Economics and Statistics Administration, U.S. Census Bureau; 2011.

National Alliance to End Homelessness. *The state of homelessness in America 2015.* http://endhomelessness.org/library/entry/the-state-of-homelessness-in -america-2015. Published 2015. Accessed August 10, 2015.

National Center for Health Statistics. *Healthy People 2000 review, 1998–99.* Hyattsville, MD: Public Health Series; 1999b:163–167.

National Center for Health Statistics. *Health, United States, 2014: with special feature on adults aged 55–64.* Hyattsville, MD: U.S. Department of Health and Human Services; 2015.

National Coalition for the Homeless. NCH fact sheet #2: How many people expe-rience homelessness? http://www.nationalhomeless.org/publications/facts /How_Many.pdf. Published 2009a. Accessed August 10, 2015.

National Coalition for the Homeless. NCH fact sheet #3: Who is homeless? http:// www.nationalhomeless.org/publications/facts/Whois.pdf. Published 2009b. Accessed August 10, 2015.

National HIV/AIDS Strategy for the United States. The White House. https:// www.whitehouse.gov/sites/default/files/uploads/NHAS.pdf. Published July 2010. Accessed August 11, 2015.

National Institute of Mental Health. Statistics: prevalence; any disorder: adults. http://www.nimh.nih.gov/statistics/index.shtml. Published 2005. Accessed August 10, 2015.

National Institute of Mental Health. Statistics: cost; mental healthcare cost data for all Americans. http://www.nimh.nih.gov/statistics/index.shtml. Published 2006. Accessed August 10, 2015.

National Institutes of Health, Office of Research on Women's Health. *Report of the National Institutes of Health: Opportunities for Research on Women's Health* (NIH Publ. No. 92–3457). Washington, DC: Government Printing Office; 1992.

National Rural Health Association. What's different about rural health care? http:// www.ruralhealthweb.org/go/left/about-rural-health. Published 2011. Accessed December 20, 2011.

Pleasant R. Minority health. In: *The Department of Health and Human Services: 50 Years of Service.* Washington DC: U.S. Department of Health and Human Services; 2003:92–95.

Regier DA, et al. One month prevalence of mental disorders in the United States: Based on five epidemiologic catchment area sites. *Arch Gen Psychiatr.* 1988;45(11):977–986.

Rodin J, Ikovics J. Women's health: review and research agenda as we approach the 21st century. *Am Psychol.* 1990;45:1018–1034.

U.S. Department of Health and Human Services. Healthy People 2020. https://www.healthypeople.gov/sites/default/files/HP2020_brochure_with_LHI_508_FNL.pdf. Published November 2010. Accessed August 11, 2015.

U.S. Department of Health and Human Services. HHS action plan to reduce racial and ethnic health disparities: a nation free of disparities in health and health care. http://minorityhealth.hhs.gov/npa/files/Plans/HHS/HHS_Plan_complete.pdf. Published April 2011. Accessed June 20, 2015. U.S. Office of Minority Health. *Racial and Ethnic Approaches to Community Health.* Rockville, MD; 2010.

Yoon E, Chien F. Asian American and Pacific Islander health: a paradigm for minority health. *JAMA.* 1996;275(9):736–737.

Chapter 12

Cost, Access, and Quality

INTRODUCTION

The effectiveness of a health care delivery system is generally evaluated in terms of cost, access, and quality. All three major outcomes of health care delivery continue to receive attention from various stakeholders. Yet, unless costs are brought down to a reasonable level, any achievements in the other two domains will remain elusive. This is because cost, access, and quality are interrelated.

From a macro prospective, costs are commonly viewed in terms of national expenditures for health care. A widely used measure for national health expenditures is the proportion of the gross domestic product (GDP) that a country spends on the delivery of health care services. In simple terms, it refers to the proportion of a country's national income that is spent on health care. From a microperspective, health care costs refer to the cost of purchasing health insurance and the out-of-pocket costs incurred by individuals when they receive health care services. Costs must be contained at both the macro and micro levels. Increased access invariably leads to higher utilization, and, in turn, higher costs. High-quality care should also be the most cost-effective care. Hence, cost is an important factor in the evaluation of quality.

This chapter discusses some of the major reasons for the dramatic rise in health care expenditures. Costs of health care in the United States are compared with those of other countries, and the impact of various cost-containment measures is examined. The government has played a significant role in cost containment and quality improvement, but access to health care by all Americans has remained an elusive dream.

COST OF HEALTH CARE

Cost can carry different meanings in the delivery of health care. The meaning depends on the perspective one takes. Three different meanings are presented here.

1. When consumers and financiers speak of the cost of health care, they are usually referring to the price of health care, such as the physician's bill or the premiums that both employers and employees pay for purchasing health insurance.

2. From a national perspective, health care costs refer to how much a nation spends on health care services, commonly referred to as *health care expenditures* or *health care spending*. These terms primarily reflect the consumption of economic resources in the delivery of health care. Such economic resources include health insurance, the skills of health care professionals, organizations and institutions of health care delivery, pharmaceuticals, medical equipment and supplies, public health functions, and new medical discoveries. Because expenditures equal price times quantity ($E = P \times Q$), growth in health care spending can be accounted for by growth in the prices charged by providers of health services as well as by increases in the utilization of services.

3. A third perspective is that of the providers, where the notion of cost refers to staff salaries, capital costs for building and equipment, rental of space, purchase of supplies, and other costs of production.

It is useful to understand which factors drive costs. This understanding can help identify which costs can be controlled to ensure that health care is delivered at an optimal value.

THE HIGH COST OF U.S. HEALTH CARE

Health care spending spiraled upward at double-digit rates during the 1970s after a massive growth in access created by the Medicare and Medicaid programs in 1965. By 1970, U.S. government expenditures for health care services and supplies had grown by 140%, from $7.9 billion to $18.9 billion (National Center for Health Statistics [NCHS], 1996). During the 1980s, the rate of increase began slowing down. In the 1990s, medical inflation was finally brought under control to a single-digit rate of growth, mostly because medical care costs and utilization were controlled through managed care. The average annual rate of growth in health spending slowed to 5.7% between 1993 and 2000 as managed care proliferated; however, the rate of growth then started to accelerate again. The recent economic recession slowed health care spending growth substantially, with only a 4.1% increase occurring in 2008 and a 4.0% increase in 2009—the slowest growth rate in more than 50 years. Simultaneously, however, federal health spending increased as more people became eligible for benefits and government revenues declined, increasing spending from 37.6% of federal revenue in 2008 to 54.2% in 2009 (Martin et al., 2011). In 2013, 17.4% of the GDP in the United States was consumed by health care.

Trends in national health expenditures are commonly evaluated by comparing medical inflation to general inflation in the economy (measured by annual changes in the consumer price index) and by comparing changes in national health spending to changes in the GDP. Typically, the rates of change in medical inflation have remained consistently above the rates of change in the consumer price index, and health care spending growth rates have consistently surpassed growth rates in the general economy. When spending on health care grows at a faster rate than the GDP, it means that a growing share of total economic resources is devoted to the delivery of health care.

Table 12.1 compares U.S. health spending with that of 30 other developed countries. In 2012, the United States spent $8,745 per capita on health—approximately $2,600 more per capita than the country with the second highest per capita spending, Norway.

Table 12.1   Health Spending in Organization for Economic Cooperation and Development Countries

	Total Health Spending per Capita, 2012			GDP per Capita, 2012			Health Spending as a Percentage of GDP, 2012	
	U.S. $PPP	% of U.S. Level	AAG, 2000–2012 (%)	U.S. $PPP	% of U.S. Level	AAG, 2001–2013 (%)	% of GDP	% of U.S. Level
United States	8,745	100.0	3.9	51,435	100.0	0.9	16.9	100.0
Luxembourg	4,578	52.3	1.9	91,754	178.4	0.6	7.1	42.0
Norway	6,140	70.2	3.4	66,358	129.0	0.5	9.3	55.0
Switzerland	6,080	69.5	2.9	55,916	108.7	0.9	11.4	67.5
Austria	4,896	56.0	2.4	44,892	87.3	1.0	11.1	65.7
Iceland	3,536	40.4	1.7	40,606	78.9	1.5	9.0	53.3
Belgium	4,419	50.5	3.8	41,684	81.0	0.7	10.9	64.5
France	4,288	49.0	2.3	37,347	72.6	0.5	11.6	68.6
Canada	4,602	52.6	3.9	42,284	82.2	1.0	10.9	64.5
Germany	4,811	55.0	1.8	42,730	83.1	1.0	11.3	66.9
Australia	3,997	45.7	4.2	43,676	84.9	1.4	9.1	53.8
Denmark	4,698	53.7	2.5	43,565	84.7	0.1	11.0	65.1
The Netherlands	5,099	58.3	4.9	46,062	89.6	0.6	11.8	69.8
Greece	2,409	27.5	1.8	25,462	49.5	−0.6	9.3	55.0
Ireland	3,890	44.5	5.4	45,210	87.9	0.4	8.9	52.7

Sweden	4,106	47.0	3.5	43,869	85.3	1.3	9.6	56.8
United Kingdom	3,289	37.6	4.0	37,383	72.7	0.9	9.3	55.0
Italy	3,209	36.7	1.4	35,054	68.2	−0.7	9.2	54.4
Japan	3,649	41.7	3.3	35,601	69.2	0.8	10.3	60.9
New Zealand	3,172	36.3	5.2	32,861	63.9	1.3	10.0	59.2
Finland	3,559	40.7	3.6	40,209	78.2	0.8	9.1	53.8
Spain	2,987	0.34	3.7	32,774	63.7	0.0	9.3	55.0
Portugal	2,457	28.1	1.0	27,001	52.5	−0.3	9.5	56.2
Czech Republic	2,077	23.8	4.4	28,647	55.7	2.1	7.5	44.4
Hungary	1,803	20.6	2.5	22,494	43.7	1.8	8.0	47.3
Korea	2,291	26.2	8.7	32,022	62.2	3.5	7.6	45.0
Slovak Republic	2,105	24.1	7.9	25,725	50.0	4.2	8.1	47.9
Poland	1,540	17.6	5.5	22,869	44.5	3.8	6.8	40.2
Mexico	1,048	12.0	4.1	16,808	32.7	1.1	6.2	36.7
Turkey	984	11.3	4.9	18,002	35.0	3.7	5.4	32.0
Organization for Economic Cooperation and Development Median	3,484	39.8	3.8	37,139	72.2	1.6	9.3	55.0

Note: PPP: Purchasing Power Parity, AAG: Annual Average Growth. Data from Organization for Economic Cooperation and Development (OECD). OECD health at a glance 2014, Annex A. Gross domestic product (GDP) (indicator). Paris: OECD; 190—197. doi: 10.1787/dc2f7oec-en. Published 2015. Accessed June 14, 2015.

REASONS FOR HIGH HEALTH CARE COSTS

The rising health care expenditures have been attributed to the complex interaction of numerous factors. General inflation in the economy is a highly visible cause of health care spending because it affects the cost of producing health care services through such tangibles as higher wages and costs of supplies. Apart from the effects of general inflation, other factors influence medical cost inflation (see **Exhibit 12.1**).

Third-Party Payment

Health care is among the few services for which a third party—not the consumer—pays the lion's share for most of the services used. Whether the government or a private insurance company foots the bill, individual patients pay a price that is far lower than the actual cost of the service (Altman & Wallack, 1996). As a result, the propensity to utilize greater quantities of health care than one would if services are fully paid out of pocket (moral hazard) leads to excessive utilization. Actually, both patient and provider have little incentive to be cost conscious when someone else is paying the bill.

Growth of Technology

In the adoption and diffusion of intensive procedures, the United States follows an early-start, fast-growth pattern (TECH Research Network, 2001). The introduction and intensive use of technology have a direct impact on the escalation of health care costs. New technology is expensive to develop, and costs incurred in its research and development are included in the total health care expenditures. Once technology is developed, it creates demand for its use. The development of new technology raises the expectations of consumers about what medical science can do to diagnose

Exhibit 12.1   Main Reasons for the High Cost of Health Care

• Third-party payment	• Multipayer system and administrative costs
• Growth of technology	• Defensive medicine
• Increase in the elderly population	• Waste and abuse
• Medical model of health care delivery	• Practice variations

and treat disease and prolong life. Unsurprisingly, attempts to limit the diffusion of certain expensive technologies in the United States have proved largely unsuccessful.

Increase in the Elderly Population

During the past 100 years, life expectancy in the United States has increased significantly. Life expectancy at birth increased by almost 30 years from 47.3 years in 1900 to nearly 78 years in 2007 (NCHS, 2010). The increased life expectancy of an aging population of the baby boom generation has added to the notable increase in the elderly population. The elderly consume more health care compared to other age groups, and they incur costs that are nearly three times as high as the general population. In 2007, the average medical expenses for a person 65 years or older amounted to $9,696 per person, compared with $3,499 per person for individuals younger than the age of 65 (NCHS, 2010, p. 377).

Medical Model of Health Care Delivery

The *medical model* emphasizes medical intervention after a person has become sick. Prevention and lifestyle/behavior changes to promote health are de-emphasized in this model. Although health promotion and disease prevention are not the answer to every health problem, these principles have not been accorded their rightful place in the U.S. health care delivery system. Consequently, more costly health care resources must be employed to treat many health problems that could have been prevented.

Multipayer System and Administrative Costs

Administrative costs include costs associated with health insurance marketing and enrollment, contracting with providers, claims processing, utilization monitoring, and handling of denials and appeals. Because of the complexity of a multipayer system, costs are often duplicated and may account for as much as 24% to 25% of total health care expenditures in the United States. It is commonly believed that a single-payer health care system has lower administrative costs.

Defensive Medicine

The U.S. health care delivery system is riddled with legal risks for providers that promote defensive medicine. The practice of *defensive medicine* leads to tests and services that are not medically justified but rather are performed by physicians to protect themselves against potential malpractice lawsuits. Unrestrained malpractice awards by the courts and increased malpractice insurance premiums for physicians significantly add to the cost of health care.

Waste and Abuse

Health care fraud has been identified as a major problem in the Medicare and Medicaid programs. It may also occur when more services are provided than are medically necessary or when services not provided are billed to third-party payers. The latter practice may include billing for a higher-priced service when a lower-priced service is actually delivered.

Practice Variations

The work of John Wennberg and others brought to light a disturbing aspect of physician behavior accounting for wide variations in treatment patterns for similar patients. These practice variations are referred to as *small-area variations*, in recognition of the fact that the observed differences in practice patterns have been associated only with certain geographic areas of the country. Such a variation in practice intensity, which can be as great as twofold, cannot be explained by age, gender, race, pricing variations, demand inducements, or health status (Baucus & Fowler, 2003). Small-area variations signal gross inefficiencies in the U.S. health care delivery system because they increase costs without appreciably better outcomes.

COST CONTAINMENT

Even though rising health care expenditures may seem innocuous to some, they must be controlled for several reasons. First, rising health care costs mean that Americans have to forgo other goods and services when more is spent on health care. Second, economic resources should be directed to their highest-valued uses, even though consumers decide how much should be spent on purchasing a product or service based on their perception of the value they expect to receive (Feldstein, 1994, p. 13).

The United States has made many attempts to control health care spending, using a combination of government regulation and market-based competition. Most of these undertakings have met with limited success, mainly because implementing a system-wide cost-control initiative has not been feasible in such a fragmented system. Cost-containment measures in the United States can be applied only in a piecemeal fashion and can affect only certain targeted sectors of the health care delivery system at one time. In contrast, national health care programs in other countries have *single-payer systems* in which effective centralized controls are feasible.

Another reason that cost-control efforts in the United States have not proven very successful is because of cost shifting between programs and sectors. *Cost shifting* refers to the ability of providers to make up for lost revenues in one area by increasing utilization or charging higher prices in other areas that are free of controls. Only system-wide controls can prevent cost shifting.

Health Planning

Health planning refers to an undertaking by the government to align and distribute health care resources in a manner that, in the eyes of the government, would achieve desired health outcomes for all people. Health planning employs supply-side rationing to control health care expenditures. The central planning function does not fit well in a system that is largely private because of the absence of a central administrative agency to monitor the system. In the United States, the types of health care services, their geographic distribution, access to these services, and the prices charged by providers develop independently of any preformulated plans.

Price Controls

In 1971, President Richard Nixon imposed the Economic Stabilization Program, which placed limits on the amount that hospitals could raise their prices from year to year (Williams & Torrens, 1993). The Economic Stabilization Program controls did generate a moderating influence on price increases for most medical services; however, the program placed no limits on the quantity of services or costs of production (Altman & Eichenholz, 1976). After the controls were lifted, inflation returned to its precontrol levels (Altman & Eichenholz, 1976).

Perhaps the most important undertaking to control prices for inpatient hospital care was the conversion of hospital Medicare reimbursement from a retrospective plan to a prospective system based on diagnosis-related groups as authorized under the Social Security amendments of 1983. This change reduced the growth in inpatient hospital spending, but it had little impact on total per capita Medicare cost inflation; costs mainly shifted from the inpatient to the outpatient sector.

Another rate-setting mechanism was the Omnibus Budget Reconciliation Act of 1989, which helped establish a national Medicare fee schedule. With this fee schedule, known as the *resource-based relative value scale*, physicians are paid according to relative value units established for more than 7,000 covered services, and a volume performance standard was implemented to contain the annual rate of growth in Medicare physician payments.

Peer Review

The term *peer review* refers to the general process of medical review of utilization and quality carried out directly by, or under the supervision of, physicians (Wilson & Neuhauser, 1985, p. 270). Under the Medicare program, peer review organizations were established in 1984 to determine whether care is reasonable, necessary, of adequate quality and provided in the most appropriate setting. These organizations are now called quality improvement organizations. They are statewide private organizations composed of practicing physicians and other health care professionals who are paid by the federal government to review the care provided to Medicare beneficiaries. They can deny payment if care does not meet certain standards.

Competitive Approaches

Competition refers to rivalry among sellers for customers (Dranove, 1993). In health care delivery, it means that providers of health care services try to attract patients who have the ability to choose from several different providers. Although competition more commonly refers to price competition, it may also be based on technical quality, amenities, access, or other factors (Dranove, 1993). In the United States, competitive reforms were given preference because of the growing interest in market-oriented approaches across many sectors of the economy during the Ronald Reagan presidency in the 1980s. Market-oriented reforms were accompanied by mounting cost-containment efforts in the private sector and the growth of managed care. Competitive strategies can be classified into four broad types: demand-side incentives, supply-side regulation, payer-driven price competition, and utilization controls.

Demand-side incentives refer to cost-sharing mechanisms that place a larger cost burden on consumers, thereby encouraging consumers to be more cost conscious in selecting the insurance plan that best serves their needs and more judicious in their utilization of services. *Supply-side regulation* typically refers to the antitrust laws passed in the United States, which prohibit business practices that stifle competition among providers, such as price fixing, price discrimination, exclusive contracting arrangements, and mergers deemed anticompetitive by the Department of Justice. Such restrictions force health care organizations to be cost-efficient to survive. *Payer-driven price competition* occurs when employers shop for the best value in terms of the cost of premiums and the benefits package (competition among insurers), and when MCOs shop for the best value from providers of health services (competition among providers). The *utilization controls* used in managed care have eliminated some of the unnecessary or inappropriate services provided to consumers by intervening in the decisions made by providers, in an effort to ensure that only services deemed appropriate and necessary are provided.

Chronic Disease Prevention and Management

Approximately 70% of all U.S. health care costs are generated by 10% of patients, who typically have one or more chronic diseases; thus there is enormous potential for cost containment through the improvement of the delivery of care for chronic conditions. So far, it has proved difficult to steer the system toward a preventive and chronic-disease–oriented model. Newer approaches, such as the medical-home model and accountable care organizations, are being investigated. There is also a notable regulatory push for providers to adopt electronic health records. Thus far, the effectiveness of these approaches in controlling costs remains inconclusive.

UNEQUAL IN ACCESS

In broad terms, *access* to care can be defined as the ability to obtain needed, affordable, convenient, acceptable, and effective personal health services in a timely manner. Access is one of the key determinants of health status, along with environment, lifestyle, and heredity factors. It also helps assess the effectiveness of the medical care delivery system and is increasingly linked to quality of care and the efficient use of needed services.

Although *access* is a familiar term used by both popular and academic media, it is associated with numerous and differing concepts. It may refer to the availability (or not) of a usual source of care for an individual, the actual utilization of health services, or the acceptability of particular services. **Figure 12.1** illustrates the system, provider, and individual characteristics that influence access to care.

Data on Access

Population-based surveys supported by federal statistical agencies are the major data sources for conducting analyses on access to care. Large national surveys such as the National Health Interview Survey and

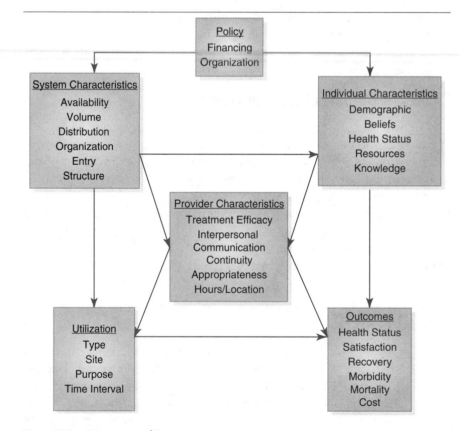

Figure 12.1   Determinants of Access

the Medical Expenditure Panel Survey are the leading data sources used to monitor access trends as well as other issues of interest. The latter comprises a series of surveys that gather data on health care use and expenditures (e.g., inpatient, outpatient, and office-based care; dental care; and prescription medications), health insurance coverage, access to care, sources of payment, health status and disability, medical conditions, health care quality, and measures of socioeconomic and demographic characteristics.

Other well-known national surveys are listed in **Table 12.2**. They include national surveys and surveys on special topics.

The federal government also collects data on special topics such as community health centers (e.g., Bureau of Common Reporting Requirement and Uniform Data System), HIV/AIDS (e.g., HIV Cost and Services Utilization Study 1994–1998), managed care (e.g., Consumer Assessment of Health Plans Study 1996), and mental health (e.g., Mental Health Care Services Study). The Medicare Current Beneficiary Survey, the Medicare Statistical System, the Medicaid Data System, and the Medicaid Demonstration Projects (1983–1984, 1992–1996) have collected data relevant to Medicare and Medicaid.

States, associations, and research institutions also regularly collect data on topics of interest to them. Examples include state health services utilization data (e.g., all-payer hospital discharge data systems), state managed care data (e.g., managed care encounter data), state Medicaid enrollee satisfaction data (e.g., Medicaid enrollee satisfaction surveys), physician data from the American Medical Association's Physician Masterfile, and hospital data from the American Hospital Association's Annual Survey of Hospitals 1946 to present. Examples of research institution–based initiatives include collection of data on the health care delivery system (e.g., Center for Evaluative Clinical Sciences: Dartmouth Atlas of Health Care in the U.S.), women's health (e.g., Commonwealth Fund: Women's Health Survey 1993), minority health (e.g., Commonwealth Fund: Health Care Services and Minority Groups: A Comparative Survey of Whites, African Americans, Hispanics, and Asian Americans 1994), health insurance (e.g., Mathematica Policy Research/Robert Wood Johnson Foundation: Family Survey on Health Insurance 1993–1994), and access to care (e.g., Robert Wood Johnson Foundation National Access Surveys, Mathematica Policy Research: Access to Care Pilot Survey of Medicaid Beneficiaries 1994).

Table 12.2   Selected National Surveys of Health Care

Survey Title	Survey Author	Survey Function
Current Population Survey and Survey of Income and Program Participation	U.S. Census Bureau	Information on population characteristics
Area Resource File	Bureau of Health Professions	Pools information on characteristics of population and health care delivery system
National Health and Nutrition Examination Survey	NCHS	Information on demographics, prevalence of selected diseases, nutrition, and behavioral risk factors
National Hospital Discharge Survey	NCHS	Data on short-stay hospital discharges and utilization
Ambulatory Medical Care Survey	NCHS	Data on ambulatory medical encounters
National Hospital Ambulatory Medical Care Survey	NCHS	Data on ambulatory hospital encounters
National Nursing Home Survey	NCHS	Data on nursing homes and utilization, nursing home residents, and nursing home staff
Behavioral Risk Factor Survey	CDC	Data on health practices and behavioral risks of illness
National Health Provider Inventory	CDC	Data on inpatient facilities
Longitudinal Survey on Aging	CDC	Data on older individuals
National Nursing Home Survey Follow-Up	CDC	Data on nursing homes
National Employer Health Insurance Survey	CDC	Data on insurance
Vital Statistics of the United States	CDC	Vital statistics information

Data from Centers for Disease Control and Prevention; NCHS, National Center for Health Statistics. http://www.cdc.gov/nchs/surveys.htm

With the growth of managed care, encounter databases have become increasingly critical in recording and evaluating access to health care. In addition to the federal government, private nonprofit research centers collect information on managed care. Examples include the National Health Maintenance Organization Census (1977 to the present, sponsored by Interstudy) and the Healthcare Effectiveness Data and Information Set (sponsored by the National Committee for Quality Assurance).

Access Disparities

Access is best predicted by race, income, and occupation. These three factors are interrelated: Those individuals belonging to minority groups tend to be poorer, less educated, and more likely to work in job environments that pose greater health risks. In the United States, both low socioeconomic status and minority group membership are associated with lower overall health care access and utilization. Racial/ethnic minorities are less likely than their white counterparts to have a specific source of ongoing care. A similar trend is observed among lower-income individuals and their higher-income counterparts. Among those persons who have a usual source of care, blacks and Hispanics are more likely than whites to have hospital-based (as opposed to office-based) care. Hispanics, in particular, are less likely to have a usual primary care provider than their non-Hispanic white counterparts (36% versus 21%). Nonwhite Medicare beneficiaries have fewer cancer screenings, flu shots, and ambulatory and physician visits than their white counterparts (Gornick, 2000).

Geographic disparities in access are also present, and individuals from rural areas face greater access barriers than those residing in urban areas. Rural Americans have higher mortality and morbidity and shorter life expectancy than their urban counterparts (Cordes, 1989; DeFriese & Ricketts, 1989; Rowland & Lyons, 1989; Sherman, 1991). Although rural residents have a greater need for health care services, there are severe limitations in the availability of services to address those needs. The main shortcomings in rural health care delivery include maldistribution of physicians, lack of both primary and specialty care services, and inability to pay for services.

Access Initiatives

Access to care has been incrementally addressed by the U.S. government through a variety of public programs. Access for disadvantaged populations is clearly established in legislative history. The Sheppard-Towner Act of

1921 exemplifies early federal attempts to provide direct primary care health services to economically disadvantaged mothers and children. Government interest in assuring access to other lower-income populations grew during World War II, when comprehensive care was extended to the wives and children of low-rank armed forces personnel. The issue of health care access among disadvantaged populations paved the way for the Great Society programs of the 1960s to help the elderly and poor through the Medicare and Medicaid programs.

Later, services such as cancer screening and immunizations were added to the Medicare program, and $24 million was allocated to states in 1997 to create the Children's Health Insurance Programs for children in low-income families who did not otherwise qualify for Medicaid. Several states have expanded their Medicaid programs under the Affordable Care Act, even though the mandate for all states to expand Medicaid was struck down by the U.S. Supreme Court.

AVERAGE IN QUALITY

Quality can be appreciated from both a microperspective and a macroperspective. **Exhibit 12.2** provides examples of micro- and macro-level quality indicators. The microview focuses on services at the point of delivery and their subsequent effects; it is associated with the performance of individual caregivers and health care organizations. The macroview looks at quality from the standpoint of populations; it reflects the performance of the entire health care delivery system.

Exhibit 12.2   Selected Quality Indicators

Micro level	Macro level
• Small-area variations	• Cost
• Medical errors	• Access
• Patient satisfaction	• Population health
• Quality of life	
• Health outcomes	

The Institute of Medicine defines *quality* as "the degree to which health services for individuals and populations increase the likelihood of desired health outcomes and are consistent with current professional knowledge" (McGlynn, 1997, p. 8). This definition has several implications:

1. Quality performance occurs on a continuum, theoretically ranging from unacceptable to excellent.
2. The focus is on services provided by the health care delivery system (as opposed to individual behaviors).
3. Quality may be evaluated from the perspective of individuals and populations or communities.
4. The emphasis is on desired health outcomes; research evidence must be used to identify the services that improve health outcomes.
5. In the absence of scientific evidence regarding appropriateness of care, professional consensus can be used to develop criteria for the definition and measurement of quality (McGlynn, 1997).

Although complete in many respects, the definition of quality proposed by the Institute of Medicine fails to include the roles of cost and access in the evaluation of quality. Even though the United States spends more of its national economic production on health care than other nations, Americans are not the healthiest people in the world. The main reasons why the United States trails behind other industrialized nations in broad population measures of health include a lack of emphasis on disease prevention and health promotion and a lack of access to primary health care. More health care expenditures or more intensive use of medical technology do not produce better health. In other words, more is not better, and more does not represent better quality.

In his well-known model to help define and measure quality in health care organizations, Donabedian (1980) proposed three domains in which health care quality should be examined: structure, process, and outcomes. Donabedian noted that all three domains are important in measuring the quality of care.

Structure, process, and outcomes are closely linked (**Figure 12.2**). The three domains are also hierarchical. Structure is the foundation of the quality of health care: Good processes require a good structure. In other words, deficiencies in structure generally have a negative effect on the

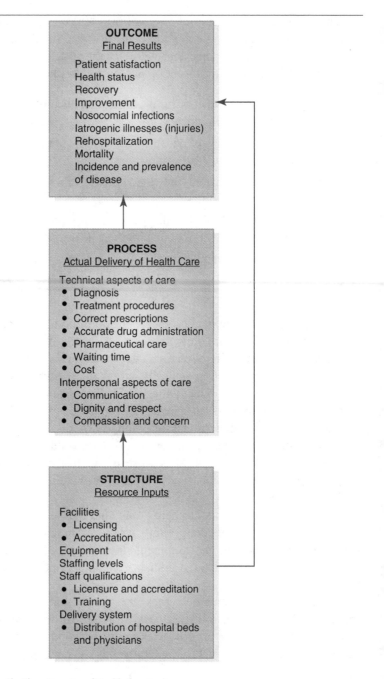

Figure 12.2   The Three Domains of Health Care Quality

processes (defined in the "Process" subsection later in this section) of health care delivery. Structure and processes together influence quality outcomes. This model views quality strictly from the delivery system's perspective; it does not account for social and individual lifestyle and behavioral factors that also have a significant influence on health status.

Structure

Structure has been defined as "the relatively stable characteristics of the providers of care, of the tools and resources they have at their disposal, and of the physical and organizational settings in which they work" (Donabedian, 1980, p. 81). Structural measures indicate the extent to which health care organizations are capable of providing adequate levels of care (Williams & Torrens, 1993). Hence, structure provides an indirect measure of quality under the assumption that a good structure enables health care delivery professionals to employ good processes that would lead to good outcomes.

A significant initiative toward improving structure is the use of electronic health records—digitally formatted medical records that provide real-time patient medical information for authorized personnel (HealthIT, 2013). To date, their effectiveness in improving quality, however, has not been clearly established.

Process

Process refers to the specific way in which care is provided. Examples of process include correct diagnostic tests, correct prescriptions, accurate drug administration, pharmaceutical care, waiting time to see a physician, and interpersonal aspects of care delivery. Just as with structure, it is important to relate process to patient care outcomes. In other words, structures and processes should be employed with the objective of achieving better outcomes. Some significant initiatives toward process improvement have occurred in recent years. Some of the main developments in this area are clinical practice guidelines, cost-efficiency, critical pathways, and risk management, which are discussed in the "Developments in Process Improvement" section later in this chapter.

Outcome

Outcome refers to the effects or final results obtained from utilizing the structure and processes of health care delivery. Outcomes are viewed by many as the bottom-line measure of the effectiveness of the health care delivery system (McGlynn & Brook, 1996). Positive outcomes suggest recovery from disease and improvement in health. They also suggest an overall improvement in a population's health status. Outcome measures include postoperative infection rates, nosocomial infections, iatrogenic illnesses, rates of rehospitalization, and patient satisfaction.

QUALITY STRATEGIES AND INITIATIVES

The CMS Quality Strategy pursues and aligns with the three broad aims of the National Quality Strategy (CMS, 2013a). These are:

- *Better care*: Improve the overall quality of care by making health care more patient-centered, reliable, accessible, and safe.
- *Healthy people, healthy communities*: Improve the health of the U.S. population by supporting proven interventions to address behavioral, social, and environmental determinants of health in addition to delivering higher quality care.
- *Affordable care*: Reduce the cost of quality health care for individuals, families, employers, and government.

Formerly known as the Physician Quality Reporting Initiative, the Physician Quality Reporting System (PQRS) encourages individual eligible professionals and group practices to report information on the quality of care to Medicare. PQRS gives participating eligible professionals and group practices the opportunity to assess the quality of care they provide. Beginning in 2015, the program was slated to apply a negative payment adjustment to individual eligible professionals and PQRS group practices who did not satisfactorily report data on quality measures for Medicare Part B Physician Fee Schedule–covered professional services in 2013. Those who report satisfactorily for the 2015 program year will avoid the 2017 PQRS negative payment adjustment (CMS, 2015b).

The Affordable Care Act requires the U.S. Department of Health and Human Services to develop quality data collection and reporting tools such as a quality rating system, a quality improvement strategy, and an enrollee satisfaction survey system. Information from the quality rating system, quality improvement strategy, and surveys will inform consumer selection of a Quality Health Plan (QHP), decisions about QHP certification, and the federal and state marketplaces' monitoring of QHP performance (CMS, 2015a).

DEVELOPMENTS IN PROCESS IMPROVEMENT

Clinical Practice Guidelines

In response to findings of small-area variations, various professional groups, MCOs, and the government have embarked on the development of standardized practice guidelines. *Clinical practice guidelines* (also called *medical practice guidelines*) are explicit descriptions of preferred clinical processes for managing a clinical problem based on research evidence, whenever possible, and on consensus in the absence of evidence (Larsen, 1996). Hence, clinical practice guidelines are designed to provide scientifically based protocols to guide physicians' clinical decisions; they are intended to promote lower costs and better outcomes. Currently, the National Guideline Clearinghouse works under the Agency for Healthcare Research and Quality to compile, update, and disseminate objective, detailed clinical practice guidelines for a variety of conditions, diseases, and treatments in the United States (AHRQ, 2015).

Cost-Efficiency

Also referred to as cost-effectiveness, cost-efficiency is an important concept in quality assessment. A service is *cost-efficient* when the benefit received is greater than the cost incurred in providing the service. In economic terms, additional services beyond the optimal point produce diminishing marginal returns. This point also represents optimal quality, which serves as a point of demarcation between underutilization and overutilization. On the one hand, *underutilization* (underuse) occurs when the benefits of an intervention outweigh its risks or costs, yet the intervention is not used (Chassin, 1991). On the other hand, *overutilization* (overuse) occurs when the costs or risks of treatment outweigh the benefits, yet additional care is delivered. When health care is overused, precious resources are wasted.

Critical Pathways

Critical pathways are outcome-based and patient-centered clinical management tools that are interdisciplinary in nature and that facilitate coordination of care among multiple clinical departments and caregivers within a health care facility, such as a hospital. A critical pathway is a timeline that identifies planned medical interventions along with expected patient outcomes for a specific diagnosis or class of medical conditions, often defined by a diagnosis-related group. In addition to technical outcomes, pathways may measure factors such as patient satisfaction, self-reported health status, mental health, and activities of daily living. Use of critical pathways reduces costs and improves quality by reducing errors, improving coordination among interdisciplinary players, streamlining clinical management functions, providing systematic data for assessing care, and reducing variation in practice patterns (Giffin & Giffin, 1994).

Risk Management

Risk management consists of proactive efforts to prevent adverse events related to clinical care and facilities operations, and it is especially focused on avoiding medical malpractice (Orlikoff, 1988). Initiatives undertaken by a health care organization to review clinical processes and establish protocols for the specific purpose of reducing malpractice litigation can actually enhance quality. Malpractice concerns result in defensive medicine; thus risk-management approaches should employ the principles of cost-efficiency along with standardized practice guidelines and critical pathways. Unfortunately, fear of litigation may lead to reluctance on the part of hospitals and physicians to disclose preventable harm and actual medical errors. In this respect, fear of litigation may actually conceal problems that may compromise patient safety (Lamb et al., 2003).

CONCLUSION

Increasing costs, lack of access, and concerns about quality pose the greatest challenges to health care delivery in the United States. To some extent, these three issues are interrelated. Increasing costs limit the system's ability to expand access; without universal coverage for all Americans, however, it is doubtful that the United States will ever match other developed countries in population health outcome.

Health care costs in the United States are the highest in the world. A move toward prospective payments and the growth of managed care can be largely credited with putting the brakes on rising health care spending during the 1990s; even so, the best current forecasts anticipate accelerated spending growth in the future, which means that a larger share of the economic resources will be devoted to the delivery of health care.

Access to medical care is one of the determinants of health status, along with environmental, lifestyle, and heredity factors. Access is also regarded as a significant benchmark in assessing the effectiveness of the medical care delivery system. Access is explained in terms of enabling and predisposing factors, as well as factors related to health policy and health care delivery.

One reason that the pursuit of quality in health care has trailed behind the emphasis on cost and access is the difficulty in defining and measuring quality. Meanwhile, growth of managed care and emphasis on cost containment have produced a heightened interest in quality because of the intuitive concern that control of costs may have a negative impact on quality; however, there is still a long way to go in specifying what constitutes good quality in medical care, how to guarantee it for patients, and how to reward providers and health plans whose outcomes indicate successes in quality improvement. One challenge in achieving such a goal is that patients, providers, and payers may all define quality differently, which translates into different expectations of the health care delivery system and, therefore, differing evaluations of its quality (McGlynn, 1997).

REFERENCES

Agency for Healthcare Research and Quality (AHRQ). National Guideline Clearinghouse. http://www.guideline.gov/about/index.aspx. Last updated June 18, 2015. Accessed August 12, 2015.

Altman SH, Eichenholz J. Inflation in the health industry: causes and cures. In: Zubkoff M, ed. *Health: A Victim or Cause of Inflation?* New York: Milbank Memorial Fund; 1976:1–32.

Altman SH, Wallack SS. Health care spending: can the United States control it? In: Altman SH, Reinhardt UE, eds. *Strategic Choices for a Changing Health Care System.* Chicago: Health Administration Press; 1996.

Baucus M, Fowler EJ. Geographic variation in Medicare spending and the real focus of Medicare reform. *Health Aff.* http://content.healthaffairs.org/cgi /content/abstract/hlthaff.w2.115v1. Published 2003. Accessed August 11, 2015.

Centers for Medicare and Medicaid Services (CMS). CMS Quality Strategy 2013— Beyond. http://www.cms.gov/Medicare/Quality-Initiatives-Patient-Assessment -Instruments/QualityInitiativesGenInfo/Downloads/CMS-Quality-Strategy.pdf. Published November 18, 2013. Accessed August 11, 2015.

Centers for Medicare and Medicaid Services (CMS). Health insurance marketplace quality initiatives. http://www.cms.gov/Medicare/Quality

-Initiatives-Patient-Assessment-Instruments/QualityInitiativesGenInfo /Health-Insurance-Marketplace-Quality-Initiatives.html. Updated March 20, 2015a. Accessed August 15, 2015.

Centers for Medicare and Medicaid Services (CMS). Physician Quality Reporting System. https://www.cms.gov/Medicare/Quality-Initiatives-Patient-Assessment -Instruments/PQRS/index.html. Updated May 29, 2015b. Accessed August 11, 2015.

Chassin MR. Quality of care: time to act. *JAMA*. 1991;266:3472–3473.

Cordes SM. The changing rural environment and the relationship between health services and rural development. *Health Serv Res*. 1989;23(6):757–784.

DeFriese GH, Ricketts TC. Primary health care in rural areas: an agenda for research. *Health Serv Res*. 1989;23(6):931–974.

Donabedian A. *Explorations in Quality Assessment and Monitoring: The Definition of Quality and Approaches to Its Assessment*. Vol. 1. Ann Arbor, MI: Health Administration Press; 1980.

Dranove D. The case for competitive reform in health care. In: Arnould RJ, Rich FR, White WD, eds. *Competitive Approaches to Health Care Reform*. Washington, DC: Urban Institute Press; 1993:67–82.

Feldstein P. *Health Policy Issues: An Economic Perspective on Health Reform*. Ann Arbor, MI: AUPHA Press/Health Administration Press; 1994.

Giffin M, Giffin RB. Market memo: critical pathways produce tangible results. *Health Care Strat Manage*. 1994;12(7):1–6.

Gornick ME. *Vulnerable Populations and Medicare Services: Why Do Disparities Exist?* New York: Century Foundation Press; 2000.

HealthIT. What is an electronic health record (EHR)? http://www.healthit.gov /providers-professionals/faqs/what-electronic-health-record-ehr. Last updated March 16, 2013. Accessed August 11, 2015.

Lamb RM, et al. Hospital disclosure practices: results of a national survey. *Health Aff*. 2003;22(2):73–83.

Larsen RR. Narrowing the gray zone: how clinical practice guidelines can improve the decision-making process. *Postgrad Med*. 1996;100(2):17–24.

Martin A, Lassman D, Whittle L, Catlin A. National Health Expenditure Accounts Team. Recession contributes to slowest annual rate of increase in health spending in five decades. *Health Aff*. 2011;30(1):11–22.

McGlynn EA. Six challenges in measuring the quality of health care. *Health Aff*. 1997;16(3):7–21.

McGlynn EA, Brook RH. Ensuring quality of care. In: Andersen RM, Rice TH, Kominski GF, eds. *Changing the U.S. Health Care System: Key Issues in Health Services, Policy, and Management.* San Francisco: Jossey-Bass; 1996.

National Center for Health Statistics (NCHS). *Health, United States, 1995.* Hyattsville, MD: U.S. Department of Health and Human Services; 1996.

National Center for Health Statistics (NCHS). *Health, United States, 2010.* Hyattsville, MD: U.S. Department of Health and Human Services; 2010.

Orlikoff JE. *Malpractice Prevention and Liability Control for Hospitals.* 2nd ed. Chicago: American Hospital Publishing; 1988.

Rowland D, Lyons B. Triple jeopardy: rural, poor, and uninsured. *Health Serv Res.* 1989;23(6):975–1004.

Sherman A. *Falling by the Wayside: Children in Rural America.* Washington, DC: Children's Defense Fund; 1991.

TECH Research Network. Technology change around the world: evidence from heart attack care. *Health Aff.* 2001;20(3):25–42.

Williams SJ, Torrens PR. Influencing, regulating, and monitoring the health care system. In: Williams SJ, Torrens PR, eds. *Introduction to Health Services.* 4th ed. Albany, NY: Delmar; 1993:421–429.

Wilson FA, Neuhauser D. *Health Services in the United States.* 2nd ed. Cambridge, MA: Ballinger; 1985.

Chapter 13

Health Policy

INTRODUCTION

Although the United States does not have a centrally controlled system of health care delivery, it does have a history of federal, state, and local government involvement in health and social policy. Perhaps the most visible policy efforts were the social programs created under the Social Security legislation during Franklin Roosevelt's presidency in the 1940s. This initiative later paved the way for the creation of Medicare and Medicaid through amendments to the Social Security Act in 1965. Recently, the Affordable Care Act (ACA) has implemented multifaceted changes to the U.S. health care system; some impacts have already been achieved and longer term impacts have yet to be assessed in the future. This chapter first defines what health policy is and explores the principal features of health policy in the United States. Next, it describes the development of legislative policy and gives examples of critical health policy issues. Finally, an overview of health policy after the ACA is provided.

WHAT IS HEALTH POLICY?

Public policies are authoritative decisions made in the legislative (congressional), executive (presidential), or judicial (courts, including the Supreme Court) branches of government that are intended to direct or influence the actions, behaviors, or decisions of others (Longest, 2002). When public policies pertain to or influence the pursuit of health, they become health policies. Thus *health policy* can be defined as "the aggregate of principles, stated or unstated, that . . . characterize the distribution of resources, services, and political influences that impact on the health of the population" (Miller, 1987, p. 15).

Different Forms of Health Policies

Health policies often come as a by-product of public social policies enacted by the government. A relevant example is the expansion of health insurance coverage. In the past, policies that excluded fringe benefits from income or Social Security taxes and a U.S. Supreme Court ruling that employee benefits, including health insurance, could be legitimately included in the collective bargaining process led to important changes in the health care system. As a result of these policies, employer-provided health insurance benefits grew rapidly in the middle decades of the 20th century (Health Insurance Association of America, 1992). In 1965, adoption of the Medicare and Medicaid legislation expanded the health sector by providing publicly subsidized health insurance to the elderly and indigent. Recently, the ACA has decreased the number of uninsured Americans by a few million.

The American health care system has developed under extraordinarily favorable public policies. For example, the federally funded National Institutes of Health (NIH) had a budget of approximately $10 million when the agency was established in the early 1930s. Today, following exponential growth in its funding, the NIH's annual budget is over $30 billion (NIH, 2015). In addition, private industry spends a significant amount on biomedical research and development, encouraged by governmental policies that permit businesses to recoup their investments in research and development.

Health policies pertain to health care at all levels, including policies affecting the production, delivery, and financing of health care services. Such policies may affect groups or classes of individuals, such as physicians, the poor, the elderly, or children. They can also affect types of organizations, such as medical schools, health maintenance organizations (HMOs), nursing homes, producers of medical technology, or employers. In the United States, each branch and level of government can influence health policy. For example, both the executive and legislative branches at the federal, state, and local levels can establish health policies, and the judicial branch can uphold, strike down, or modify existing laws affecting health and health care at any level.

Statutes or laws are also considered policies—for example, the statutory language contained in the 1983 amendments to the Social Security Act that authorized the prospective payment system (PPS) for reimbursing hospitals for Medicare beneficiaries. Another example comprises the certificate-of-need programs through which many states seek to regulate capital expansion in their health care systems.

Regulatory Tools

Health policies can be used as *regulatory tools* (Longest, 2002). They may call upon the government to prescribe and control the behavior of a particular target group by monitoring the group and imposing sanctions if it fails to comply. Federally funded quality improvement organizations, for instance, develop and enforce standards concerning appropriate care under the Medicare program. State insurance departments across the country regulate health insurance companies in an effort to protect customers from excessive premiums, mendacious practices, and defaults on coverage in case of financial failure of an insurance company.

Some health policies are self-regulatory. For example, physicians set standards of medical practice, and schools of public health decide which courses should be part of their graduate programs in public health (Weissert & Weissert, 1996).

Allocative Tools

Health policies can also be used as *allocative tools* (Longest, 2002); that is, they may involve the direct provision of income, services, or goods to certain groups of individuals or institutions. Allocative tools in the health care arena are of two main types: distributive and redistributive. *Distributive policies* spread benefits throughout society. Typical distributive policies include funding of medical research through the NIH, the construction of facilities (e.g., hospital construction under the Hill-Burton program during the 1950s and 1960s), and the establishment of new institutions (e.g., HMOs). *Redistributive policies*, in contrast, take resources from one group and give it to another—a system that often creates visible beneficiaries and payers. As a consequence, health policy is often most visible and politically charged when it performs redistributive functions. Redistributive policies include the Medicaid program, which takes tax revenue from the public and spends it on the poor in the form of free health insurance.

PRINCIPAL FEATURES OF U.S. HEALTH POLICY

Several features characterize U.S. health policy, including the government acting as a subsidiary to the private sector; fragmented, incremental, and piecemeal reform; pluralistic (interest group) politics; a decentralized role for the states; and the impact of presidential leadership. These features often act or interact to influence the development and evolution of health policies.

Government as Subsidiary to the Private Sector

In the United States, health care is not seen as a right of citizenship or a primary responsibility of government. Instead, the private sector plays a dominant role. Much as with many other public policy issues, Americans generally prefer market solutions over government intervention in health care financing and delivery, and for this reason, they have a strong preference for minimizing the government's role in the delivery of health care. One result is that Americans have been far more reluctant than their counterparts in most industrialized democracies to develop social insurance programs. In addition, public opinion in the United States often presumes such programs to be overly generous.

Generally speaking, the role of government in U.S. health care has grown incrementally, mainly in response to perceived problems and negative consequences. Some of the most cited problems associated with government involvement include escalating costs, bureaucratic inflexibility and red tape, excessive regulation, irrational paperwork, arbitrary and sometimes conflicting public directives, inconsistent enforcement of rules and regulations, fraud and abuse, inadequate reimbursement, arbitrary denial of claims, insensitivity to local needs, consumer and provider dissatisfaction, and charges that such efforts tend to promote welfare dependence rather than a desire to seek employment (Longest, 2002).

The most credible argument for policy intervention begins with the identification of situations in which markets fail or do not function efficiently. Health care in the United States is a big industry, but certain specific characteristics and conditions of the health care market distinguish it from other types of businesses. Notably, the market for health care services in the United States violates the conditions of a competitive market in several ways.

For example, the complexity of health care services almost eliminates the ability of the consumer to make informed decisions without guidance from the sellers (providers). In addition, the entry of sellers into the health care market is heavily regulated. Widespread insurance coverage also affects the decisions of both buyers and sellers in these markets. These and other factors mean that the markets for health care services do not operate competitively, which in turn invites policy intervention to rectify perceived inequities.

Government spending for health care has largely been confined to filling the gaps in the private sector. Such interventions have, for example, included environmental protection, preventive services, communicable disease control, care of special groups, institutional care of the mentally and chronically ill, provision of medical care to the indigent, and support for research and training. With health coverage considered a privilege for those who are offered insurance through their employers, the government is left in a gap-filling role for the most vulnerable of the uninsured population.

Fragmented, Incremental, and Piecemeal Reform

The subsidiary role of the government and the attendant mixture of private and public approaches to the delivery of health care also result in a complex and fragmented pattern of health care financing in which (1) the employed are predominantly covered by voluntary insurance provided through contributions made by themselves and their employers; (2) the aged are insured through a combination of coverage financed out of Social Security tax revenues (Medicare Part A), voluntary insurance for outpatient and prescription drug coverage (Medicare Part B and Part D), and voluntary purchase of Medigap plans; (3) the poor are covered through Medicaid via federal, state, and local revenues; and (4) special population groups, such as veterans, Native Americans, and members of the armed forces, have coverage provided directly by the federal government.

Health policies in the United States have been incremental and piecemeal. An example is the gradual reforms in the Medicaid program since its establishment in 1965. In 1984, the first steps were taken to mandate coverage of pregnant women and children in two-parent families who met income eligibility requirements and to mandate coverage for all children aged 5 years or younger who met financial eligibility requirements. In 1986, states were given the option of covering pregnant women and children up to 5 years of age in families with incomes below 100% of federal poverty income guidelines. In 1988, that option was increased to cover families at 185% of the federal poverty level. In 1988, as part of the Medicaid Catastrophic Act (which remains in effect today), Congress mandated coverage for pregnant women and infants in families with incomes below 100% of federal poverty guidelines. (In 1989, this criterion was expanded to 133% of the poverty income, and coverage of children was extended to include children aged 6 years or younger.) In 1988, Congress required that Medicaid coverage be continued for 6 months for families leaving the Aid to Families with Dependent Children program and allowed states the option of adding 6 months to that extension. The Children's Health Insurance Program (CHIP) allows states to use Medicaid expansion to extend insurance coverage to uninsured children who otherwise are not qualified for existing Medicaid programs.

These examples illustrate how a program may be reformed and expanded through successive legislative enactments over several years. In typical American fashion, the Medicaid program has been reformed through incremental change, but without ensuring access to medical care for all of the nation's uninsured. Among the uninsured population are millions of Americans who are not categorically eligible for services—mostly adults younger than age 65 with no dependent children. Congress has demonstrated the desire and political will to address the needs of a small number of the uninsured perceived as being the most vulnerable (e.g., pregnant women and children) but had not developed a consensus on more dramatic steps until the passage of the ACA. The ACA greatly increases insurance options for Americans previously lacking coverage, including a Medicaid expansion for adults with incomes up to 133% of the federal poverty level (in states that have chosen to expand Medicaid), the creation of state and federal health insurance exchanges for better regulation of private plans, and a prohibition on insurers against denying coverage due to preexisting medical conditions.

The process of legislative health policy development offers another vivid case of institutional fragmentation. Thirty-one different congressional committees and subcommittees try to claim some fragment of jurisdiction over health legislation. The reform proposals that emerge from these committees face a daunting political challenge because proposals undergo separate consideration and passage in each chamber of Congress, are subject to negotiations in a joint conference committee to reconcile bills passed by the two houses, and then head back to each chamber for approval. In the Senate, 41 of the 100 members can thwart the entire process at any point.

After a specific bill has passed in Congress, however, its journey is far from over. Multiple levels of federal and state bureaucracy must interpret the legislation, and rules and regulations must be written for its implementation. During this process, political actors, interest groups, or project beneficiaries may influence the ultimate design of the program. At times, the final result may differ significantly from the initial intent of the bill's congressional sponsors.

This complex and seemingly anarchic process of policy formulation and implementation makes fundamental, comprehensive policy reform extremely difficult. Ideology and the organization of government reinforce the tendency toward maintaining a standstill. It usually takes a great political event—a landmark election, a mass popular upheaval, a war, or a domestic crisis—to shake off (even temporarily) the normal tilt toward inaction and the status quo. The passage of the ACA was a notable accomplishment in this regard, but it remains to be seen how effectively the law actually works to reduce health care costs while increasing insurance coverage and medical care access.

Pluralistic and Interest Group Politics

Perhaps the most common explanation for health policy outcomes in the United States is one based on the role of interest groups and the incremental policies that result from compromises designed to satisfy their demands. Traditionally, the membership of the policy community has included (1) the legislative committees with jurisdiction in a policy domain, (2) the executive branch agencies responsible for implementing policies in the public domain, and (3) the interest groups in the private domain. The first two categories are the suppliers of the policies demanded by the third category.

Innovative, non-incremental policies are resisted by the established groups because such measures undermine the bargaining practices designed to reduce threats to established interests. The stability of the system is ensured because most groups are satisfied with the benefits that they receive; however, the result for any single group is less than optimal.

Interest Groups

The most effective demanders of policies are the well-organized interest groups. Interest groups' pluralism affects health policy just as it does any other policy debate in American politics. Powerful interest groups involved in health care politics are adamant about resisting any major change (Alford, 1975). Each group fights hard to protect its own interests.

By combining and concentrating the resources of their members, organized interest groups can dramatically change the ratio between the costs and benefits of participation in the political arena for policy change. Interest groups represent a variety of individuals and entities, such as physicians in the American Medical Association, senior citizens allied with the AARP (American Association of Retired Persons), institutional providers such as hospitals belonging to the American Hospital Association, nursing homes belonging to the American Health Care Association or the American Association of Homes and Services for the Aging, and the member companies in the Pharmaceutical Research and Manufacturers of America. In recent years, physicians have often found it difficult to establish a unified voice to lobby for their interests because of the many specialty groups that exist among them.

The policy agenda of interest groups is typically reflective of their own interests. For example, AARP advocates programs to expand financing for long-term care for the elderly. Organized labor was among the staunchest supporters of national health insurance during the 1950s and again in the 1990s. Educational institutions and accrediting bodies have their primary concerns embedded in policies that would enable them to receive higher funding to educate health professionals.

Employers

The health policy concerns of American employers are mostly shaped by the degree to which employers are involved in the provision of health insurance benefits for their employees, their dependents, and their retirees.

Many small business owners adamantly oppose health policies that would mandate them to provide coverage for employees because they believe they cannot afford to do so. Health policies that affect the health of workers or the health of the labor–management relations experienced by employers also attract their attention. For example, employers must comply with federal and state regulations regarding the health and well-being of their employees and engage in measures to prevent job-related illnesses and injuries. Employers are often subject to inspection by regulatory agencies to ensure that they are adhering to health and safety policies applicable to the workplace.

Consumer Groups

The interests of consumers are not uniform, nor are the policy preferences of their interest groups. Often, consumers do not have sufficient financial means to organize and advocate for their own best interests.

The health policy concerns of consumers and the groups that represent them reflect the rich diversity of the American people. African Americans and, more recently, the rapidly growing numbers of Hispanics face special health problems. Both groups are underserved for many health care services and are underrepresented in all of the health professions in the United States. Their health policy interests include getting their unique health problems (e.g., higher infant mortality, higher exposure to violence among adolescents, higher levels of substance abuse among adults, and earlier deaths from cardiovascular disease and various other causes) adequately addressed.

Manufacturers of Technology

The health policy concerns of pharmaceutical and medical technology organizations include discerning changes in health policy areas and exerting influence over the formulation of policies. Health policy concerns regarding medical technology (including pharmaceuticals) are driven by three main factors: (1) Medical technology plays an important role in rising health costs, (2) medical technology often provides health benefits to people (albeit not always), and (3) the use of medical technology provides economic benefits aside from its potential to provide health benefits. These factors are likely to remain important determinants of the nation's policies toward medical technology.

Another factor driving the United States' current medical technology policy is policy makers' desire to develop cost-saving technology and to expand access to it. The government is spending an increasing amount of money on technology assessment. The goal is to identify the relative values among alternative technologies, presumably so that the government can support the best values in technology.

Alliances

To overcome pluralistic interests and maximize policy outcomes, diverse interest groups may form alliances among themselves and with members of the legislative body to protect and enhance the interests of those receiving benefits from government programs. Each member of these alliances receives some benefits from the current programs. Legislators are able to demonstrate to their constituencies the economic benefits from government spending in their districts, agencies are able to expand their programs, and interest groups are the direct recipients of benefits bestowed by government programs.

Decentralized Role of the States

In the United States, individual states play a significant role in the development and implementation of health policies. The importance of the role of individual states can be seen in programs involving the following:

- Financial support for the care and treatment of the poor and chronically disabled, which includes the primary responsibility for the administration of the federal/state Medicaid program and CHIP
- Quality assurance and oversight of health care practitioners and facilities (e.g., state licensure and regulation)
- Regulation of insurance, including health insurance
- Control of Medicaid costs
- Health personnel training (states provide the major share of the cost for the training of health care professionals)
- Authorization of local government health services

States are vested with broad legal authority to regulate almost every facet of the health care system. They license and regulate health care facilities and health professionals; restrict the content, marketing, and price of health insurance (including professional liability or malpractice insurance); set and enforce environmental quality standards; and enact a variety of controls on health care costs. All states bear a large responsibility for financing health services for the poor, primarily through the Medicaid program, for which financing is shared with the federal government. In addition, most states subsidize some of the costs of delivering health services to those persons with neither public nor private coverage. Personal health services funded or provided by states, often in cooperation with local government, include a range of services, such as public health nursing, communicable disease control, family planning and prenatal care, nutrition counseling, and home health services.

Most of the incremental policy actions of recent years originated in state governments. One action was to create a special program called an insurance risk pool. This measure was intended to help persons who were otherwise unable to acquire private insurance because of the medical risks that they posed to insurance companies to do so. Most of these programs are financed by a combination of individual premiums and taxes on insurance carriers. Other state-initiated programs have addressed additional vulnerable populations. New Jersey developed a program to ensure access to care for all pregnant women. Florida began a program, called Healthy Kids Corporation, which linked health insurance to schools. Massachusetts, Hawaii, and Oregon have experimented with more comprehensive programs designed to provide universal access to care within their jurisdictions. All states have to decide whether to expand or not expand Medicaid under the ACA and to establish or not establish a state-run exchange.

Arguments have been made against too much state control over health policy decisions. The greater the amount of control states have, the more difficult it becomes to develop a coordinated national strategy. For example, it is difficult to plan a national disease control program if all states do not participate in the program or if they do not collect and report data in the same way. Moreover, some critics argue that disparities among states may lead to inequalities in access to health services. This factor, in turn, might lead to migration from states with poor health benefits to those with more generous programs.

Impact of Presidential Leadership

Americans often look to strong presidential leadership to catalyze major change in health policies, and presidents have important opportunities to influence congressional outcomes through their efforts to achieve political compromises that allow bills with at least some of their preferred agendas to be passed.

President Lyndon Johnson's role in the passage of Medicare and Medicaid is often cited as a prime example. Johnson shepherded the passage of Medicare and Medicaid in 1965 in the context of an unusually favorable level of political opportunity and by effectively using his leadership skills.

The major piece of health legislation that passed under President Harry Truman was the Hill-Burton Hospital Construction Act. Two major pieces of health legislation were passed during Richard Nixon's presidency: (1) the actions leading to federal support of HMOs in 1973 and (2) the enactment of the National Health Planning and Resources Development Act of 1974. Under President Ronald Reagan, new Medicare cost control approaches for hospitals and physicians were created, and additional Medicare coverage for the elderly was established. Even though President Bill Clinton's comprehensive reform efforts failed, many of his incremental initiatives succeeded; examples include the Health Insurance Portability and Accountability Act of 1996 and CHIP.

Many political lessons can be learned from the failure of Clinton's health care reform initiative (Litman & Robins, 1997). Presidential leadership in achieving landmark changes in health policies can be successful only when a convergence of political opportunity, political skill, and commitment occurs. Opportunities were uniquely abundant for Johnson in 1965, and he effectively handled his legislative role. Presidents Truman, John Kennedy, and Jimmy Carter might have promoted their proposals with greater skill, but they were fundamentally thwarted by the lack of a true window of opportunity. Clinton enjoyed a uniquely high level of public interest in health care reform but failed in part because of other weaknesses related to his level of opportunity, especially his failure to act within the first 100 days after his inauguration. The complexity of the ever-changing details of his proposal was another major flaw and ultimately proved too much for the general public to comprehend and too easy for adversaries to distort.

The 2008 presidential race, from which Barack Obama emerged victorious, offered another opportunity for Democrats to take up health care reform. While campaigning for the presidency, Obama presented a framework for health care reform to achieve three goals: (1) modernize the health care system to improve quality and reduce costs, (2) expand coverage to all Americans, and (3) improve prevention and public health. The ACA represents the most ambitious expansion of public health insurance since the creation of Medicare and Medicaid.

DEVELOPMENT OF LEGISLATIVE HEALTH POLICY

The making of health policy in the United States is a complex process involving both private and public sectors (including multiple levels of government).

Policy Cycle

The formation and implementation of health policy occur in a policy cycle comprising five components: (1) issue raising, (2) policy design, (3) building of public support, (4) legislative decision making and building of policy support, and (5) legislative decision making and policy implementation. These activities are likely to be shared with Congress and interest groups in varying degrees.

Issue-raising activities are clearly essential in the policy formation cycle. The enactment of a new policy is generally preceded by a variety of actions that first create a widespread sense that a problem exists and needs to be addressed. The president may form policy concepts from a variety of sources, including campaign information; party ideology; recommendations from advisers, cabinet members, and agency chiefs; personal views; expert opinions; and public opinion polls.

The second component of policy-making activity involves the design of specific policy proposals. Presidents have substantial resources at their disposal for developing new policy proposals. For example, they may call on segments of the executive branch of government, such as the Centers for Medicare and Medicaid Services, or policy staffs within the U.S. Department of Health and Human Services.

In building public support, presidents can choose from a variety of strategies, including major addresses to the nation, efforts to mobilize their administrations to make public appeals, and organized attempts to increase support among interest groups.

To facilitate legislative decision making and the building of policy support, presidents, key staff, and department officials interact closely with Congress. Presidents generally meet with legislative leaders several times a month in an effort to shape the coming legislative agenda and to identify possible problems as bills move through various committees.

Legislative Process

When a bill is introduced in the House of Representatives, it is assigned to an appropriate committee by the speaker. The committee chair forwards the bill to the appropriate subcommittee. The subcommittee then forwards proposed legislation to agencies that will be affected by the legislation, holds hearings and debates (markup), receives testimony, and may add amendments. The subcommittee and committee may recommend the bill, not recommend it, or recommend that it be tabled. Diverse interest groups, individuals, experts in the field, and business, labor, and professional associations often exert influence over the bill through campaign contributions and intense lobbying. The full House then hears the bill and may add amendments. The bill can be approved with or without amendments. The approved bill is sent to the Senate.

In the Senate, the bill is sent to an appropriate committee and then forwarded to an appropriate subcommittee. The subcommittee may send the bill to agencies that will be affected. It also holds hearings and receives testimony from all interested parties (e.g., private citizens, business, labor, agencies, experts). The subcommittee votes on and forwards the proposed legislation with appropriate recommendations. Amendments may or may not be added. The full Senate hears the bill and may add amendments. If the bill and House amendments are accepted, then the bill goes to the president. If the Senate adds amendments that have not been voted on by the House, then the bill must go back to the floor of the House for a vote.

If the amendments are minor and noncontroversial, the House may vote to pass the bill. If the amendments are significant and controversial, the House may call for a conference committee to review the amendments. The conference committee consists of members from the equivalent committees of the House and Senate. If the recommendations of the conference committee are not accepted, then another conference committee is called.

After the bill has passed both the House and Senate in identical form, it is then forwarded to the president for signature. If the president signs the legislation, it becomes law. If the president does not sign it, at the end of 10 days (excluding Sundays), it becomes law unless the president vetoes it. If less than 10 days are left in the congressional session, then inaction on the part of the president results in a veto—a situation called a pocket veto. The veto can be overturned by a two-thirds majority vote of the Congress; otherwise, the bill is dead.

After legislation has been signed into law, it is forwarded to the appropriate agency for implementation. The agency publishes proposed regulations in the *Federal Register* and then holds hearings regarding how the law is to be implemented. A bureaucracy only loosely controlled by either the president or Congress writes (i.e., publishes, gathers comments about, and rewrites) regulations. At that point, the program goes on to the 50 states for enabling legislation, if appropriate. There, organized interests hire local lawyers and lobbyists, and a whole new political cycle begins. Finally, all parties may adjourn to the courts to settle disputed issues, with potentially long rounds of litigation shaping the final outcome.

CRITICAL POLICY ISSUES

Government health policies have been enacted to resolve or prevent perceived deficiencies in health care delivery. Over the last 4 decades, most health policy initiatives and legislative efforts have focused on access to care (e.g., expanding insurance coverage, outreach programs in rural areas), cost of care (e.g., PPS, resource-based relative value scale), and quality of care (e.g., creating the Agency for Health Care Policy and Research, later renamed as the Agency for Healthcare Research and Quality, and calling for clinical practice guidelines).

Access to Care

Policies on access are aimed primarily at providers and financing mechanisms, with the purpose of expanding care to the most needy and underserved populations, including the elderly, minorities, rural residents, individuals with low incomes, and persons with AIDS. In addition to the coverage provisions included in the ACA, other programs, such as an expansion of the Community Health Center program to add 263 new centers (serving 1.25 million additional patients total), are intended to increase access to health care services (Bureau of Primary Health Care, 2013).

Providers

Several groups of providers are involved in delivering health care. Policy issues include ensuring that there is a sufficient number of providers and that their geographic distribution is desirable. The debate over the supply of physicians is an important public policy issue because policy decisions influence the number of persons entering the medical profession; that number, in turn, has implications for other policies. The number of new entrants into the profession is influenced by programs of government assistance for individual students and by government grants given directly to educational institutions. On the downside, an increasing supply of physicians may result in increased health care expenditures because of provider-induced demand. On the positive side, an increasing supply of physicians may also help alleviate shortages in certain regions of the country. Policy approaches to expanding access have included the National Health Service Corps, legislation supporting rural health clinics to expand geographic access, student assistance programs to expand the pool of health care workers, and legislation to expand a system of emergency medical services.

Public Financing

In the United States, public financing has been largely used to assist vulnerable groups in obtaining health care. These groups include the elderly (Medicare), poor children (Medicaid), poor adults (Medicaid and local or state general assistance), the disabled (Medicaid and Medicare), veterans (Veterans Health Administration), Native Americans (Indian Health Service), and patients with end-stage renal disease (Medicare and Social Security benefits for kidney dialysis and transplants). Access continues to be a problem in many communities, partly because health policies enacted since 1983 have focused on narrowly defined elements of the delivery system.

Access and the Elderly

Two main concerns dominate the debate about Medicare policy. First, spending must be restrained to keep the program solvent. Second, the program must be made truly comprehensive by adding services not currently covered or covered inadequately (e.g., comprehensive nursing home coverage). This is a paradox, however, because the two policy goals are at odds.

Access and Minorities

Minorities are more likely than whites to face access problems. Hispanics, blacks, Asian Americans, and Native Americans, to name the most prevalent minorities, all experience difficulties accessing the health care delivery system. In some instances, the combination of low income and minority status creates difficulties; in others, the interaction of special cultural habits and minority status causes problems in accessing health care. Resolving the problems confronting these groups would require policies designed to encourage professional education programs sensitive to the special needs of minorities and programs to expand the delivery of services to areas populated by minorities. Many of these areas have been designated as having shortages of health care workers.

Access in Rural Areas

Delivery of health care services in rural communities has always posed the problems of how to make advanced medical care available to residents of sparsely settled areas. Purchasing high-tech equipment to serve a few people is not cost-efficient, and finding physicians who want to reside in rural areas is difficult. Thus specialists and expensive diagnostic equipment are not readily available in rural medical practices. Reimbursement systems based on average costs make it difficult for rural hospitals with few patients to survive financially.

Funding the National Health Service Corps is one step toward addressing the problem of personnel shortages in rural areas; however, the Corps affects only the percentage of graduating physicians who practice in manpower shortage areas, and only for a limited time period for each student. Additional programs that increase the total supply of physicians and create incentives for permanent practice in rural areas are needed.

Access and Low Income

Low-income mothers and their children have problems accessing the health care system, both because they lack insurance and because they generally live in medically underserved areas. Pregnant women in low-income families are far less likely to receive prenatal care than are women in higher income categories. The CHIP program, signed into law in 1997, has given states some flexibility in how they spend federal funds allocated for investment in children's health coverage ("States Face a Welcome Dilemma," 1997).

Smoking and Tobacco Use

In the United States, lung cancer is the leading cause of death by cancer, killing 157,000 people annually. Overall, tobacco use causes almost 1 in 5 deaths in the United States. From 2000 to 2004, tobacco was responsible for approximately 443,000 early deaths annually. In 2007, the Institute of Medicine (IOM) released a report entitled *Ending the Tobacco Problem: A Blueprint for the Nation*, with the purpose of reducing smoking rates in the country. This goal is to be achieved through a two-pronged strategy involving strengthening and fully implementing traditional tobacco control measures and changing the regulatory landscape to permit policy innovations. The report concluded that if states maintained a comprehensive integrated tobacco control strategy at the CDC-recommended level of $15 to $20 per capita, tobacco use could be effectively reduced. Research has shown that more capital and time invested in tobacco control programs result in greater and quicker impact. For example, in California, the state with the longest-running tobacco control program, smoking rates fell from 22.7% in 1988 to 13.2% in 2008. Residents of the state now buy approximately half the number of cigarettes as the rest of the nation, and California was the first state to pass electronic tax stamp laws, making it easier to collect sales taxes and prevent tax evasion (California Tobacco Control Program, 2010).

In addition to supporting control programs, the U.S. government teams up with national partners to run nationwide campaigns directed at smoking cessation. The American Legacy Foundation administers the truth campaign that supports state-based youth prevention efforts. The Americans for Nonsmokers' Rights group provides states and municipalities with assistance and guidance in the process of passing and implementing smoke-free indoor air policies. The American Cancer Society, American Heart Association, and American Lung Association provide advocacy leadership on tobacco control policy issues, while also providing support at the community level through offices across the nation.

Cost Containment

To a large extent, the strengths of the U.S. health care delivery system also contribute to its weaknesses. The United States boasts both the latest developments in medical technology and a supply of well-trained specialists, but these advances amount to the most expensive means possible to provide care to patients, making the U.S. health care system the most costly in the world. No other aspect of health care policy has received more attention during the past 30 years than efforts to contain increases in health care costs. Two major policy initiatives enacted by the federal government have targeted hospitals (PPS) and physicians' services (resource-based relative value scale) for price controls.

The National Health Planning and Resources Development Act of 1974 marked the transition from improvement of access to cost containment as the principal theme in federal health policy. Health planning, through certificate-of-need review, was used as a policy tool to contain hospital costs. One major change in the health policy environment was a new system of paying hospitals for Medicare clients—the PPS, which was enacted in 1983 (Mueller, 1988). The PPS method of reimbursement has proved to be the most successful tool for controlling hospital expenditures (Wennberg et al., 1984). Government programs, especially Medicare and Medicaid, federal employee benefit programs, and those of the Veterans Health Administration and armed services, face constant pressure from Congress to keep costs down.

Expenditures are a function of the price of services times the quantity of services delivered. In the past, most policies enacted have focused on the price of services. Policy makers are reluctant to consider restricting the quantity of services, fearful of a backlash because of rationing of care.

Increased debate over the right to die and the value of life-extending services provides an opportunity to discuss limiting reimbursable services. So far, the federal government has been reluctant to adopt an explicit rationing strategy to contain expenditures, but state governments can be expected to experiment with other means of cost containment.

The private sector also influences the policy focus on cost containment. Major corporations are now aggressively pursuing ways to restrain the escalation of health insurance costs for their employees. Large employers have started to offer discounts toward the purchase of health insurance when employees enroll in healthy lifestyle programs and achieve certain health goals.

The ACA includes some cost control measures. It is too early to assess their effectiveness.

Quality of Care

Along with access and cost, quality of care is the third main concern of health care policy. The Health Care Quality Act of 1986 mandated the creation of a national database within the U.S. Department of Health and Human Services to provide data on legal actions against health care providers. This information allows people recruiting physicians in one state to discover actions against those physicians in other states.

In the Omnibus Budget Reconciliation Act (OBRA) of 1989, Congress created a new agency, the National Center for Health Services Research (now called the Agency for Healthcare Research and Quality [AHRQ]), and mandated it to conduct and support research with respect to the outcomes, effectiveness, and appropriateness of health care services and procedures (U.S. House of Representatives, 1989). AHRQ has established funding for patient outcomes research teams that focus on particular medical conditions. The patient outcomes research teams are part of a broader effort, the medical treatment effectiveness program, which "consists of four elements: medical treatment effectiveness research, development of databases for such research, development of clinical guidelines, and the dissemination of research findings and clinical guidelines" (Salive et al., 1990). The development of clinical guidelines was carried out by AHRQ from 1992 to 1996; this effort has now broadened to become the National Guideline Clearinghouse, responsible for the analysis and dissemination of clinical guidelines across the United States (National Guideline Clearinghouse, n.d.). AHRQ also focuses on improving quality of care through comparative-effectiveness research, health information technology initiatives, preventive medicine (through the U.S. Preventive Services Task Force in particular), and health care value analyses.

Research and Policy Development

The research community can influence the making of health policy through documentation, analysis, and prescription (Longest, 2002). The first role of research in policy making is documentation—that is, the gathering, cataloging, and correlating of facts that depict the state of the world that policy makers face. This process may help define a given public policy problem or raise its political profile.

A second way in which research informs, and thereby influences, policy making is through analysis of what does and does not work. Program evaluation and outcomes research fall under this domain. Often taking the form of demonstration projects intended to provide a factual basis for determining the feasibility, efficacy, or practicality of a possible policy intervention, analysis can help define solutions to health policy problems.

The third way in which research influences policy making is through prescription. Research demonstrating that a particular course of action being contemplated by policy makers may (or may not) lead to undesirable or unexpected consequences can make a significant contribution to policy making.

Health Policy After the Affordable Care Act

According to the Commonwealth Fund (2015), challenges related to health policy and the ACA include: (1) The Supreme Court made it optional for states to expand Medicaid eligibility, resulting in significant consequences for residents in states that have opted out. Millions in those states are now trapped in a coverage gap, earning too much to qualify for Medicaid but not enough for subsidies offered in the marketplaces (Commonwealth Fund, 2015). (2) Undocumented immigrants are excluded from the law; consequently they cannot purchase marketplace coverage or qualify for Medicaid (Commonwealth Fund, 2015). The Congressional Budget Office estimates that 30 percent of the remaining uninsured will be unauthorized immigrants by 2020 (Commonwealth Fund, 2015). (3) Some individuals with higher incomes are having more issues affording their premiums and deductibles due to subsidies becoming less generous with higher household income (Commonwealth Fund, 2015):

> Sixty-five percent of individuals with annual incomes just under $30,000 and families of four with incomes of $60,000 reported it was very or somewhat easy to afford their premiums. However, just over half (54%) with incomes above these levels said it was very or somewhat easy to pay … A number of Republicans in Congress continue to promise a repeal of the ACA. While previous attempts haven't gained traction, repeal—or wholesale changes—remains a possibility. A dismantling of the ACA's reforms would mean that millions who have gained coverage and access to affordable health care might once again join the ranks of the uninsured. (Commonwealth Fund, 2015, What's Next for the ACA section, p. 4)

INTERNATIONAL HEALTH POLICY: COMPARISONS

Looking abroad, international analyses of health policy and health care systems show both similarities with and differences from the U.S. approach to health. One of the largest studies, the 2014 Commonwealth

Fund International Health Policy Survey, sought to characterize the experience of patients in eleven countries: the United States, the United Kingdom, Australia, Canada, France, Germany, the Netherlands, New Zealand, Norway, Sweden, and Switzerland. All are industrialized, high-income countries, and all face challenges from rising health care costs. Nonetheless, each of these countries differs greatly in terms of issues such as insurance benefits (all except the United States have a universal coverage structure), patient referral processes (all except Germany and the United States enforce gatekeeping methods before specialist services can be obtained), cost sharing (the United Kingdom and the Netherlands have the most comprehensive programs, while the other countries use methods of cost sharing or benefit gaps in coverage), and uses of medical technology (practices in Canada and the United States are least likely to have electronic medical records) (Schoen et al., 2007).

Despite these broad differences, the United States expends vastly more for medical care both per capita ($9,255 average per person—twice as much as the average in the next-highest-cost country) and as a percentage of gross domestic product (a total of 17.4% of the 2013 U.S. gross domestic product went to health care spending). Additionally, all other profiled countries had uninsured rates less than 2% (versus the 2014 estimate of 12% in the United States) and significantly lower barriers to access. In light of these findings, it becomes even more important to look critically at the shortfalls of the U.S. health care system and identify and implement fundamental changes that could work in this country to reduce costs, increase access, and improve quality.

CONCLUSION

Health policies are developed to serve the public's interests; however, public interests are diverse, and members of the public often hold conflicting views. Although the public consistently supports the goal of national health insurance, it also rejects the idea of the federal government running the health care delivery system. Similarly, although the American public wants the government to control health care costs, it also believes that the federal government already exerts too much control over Americans' daily lives. The challenge for policy makers is to find a balance between governmental provisions (i.e., control) and the private health care market to improve coverage and affordability of care. Successful health policies are more likely to be couched in terms of cost containment (a market-justice, economic, business, and middle-class concern) than in improved or expanded access and reduction or elimination of health disparities (a social-justice, liberal, labor, low-income issue); however, cost-related policies are likely to have very little impact on improving the quality of care or reducing health disparities.

REFERENCES

Alford RR. *Health Care Politics: Ideology and Interest Group Barriers to Reform.* Chicago: University of Chicago Press; 1975.

Bureau of Primary Health Care. HHS awards Affordable Care Act funds to expand access to health care. http://www.hhs.gov/news/press/2013pres/11/20131107a .html. Published August 9, 2011. Accessed August 12, 2015.

California Tobacco Control Program. Two decades of the California Tobacco Control Program: California tobacco survey, 1990–2008. https://www.cdph .ca.gov/programs/tobacco/Documents/Resources/Publications/CDPH _CTS2008%20summary%20report_final.pdf. Published 2010. Accessed August 12, 2015.

The Commonwealth Fund. The Affordable Care Act at five years: how the law is changing health coverage in the U.S. http://www.commonwealthfund.org /ACAat5/coverage-reform/. Published 2015. Accessed August 12, 2015.

Health Insurance Association of America. *Source Book of Health Insurance Data.* Washington, DC: Health Insurance Association of America; 1992.

Institute of Medicine (IOM). *Ending the Tobacco Problem: A Blueprint for the Nation.* Washington DC: IOM; 2007.

Litman T, Robins L. The relationship of government and politics to health and health care: a sociopolitical overview. In: Litman T, Robins L, eds. *Health Politics and Policy.* 3rd ed. New York: John Wiley and Sons; 1997:3–45.

Longest BB. *Health Policymaking in the United States.* Ann Arbor, MI: Health Administration Press; 2002.

Miller CA. Child health. In: Levine S, Lillienfeld A, eds. *Epidemiology and Health Policy.* New York: Tavistock; 1987:15.

Mueller KJ. Federal programs do expire: the case of health planning. *Public Admin Rev.* 1988;48:719–735.

National Guideline Clearinghouse. http://www.guideline.gov/about/index.aspx. n.d. Accessed August 12, 2015.

National Institutes of Health (NIH). NIH budget. http://www.nih.gov/about /budget.htm. Reviewed January 29, 2015. Accessed August 12, 2015.

Salive ME, et al. Patient outcomes research teams and the Agency for Health Care Policy and Research. *Health Serv Res.* 1990;25:697–708.

Schoen C, Osborn R, Doty MM, et al. Toward higher-performance health systems: Adults' health care experiences in seven countries, 2007. *Health Aff.* 2007;26(6);w717–w734.

States face a welcome dilemma: how to best spend $24 billion to cover nation's uninsured children. *State Health Watch.* 1997; 4(8):1, 4.

U.S. House of Representatives. *Omnibus Budget Reconciliation Act of 1989: Conference Report to Accompany H.R. 3299.* Washington, DC: Government Printing Office; November 21, 1989.

Weissert C, Weissert W. *Governing Health: The Politics of Health Policy.* Baltimore, MD: Johns Hopkins University Press; 1996.

Wennberg JE, et al. Will payment based on diagnosis-related groups control hospital costs? *N Engl J Med.* 1984;311(5):295–300.

Chapter 14

The Future of Health Services Delivery

INTRODUCTION

Fundamental features of U.S. health care delivery, such as a largely private infrastructure and traditional American values, have, in the past, resisted any proposals for a sweeping transformation of health care. How certain forces of change play out in the future will be particularly significant. The main forces include social, demographic, and cultural trends; economic conditions; political will and legal rulings; technological innovation; global health issues; and ecological events, such as the emergence of new diseases and catastrophic occurrences. Among these, certain forces such as demographic trends project a foreseeable course, based on which some predictions can be made. For other factors, even short-term predictions are difficult. For instance, it is impossible to predict the future course of the U.S. economy, employment, and family incomes, all of which will affect what individual Americans and the nation may or may not be able to afford in the wake of rising health care costs. U.S. health care stands at a tipping point—a convergence of a growing, graying, and highly consumptive population with increasingly limited financial and human capital resources (Frist, 2014).

Despite the intents and promises of the Affordable Care Act (ACA), serious issues remain in the areas of coverage, cost, access, and affordability. Although the ACA—also known as Obamacare—has remained highly unpopular, many Americans have had no choice but to enroll. Many had their previous health insurance cancelled because the plans they had did not comply with the ACA's new mandates. Although preliminary information in the areas of coverage, cost, access, and affordability may be harbingers of what may be forthcoming, better research in the future is expected to provide more definitive answers. Nevertheless, despite opposition, the ACA has already found a firm footing within the U.S. health care delivery system. Regardless of the ACA's final fate, the ongoing transformative changes that have occurred and are still occurring under the law will have far reaching effects on U.S. health care.

FORCES OF FUTURE CHANGE
Social, Demographic, and Cultural Trends

It is no secret that the rising tide of the elderly in America, concomitant with dropping birth rates, will put serious strains on Medicare and Social Security—government-run medical and retirement programs respectively funded through workers' payroll taxes. For example, according to the recent Medicare trustees reports, the program faces a substantial financial short-fall with looming negative consequences for beneficiaries, providers, and taxpayers. This is despite the 165 some provisions contained in the ACA to reduce Medicare costs, increase revenues, and combat program fraud and abuse (Centers for Medicare and Medicaid Services [CMS], 2014).

Social changes are reflected in drops in labor participation, upticks in welfare and disability rolls, and a continuous rise in illegal immigration. For example, the labor participation rate[1] in 2015 reached around 63%—the lowest point since 1978 (Farley, 2015)—meaning that 37% of working age

---

[1]Percentage of the population (16 years and older) that is either employed or actively seeking work.

Americans were not working and had given up looking for work. This is mostly attributed to the retiring baby boomers[2] and an economy that has remained sluggish all through the Barack Obama presidency. Rolls of the nonelderly disabled have consistently risen from 13.6% of Medicare beneficiaries in 2000 to 16.7% in 2015 (National Center for Health Statistics [NCHS], 2004, 2015) under fairly loose eligibility criteria, as if an increasing proportion of working-age Americans were disqualified from working. Medicaid rolls have increased from covering 15% of the population in 2000 to an estimated 25% in 2015. Since the ACA's implementation, of the 12.6 million newly enrolled in Medicaid, 6.1 million previously had health insurance (Carman, 2015). Illegal immigration has been a long-standing issue that neither Democrats nor Republicans have had the political will to address. Even though illegal immigrants are not covered by the ACA, they do get health care through a variety of sources that include emergency rooms, community health centers, and charity from hospitals. Increasing dependency on government handouts and haphazard immigration that does not promote cultural assimilation have already resulted in a gradual erosion of the traditional American belief and value system.

Aside from political rhetoric and spins put on reality, basic economics informs us that rising consumption along with reduced production will result in higher expenditures. After an average annual increase of about 4% between 2009 and 2013 in national health expenditures (data from NCHS, 2015), before the ACA went into effect, national health spending picked up speed throughout 2014 (Altman, 2015). The trend is on an upswing.

Economic Forces

Expenditures can rise as long as people can afford them. Hence, affordability of health care at both individual and national levels is critical. Household income in relation to economic inflation is a fundamental determinant of affordability, and both employment and personal income depend on the nation's economic health. According to Sentier Research, the median household income in April 2015 was $54,578, which was 1.1% lower than the median income in June 2009 when the recent recession ended. During this time period, consumer prices (a measure of inflation) increased by 9.9%. Further, the 2015 median income was 4%

---

[2]Those born between 1946 and 1964, when there was a significant rise in birth rates.

lower than what it was in 2000 (Green & Coder, 2015). Hence, over a span of 15 years average family incomes have gone down, not up. It is tragic indeed that apart from the bloated welfare state that America is becoming, working Americans are earning less. Research on affordability at the individual level should be forthcoming to assess how the average American is able to afford health care in an environment of rising costs and dwindling incomes.

At the national level, opinions vary on whether a stagnant economy and downward sloping labor participation rate have become the new normal. But, again, basic economics tells us that overreaching government regulations have a cost that society must bear. For example, mandates to insure regardless of preexisting medical conditions and to include all prescribed benefits in all health plans, regardless of whether or not people need those services, will raise health insurance premiums. Federal subsidies paid to insurers under the ACA mask the true costs of health insurance, but as the subsidies are phased out starting in 2016, we can expect premiums to rise more rapidly.

Political Will, Ideologies, and Legal Rulings

The ACA is a textbook case that illustrates political will on the part of the president and his political party in passing and rolling out a substantial piece of legislation. As pointed out in previous sections, there will be fallouts. Much will depend on the quality of political leadership, resolve to take action despite political consequences, ideological differences between the two main political parties, and the involvement of American people regarding how critical issues get addressed in the future.

The U.S. Supreme Court has played a pivotal role in upholding the constitutionality of major portions of the ACA. The Court is evenly divided along ideological lines, and a shift in either direction, to the left or to the right, will have a bearing on future rulings.

Technological Innovation

Thus far, the overall effect of medical technology has been to increase costs. Yet, Americans strongly favor ongoing innovation, availability, and use of new technology, particularly for diagnostics and treatments. Future focus will be on technologies that promote a greater degree of self-reliance and self-care, with remote monitoring to ensure effectiveness and safety.

Global Health Issues

In many respects, the world has become progressively interconnected and interdependent through ease of trade and travel. Globalization presents both opportunities and challenges. For example, manufacture of generic and other drugs by Asian countries for export to Europe, Canada, and the United States helps the economies of both manufacturing and importing countries. But, safety becomes an issue. The Food and Drug Administration (FDA) has warned that consumers continue to buy potentially risky drugs over the Internet with no guarantee of their effectiveness or safety.

On other fronts, the prevention and control of infectious diseases globally will continue to pose major challenges. For example, increase in cross-border travel resulted in the spread of a previously unknown communicable disease called severe acute respiratory syndrome (SARS) from China to Canada in 2003 and of polio virus from India to northern Minnesota in 2005 (Milstein et al., 2006). In 2014, at least 11 people infected with the deadly Ebola virus were treated in U.S. hospitals and had raised serious alarms in some parts of the country. Almost all the victims had traveled from sub-Saharan Africa. Similarly, the Centers for Disease Control and Prevention (CDC) identified 401 cases of the deadly MERS virus—short for Middle East respiratory syndrome and first reported in 2012 in Saudi Arabia—in 12 countries between 2012 and 2014 (Weintraub & Stanglin, 2014). Current efforts to strengthen global health security include disease surveillance for outbreaks of international importance and urgency, exchange of technical information on new pathogens, and early warning and control of serious animal disease outbreaks. In a rapidly changing world, however, renewed efforts and cooperation among nations will become necessary. Worldwide shortage of trained health care workers is another area of alarming concern, as lack of treatment and isolation capabilities often result in deadly pandemics, affecting large segments of a population.

Ecological Events

New diseases, natural disasters, and bioterrorism have major implications for public health. Diseases that are communicable—such as new strains of influenza—and those related to environmental agents—such as vector-borne diseases (for example, West Nile virus and chikungunya virus)—can bring about mass hysteria particularly in large population centers, especially when some disease may remain mysterious and treatments are not readily available, as was the case with Ebola. Growth of populations around the globe will intensify human–animal-ecosystems interface, raising the probability of engendering diseases that are yet unknown. When a significant number of people are affected or threatened by disease, research and technological innovation go into high gear. Technologies, such as remote sensing and geographic information systems, will find ongoing applications in public health and safety.

Natural disasters disrupt not only people's daily lives but also create conditions that pose serious health risks through contamination of food and water. Health problems and psychological distress often follow. Initiatives, such as biosurveillance and infrastructure upgrades will be constantly needed to cope with natural and man-made disasters. Roles of the CDC and other partnering agencies will continue to evolve as new challenges emerge. On the downside, the growing need for combatting new ecological threats will divert resources from providing routine health care to patients in most need of those services.

CHALLENGES OF COVERAGE, ACCESS, AND COST

Despite the promise that the ACA would be designed to cover all Americans, unacceptable gaps in coverage still remain. Before the ACA was implemented, somewhere between 15% and 16% of the U.S. population was uninsured. That number dropped to 11.9% in 2014 (Kutscher, Herman, & Meyer, 2015)—an improvement, but still off the mark. Under the ACA, a net number of 16.9 million gained health insurance—22.8 million gained while 5.9 million lost coverage (Carman, 2015). According to estimates by the Congressional Budget Office (CBO), the uninsured population was 35 million in 2015 (CBO, 2015a); hence, achieving universal coverage will remain a challenge well into the future.

One important test of a robust health care system is whether the insured get timely access to health care services. Health insurance facilitates access; it does not guarantee it. Currently, research on the ease with which people can gain access and satisfaction with access under the ACA is not available. For example, whether enrollees who had to change health plans and doctors—despite President Obama's hollow rhetoric, "If you like your health care plan, you'll be able to keep your health care plan" and "If you like your doctor, you can keep your doctor"—are now satisfied with the switches they had to make is still unknown. On the other hand, according to limited-focus group research that provides preliminary insights into the experiences of those who gained health insurance through Medicaid, many are encountering roadblocks to receiving the care they want. Finding a primary care physician appears to be the biggest hurdle; finding a specialist or a dentist is even tougher (Millman, 2014). This is despite the fact that the ACA provided for reimbursement bumps in 2013 and 2014 as an incentive for physicians to take Medicaid patients. So, despite gaining coverage, Medicaid beneficiaries will continue to receive services from the sources they have traditionally relied upon—hospital emergency departments and government-subsidized community health centers in areas where these services are available. Nevertheless, these indications are preliminary and need to be verified through more robust research.

The capacity of the health care system to meet the demand for services is a major issue that threatens future access to health care for most Americans. Hospital executives, for example, believe that across the nation there are shortages of physicians, nurses, and advanced practitioners (American Nurse, 2014). Economists estimate that one-third of the physicians and at least half of nurses could retire by 2021. It is also projected that the nation will require 10 to 12 million new and replacement direct care workers—medical assistants, nursing aides, home health aides, etc. (Okrent, 2011). The ACA has some provisions to address the looming shortage of health care personnel. However, any positive effects would not be apparent for some time.

Reporters such as Volsky (2013) quite erroneously jumped to the conclusion that the ACA, even before it was fully implemented in 2014, had somehow led to the moderation in health insurance premiums and other health care costs. In a comprehensive analysis by Kowalski (2014), "Across all states, from before the reform to the first half of 2014, enrollment-weighted premiums in the individual health insurance market increased by 24.4 percent beyond...state level trends." For 2015, the average premium rise is around 4–5%, but there are significant variations both across and within states (PricewaterhouseCoopers LLP, 2015).

Depending on the health utilization experience of the enrollees, future premiums could moderate somewhat or they could rise, even dramatically. There has been a moderation in the rise of premium costs in 2015; however, besides insurance premiums, the true cost burden at the individual level must include the actual out-of-pocket costs—deductibles and copayments—that individuals actually bear when they utilize health care services. We will have to wait for future research to address such questions. In the meantime, it is reported that the 2015 maximum out-of-pocket limits of $6,600 for an individual plan and $13,200 for a family plan are making health care unaffordable for many patients, especially those with lower incomes (Herman, 2015).

The net cost of coverage provisions of the ACA has been estimated to be $1.2 trillion between 2016 and 2025 (CBO, 2015a). It is almost impossible to estimate the total economic cost attributable to job losses, reduced working hours, businesses taking their operations overseas, higher operating costs passed on to consumers, and increased taxes that would reduce consumers' purchasing power. Such negative trends will have consequences for the overall economy, not just health care. On the other hand, the economy could somehow start humming at a rapid pace as a number of entrepreneurs, innovators, and small businesses spring up all across the nation. This, however, has not happened in the past 7 years or so; hence, it dims the prospects of exponential economic growth at least in the foreseeable future. It also questions the nation's ability to spend another $1.2 trillion on a program that does not even bring health care to all citizens, which, if it could be realized in some rational way, would indeed be a much desired and noble goal.

THE FUTURE OF HEALTH CARE REFORM

Speculations abound that the ACA would eventually lead to a *single-payer system*, which is a national health care program in which the financing and insurance functions are taken over by the federal government. A single-payer system in the United States would be fairly similar to today's Medicaid in which the beneficiaries get tax-financed health care, but with more controls over how that health care is delivered. As an alternative, a single-payer system could resemble today's Medicare in which the beneficiaries get subsidized health care. Over time, however, such a program will start leaning toward Medicaid, with some out-of-pocket cost sharing still in place. On the other hand, unlike Medicaid and Medicare, single-payer does not generally have eligibility criteria. It aims to provide *universal coverage*—that is, all legal residents get health insurance and some form of *universal access*—that is, all the insured get some degree of access to health care services. It is well to keep in mind that the ACA currently does not achieve these goals.

Will a Single-Payer System Emerge?

In an interview, Senator Harry Reid (D), one of the chief architects of the ACA, confessed that a number of Democrat lawmakers were ready to support a single-payer system (McHugh, 2013). Reid confessed that the option was on the table during negotiations with other Democrats over the ACA. So, will the United States have a single-payer system in the future? For a single-payer system to materialize, certain forces have to be in the right alignment.

Throughout the history of health care reform, political forces have taken center stage in the debates. Also, for political reasons, the central features of the ACA were not scheduled to be implemented until 2014, after Obama's second-term election in 2012. During this election, calls by Obama's opponent, Mitt Romney, to repeal Obamacare were ignored by the electorate for two main reasons. Romney did not have a plan that would replace Obamacare; if he had one, he did not articulate it. Secondly, people relied on Obama's promises referred to earlier. Additionally, Obama had pledged that an average family would save $2,500 a year on health insurance—like his other promises, this one has also turned out to be hollow rhetoric. In contrast to the 2012 presidential election, the 2014 congressional elections, in which Democrats had to concede both the houses to Republicans, may well have hinged on the widespread disenchantment with the promises of Obamacare and the experiences of those who lost the coverage they had liked. Following the 2014 elections, Senator Chuck Schumer, an influential Democrat, said that whatever the merits or demerits of health reform, it was bad politics (Goodman, 2014). In future, politicians will have to assess the political cost they would personally incur for taking a position in favor of a single-payer system, if it comes to that. Also, control of the presidency and the Congress will have to be in the hands of the Democratic Party, just as it was with the passage of the ACA.

Morphing the ACA into a single-payer system will also depend on social and economic factors. For example, if health insurance premium costs and out-of-pocket costs rise beyond what most people consider to be affordable, there could be a push for a single-payer system. Conversely, mass dissatisfaction with the ACA may kill the prospects of a single-payer system, unless crafty politicians could put the blame on corporate America and if Americans buy into that spin. Corporations could be accused of being insensitive to the rising cost of health insurance, and insurance companies could be labeled as profit mongers. On the economic front, individual income taxes have already risen to pay for Obamacare. But, tax hikes in the future are not out of the question. That is just the nature of government programs; the amount of money needed to pay for them never seems to be adequate, as the experience with Medicare and Medicaid has shown. Much remains unknown at present. For example, will the health care industry support a single-payer system, just as it supported Obamacare? Will voting Americans buy into the idea of a government-run program? Will the two political parties be able to build consensus, or will one party be in a position to boycott the other, as it happened with the ACA?

The Cost Control Imperative

For a system to remain solvent, any expansion of coverage must be accompanied by cost control measures. To control costs materially, it is necessary to manage utilization, limit reimbursement to providers, and employ some sort of rationing for the supply of health care services. Only the government is in a position to wage war against costs on all three fronts, particularly in a single-payer national health care system. The extent of controls needed to limit rising health care costs cannot be accomplished under the ACA as it exists now. Moreover, at least theoretically, heavy-handed government controls would be strongly opposed by most Americans. Hence, it is not seen as a practical alternative for future reforms. In the short term, we may actually see some relaxations in the rules crafted to implement Obamacare.

There is a dire need to control costs. According to CBO's latest report:

Federal spending for Social Security and the government's major health care programs—Medicare, Medicaid, the Children's Health Insurance Program, and subsidies for health insurance purchased through the exchanges created by the Affordable Care Act—would rise sharply, to 14.2 percent of GDP by 2040 (CBO, 2015b).

National Debt

Any meaningful health care reform cannot be undertaken in isolation of broader economic realities. U.S. budget deficits (overspending) and the rising national debt (borrowing money to pay for the overspending) will affect all aspects of the economy, including health care, which accounts for an estimated 18% of the U.S. economy. According to the U.S. Department of the Treasury (2015), national debt now exceeds $18 trillion. Since the previous edition of this book was prepared, the United States has racked up an additional $3 trillion in debt. If at some point in the future (no one knows when, and it may not happen for a few years to come), the United States defaults on its obligation to repay the debt there would be unimaginable consequences that will reverberate throughout the world's economies. To put this in perspective, each time the prospects of a default by Greece—its national debt is just 2% that of the United States—are in the news, it sends jitters throughout the financial markets. The national debt has consequences for the world's economies and the standard of living that Americans have been taking for granted.

This is what the CBO recently said about the mounting debt:

> The rising debt could not be sustained indefinitely; the government's creditors would eventually begin to doubt its ability to cut spending or raise revenues by enough to pay its debt obligations, forcing the government to pay much higher interest rates to borrow money (CBO, 2015b).

Higher interest rates will only exacerbate the problem.

Generational Impact

The financing of Medicare is essentially a generational transfer system in which current taxpayers pay for the benefits of current beneficiaries. Shortfalls in such a financing system must be paid by future generations. Data from the three most recent reports (2011–2013) of the boards of trustees of the Federal Hospital Insurance and Federal Supplementary Medical Insurance Trust Funds (trustees' report) on annual Medicare deficits are presented in **Table 14.1**. Even though the estimated date for Medicare's bankruptcy fluctuates from year to year, there is no denial that within the next 12 to 15 years the system will be insolvent. No meaningful health care reform can ignore the serious steps needed to address this impending disaster that will otherwise affect the lives of not only millions of senior citizens but of working Americans as well. The 2014 trustees' report projects that Medicare spending will rise faster than workers' earnings and the nation's economic output.

The ACA includes some cost-saving measures for Medicare, but their long-term impact is not clear. The CMS has projected short-term savings

Table 14.1 Deficits in Medicare Funding: 2011–2013 (Billions of Dollars)

	2011	2012	2013
Total income	$530.0	$536.9	$575.8
Total expenditures	$549.1	$574.2	$582.9
Deficit (expenditures exceeding income)	$19.1	$37.3	$7.1

Data from Centers for Medicare and Medicaid Services 2013, 2014, 2015 Annual report of the boards of trustees of the federal hospital insurance and federal supplementary medical insurance trust funds.

of over $200 billion through 2016 (CMS, 2012). States are also grappling with cost-saving measures applied to Medicaid, which is managed by the states. There is a push toward enrolling more beneficiaries in managed care and paying managed care organizations capitated monthly fees to cover all health care expenses for Medicaid beneficiaries. Such changes may be just the beginning of austerity measures, however, as states are experiencing budget deficits of their own.

FUTURE MODELS OF CARE DELIVERY

There is widespread consensus that the existing model of health care delivery in the United States must change. Several issues in the existing system, which is driven by the medical model of health, remain to be resolved:

1. There is inadequate emphasis on wellness, disease prevention, and health promotion.

2. Despite a dramatic rise in chronic conditions and ensuing disabilities, the existing health care system focuses primarily on addressing acute illnesses.

3. Inadequate access to primary care results in the overuse of costly emergency room services.

4. Undue emphasis on specialization increases the cost of health care without being accompanied by noteworthy improvements in the health status of the U.S. population.

5. The delivery of care remains fragmented, instead of continuous and coordinated.

The ACA is intended to make some headway in these areas by emphasizing wellness and disease prevention and care coordination. Three emerging models of health care delivery were discussed in previous chapters—namely, the medical home model, community-oriented primary care, and accountable care organizations. In addition, two lesser known models—the teamlet model and connected health care—are worth mentioning. All of these models are still in their infancy. There will be successes and failures along the way, but there will be room for more than one model of care. Regardless, the challenge of providing better access to more people, improved health outcomes, care coordination, and continuity of care, all while reducing the cost of health care, is likely to remain.

Teamlet Model

A teamlet refers to a small team consisting of a clinician—such as a primary care physician, nurse practitioner, or physician assistant—and one or two allied health professionals who function as a health coach. The teamlet works together collaboratively. The main function of the health coach is to assist patients with gaining the knowledge, skills, and confidence to self-manage their chronic conditions. The health coach also coordinates care by scheduling clinical visits, helping patients adopt healthy lifestyles, helping patients understand and adhere to their medication regimen, and providing other types of support (Ngo et al., 2010). The model has been tried within the veterans' health system. Early indications are that the model holds promise, but its success would require comprehensive training, stability of teamlets, clear cross-coverage policies, and clearly defined responsibilities (Rodriguez et al., 2014).

Connected Health Care

Connected health care incorporates the use of communication technology, patient self-management, and distant monitoring technology for chronic care management. New monitoring technology has the capability of enabling just-in-time provider interventions when needed (Kvedar et al., 2011). One main objective of connected care is to keep chronically ill patients connected to necessary clinical expertise in between office visits so as to avert medical crises that might otherwise land these patients in the emergency room (Moore, 2009). Wearable devices for health monitoring and diagnostics will proliferate if they can help prevent serious medical onsets or enable fast intervention and provided more people can afford them. Today's wearables give the advantage of continuous real-time monitoring of critical body functions.

FUTURE WORKFORCE CHALLENGES

An adequate and well-trained workforce is a critical component of the health care delivery infrastructure. Shortage of health care professionals has been pointed out previously. Hence, the most productive use of existing resources must be emphasized.

According to a report produced by the National Academy of Sciences (2010), nurses should practice to the full extent of their education and training. Licensing requirements and rules governing the scope of practice across states need to be unified for advance practice nurses who have master's or doctoral degrees. Residency programs for nurses need to incorporate training in community health, public health, and geriatrics.

Primary care physicians need training so they can adequately function as "comprehensivists" to address the needs of a growing number of people with complex chronic conditions. They must be prepared to manage complex pharmacology, understand end-of-life issues and medical ethics, and lead health care teams.

A shortage of health care professionals trained in geriatrics is a critical challenge with serious implications, as the elderly population will keep increasing. This problem is compounded by the shortage of faculty in colleges and universities who are trained in geriatrics. The elderly use the majority of home health care services and nursing home care, account for roughly half of hospital inpatient days, and represent approximately one-fourth of all ambulatory care visits. Many elderly patients suffer from chronic conditions, and their care is often complicated by the presence of comorbidities, the use of multiple prescription drugs, and an increased prevalence of mental conditions and dementia. Evidence shows that care of older adults by health care professionals prepared in geriatrics yields better physical and mental outcomes without increasing costs (H.J. Cohen et al., 2002). How to incentivize future workers to train for geriatric care is a challenge that is likely to remain. Under alternative demographic scenarios, an additional 2.5 to 3 million professionals in various occupations (nurses, assistants, social workers, etc.) will be needed to meet future demand for long-term care services by 2030 (Spetz et al., 2015).

Integration of a racially and culturally diverse workforce is also a growing necessity. It is estimated that somewhere near the middle of the 21st century, more than half of all U.S. citizens will be nonwhite (U.S. Census Bureau, 2001). Developing skills in cultural competence will divert some resources from health care. The term *cultural competence* refers to knowledge, skills, attitudes, and behavior required of a practitioner to provide optimal health care services to persons from a wide range of cultural and ethnic backgrounds. To do so effectively, health care providers need to understand how and why different belief systems, cultural biases, ethnic origins, family structures, and many other culture-based factors influence the manner in which people experiencing illness comply with medical advice and respond to treatment. Such variations have implications for outcomes of care (J.J. Cohen et al., 2002).

GLOBAL CHALLENGES

As pointed out previously, global issues can affect health care in America. Each year, more than 350 million foreign travelers arrive in the United States. To safeguard the public's health, the CDC operates quarantine stations at several major entry points. American businesses have spread worldwide. Hence, the CDC is actively involved in global surveillance and early detection of health threats and works closely with U.S. embassies overseas. The CDC operates over 60 Global Disease Detection Centers and other offices worldwide. Even though international cooperation is absolutely critical for combatting health threats, it has been an ongoing challenge. Since 2007, International Health Regulations (IHRs) have been binding on 196 countries under the aegis of the World Health Organization (WHO). The IHRs require countries to report certain disease outbreaks and other public health events to WHO (WHO, 2015). However, 80% of the countries have failed to meet the requirements of the IHRs, according to the Office of Global Affairs of the U.S. Department of Health and Human Services (DHHS). Neither the United States nor the United Nations has the authority to enforce compliance. Yet, when threats to public health arise anywhere in the world, the affected nations look to the United States and other developed countries to come to their rescue.

U.S. government agencies lend their assistance primarily through critically needed scientific knowledge and technical expertise to address a wide range of health issues. Many U.S.-based private philanthropic organizations send supplies and aid workers to affected areas. The irony is that when major disturbances occur, the affected areas are not safe either for the locals or for foreign aid workers.

Ongoing armed conflicts, in places such as the Middle East, affect medical care and public health services. In war zones, diseases such as diarrheal episodes and acute respiratory infections spread. Health care infrastructure sustains damage. Health workers are injured, killed, or evacuated. Supplies dwindle. Refugees migrate in large numbers, putting a strain on food and water supplies and sanitation. Hence, both morbidity and mortality increase. Large-scale bioterrorism has not yet occurred, but global unrest amid the rise of extremism makes it a real possibility in the future. Conflicts occurring in other parts of the globe can be "exported" to countries such as the United States.

NEW FRONTIERS IN CLINICAL TECHNOLOGY

Despite its role in cost escalation, technological progress will continue; but increased efforts in technology assessment will also take place. At some point, assessment and use of technology based on cost-effectiveness is likely to influence health policy. Yet, technology is already affecting many aspects of medical practice. It is currently driving much of the growth in the health services industry. Several areas of technological advance are noteworthy.

1. *Genetic mapping* is the first step in isolating a gene. Human genetic information has opened the way for the new field of *molecular medicine*, a branch of medicine that deals with the understanding of the role that genes play in disease processes and treatment of diseases through gene therapy. Gene therapy is a therapeutic technique in which a functioning gene is inserted into targeted cells to correct an inborn defect or provide the cell with a new function. This technique is expected to replace treatment with medications or surgery in some areas. Cancer treatment is receiving much attention as a prime candidate for gene therapy since current techniques (surgery, radiation, and chemotherapy) are effective in only one-half the cases and can greatly reduce a patient's quality of life.

2. *Personalized medicine and pharmacogenomics* are relatively new fields. Pharmacogenomics is the study of how genes affect a person's response to drugs. Personal characteristics of individual patients can vary so much that not all medications work for everyone. In

personalized medicine, specific gene variations among patients will be matched with responses to particular medications to increase effectiveness and reduce unwanted side effects.

3. *Drug design and delivery*: Rational *drug design* will shorten the drug discovery process. The chief candidates for this process are drugs to treat neurological and mental disorders and antiretroviral therapies for HIV/AIDS, encephalitis, measles, and influenza. New *drug delivery* systems will be used to target specific cells, for example, in treating cancer tumors without damage to healthy tissues.

4. *Imaging technologies* have made one of the most dramatic advances in health care. For example, focused energy beams can avoid damage to adjacent tissue, 3-D technology can allow faster and more accurate analysis of images, and neuroimaging will help in early detection of strokes and Alzheimer's disease.

5. *Minimally invasive surgery* is undergoing advances that include image-guided brain surgery, minimal access cardiac procedures, and the endovascular placement of grafts for abdominal aneurysms. The use of robotic surgery is in its early stages.

6. *Vaccines* have traditionally been used prophylactically to prevent specific infectious diseases. However, the therapeutic use of vaccines in the treatment of noninfectious diseases, such as cancer, has opened new fronts in medicine. At the same time, development of new vaccines for emerging infectious diseases remains on the research agenda.

7. *Blood substitutes* would likely be available one day for large-scale use. Substitutes for real blood are necessary when supplies fall short, particularly in war and in natural disasters.

8. *Xenotransplantation*, in which animal tissues are used for transplants in humans, is a growing research area. It presents the promise of overcoming the critical shortages of available donor organs. Organs from genetically engineered animals may one day be available for transplantation (Schneider & Seebach, 2013).

9. *Regenerative medicine* holds the promise of regenerating damaged tissues and organs in vivo (in the living body) through reparative techniques that stimulate previously irreparable organs into healing themselves. Regenerative medicine also enables scientists to grow tissues and organs in vitro (in the laboratory) and safely implant them when the body cannot be prompted into healing itself.

CARE DELIVERY OF THE FUTURE

Gossink and Souquet (2006) paint a picture of what medical care in the future may look like. This will be achieved mainly through advancements in medical imaging, molecular medicine, and distant monitoring. Medical care will shift its focus from the acute phase of illness to prevention and aftercare. Lifestyle, family history, and genetic factors will be used to develop a patient's risk profile. Patients with an elevated risk profile will be regularly screened for possible onset of acute disease and to follow the course of chronic disease. Some screening will be possible at home with the patient in wireless contact with the physician. If molecular diagnosis detects disease, the extent and location of the disease will be assessed through molecular imaging. Image-guided, minimally invasive procedures will be used if surgery is recommended. Pharmaceutical treatment will be individualized. A feedback system will determine needed drug dosage by a continuous measurement of drug concentration at the targeted site in the body. Miniature implanted devices will take over damaged body functions. Regenerative medicine and cell therapy will revive organs, such as a damaged heart. If needed, complete artificial organs, such as the pancreas, liver, and even heart, could be implanted. Physicians will be able to continuously monitor the condition of elderly patients with chronic conditions, and help could be dispatched in case of an emergency.

CONCLUSION

Some features of U.S. health care delivery have remained stable, but the future will be determined by how certain forces of change interact. The ACA was passed in late 2010, but serious issues remain in the areas of coverage, cost, access, and affordability. Nevertheless, the ACA is expected to transform U.S. health care in ways that are yet unknown. Serious challenges lie ahead unless the nation can control rising consumption of health care resources, the costs associated with them, and mend an economy that has not meaningfully improved in several years. Eventually, the nation will have to come to grips with what it can reasonably afford.

The existing model of health care delivery must also change. The ACA is intended to make some headway in emphasizing wellness, disease prevention, and care coordination. New models of care delivery are also being investigated.

Another critical area that must be addressed is the shortage of health care professionals. While the population is rapidly aging, little has been done to address the need for geriatric care. Addressing workforce diversity and training are other looming challenges that could otherwise threaten the adequacy of health care workforce in a changing demographic landscape.

To combat global health threats, international readiness has remained questionable. Armed conflicts in unstable areas of the world not only create new health crises, they also syphon off limited resources. Catastrophic consequences could follow.

Technological innovations in the areas of advanced imaging, minimally invasive surgery, genetic mapping, regenerative medicine, etc., will help shape the delivery of medical care in ways never before imagined. Many of these developments will likely shift the focus of medicine from the acute phase of illness to prevention and aftercare.

REFERENCES

Altman D. New evidence health spending is growing faster again. *Washington Wire*. http://blogs.wsj.com/washwire/2015/06/11/new-evidence-health -spending-is-growing-faster-again. Posted June 11, 2015. Accessed June 2015.

American Nurse. Hospital executives: continued shortage of nurses, advanced practitioners, physicians. *Am Nurse*. 2014;46(1):10.

Carman KG. Health coverage grows under Affordable Care Act. RAND Corporation. http://www.rand.org/news/press/2015/05/06.html. Published May 6, 2015. Accessed June 2015.

Centers for Medicare and Medicaid Services (CMS). The Affordable Care Act: lowering Medicare costs by improving care. http://www.cms.gov/apps/files /aca-savings-report-2012.pdf. Published 2012. Accessed June 2015.

Centers for Medicare and Medicaid Services (CMS). The 2014 annual report of the boards of trustees of the Federal Hospital Insurance and Federal Supplementary Medical Insurance trust funds. http://www.cms.gov /Research-Statistics-Data-and-Systems/Statistics-Trends-and-Reports /ReportsTrustFunds/Downloads/TR2014.pdf. Published 2014. Accessed June 2015.

Cohen HJ, et al. A controlled trial of inpatient and outpatient geriatric evaluation and management. *N Engl J Med*. 2002;346(12):906–912.

Cohen JJ, et al. The case for diversity in the health care workforce. *Health Aff*. 2002;21(5):90–102.

Congressional Budget Office (CBO). Insurance coverage provisions of the Affordable Care Act—CBO's March 2015 baseline. http://www.cbo.gov/sites/default/files/cbofiles/attachments/43900-2015-03-ACAtables.pdf. Published 2015a. Accessed June 2015.

Congressional Budget Office (CBO). The 2015 long-term budget outlook. https://www.cbo.gov/publication/50250. Published June 16, 2015b. Accessed June 2015.

Farley R. Declining labor participation rates. *FactCheck.org*. http://www.factcheck.org/2015/03/declining-labor-participation-rates. Posted March 11, 2015. Accessed June 2015.

Frist WH. Connected health and the rise of the patient-consumer. *Health Aff.* 2014;33(2):191–193.

Goodman JC. Why the Democrats lost the election: Obamacare. *Forbes*. http://www.forbes.com/sites/johngoodman/2014/11/28/why-the-democrats-lost-the-election-obamacare. Published November 28, 2014. Accessed June 2015.

Gossink R, Souquet J. Advances and trends in healthcare technology. In: Wendler T, Spekowius G, eds. *Advances in Healthcare Technology: Shaping the Future of Medical Care*. Dordrecht, The Netherlands: Springer; 2006:1–14.

Green G, Coder J. Household income trends, April 2015. Sentier Research. http://www.sentierresearch.com/reports/Sentier_Household_Income_Trends_Report_April2015_05_28_15.pdf. Issued May 2015. Accessed June 2015.

Herman B. Deductible debate. *Mod Healthc*. 2015;45(24):22–24.

Kowalski AE. *The early impact of the Affordable Care Act, state by state.* Brookings Papers on Economic Activity. Washington, DC: The Brookings Institution; 2014.

Kutscher B, Herman B, Meyer H. Uninsured drop as ACA faces threats. *Mod Healthc*. 2015; 45(22):0011.

Kvedar J, et al. E-patient connectivity and the near term future. *J Gen Intern Med*. 2011;26:636–638.

McHugh K. Reid says Obamacare will lead to a single-payer healthcare system. *The Daily Caller*. http://dailycaller.com/2013/08/10/absolutely-yes-reid-says-obamacare-will-lead-to-a-single-payer-healthcare-system. Published August 10, 2013. Accessed June 2015.

Millman J. Millions have joined Medicaid under Obamacare. Here's what they think of it. *The Washington Post*. http://www.washingtonpost.com/blogs/wonkblog/wp/2014/09/19/millions-have-joined-medicaid-under-obamacare-heres-what-they-think-of-it. Published September 19, 2014. Accessed June 2015.

Milstein JB, et al. The impact of globalization on vaccine development and availability. *Health Aff*. 2006;25(4):1061–1069.

Moore R. Telehealth connected care. *Health Manage Technol*. 2009;30(3):39–40.

National Academy of Sciences. *The Future of Nursing: Leading Change, Advancing Health*. Washington, DC: Institute of Medicine; 2010.

National Center for Health Statistics (NCHS). *Health, United States, 2004*. Hyattsville, MD: U.S. Department of Health and Human Services; 2004.

National Center for Health Statistics (NCHS). *Health, United States, 2014*. Hyattsville, MD: U.S. Department of Health and Human Services; 2015.

Ngo V, et al. Health coaching in the teamlet model: a case study. *J Gen Intern Med*. 2010;25(12):1375–1378.

Okrent D. *Health Care Workforce: Future Supply vs. Demand*. Washington, DC: Alliance for Health Reform; 2011.

PricewaterhouseCoopers LLP. A look at state ACA participation and 2015 individual market health insurance rate filings. http://www.pwc.com/us/en/health -industries/health-research-institute/aca-state-exchanges.jhtml. Published 2015. Accessed August 16, 2015.

Rodriguez H, et al. Teamlet structure and early experiences of medical home implementation for veterans. *J Gen Intern Med*. 2014;29(2):623–631.

Schneider MKJ, Seebach JD. Xenotransplantation literature update, July–August 2013. *Xenotransplantation*. 2013;20(5): 308–310.

Spetz J, et al. Future demand for long-term care workers will be influenced by demographic and utilization changes. *Health Aff*. 2015;34(6):936–945.

U.S. Census Bureau. *Statistical Abstract of the United States, 2001*. Washington, DC: U.S. Census Bureau; 2001.

U.S. Department of the Treasury. The debt to the penny and who holds it. http:// www.treasurydirect.gov/NP/debt/current. Published 2015. Accessed June 2015.

Volsky I. The remarkable slowdown in health care costs since the passage of Obamacare: Think Progress. http://thinkprogress.org/health/2013/08/20/2498391 /growth-in-health-care-costs-continues-to-decrease-since-passage-of-obamacare. Published August 20, 2013. Accessed June 2015.

Weintraub K, Stanglin D. Deadly MERS virus turns up in the U.S. for the first time. *USA Today*. http://www.usatoday.com/story/news/nation/2014/05/02 /mers-deadly-virus-cdc-indiana/8619665. Published May 2, 2014. Accessed June 2015.

World Health Organization (WHO). International health regulations. http://www .who.int/topics/international_health_regulations/en. Published 2015. Accessed June 2015.

Appendix

Essentials of the Affordable Care Act (ACA)

THE LEGISLATION AND COURT RULINGS

- The Affordable Care Act, or the ACA, nicknamed Obamacare, is short for Patient Protection and Affordable Care Act of 2010 as amended by the Health Care and Education Reconciliation Act of 2010.
- The ACA represents the most sweeping reform of the U.S. health care system since the creation of Medicare and Medicaid in 1965.
- The U.S. Supreme Court ruled, in 2012, that the ACA was constitutional, but that the federal government could not coerce states to expand their state Medicaid programs.
- In a 2014 ruling, the U.S. Supreme Court held that the ACA violated the Religious Freedom Restoration Act of 1993 when it forced corporations run by owners who held deeply religious beliefs against providing contraceptives that may be deemed to induce abortions.

- In 2015, the U.S. Supreme Court ruled that certain low-income individuals could not be disqualified from obtaining federal subsidies when they purchase health insurance through the exchange established by the federal government.

HEALTH INSURANCE

- The ACA's primary goal was to expand health insurance to the previously uninsured, but it was not designed to achieve universal coverage.
- Between 16.4 and 16.9 million Americans gained health insurance under the ACA.
- Nearly 12% of Americans still did not have health insurance during the first 3 months of 2015, one year after the insurance features of the ACA went into effect. In 2015, the uninsured population stood at 35 million, according to government's estimates.
- Health plans are mandated to provide "minimum essential coverage."
- Employers with 100 or more full-time equivalent workers must cover at least 70% of their full-time workers (those working 30 hours or more per week) starting in 2015 and 95% by 2016. Employers that have between 50 and 99 workers must comply by 2016.
- It is illegal for health insurance companies to deny coverage to people with preexisting medical conditions.
- Children and young adults under the age of 26 can be covered under their parents' health insurance plans.
- The coverage gap (donut hole) in Medicare Part D will gradually close, and will be eliminated by 2020.

ACCESS AND CARE DELIVERY

- The ACA puts greater emphasis on preventive care than previously.
- To enable access to the expanded number of insured, additional primary care providers are needed. An estimated demand is for 16,000 to 17,000 additional physicians.

- The ACA includes some provisions to address the looming physician shortages through additional funding for medical residency training programs and proposals to expand the nonphysician workforce of clinicians with advanced training.
- The FDA is authorized to approve "biosimilars" under a process similar to the approval of generic drugs. It is believed that the introduction of biosimilars will create competition and drive down the cost of biologics.
- The ACA provides special funding to expand community health centers to provide increased access to underserved populations.
- Requirements to provide community benefits by nonprofit hospitals have been tightened.
- Managed care organizations must spend at least 80% of the insurance premium dollars on the delivery of medical care, keeping no more than 20% for administrative expenses.
- The ACA authorized formation of accountable care organizations to serve Medicare beneficiaries enrolled in the traditional fee-for-service program.
- Increased federal funding is provided to the states to deliver home- and community-based attendant services to long-term care patients under a program called Community First Choice.
- The Elder Justice Act of 2010 was incorporated into the ACA to counter elder abuse, neglect, and exploitation of patients in nursing homes.
- The U.S. Department of Health & Human Services is required to develop data collection and reporting tools on quality of care.

COST

- Between 2014 and 2015, premiums on health insurance purchased through the government exchanges went up by 8% before subsidies (28% after subsidies).
- With some exceptions, out-of-pocket annual costs are limited to $6,350 for single plans and $12,700 for family plans.
- The net cost of coverage provisions of the ACA has been estimated to be $1.2 trillion between 2016 and 2025.

REIMBURSEMENT TO PROVIDERS AND HEALTH PLANS

- The ACA requires reduction in payments to hospitals that incur excessive Medicare readmissions within 30 days of discharge.
- The ACA requires value-based payment to providers. These payment arrangements will be designed to incentivize and hold providers accountable for the total cost and quality of care for a population of patients.
- Medicare star ratings are used to reward higher-quality health plans with incentive payments.
- A Shared Savings Program will be used to reward accountable care organizations that lower the growth of health care expenditures while meeting certain quality of care criteria.

TAXES

- The ACA imposes a 2.3% excise tax on the manufacturers and importers of certain medical devices.
- In its decision on the constitutionality of the ACA, the U.S. Supreme Court regards penalties to be paid by individuals for not having health insurance as a tax.
- New taxes are imposed on the health insurance industry, based on premiums collected.
- Tax deduction for individual taxpayers on medical expenses has been reduced.

Glossary

Academic medical center: An organization in which there is active collaboration among a university, medical school, hospital/health system, and health care professionals.

Access: The ability of persons needing health services to obtain appropriate care in a timely manner.

Accountable care organization (ACO): An integrated group of providers—including hospitals, physicians, and post-discharge care delivery organizations—who work together to deliver coordinated care and take responsibility for quality and efficiency of services delivered.

Acquisition: Purchase of one organization by another.

Activities of daily living (ADLs): The most commonly used measure of disability. ADLs determine whether an individual needs assistance to perform basic activities, such as eating, bathing, dressing, toileting, and getting into or out of a bed or chair. *See* **instrumental activities of daily living (IADLs)**.

Acute condition: Short-term, intense medical care for an illness or injury usually requiring hospitalization. *See* **subacute care**.

Adaptive rehabilitation: Care that improves function despite deficits that remain.

Administrative costs: Costs associated with health insurance marketing and enrollment, contracting with providers, claims processing, utilization monitoring, and handling of denials and appeals.

Administrative information systems: Designed to assist in carrying out financial and administrative support activities such as payroll, patient accounting, materials management, and office automation.

Adult day care: A community-based, long-term care service that provides a wide range of health, social, and recreational services to elderly adults who require supervision and care while members of the family or other informal caregivers are away at work.

Adult foster care: LTC services provided in small, family-operated homes, located in residential communities, which provide room, board, and varying levels of supervision, oversight, and personal care to nonrelated adults.

Advance directives: A patient's wishes regarding continuation or withdrawal of treatment when the patient lacks decision-making capacity.

Advanced-practice nurse (APN): A general name for nurses who have education and clinical experience beyond that required of a registered nurse (RN). APNs include four areas of specialization in nursing: clinical nurse specialists (CNSs), certified registered nurse anesthetists (CRNAs), nurse practitioners (NPs), and certified nurse midwives (CNMs).

Alliance: A joint agreement between two organizations to share their resources without joint ownership of assets.

Allied health professional: A professional who is educated and trained in a specialized field of health care and has responsibility for the delivery of services associated with medical care.

Allocative tool: Designates a use of health policy in which there is a direct provision of income, services, or goods to groups of individuals who usually reap benefits in receiving them.

Allopathic medicine: A philosophy of medicine that views medical treatment as active intervention to counteract the effects of disease through medical and surgical procedures that produce effects opposite those of the disease. *See* **osteopathic medicine.**

Almshouse: Also a poorhouse, was an unspecialized institution existing during the 18th and mid-19th centuries that mainly served general welfare functions, essentially providing shelter to the homeless, the insane, the elderly, orphans, and the sick who had no family to care for them.

Alternative medicine: Also called *alternative and complementary medicine.* Nontraditional remedies, for example, acupuncture, homeopathy, naturopathy, biofeedback, yoga exercises, chiropractic, and herbal therapy.

Ambulatory: Related to walking, typically used as the opposite of inpatient.

Ambulatory care: Also referred to as *outpatient services.* Ambulatory care includes (1) care rendered to patients who come to physicians' offices, outpatient departments of hospitals, and health centers (2) outpatient services intended to serve the surrounding community (community medicine); and (3) certain services that are transported to the patient.

Asylum: Forerunner of today's inpatient psychiatric facilities. Built by state governments for patients with untreatable, chronic medical illness.

Average daily census: Average number of hospital beds occupied daily over a given period of time. This measure provides an estimate of the number of inpatients receiving care each day at a hospital.

Average length of stay (ALOS): The average number of days each patient stays in the hospital. For individual or specific categories of patients, this measure indicates severity of illness and resource use.

Balance bill: Billing of the leftover sum by the provider to the patient after insurance has partially paid the charge initially billed.

Behavioral factors: Individual lifestyles that include diet, exercise, a stress-free lifestyle, risky or unhealthy behaviors, and other individual choices that may contribute to significant health problems.

Beneficence: The ethical obligation of a health services organization to do all it can to alleviate suffering caused by ill health and injury.

Beneficiary: Anyone covered under a particular health insurance plan.

Benefit period: Under Medicare rules, benefits for an inpatient stay are based on a benefit period. A benefit period is determined by a spell of illness beginning with hospitalization and ending when the beneficiary has not been an inpatient in a hospital or a skilled nursing facility for 60 consecutive days.

Biologics: Biological products that include a wide range of products such as vaccines, blood and blood components, allergenics, somatic cells, gene therapy, tissues, and recombinant therapeutic proteins.

Biosimilar: A product that is highly similar to, or is interchangeable with, a biologic that has already been approved by the FDA.

Bundled payments: Payment scheme in which a number of related services are included in one price.

Capacity: The number of beds set up, staffed, and made available by a hospital for inpatient use.

Capitalism: Political and economic system that relies primarily on market forces in the production and distribution of goods and private ownership, as opposed to socialism where collective or governmental forces prevail.

Capitation: A reimbursement mechanism under which the provider is paid a set monthly fee per enrollee (sometimes referred to as per member per month or PMPM rate) regardless of whether or not an enrollee sees the provider and regardless of how often an enrollee sees the provider.

Carve-out: The assignment through contractual arrangements of specialized services to an outside organization because these services are not included in the contracts managed care organizations (MCOs) have with their providers or the MCO does not provide the services.

Case management: An organized approach to evaluating and coordinating care, particularly for patients who have complex, potentially costly problems that require a variety of services from multiple providers over an extended period.

Case mix: An aggregate of the severity of conditions requiring medical intervention. Case-mix categories are mutually exclusive and differentiate patients according to the extent of resource use.

Categorical programs: Public health care programs designed to benefit only a certain category of people.

Census: The number of patients in a hospital on a given day or the number of beds occupied on a given day.

Certification: Conferred by the U.S. Department of Health and Human Services, it entitles an organization to participate in Medicare and Medicaid. The organization must comply with the conditions of participation.

Chronic condition (chronic disease): A long-lasting medical condition that can be controlled but not cured.

Clinical decision support systems Interactive software systems designed to help clinicians with decision-making tasks, such as determining a diagnosis or recommending a treatment for a patient.

Clinical information systems: Systems that involve the organized processing, storage, and retrieval of information to support patient care processes.

Clinical practice guidelines (medical practice guidelines): Standardized guidelines in the form of scientifically established protocols, representing preferred processes in medical practice.

Clinical trial: A research study, generally based on random assignments, designed to study the effectiveness of a new drug, device, or treatment.

Cognitive impairment: A mental disorder that is indicated by a person having difficulty remembering, learning new things, concentrating, or making decisions that affect the individual's everyday life.

Coinsurance: Cost sharing in the form of a percent amount. A plan with an 80:20 coinsurance, for example, pays 80% of all covered medical expenses after the deductible requirement has been met until the maximum out-of-pocket liability in a given year has been met.

Community hospital: Nonfederal (i.e., VA and military hospitals are excluded), short-term, general or special hospital whose services are available to the public.

Community-oriented primary care (COPC): Incorporates the elements of good primary care delivery and adds to this a population-based approach to identifying and addressing community health problems.

Comorbidity: Presence of more than one health problem in an individual.

Conditions of participation: Standards developed by the Department of Health and Human Services (DHHS) that a facility must comply with in order to participate in the Medicare and Medicaid programs.

Consumer-driven health plan: A high-deductible health plan that carries a savings option to pay for routine health care expenses.

Consumer price index: A measure of inflation in the general economy.

Copayment (coinsurance): A portion of health care charges that the insured has to pay under the terms of his or her health insurance policy. *See* **deductible**.

Corporate era: A recent period in the evolution of the U.S. medical delivery system that is characterized by the domination of corporations rather than individuals in decision making regarding care delivery and payment.

Corporatization: In this text, the ways in which health care delivery in the United States has become the domain of large organizations.

Cost-effectiveness Evaluation of overall usefulness of medical technology, including evaluation of the safety and efficacy of a technology in relation to its cost. *See* **cost-efficiency.**

Cost-efficiency: A service is cost efficient when the benefit received is greater than the cost incurred to provide the service.

Cost sharing: Sharing in the cost of health insurance premiums by those enrolled and/or payment of certain medical costs out of pocket, such as copayments and deductibles.

Cost shifting (cross-subsidizing): In general, shifting of costs from one entity to another as a way of making up losses in one area by charging more in other areas. For example, when care is provided to the uninsured, the provider makes up the cost for those services by charging more to the insured.

Critical access hospital (CAH): Medicare designation for small rural hospitals with 25 beds or fewer that provide emergency medical services besides short-term hospitalization for patients with noncomplex health care needs. CAHs receive cost-plus reimbursement.

Critical pathways: Outcome-based, patient-centered case management tools that are interdisciplinary, facilitating coordination of care among multiple clinical departments and caregivers. A critical pathway identifies planned medical interventions in a given case, along with expected outcomes.

Custodial care: Nonmedical care provided to support and maintain the patient's condition, generally requiring no active medical or nursing treatments.

Days of care: Cumulative number of patient days over a given period of time.

Decision support systems: Computer-based information and analytical tools to support managerial decision making in health care organizations.

Deductible: The portion of health care costs that the insured must first pay (generally up to an annual limit) before insurance payments kick in. Insurance payments may be further subject to copayment.

Deemed status: A designation used when a hospital, by virtue of its accreditation by the Joint Commission or the American Osteopathic Association, does not require separate certification from the DHHS to participate in the Medicare and Medicaid programs.

Defensive medicine: Excessive medical tests and procedures performed as a protection against malpractice lawsuits, otherwise regarded as unnecessary.

Demand-side incentive: Cost-sharing mechanism that places a larger cost burden on consumers, thereby encouraging consumers to be more cost conscious in selecting the insurance plan that best serves their needs and more judicious in their utilization of services.

Demand-side rationing: Barriers to obtaining health care faced by individuals who do not have sufficient income to pay for services or purchase health insurance.

Dependency: (1) A person's reliance on another for assistance with common daily functions, such as bathing and grooming. *See* **activities of daily living.** (2) Children's reliance on adults, such as parents or school officials, to recognize and respond to their health needs.

Determinants of health: *See* **health determinants.**

Developmental disability: A physical incapacity that generally accompanies mental retardation and often arises at birth or in early childhood.

Developmental vulnerability: Rapid and cumulative physical and emotional changes that characterize childhood and the potential impact that illness, injury, or untoward family and social circumstances can have on a child's life-course trajectory.

Discharge: Release of a patient who has received inpatient services. Total number of discharges indicates access to hospital inpatient services as well as the extent of utilization.

Discharge planning: Part of the overall treatment plan designed to facilitate discharge from an inpatient setting. It includes, for example, an estimate of how long the patient will be in the hospital, what the expected outcome is likely to be, whether any special requirements will be needed at discharge, and what needs to be facilitated for postacute continuity of care.

Disease: Condition determined by a medical professional's evaluation, unlike an illness, which is based on the patient's assessment. *See* **illness.**

Dispensary: A clinic during the Preindustrial period that provided charity care in urban areas.

Distributive policies: Spread benefits throughout society. Examples are funding of medical research through the National Institutes of Health, the training of medical personnel through the National Health Services Corps, the construction of health facilities under the Hill-Burton program, and the initiation of new institutions (e.g., HMOs).

E-health: Health care information and services offered over the Internet by professionals and nonprofessionals alike.

E-therapy: Any type of professional therapeutic interaction that makes use of the Internet to connect qualified mental health professionals and their clients.

Efficacy The health benefit to be derived from the use of technology or how effective a given technology is in diagnosing or treating a condition.

Enabling characteristics Within the access to care framework, factors that make it possible (or easier) for individuals to use available health care resources

Enrollee: A person enrolled in a health plan, especially in a managed care plan.

Environmental factors: Factors that encompass the physical, socioeconomic, sociopolitical, and sociocultural dimensions of life.

Ethics committee: An interdisciplinary committee responsible for developing guidelines and standards for ethical decision-making in the provision of health care and for resolving issues related to medical ethics.

Financing: Any mechanism that gives people the ability to pay for health care services.

Gatekeeping: The use of primary care physicians to coordinate health care services needed by an enrollee in a managed care plan.

General hospital: A hospital that provides general and specialty medical services for a variety of medical needs.

Generalist: A physician in family practice, general internal medicine, or general pediatrics. *See* **specialist.**

Genetic mapping: The first step in isolating a gene.

Globalization: Various forms of cross-border economic activities driven by global exchange of information, production of goods and services more economically in developing countries, and increased interdependence of mature and emerging world economies.

Health: A state of physical, mental, and social well-being (WHO 1948).

Health care delivery: The provision of medical care or illness care.

Health care reform: Systematic changes in how medical care is financed or delivered.

Health care system: Organizations, personnel, and activities associated with promoting, restoring, and maintaining health.

Health determinants: Factors that contribute to the general well-being of individuals and populations.

Health informatics: The application of information science to improve the efficiency, accuracy, and reliability of health care services. Health informatics requires the use of information technology (IT) but goes beyond IT by emphasizing the improvement of health care delivery.

Health plan: The contractual arrangement between the MCO and the enrollee, including the collective array of covered health services that the enrollee is entitled to.

Health planning: Decisions made by governments to limit health care resources, such as hospital beds and diffusion of costly technology.

Health policy: Public policy that pertains to or influences the pursuit of health.

Health technology assessment: Any process of examining and reporting properties of a medical technology used in health care, such as safety, effectiveness, feasibility, and indications for use, and cost-effectiveness.

Heredity: A key determinant of health that predisposes individuals to certain diseases.

Holistic medicine: A philosophy of health care that emphasizes the well-being of every aspect of a person, including the physical, mental, social, and spiritual aspects of health.

Horizontal integration: A growth strategy in which an organization extends its core product or service. *See* **vertical integration**.

Hospice: A cluster of special services for the dying, which blends medical, spiritual, legal, financial, and family-support services. The venue can vary from a specialized facility to a nursing home to the patient's own home.

Hospitalist: A physician who specializes in the care of hospitalized patients.

Illness: Patient condition recognized by the patient's perceptions and evaluation of how he or she feels, unlike disease, which is determined by a medical professional. *See* **disease**.

Information technology (IT): Technology used for the transformation of data into useful information. IT involves determining data needs, gathering appropriate data, storing and analyzing the data, and reporting the information generated in a user-friendly format.

Informed consent: A fundamental patient right to make an informed choice regarding medical treatment based on full disclosure of medical information by the providers.

Inpatient: Services delivered on the basis of an overnight stay in a health care institution.

Inpatient day: A night spent in the hospital by a person admitted as an inpatient. It is also called a patient day or a hospital day.

Instrumental activities of daily living (IADLs): A person's ability to perform household and social tasks, such as home maintenance, cooking, shopping, and managing money. *See* **activities of daily living (ADLs)**.

Insured: The individual who is covered for risk by insurance.

Integrated care: Care that embodies the concepts of comprehensive, coordinated, and continuous services that provide a seamless process of care.

Integrated delivery system (IDS): A network of organizations that provides or arranges to provide a coordinated continuum of services to a defined population and is willing to be held clinically and fiscally accountable for the outcomes and health status of the population serviced.

Interoperability The ability to share and access patient information by various users.

Item-based pricing: The costs of ancillary services that often accompany major procedures such as surgery.

Joint venture: Creation of a new organization in which two or more institutions share resources to pursue a common purpose.

License: Permission granted by the state for an organization to legally operate.

Long-term care: A variety of individualized, well-coordinated services that are designed to promote the maximum possible independence for people with functional limitations. These services are provided over an extended period to meet the patients' physical, mental, social, and spiritual needs, while maximizing quality of life.

Maintenance rehabilitation Care that aims to preserve the present level of function and prevent further decline.

Managed care: A system of health care delivery that (1) seeks to achieve efficiencies by integrating the four functions of health care delivery, (2) employs mechanisms to control (manage) utilization of medical services, and (3) determines how much the providers get paid.

Market justice: A distributional principle according to which health care is most equitably distributed through the market forces of supply and demand rather than government interventions. *See* **social justice**.

Meaningful use Specific criteria in quality, safety, efficiency, etc. that providers are required to meet to comply with the Health Information Technology for Economic and Clinical Health Act of 2009.

Means-tested program: A program in which eligibility depends on income.

Mediating factors Mediating factors are forces or conditions that moderate the effects of the intervention studied, either positively or negatively.

Medicaid: A joint federal–state program of health insurance for the poor.

Medical center: A hospital with a high level of specialization and a wide scope of services.

Medical home: Primary care delivery based on a partnership between the patient and the provider with a focus on chronic care.

Medical loss ratio: The percentage of premium revenue spent on medical expenses.

Medical model: Delivery of health care that places its primary emphasis on the treatment of disease and relief of symptoms instead of prevention of disease and promotion of optimum health.

Medical practice guidelines: *See* **clinical practice guidelines**.

Medical system: Large organizations that may include more than one hospital to serve a large geographical area.

Medical technology: Practical application of the scientific body of knowledge for the purpose of improving health and creating efficiencies in the delivery of health care.

Medicare: A federal program of health insurance for the elderly, certain disabled individuals, and people with end-stage renal disease.

Medigap: Commercial health insurance policies purchased by individuals covered by Medicare to insure the expenses not covered by Medicare.

Member: An enrollee in a private health insurance plan.

Merger: Unification of two or more organizations into a single entity through mutual agreement.

Molecular medicine: A branch of medicine that deals with the understanding of the role that genes play in disease processes and treatment of diseases through gene therapy.

Moral hazard: Consumer behavior that leads to a higher utilization of health care services because people are covered by insurance.

Nanomedicine: A developing area of medicine in which materials are manipulated on the atomic and molecular level (one nanometer is one-billionth of a meter).

Need: Need for health services (in contrast to demand for health services) is based on individual judgment of the patient or a health care professional.

Need attributes: Within the access to care framework, factors that reflect the health status of the individual, either from a self-perceived perspective or from professional assessment.

New morbidities: Dysfunctions, such as drug and alcohol abuse, family and neighborhood violence, emotional disorders, and learning problems, from which older generations do not suffer.

Nonmaleficence: The moral obligation of health services personnel not to harm the patients. This principle requires physicians to use their best professional judgment in choosing interventions that maximize the potential health benefits at minimum risk.

Nonphysician practitioners (NPPs): Clinical professionals, such as nurse practitioners and physician assistants, who practice in many areas similar to those in which physicians practice but who do not have an MD or a DO degree.

Occupancy rate: The percentage of a hospital's total inpatient capacity that is actually utilized.

Organized medicine: Concerted activities of physicians, mainly to protect their own interests, through such associations as the American Medical Association (AMA).

Orphan drugs: Certain new drug therapies for conditions that affect fewer than 200,000 people in the United States.

Osteopathic medicine: A medical philosophy based on the holistic approach to treatment that also emphasizes correction of the position of the joints or tissues and diet and environment as factors that might destroy natural resistance. *See* **allopathic medicine**.

Outcome: The end result of health care delivery; often viewed as the bottom-line measure of the effectiveness of the health care delivery system.

Outpatient: In contrast to inpatient, *see* **Ambulatory**.

Outpatient services: As opposed to inpatient services, outpatient services include any health care services that are not provided based on an overnight stay in which room and board costs are incurred. *See* **ambulatory care**.

Overutilization (overuse): Utilization of medical services, the cost of which exceeds the benefit to consumers or the risks of which outweigh potential benefits.

Package pricing: Bundling of fees for an entire package of related services.

Palliation: Serving to relieve or alleviate, such as pharmacologic pain management and nausea relief.

Palliative care: Pain and symptom management; it is a primary area of emphasis in hospice care.

Part A: A part of Medicare which mainly covers hospital care and limited nursing home care.

Part B: A part of Medicare in which government-subsidized voluntary insurance covers physician services and outpatient services.

Patient days: The cumulative census over a given period of time. *See* **days of care** and **inpatient day**.

Payer-driven competition: Competitive strategy used by employers who shop for the best value in terms of the cost of premiums and the benefits package (competition among insurers), and when MCOs shop for the best value from providers of health services (competition among providers).

Peer review: The general process of medical review of utilization and quality when it is carried out directly or under the supervision of physicians.

Per diem: A type of reimbursement that pays a flat rate for each day of inpatient stay.

Personalized medicine: Matching of gene variations with responses to particular medications to increase effectiveness and reduce unwanted side effects.

Pesthouse: An institution that existed in preindustrial America to quarantine people with contagious diseases such as cholera, smallpox, or typhoid.

Pharmaceutical care: A mode of pharmacy practice in which the pharmacist not only dispenses drugs but also informs patients on the proper use of drugs and their potential misuse. When asked, the pharmacist also assists prescribers in appropriate drug choices.

Pharmacogenomics: The study of how genes affect a person's response to drugs.

Physician–hospital organization (PHO): A legal entity formed between a hospital and a physician group to achieve shared market objectives and other mutual interests.

Planned rationing: *See* **supply-side rationing**.

Poorhouse: *See* **almshouse**.

Postindustrial era: Phase of the medical delivery system that began in the late 19th century. The medical profession grew as a result of urbanization, new scientific discoveries, and reforms in medical education.

Precertification Requirement by some insurance plans that the enrollee or the provider call the plan administrators for approval before certain services are provided.

Preindustrial era: Phase of the medical delivery system from the middle part of the 18th century until the latter part of the 19th century. Health care was not grounded in science and was delivered in a free market.

Premium: The insurer's charge for insurance coverage; the price for an insurance plan.

Process: The specific way in which care is provided. Examples of process include correct diagnostic tests, correct prescriptions, accurate drug administration, pharmaceutical care, waiting time to see a physician, and interpersonal aspects of care delivery.

Proprietary hospital: A for-profit hospital owned by individuals, a partnership, or a corporation. Also referred to as *investor-owned hospital*.

Prospective reimbursement: A method of payment in which certain preestablished criteria are used to determine in advance the amount of reimbursement.

Provider-induced demand: Artificial creation of demand by providers that enables them to deliver unneeded services to boost their incomes.

Public health: A wide variety of activities undertaken by state and local governments to ensure conditions that promote optimum health for society as a whole.

Public health system: A system whose mission is to improve and protect community health.

Public hospital: A hospital owned by the federal, state, or local government.

Public policies: Authoritative decisions made in the legislative, executive, or judicial branches of government that are intended to direct or influence the actions, behaviors, or decisions of others.

Quality: The degree to which health services for individuals and populations increase the likelihood of desired health outcomes and are consistent with current professional knowledge.

Quality of life: (1) Factors considered important by patients, such as environmental comfort, security, interpersonal relations, personal preferences, and autonomy in making decisions when institutionalized. (2) Overall satisfaction with life during and following a person's encounter with the health care delivery system.

Quality-of-life indicators: Measures that demonstrate the general well-being of individuals and societies.

Redistributive policies: Policies that take money or power from one group and give it to another. An examples is the Medicaid program, which takes tax revenue and spends it on the poor in the form of health insurance.

Regenerative medicine: Regeneration of damaged tissues and organs in vivo through techniques that stimulate previously irreparable organs into healing themselves. Can also be done in vitro and implanted when the body cannot be prompted to heal itself.

Regulatory tools: Health policies in which the government prescribes and controls the behavior of a particular target group by monitoring the group and imposing sanctions if it fails to comply.

Reimbursement: The amount insurers pay to a provider. The payment may only be a portion of the actual charge.

Reinsurance Stop-loss coverage that self-insured employers purchase to protect themselves against any potential risk of high losses.

Residency: Graduate medical education in a specialty that takes the form of paid on-the-job training, usually in a hospital.

Resource-based relative value scale (RBRVS): A payment method instituted by Medicare for determining physicians' fees. Each treatment or encounter by the physician is assigned a relative value based on the time, skill, and training required to treat the condition.

Respite care: A service that provides temporary relief to informal caregivers, such as family members.

Restorative care: Short-term therapy treatments to help a person regain or improve physical function.

Retail clinic: A type of proprietary, community-based, freestanding medical facility found across the country in retail establishments such as Walmart, Walgreens, and CVS pharmacies.

Retrospective reimbursement: Reimbursement rates based on costs actually incurred.

Risk: The possibility of a substantial financial loss from an event of which the probability of occurrence is relatively small.

Risk management: Limiting risks against lawsuits or unexpected events.

Rural hospital: A hospital located in a county that is not part of a metropolitan statistical area.

Safety Protection against unnecessary harm from the use of technology.

Secondary care: Routine hospitalization, routine surgery, and specialized outpatient care, such as consultation with specialists and rehabilitation.

Self-insurance: Health insurance provided by large employers who can afford to assume the risk by budgeting funds to pay medical claims incurred by their employees.

Senior centers: Local community centers for older adults that provide opportunities to congregate and socialize, and in some cases have a midday meal.

Single-payer system: A national health care program in which the financing and insurance functions are taken over by the federal government.

Skilled nursing care: Medically oriented long-term care provided mainly by a licensed nurse under the overall direction of a physician.

Small area variations: Unexplained variations in the treatment patterns for similar patients and medical conditions.

Social justice: A distribution principle according to which health care is most equitably distributed by a government-run national health care program. *See* **market justice**.

Socialism: Political and economic system that advocates collective or governmental ownership and administration of the means of production and distribution of goods, as opposed to capitalism where private and market forces dominate.

Socialized medicine: Any large-scale government-sponsored expansion of health insurance or intrusion in the private practice of medicine.

Socioeconomic status: A measure of one's social position in relation to others, typically based on income, education, and occupation.

Special populations: Those with health needs but with inadequate resources to address those needs.

Specialist: A physician who specializes in specific health care problems, for example, anesthesiologists, cardiologists, and oncologists. *See* **generalist**.

Specialty hospital: A hospital that admits only certain types of patients or those with specified illnesses or conditions. Examples include rehabilitation hospitals, tuberculosis hospitals, children's hospitals, cardiac hospitals, orthopedic hospitals, etc.

Stop-loss: An insurance provision in which an insured has a maximum out-of-pocket liability in a given year.

Structure: "The relatively stable characteristics of the providers of care, of the tools and resources they have at their disposal, and of the physical and organizational settings in which they work" (Donabedian, 1980, p. 81).

Subacute care: Clinically complex services that are beyond traditional skilled nursing care.

Subacute condition: Technically complex services that are beyond traditional skilled nursing care.

Supply-side rationing: Also called *planned rationing;* rationing that is generally carried out by a government to limit the availability of health care services, particularly expensive technology.

Supply-side regulation: The antitrust laws passed in the United States, which prohibit business practices that stifle competition among providers, such as price fixing, price discrimination, exclusive contracting arrangements, and mergers deemed anticompetitive by the Department of Justice.

Surgicenter: A freestanding, ambulatory surgery center that performs various types of surgical procedures on an outpatient basis.

Teaching hospital: A hospital with an approved residency program for physicians.

Technological imperative: Use of technology without cost considerations, especially when the benefits to be derived from the use of technology are small compared to the costs.

Technology assessment: *See* **health technology assessment**.

Technology diffusion: The proliferation of technology once it is developed.

Telemedicine: Use of telecommunications technology that enables physicians to conduct two-way, interactive video consultations or transmit digital images, such as X-rays and MRIs, to other sites.

Tertiary care: The most complex level of care. Typically, tertiary care is institution based, highly specialized, and highly technological. Examples include burn treatment, transplantation, and coronary artery bypass surgery.

Third-party payers: In a multipayer system, the payers for covered services, for example, insurance companies, managed care organizations, and the government. They are called third parties because they are neither the providers nor the recipients of medical services.

Title 18: The Medicare program. More precisely known as Title XVIII (18) of the Social Security Amendment of 1965.

Title 19: The Medicaid program. More precisely known as Title XIX (19) of the Social Security Amendment of 1965.

TriCare: An insurance program financed by the U.S. Department of defense to permit beneficiaries to receive care from both private and military medical care facilities.

Underutilization: Occurs when medically needed health care services are withheld. This is especially true when potential benefits are likely to exceed the cost or risks.

Underwriting: A systematic technique used by an insurer for evaluating, selecting (or rejecting), classifying, and rating risks.

Universal access: The ability of all citizens to obtain health care when needed. It is a misnomer because timely access to certain services may still be a problem because of supply-side rationing.

Universal coverage: Health insurance coverage for all citizens.

Urgent care center: A walk-in clinic generally open to see patients after normal business hours in the evenings and weekends without having to make an appointment.

Usual source of care A single provider or place where patients obtain, or can obtain, the majority of their health care.

Utilization control: Limiting utilization of medical services to only those deemed appropriate and necessary.

Utilization review: A process by which an insurer reviews decisions by physicians and other providers on how much care to provide.

Value: Greater benefits or higher quality at the same or lower price levels (costs).

Vertical integration: Linking of services that are at different stages in the production process of health care. For example, a hospital system that launches hospice, long-term care, or ambulatory care services. *See* **horizontal integration**.

Veterans Integrated Service Networks (VISNs): Components of the Veterans Administration system. There are 21 geographically distributed networks that are responsible for coordinating the activities of the hospitals and other facilities located within its jurisdiction.

Virtual integration: The formation of networks based on contractual arrangements.

Virtual organization New organization that is formed by contractual arrangements between two or more organizations; it is an organization without walls.

Virtual visits: Online consultations between physicians and patients.

Voluntary health insurance: Private health insurance (in contrast to government-sponsored compulsory health insurance).

Voluntary hospital: A nonprofit hospital.

Vulnerability Susceptibility to negative events that result in poor health or illness. Poor health can be manifested physically, psychologically, and socially.

Walk-in clinic: A freestanding, ambulatory clinic in which patients are seen without appointments on a first-come, first-served basis.

Xenotransplantation: Also called xenografting. Transplanting of animal tissue into humans.

REFERENCES

Donabedian A. *Explorations in Quality Assessment and Monitoring: The Definition of Quality and Approaches to Its Assessment.* Vol. 1. Ann Arbor, MI: Health Administration Press; 1980.

World Health Organization (WHO). *Preamble to the Constitution.* Geneva, Switzerland: World Health Organization; 1948.

Index